CW00549534

*The Classical
Origins of Modern
Homophobia*

The Classical Origins of Modern Homophobia

Robert H. Allen

McFarland & Company, Inc., Publishers
Jefferson, North Carolina, and London

LIBRARY OF CONGRESS CATALOGUING-IN-PUBLICATION DATA

Allen, Robert H. (Robert Howard) 1949–
The classical origins of modern homophobia / Robert H. Allen.
p.   cm.
Includes bibliographical references and index.

ISBN-13: 978-0-7864-2349-1
softcover : 50# alkaline paper ∞

1. Homophobia — History — To 1500.   2. Civilization, Classical.   I. Title.
HQ76.4.A44 2006   306.76'6 — dc22   2006004313

British Library cataloguing data are available

Cover photograph ©2006 Photodisc

Manufactured in the United States of America

*McFarland & Company, Inc., Publishers
Box 611, Jefferson, North Carolina 28640
www.mcfarlandpub.com*

In loving memory of
Jacob J. Collins — "Toth"
1974–1998

Whoever he was, wherever he is.

Table of Contents

Preface

The subject of this book is a vast cultural shift in Western civilization: the central ethical understanding of why the Greco-Roman world went from one that valued and used homosexuality in the training of young men to one that regarded homosexuality with horror and contempt and outlawed it, with severe penalties. The book begins with a review of the honorable position male homosexuality held in Athens and the Greek culture generally during the period of Greece's greatest cultural achievements. The last chapter reviews the quite modern-sounding attitudes of lawmakers and religious leaders at the end of the Roman period, when homosexuality was punished with the severest civil penalty — burning at the stake. The intervening chapters carefully examine the complex cultural forces that brought about this change.

The book is ambitious, in that it attempts to cover the range of factors in classical culture that interacted to bring about the change from a gay-friendly to a violently homophobic attitude. The work is as polyphonic, so to speak, as I could make it in the approaches taken to the topic. Because the topic is so wide-ranging and because the amount and variety of evidence that survives regarding the classical world is so great, it seemed clear from the beginning of the project that no one intellectual discipline would suffice to produce a full and satisfactory explanation of that change. Philosophy and the history of ideas, political history, anthropology, the history of religions, mass psychology and the analysis of texts all are used to diagnose the slow erosion of respect for homosexuality in the Greco-Roman world.

The importance of this book is, alas, written across history down to today's newspapers in letters of blood and flame. Homophobia is not a harmless notion that originated in antiquity and has been kept around as a quaint relic. Homophobia has caused the deaths of countless thousands of innocent men and women in the Western world for the last 1,500 years, and it has blighted and warped the lives of far more. Some careful account of where this infamous thing came from and how it came to take hold on an entire culture seemed an important addition to the intellectual understanding of a whole culture. It is not unimportant, either, that a fully documented account be presented of the irrational, tyrannical and sorry roots of a notion so bloody.

My research was fairly extensive, as the more than 300 sources cited in the bibliography will attest. I read widely in classical Greek and Roman texts of course — quite literally from Aristotle to Zeno, as well as commentaries on those texts, histories of antiquity, anthropological studies of the nature of prejudice, psychological studies of the nature of homosexuality, and specifically studies of the nature of homophobia in the modern world. The research and writing of this book covered six years.

Other than one popular and poorly written and researched book on the topic, I found no clear or comprehensive study that dealt with the topic seriously or at any length. One the other hand, I found several books that promoted misreading of texts on the topic of ancient attitudes toward homosexuality, and part of the writing of this book was simply to set the record straight.

Classical scholars seem all too often to ignore homosexuality altogether, and modern writers on homosexuality tend to give no more than a nod toward the gay-friendly attitudes of the Greeks and pass over the growth of homophobia in that culture in embarrassed silence. The result is a gap in the full picture of a whole culture. I hope this work will fill the significant gap in our understanding of both the classical world and the modern world.

The Heard Library at Vanderbilt University was a major source for classical texts, as well as the Library of the University of Tennessee at Martin; my grateful acknowledgment is extended to the librarians at both places. Without the patient organizing and savvy text finding of librarians, scholarship simply could not exist. I must also thank Helen Roulston of the University of Kentucky at Murray, for her labors at proofreading a most difficult text, and Dr. Jean Lorrah at the same university for her advice and encouragement all through the project.

Robert H. Allen
Madisonville, Tennessee

Introduction

Why were Walt Whitman fired, Oscar Wilde imprisoned and Matthew Shepard murdered? The simple answer is "all three were gay." The next, seemingly simple question, however, caused me to write this book: "Why is that bad?" I grew up with a fondness for the Greek classics and I knew perfectly well that homosexuality was regarded with indifference or even esteem in ancient Greece. I knew myself to be living in a culture that looks back on Greek and Roman antiquity with esteem, as our parent culture: Greek and Latin are still taught in schools (though less than they were a century ago); those ancient languages are still used to name medications and plants and such like; the small post office in the small Southern town where I was born had Corinthian columns supporting its porch, and the courthouse across the street had Doric columns. In my imagination now I can feel the solidity of their gray granite drums. Olympic games are still celebrated and those who lose the marathon are encouraged to be stoic about it — all Greek designs, Greek words, Greek institutions, Greek systems of thought and all venerable, admired and worthy.

But why and how did Western civilization become homophobic? That it is homophobic is a fact as solid and unbendable as the gray granite drums that supported the entablature of the courthouse. As a gay man myself I knew perfectly well that words like "faggot" and "pansy" were the worst insults that could be hurled at me. Dusty law books in that courthouse, the *Tennessee Code Annotated*, threatened jail to those who committed sodomy, even with consenting adults; preachers, their faces red with passion and dripping sweat, paced about the pulpits ranting about the sin of Sodom; "pervert" was a word almost too shocking to be whispered on television, though the swishy antics of Jonathan Harris as Dr. Smith in *Lost in Space* were universally thought funny. How, I wondered, did one particular aspect of Greek behavior come to be isolated from the total culture and so violently stigmatized?

As often happens, simple questions have complex answers; I was to spend the next six years reading, making notes and writing the answers presented here tentatively. Early in my thoughts I came to realize that homophobia is only one, and perhaps not the worst, in the long array of attitudes of prejudice that have disturbed and sometimes bloodied the world. Racism has disgraced the American South and anti–Semitism made Nazi Germany unspeakably wicked. Nationalism and the wars it has provoked have killed their millions, while religious bigotry has disgraced the prophets. All these attitudes of prejudice come from the same vile bucket. Homophobia is only one stripe in that great, dark anti-rainbow of hatred and prejudices to which much of the evils that humans have wrought on the earth can be attributed.

Attitudes of prejudice, be they racial, religious, nationalistic, or linguistic, share one central quality: monster-making. Hannah Arendt[1] has documented eloquently the process by

3

which Nazi propagandists systematically denied human attributes to the Jews, and made a harmless and talented people into hideous, inhuman and threatening monsters in the eyes of the Germans. A similar "monsterfication" happened to the African American in the New World, to Jesuits in Elizabethan England and to witches in Salem. Life is too short and the heart too vulnerable to pain to catalogue and describe all the evils done by prejudice in the world. One wishes to rise like Voltaire and shout, "Crush the infamy!"

Yet a word of caution seems in order if one would oppose homophobia in the name of justice and humanity. One must not make monsters out of those homophobes one opposes. As a boy in the South I knew many a racist old man and woman. Some of them were, as the saying went, "meaner than the devil wants a man to be." Yet some of them were not. Many a person might say that "those people ought to stay in their place," meaning that the African Americans ought to be consigned to roles at the bottom of society. Yet those racists were in their way as kindly and fair minded a lot of people as you will meet anywhere. The fact is that attitudes of prejudice are inherited along with so much else as part of a culture. A great many people inherit their culture and never stop to question if any part of it is unfair, illogical or unjust. Now and then, often under the pressure of some perceived threat, some latent prejudice in a society may be awakened and an orgy of Jew-baiting, fag-bashing or witch-burning will result. Yet to say that the ordinary person who has never thought very seriously about the matter yet feels that "they" ought to stay in their place is criminal seems to me as much a matter of monster-making as any other.

1

Harmodios and Aristogeiton: The Political Lovers

It was a democracy such as the world — with its rewards and penalties, its competition, its snobbery — never permits, but which flourished in this little room ... because its central principle was the most anarchic of all: erotic love.

> — Andrew Holleran, describing a gay
> disco in New York about 1970, in
> *The Dancer from the Dance*

A statue of two young men stood in the swarming center of ancient Athens, and no one passed them without noticing. They thrust out and hacked down with their swords, defending against unseen enemies. They were defending the city, the nourisher of every Athenian, and subtly every Athenian man who passed them imagined himself fighting beside them for all he held dear. Some who passed almost worshiped, though the young men in bronze were not gods, nor heroes from legend. Harmodios and Aristogeiton were looked upon as the founding fathers of the freedom that made the city what it was. Boys on their way to school looked up at them and hoped that they too might be as great as the Tyrant Slayers. Old men remembered battles they had fought against other tyrants. The two men were sculpted nude, and it was common knowledge that they had been lovers. The homosexual relationship of Harmodios and Aristogeiton was not a shocking secret to the Athenians, nor even a private matter that might or might not be mentioned. Rather it was part of the reason that they were admired. The bronze men were as revered in fourth-century Athens as George Washington and Alexander Hamilton are in modern Washington, D.C., and they were heroes and examples to the youth of Athens partly because of their sexual relationship. Homosexuality entered the history of the Western world not simply as a variant on the spectrum of sex, but as a crucial factor in the education of Athenian teens to make them free Athenian men. They were heroes because they had killed the last Athenian-born tyrant, but the homosexual relationship of the two men was thought of as the essential factor that empowered them to try to kill the tyrant, that made them love freedom and gave them the courage to dare to do and die.

The story is told or alluded to by classical writers from Herodotus to Aristotle, and for centuries Athenian men at symposia sang the glory of Harmodios and Aristogeiton. It is a curious crossing of the warp of politics and the woof of sexual desire, one that illustrates well the nature of pederasty in Athens in the sixth, fifth and fourth centuries BCE. Before we inquire why and how attitudes toward homosexuality changed, we must look carefully at what it was and how it was located in the culture from which modern Western culture is directly descended. This was the golden age of art, philosophy and politics in Greece and the age, too, when homosexual relationships were valued and tied in to the welfare of the community as a whole. Two substantial accounts of the Tyrant Slayers have come down to us, Thucydides in the sixth book of his *History of the Peloponnesian War*, and Aristotle in the eighteenth chapter of his *Constitution of Athens*. I have generally followed Thucydides, since the account in Aristotle has internal contradictions[1] and he gives no sources for his statements, while Thucydides carefully cites sources and generally seems favorable to the tyrannicide, while he was likewise favorable to the tyrants.[2]

Peisistratos was by all accounts a moderate and genial tyrant. He took power in Athens in the 560s BCE, riding the wave of general discontent that followed the reforms of the lawgiver Solon (who is said to have been the lover of Peisistratos).[3] Solon had canceled debts thus impoverishing many, and Peisistratos, leader of the party of the Hillmen, was a populist tyrant.[4] His sons, however were not so benevolent. Peisistratos left two legitimate sons: Hippias, who succeeded him in power, and the younger, Hipparchus. Hipparchus was something of a dilettante, following his father's taste for literature (Peisistratos had had the first definitive text of Homer made, using the skill of a certain Onomakritos). Hipparchos invited Anachreon, the great love poet, to Athens[5] to sing of the love of boys and wine, as he had done in the court of Polykrates on Samos. It was this taste for boys that was the overthrow of Hipparchos and the tyranny of the Peisistratids, for he desired Harmodios.

Harmodios was a young man of the aristocratic Gephyraei tribe.[6] He was "most beautiful, in the flower of his youth,"[7] Thucydides says, and Hipparchos was smitten with him.[8] However, Harmodios already had a lover, his kinsman, one Aristogeiton, both middle-class citizens. Their relationship was a complicated mixture of private desire and public responsibility. Aristogeiton received sexual pleasure from his somewhat younger kinsman, and educated him in the more advanced skills an adult man needed in that society; at the same time Aristogeiton did not coerce the young man who had chosen him and he fully expected that Harmodios would marry and eventually take other young men as his lovers. Harmodios on the other hand was expected to be or become a fully self-possessed person, able to negotiate his own desire and that of his friend so that he would neither be owned by Aristogeiton nor the owner of him. Both men were expected by their society to keep the relationship free from any suspicion of prostitution; it was expected to be a deeply personal, noncommercial relationship, very much apart from the notion of "I'll do this for you if you'll teach me that."

When Harmodios rejected the advances of the tyrant's brother a second time, Hipparchos decided to get revenge. He invited Harmodios' sister to be a basket carrier at the Panathena Festival in 514 BCE—it was a considerable public honor for a young woman to carry the basket holding the ritual implements at the great public religious event—then at the last moment forced her to withdraw.[9] Just how this last turn was accomplished is not clear; perhaps it was implied that she was not a virgin; Aristotle says that Hipparchos called Harmodios *malakon*.[10] The word essentially means "soft," though at this distance of time it is difficult to say exactly what was implied—perhaps that Harmodios was effeminate, sexually "easy" or a coward; whatever it meant, it reflected upon the sister as well. At any rate, the combined insults were enough to set the conspiracy in motion. They killed Hipparchos in the street of Athens. Harmodios was killed on the spot by Hipparchos' bodyguard, the conspiracy fell apart, and Aristogeiton was captured and died under torture, having implicated many friends of the tyrant who were in fact innocent.[11]

Hippias remained in power for another three years, but the charm was gone from his rule. The brutal repression following the murders forced him to remove the velvet glove from his iron fist. The dying Aristogeiton had seen to it that there was no one he could trust, and he killed or exiled many innocent as well as guilty. Hippias set about to fortify the hill near the port of Munychia as a fortress to control the city,[12] and gave his daughter as a wife to a friend of Darius, the king of Persia.[13] The Greek word *turantos*, which has come over into English as "tyrant," seems to have come from a word in Minoan for "tower" or "fortress," referring to the towers the Minoans built to control the colonized Greek population. When certain of the family of Alkmaeon (which had been exiled more than a century earlier) got help from the Spartans (backed by the Pythian oracle) and overthrew Hippias, there was little resistance by the Athenians. A solemn ceremony of cursing the Peisistratidae was held to mark their departure.[14] Hippias himself fled to the court of Darius. He was rejoined there by Onomakritos, who again proved useful — he used his oracles to help persuade Darius that an invasion of Greece would be successful.[15] Twenty years later Hippias would return, an old man[16] and surely bitter, with the conquering armies of Persia, which burned the Acropolis and took the statues of Harmodios and Aristogeiton back to Persopolis.

The immediate results of the killing of Hipparchos and the fall of Hippias were varied. These events were generally attributed, as by Thucydides, to pederastic love, and for centuries after, pederastic love was regarded as a particularly democratic institution. In Athens about 509 BCE[17] that double portrait statue we have already mentioned of Harmodios and Aristogeiton by Antenor was set up in the Agora, a law being made that no other statue might be placed near them.[18] The two men were buried in the Road of the Heroes, the Kerameikos,[19] and their descendants (it seems they both had married and both left children) were granted public maintenance in the Prytaneion and *ateleia* (exemption from taxes and other public burdens).[20] Simonides, who perfected the art of the epitaph, wrote one for the base of their statues, praising them for "bringing light to Athens," and for centuries men sang of them at the symposiums of Athens.[21]

However, on Samos, another tyrant contemporary with Harmodios and Aristogeiton, Polykrates, took the lesson to heart too — he had the wrestling courts closed because they were the main places were young men and boys met to form relationships.[22] This is the first known quasihomophobic act in all history. Not that Polykrates was averse to same-sex love. He is said to have been the rival of Anachreon for the love of a boy named Bathulos.[23] Polykrates won the boy; and, when Bathulos cut his long hair off as a symbol of entering adulthood by taking a lover,[24] the tyrant dedicated the hair as a trophy in the splendid temple of Hera he had built. The impression one gets of this relationship was that it was purely for the sake of Polykrates' pleasure — no effort seems to have been made to educate Bathulos in anything. Indeed, what could he teach the boy — the art of tyranny? Such pleasure — unlimited enjoyment of the good things of life (including pretty boys) — was the mark of tyrants, "since pleasure makes men's nature more lordly."[25]

The genuine fragments of Anachreon's poetry are scant, but they convey the same impression of his attitude toward boys. Here is fragment 360:

> O boy with the virgin glance,
> I peruse you and you do not notice
> Not seeing that, of my soul,
> You pull the reins.

The adjective here translated "virgin" (*parthenion*) generally has the same connotation in Greek as English — a sexually untouched female.[26] It seems clear that Anachreon was with some irony reducing the boy who controlled his heart like a charioteer to a passive female child. Again, in fragment 388 Artemon, a newly rich social upstart, is satirized for carrying an ivory-handled parasol "like the women" (*gunaixin*). Fragment 348 tells us something of Anachreon's politics:

> I beg on my knees, Deer-shooter
> Fair-haired child of Zeus, Artemis,
> Ruler of wild beasts, who now
> By the swirls of Lethaeos
> Looks down on a city of bold-hearted men
> Since the citizens whom you shepherd
> Are not untamed.

The citizens must have been natives of Magnesia (on the river Lethaeos), capital in Anachreon's time of a Persian satrapy. Again with some irony, he begs the favor of Artemis, goddess of wild beasts, on them precisely because they are so well tamed by the Persians.

Polykrates' act in closing the wrestling arena was against a specific manifestation of male-male love — pederastic union — which he saw as dangerous to his power. His pursuit of the boy Bathulos and his patronage of the homosexual love poet Anachreon were not hypocritical acts, violations of his own law. Rather they were an implicit recognition that there was more than one form of boy love. One might have sexual relations with same-gendered persons quite freely under the tyrant Polykrates as long as no pedagogy was mixed with the love-making. Homosexual activity as a pure power relationship reflected the power of a tyrant over his people and might be not just permitted but glorified. The wrestling court he closed was primarily a training place for young men who were preparing for the rigors of a soldier's life. That older young men came there to find sex partners was a secondary feature to the role of training place, and it was the more mature men who acted as the trainers. However, the young men chose their older partners freely, and an older man was powerless before the beauty of a youngster. Pederasty on the model that the Athenians thought conducive to democracy was one feature in a larger context of placing young men in their roles in an orderly democratic society. Merely having sex with young men because one or both partners found it pleasant had little to do with any democratic goal. Essential to true pederasty was not the sex-act and the private gratification it might afford, so much as the social context.

In Athens in the fifth century BCE a boy became an acceptable object for an older male's affection when the boy (probably on his parents' advice) cut his hair — usually in his mid-teens. Seduction of younger boys was a serious crime.[27] Great care was taken to ensure that the relationship between the older and younger male was not commercial — prostitution was forbidden to freeborn Athenians.[28] The older man might give the younger gifts, but tradition seems to have limited these to love tokens of no great monetary value: a rooster or a rabbit or a ball or a garland.[29] The older man taught the younger the arts expected of a citizen — war particularly — but as Greek culture matured the youth might be taught the arts of peace as well, even philosophy. In Athens beginning about 510 BCE male pederasty was linked closely to public policy and the tradition of Athenian democracy.

Aristotle says that liberty is a basic principle of democracy, along with equality and the principle that in a democracy each person may live as he likes.[30] Clearly the relationship of Aristogeiton and Harmodios was based on the free choice of both persons involved. They were unequal only in terms of their ages; and the point of the relationship, as far as society was concerned, was to prepare Harmodios for full and equal citizenship. The very factor of age inequality was essential to the training, since an adult Harmodios would soon encounter persons who were in fact not his real equals in various ways. Hipparchos was a wealthy, powerful and superbly well-educated man. Had Harmodios merely wished to promote his personal *arête* (excellence) by the most direct and obvious manner, he would have become Hipparchos' lover without a second thought. Furthermore, had he been merely passive, then the man with the greater power would have become his lover without further ado. But Harmodios chose Aristogeiton and Aristogeiton chose Harmodios. The two free men chose each other; Hipparchos offered a relationship based on power and was rejected. Clearly the relationship of Harmodios and Aristogeiton was democratic in the sense that is was based upon personal choice and personal liking; and — at least in the eyes of the lover — all men were considered equal, the common citizen and the ruler's brother. By contrast, in Sparta young men had their lovers assigned to them on the basis of their personal merit,[31] which suggests that society was the primary forming agent, not same-sex desire.

Sexual desire is by its nature an anarchic force, one that all tyrants must seek to control; in classical Greece all marriages, at least in the propertied classes, were arranged; young men often never saw their brides till the wedding night. Sexual union with slaves was thought shameful, so the only free sexual relationship that a free male ever entered into of his own volition was the pederastic union. When we say that young men entered freely into pederastic unions, we must qualify that to the extent that there was pressure on young men to enter such a union. Athens and all the cities — *polloi* — in the Greek world before Alexandria were what we would call small towns, a few thousand people who knew each other and minded each other's business with gusto. A young man in his mid- to later teens was expected to take a same-sex lover rather in the way that a young man in a small town today may be expected to play sports or join a church regardless of how athletic or religious in fact he is. It was shameful if he did not. The Greeks were timocratic; a sense of honor was as powerful as formal law in compelling their actions. The ultimate purpose was for the young man to enhance his virtue, his *arete*. Taking an older male lover accomplished this in ways that we might consider both rational and magical. Rationally the young man learned from the older — anything and everything the older man had to teach — as well as acquiring in sexual acts the rare and difficult art of giving and receiving pleasure and maintaining the poise between selfishness and self-abnegation. It also seems that the young man was thought to absorb essences and subtle spiritual qualities from the older man's semen, though the Greeks seem not to have thought in blatant magical terms in regard to pederasty.[32]

One suspects that many young men who were not what we might call homosexual entered into such unions for the sake of appearance. What they did with their lovers in the dark is more than history knows. Moreover, one suspects that many young men and older men who had little or no real interest in same-sex unions actively sought each other out so that they might pretend publicly to be lovers, constituting what we may call a heterosexual underground. Nevertheless, the choice of a lover was left to the young man in Athens of the fourth century; that he choose wisely was much of the point of the activity. In what must have been a life severely hedged about with restraints and choices made for him, a man found his freedom in the public arena of politics and alone with another man.

Richard D. Mohr in *Gay Ideas* has written a perceptive study of the relationship between democracy and male-male love; Mohr's interest is the modern United States, but his ideas seem equally valid for a clearer understanding of pederastic love in relation to democracy in classical Greece. Mohr is unequivocal; he suggests that "male homoerotic relations, if institutionalized in social ritual, provide *the* most distinctive symbol for democratic values and *one* of their distinctive causes."[33] Homosexual relations can both symbolize and create democracy for three reasons:

I. They cut across all social classification — same-sex lovers may belong to any class, race, denomination or social strata, and such relationships "draw into doubt the fixedness of social strata."[34]

II. Homosexual relations produce friendships that assume equality, rather than the sham "friendships" of role-divided marriages.[35]

III. "Democratic equality emerges from gay sexuality as a mode of cognition."[36] This again in four ways: (1) In the intimacy of the sex act a person's ability to care for another and respect himself are known. (2) Because men know maleness, their lovemaking is more affectionate than opposite-sex couples.[37] (3) Each male in a male-male relationship has complete control over himself, reducing possessiveness and jealousy. (4) After sex, men tell each other their life stories, affirming their own uniqueness.

Most of Mohr's statements can be exemplified from classical sources. A few brief examples:

No social distinction was greater in Athens than that between Athenians and resident aliens. In the classical period Athens was a prosperous trade city, linked to the harbor of Piraeus, and much of the population were *metics*, resident aliens (perhaps resident for generations) who occupied a position far inferior to the "natives." A *metic*, however wealthy or respected, could not own property in Athens. Zeno of Kittium (Cyprus), the philosopher, was forced to teach in the public porches (*stoa*) of Athens because, unlike Plato, who owned the Academy, Zeno could not buy a place for a school — hence his followers were called Stoics, "porchers." Yet male-male love cut across the bound between *metic* and citizen; the altar to Eros in Athens was specifically dedicated to Anteros (Avenging Love) because one Timagoras, a resident alien, fell deeply in love with Meles, a citizen. Meles rejected Timagoras and told him to leap off a certain high rock. In love or despair or both, leap he did, killing himself. Then Meles in remorse threw himself off the same rock.[38]

Less dramatic perhaps, but nevertheless illustrating how homosexual love cut across the bounds of class, is the love of the noble and aristocratic Alkibiades for the peasant-born Socrates. Clearly his love was erotic, sexually based, although it was (as the *Symposium* leaves us to suppose) unconsummated. The Seventh Letter of Alciphron, though it dates from the third century CE, is much in the spirit of idealized classical pederasty and contrasts the love of a rich man and that of a poor man for a boy; the poor man speaks to his boy:

> The Rich Man calls you his beloved [*eromenon*]: I call you my master [*kurion*]; he calls you his servant [*huparetan*], I call you my god. He calls you part of his property; I call you my all. Hence if he falls in love again with someone else he will behave the same to him whereas the poor man falls in love but once. Who can remain at your side when you are ailing? Who can go to the camp with you? Who can put himself in front of you when the arrow is sped? Who can fall in death for you? In all these ways I am rich.[39]

Individual young men could and very often did refuse an older man, so that they were as much in control as their older lovers.[40] The older man was expected to "inspire" the youth with desire.[41] When the young man reached his early twenties or so, he usually married and began to father children, becoming in his turn the older lover of young men. (There was, at least in Archaic Crete, a rite of passage for youths leaving the state of adolescence involving the gift of a wine cup as a sort of diploma.) These pederastic relationships were generally temporary, the younger male becoming a lover and guide of other boys as he aged and the older male moving on to other young men, though there are cases in the surviving documents of what seem to be lifelong, marriage-like associations between two men.[42] There is little evidence of anxiety caused by this transition, since the Greeks saw gender as determined by appearance and social activity, rather than (as we are apt to) by direction of sexual desire. As Eva Cantarella has pointed out, Greek homosexuality might be better termed bisexuality since persons who directed their sexual attentions exclusively to one or the other gender seem to have been the exception rather than the rule. The whole picture in classical Greece is a positive attitude toward all forms of same-sex relationships, gay or lesbian, pederastic or casual; but pederasty was at the heart of the Greek understanding of same-sex relations, and when it ended, other forms went down with it.

We know little of the lives of the Tyrant Slayers beyond their dramatic deaths, but we may assume that they both grew up in typical Athenian middle-class backgrounds in a pattern that was set throughout the sixth and lasted to the end of the fourth centuries. Greek culture and thought was highly polarized. The Greeks thought in pairs of opposites: male-female, free-slave, Greek-barbarian. The dichotomy between males and females was pronounced, and none too favorable to women. Especially in the cities, women lived in seclusion. Most large houses were divided into men's quarters and women's.[43] A male child was kept in the women's quarters till he was about five, then lived in the men's quarters the rest of his life. Except for slaves, Harmodios and Aristogeiton probably saw few females during their lives and would have seen very little physical affection between human beings, except possibly between their fathers and their fathers' male lovers.

Richard Isay in *Being Homosexual: Homosexual Men and Their Development* has put forth a milder form of the Freudian understanding of sexuality and applied it to the development of gay men. Isay believes that effeminacy in males results when a young man who is perhaps biologically disposed to homosexuality sees his father express affection toward his mother. The young man desires his father, and seeing him express love to someone who has whatever the culture determines to be feminine characteristics, tries to acquire those characteristics. The fact that young men seldom if ever saw free men and women together in classical Greece seems to account for the scarcity of transvestism and the dominance of a sort of hypermasculinity to the end of the classical period.

The desire for love is, of course, always the desire for another person, another self. Part of this in a child must be the desire for a person who is a caregiver, a teacher and nourisher. In societies where this routinely is a woman for both males and females, males seem to develop a stronger sense that those attributes, caregiving, teaching and nourishing, can only come from persons who are different from themselves, can come only from the female. In such societies caregiving, teaching, nourishing take on a more mysterious quality, and males may think themselves less capable of performing them — indeed in strongly homophobic contexts, males who strongly wish to be caregivers, teachers, nourishers, may think themselves sick for so wishing. But in the Greek context, it seems that men were encouraged by the structures of the society to see themselves as fully able to perform all the roles that were required for at least part of the emotional life of maturing children. Without homophobia the image of the inner self unfolded complete and self-sufficient, feeling it needed no mysterious outer something to be complete; small wonder that the Greek culture achieved as much as it did in so little time. For males in classical Greece the notion that they could be anything, that the "good life" was readily possible from within themselves, must have been almost innate.

For psychological reasons to be discussed below, homosexuality among males and females became in the Hellenistic period increasingly transgendered in its nature. The cult of Hermaphroditos grew in popularity, and the image of the male ideal changed from the clearly masculine youths of the fifth and fourth centuries BCE to the more feminine youth of

Hellenistic times. The growing effeminacy of young gay men seems to have brought homosexuality into further disfavor.[44]

After the fall of Hippias, the Athenians put up the pair of portrait statues of Harmodios and Aristogeiton. Xerxes took the statues with him to Persia, and in the rebuilding of the city under Pericles the lost statues were replaced by a pair of statues of the lovers by Critios[45] and Nesiotes. Roman copies of this second monument survive.[46] It is not likely that either the original pair of statues nor the pair that replaced them were portraits in the strict sense of a recognizable likeness of the originals; rather the statues represent the ideal of pederastic lovers as they were conceived in fifth century Athens. In this sense they tell us a good deal about the institution of pederasty in that time and place. The statues show two fully grown men. Harmodios is perhaps 20, clean shaven, his body clearly that of an adult. Aristogeiton is perhaps four or five years older.[47] He has a short beard, and his face is a bit more mature, but this is the only real difference; the bodies of the two men are virtually indistinguishable.[48] The ideal as represented by these two statues is a relationship between a younger and a slightly older adult; this is pederasty in name only — there is no boy here.

The two are shown naked, in the act of striking at the tyrant; Aristogeiton is about to stab, while Harmodios has his sword raised to hack. Both smile the archaic smile as they cover each other's backs as good warriors would; Aristogeiton has a robe draped over one forearm; his sword was concealed in it, and now he uses it to protect his younger companion. The statues have a curious quality of spiraling both in and out, in toward the intimacy of the two, yet at the same time outward, in attacking their enemy. This aspect of the statues, the lovers as good warriors, is at the heart of the institution of pederasty.

The nudity is significant. Male nudes are the rule in Greek art from the Archaic period onward; the female nude was a late invention. It was from the male nude that all Greek sculpture took its origin. The ultimate origin of the male nude, indeed of much of Greek sculpture, is in the *kuros*— statues of naked young men that begin to appear in the late Archaic era. The *kuros* originated on Crete and shows clear derivations from the funerary statues of Egypt.[49] The pharaohs of the New Kingdom had a cult of personal athleticism, seeking to preserve an idealized image of their bodies at their peak in their tombs with idealized sculptures, sometimes nude. It was at the festivals of dead heroes that Greek athletic contests originated — witness the funeral games for Patroclus in the *Iliad*— and we know from many sources that it was at the gymnasia where men exercised nude that men and boys sought each other out.[50] The *kuros* statue commemorated the young man at his peak of physical development and often was placed over his grave, even if he had lived into old age, like the statues in Egyptian tombs; the *kuros* statues are the idealized selves of Greek athletes. It is said that the cult of the dead hero originated in Crete,[51] and some Greeks believed that pederasty came from Crete. These statues both portray the flesh and imply the spirit. They imply at a very early age the separation of soul and body in Greek thought, a dualism deeply imbedded in their thought.

It is of course by seeing the genitals that persons most readily identify the gender of another person. Nudity made it obvious to young men in Greece that the other person was male, sexually endowed and hence like himself. The most important fact was that the nudity, complete exposure, was taken as a sign of complete self sufficiency; a naked man was all he was or needed to be, hence he was, like the Greek young man beholding him, fully capable of giving love to another man. Small wonder that a few centuries later homophobic Roman philosophers like Cicero would claim that the nudity of the athletic courts was the cause of Greek pederasty; the Romans, if they exercised at all, did it with at least some minimum garment on.

From as early as the seventh century BCE, pederasty was a means of training young warriors in the Greek city states. The initiation of young men was presided over by Apollo. Women in ancient Greece were largely silent, so we know less about the initiation of girls, but we hear of lesbian choruses sung by choirs of girls; and there is a suggestion that Artemis, sister of Apollo, may have presided over the education of girls in a same-sex context as did Athena.[52] Homoerotic activity among women in ancient Greece is much less documented because women in general are less well documented. Often what survives is the work of men whose point of view is not always trustworthy. Indeed, as Bernadette Brooten has written, homoerotic activity between females is less clearly defined than that among males; the penetration of the body of a male by the penis of another male serves as a clear-cut definition of homoerotic activity, while there is no parallel act to define lesbian activity.[53] The term "lesbian" is Greek, originally meaning merely a person from the island of Lesbos in the Aegean sea; the word did not achieve its modern meaning until the Middle Ages in Byzantium.[54] In the following work we take it to mean "a woman who behaves like a man and is oriented toward female companions for sex."[55]

In the Archaic period of ancient Greece we hear of schools for women where they were taught by other women to sing the praises of gods, goddesses and each other; women in such choruses were often linked as couples in a marriage-like state, called *suzxu*.[56] Plutarch, writing in the early Imperial era, describes girls in Sparta in earlier ages who danced naked in public, though this seems to have been as much for the sake of the young men who watched as for the girls themselves.[57] Some lyrics written for such a female chorus by a man have survived. Here are some lyrics Alkman wrote for the woman Hageschora to sing:

> Of radiant Agido my lay
> shall be — her radiance as clear
> as the sun, whose morning ray
> she conjures to appear.
> ....
> my cousin — fair is she
> and her tresses have the grace
> of a golden filigree;
> beneath the gold a silver face.[58]

Similar beauty contests (called *partheneia*) for, and judged by, women were held in Elis and on the island of Lesbos, always with some homoerotic elements.[59]

The name of Sappho is inextricably linked to female homoeroticism. In the first quarter of the sixth century BCE she wrote passionate lyric poetry, addressing young women in the same terms that were used by men to speak of the pederastic male-male relationship.[60] Our information on lesbian activity has suffered from the general silence imposed on women in antiquity, but there are hints in mythology that a pair composed of a goddess and a mortal woman may have been the mythic founders of Athens. We know that a god and his boy-love were regarded as the founders of several ancient Greek cities (e.g., Herakles and Iolous founded Sparta). Quite possibly Athena and a mortal woman named Myrmix were the founding couple of Athens. Athena was a goddess older than Zeus, going back to the Minoan snake goddess; the wisdom of Athena, *metis*, is essentially feminine. "Cities are the gift of Athena," the saying went.[61] Mirmex was beloved of Athena because of her upright life and the skill with which she used her hands; Mirmex claimed to have invented the plow[62] — perhaps a sexual innuendo lurks under the myth.

MYTH IN THE ORIGIN OF GREEK PEDERASTY

If we seek the ultimate origins of Greek pederasty and the myths that supported it, we must look very far afield indeed. We may begin with biology. Frank Muscarella, building on the work of a number of other scientists, has published a remarkable essay, "The Evolution of Homoerotic Behavior in Humans."[63] A shallow understanding of natural selection would suggest that homosexual activity, since it does not produce offspring, would not be likely to become a permanently inherited genetic factor. Muscarella has shown that quite likely the very opposite is true: "Same-sex friendships reinforced by erotic behavior may have helped individuals of both sexes to attain personal survival."[64] Homosexual activity in humans is shown in cave paintings as early as 17,000 years before the present, and other evidence suggest it may go back as much as 116,000 years.[65] Homoerotic behavior, particularly between older and younger individuals in both humans and other primates, evolved and has continued as a genetic trait because it offers distinct survival advantages. When young males are forced into the edge of society they are exposed to greater personal danger from outside society, and may not be able to find females to mate with. However, if an older male takes a sexual interest in such marginalized younger male he may make it possible for that male to return with advantages to society and eventually find an opposite-sex mate.[66] Likewise, young females who form sexual bonds with older females have a greater likelihood of personal survival and of raising their own offspring.[67] Muscarella points to the legendary relationship of Patroclus and Achilles in the *Iliad* as a perfect example of such homoerotic survival advantages: Patroclos is lower class, a fugitive, and becomes the friend and lover of the upper-class Achilles; thereby Patroclus gets both protection from Achilles and access to females. It becomes more likely that Patroclus will live longer (although he doesn't in Homer's tragic epic) and pass on his homoerotically charged genes.[68]

Hence, the Greek institution of pederasty was a mythically delineated and socially sanctioned embodiment of biological realities far older than history. To understand the origins of the myth that underlies Greek pederasty we must follow a chain of myth to the very dawn of written history — to Sumer. The Epic of Gilgamesh is perhaps the oldest story we have, written down around the third millennium BCE, from an oral tradition much older.[69]

In the Babylonian version the story begins with an invocation of the walls of the city of Uruk, already ancient when the epic was written:

> He built the walls of ramparted Uruk,
> The lustrous treasury of hallowed Eanna!
> See its upper wall whose facing gleams like copper
> Gaze at the lower course which nothing will equal
> [Tablet I, lines 11–14].

When the epic opens Gilgamesh is the proud, haughty king of the great city of Uruk; Enkidu, a beautiful young man, comes into the city from the wilds of the steppe. Gilgamesh and Enkidu wrestle and while they do, they fall in love[70]: "They kissed each other and made friends."[71]

The two join in fighting various monsters, the giant Humbaba, the Bull of Heaven. Ishtar, the great goddess of love and sex, attempts to seduce Gilgamesh, but he refuses her rudely, saying that all her other human lovers have met with bad ends.[72] The goddess pouts like a teenager, and demands her father punish Gilgamesh for his arrogance and for killing the Bull of Heaven. The gods decide that one of the two heroes must die, and Enkidu is chosen.[73] Gilgamesh is heartbroken at the death of his friend and begins to realize his own mortality in the death of the man who was so much like him. He goes off on a long and futile quest for immortality, and returns eventually to Uruk a sadder, wiser and kinder king. He has learned the meaning of life, love, and compassion from Enkidu.[74] According to later versions of the myth, after his death Gilgamesh became a judge of the dead in the underworld.[75]

The story of Gilgamesh and Enkidu traveled far in the ancient world. Pieces of the text in various languages have been found as far north as Sultantepe in southern Turkey and as far west as Megiddo in Palestine.[76] The parallels between Achilles and Patroclus and the heroes of the Gilgamesh epic have been widely noted.[77]

Translations and retellings of the Epic of Gilgamesh had a wide influence. The western Semites adopted and adapted Babylonian mythology and legends. In the Syrian-Palestinian religious context they reappear as a set of paired divinities: Melqart and Eshmun.[78] The late addition to the epic of Enkidu suggests he was being assimilated to the dying and rising-again god of ancient Sumer at a very early period. We first glimpse Melqart in texts at Ugrit, on the sea-coast, where he is the god termed "the valiant shepherd" and named Hauron about 1400 BCE.[79] The term "valiant shepherd" opens upon a vast mythic realm. Tammuz or Damuzi was the dying and rising-again god of the Sumerians from before history, and his worship spread throughout the Semitic world at a very early date. There he was known as Adonis,[80] and Adonis is very close to Eshmun, and both to Gilgamesh-Enkidu.[81]

In broad general terms the myth-pattern may be stated as follows. Two paired male deities were thought of as linked, often erotically. One was the sun god, daily resurrected; he was armed with a bow or spear or club as was the god who fought and defeated a serpent deity of chaos. This sun god was associated with health, healing and purification; in the Semitic context he was called Melqart, Haroun and Ba'al, while in the Greek context he was called Herakles, and well as Apollo and Melikertes. The other god, often younger, was a vegetation deity, hence also a dying and rising-again god and associated with the flowers and fertility of spring. He was castrated by a wild animal, or in association with the Mother Goddess, and his sexuality was often thought of as effeminate, or bisexual; in the Semitic context he was called Eshmun or Adon while the Greeks called him Iolaos, Aesculapius, Atthis or Adonis, Hyacinthus, Kyparissos (and probably Dionysus). The pattern of paired male deities whose relationship is homosexual and is somehow essential to the welfare of the city appears again as a mythology that originated in Sumer, was adapted and adopted in Babylon, and was adapted and adopted again in Greece, as the systemic pederasty that was very much a part of the Greek polis.

As Apollo was the primary god of the initiation of young men into manhood among the Greeks, we also find he has strong roots in Semitic and ultimately Sumerian myth that point to a derivation from the same mythic archetype as Gilgamesh and Enkidu. Almost certainly Apollo began as god of the non–Greek peoples of Anatolia.[82] One of the most common titles Apollo carried was "Lukeios," which older scholars interpret as having to do with either light or a wolf; more probably it was derived from Lukia (Lycia), a region in Anatolia that had once been part of the Hittite Empire. Very likely Apollo (Apollon, in Greek) began as the god Apulanas of the Hitties.[83] The Hittites were a people who spoke a language related to Indo-European; from about 1350 BCE till their final overthrow by Sargon II in 717 BCE they were a major influence in the politics and culture of the area from northern Mesopotamia to the center of what is now Turkey. The names of a number of legendary Greek rulers in the Mycenaean period have been found in the inscriptions of contemporary Hittite kings at Borghazheui, showing the Myceneans and the Hittites were in direct contact. Hittite priests and scholars translated and adapted Babylonian myths, legends and epics on a large scale. At least 15 tablets in the Hittite Khurrish language survive of the *Songs of Galgamishul*, an adaptation of the

Gilgamesh epic, which clearly influenced both the *Iliad* and the *Odyssey*.[84] We know a good deal about Hittite law, and the only prohibitions against homosexual activity in it involve homosexual activities between son and father, or with a ghost.[85] Like Eshmun in the Palestinian myth, the priests of the Great Mother castrated themselves and presented their severed genitals to the goddess; afterward they would engage in passive homosexual activity as prostitutes, as well as publicly cut themselves with knives and axes without flinching.[86] Such behavior is explained by Iambilikhos, the Syrian philosopher in the fourth century CE, as evidence that a god or goddess was possessing the priest: "Their senses, their will, their life are neither those of man nor of beast, but they lead another, diviner life instead, whereby they are ... wholly possessed."[87]

We hear of Apollo first in Homer, where he seems to be a god more attached to the central shrine of Troy than a god of the invading Greeks,[88] and he is said to have built the walls of Troy personally, suggesting a memory of the walls of Uruk in the Gilgamesh myth. Almost certainly the legend of Apollo taking over the shrine at Delphi from the goddess Themis is a memory of the introduction of a new, probably Lukian, deity among the Greeks. Themis was one of the ancient Olympian deities, a goddess who guarded the law of the city and the marketplace. The story went that Apollo killed the fearsome serpent Python (obviously a version of the monster of chaos), he buried the monster at Delphi on the island of Delos, and Themis relinquished her shrine there to Apollo.[89] The point was that with Apollo, a new law arrived among the Greeks, one that superseded the ancient, matriarchal laws of Themis and included a significant place for homosexuality in the ordering of the Polis, the City.

Like Enkidu, the boy-loves of Apollo did not live long. Ovid tells the story of Hyacinthus, a mortal young man whom Apollo loved. One day, just at noon when the sun was overhead, the god and the lad were exercising with the discus (nude, as the Greeks did)[90] when a tragic accident happened. Apollo threw the discus and, perhaps blown off course by the wind, it hit Hyacinthus and killed him. Apollo was heartbroken and caused the young man to rise again from the ground as the hyacinth flower that will bloom again each spring:

> As watery Pisces giveth place to Aries that the soft
> And gentle springtide doth succeed the winter hard and stower
> So often thou renewest thyself, and on the fair green clower [turf]
> Dost shoot out flowers....[91]

The hyacinth flower has each of its petals engraved with the letters "ai," the Greek word of lamentation.

The story is a thinly disguised allegory of the vegetation narrative; the hot sun of midsummer kills the young flowers and plants of spring, only to cause them to return again the following year.[92] Apollo is the sun god and the sun itself and his eye-beams striking the nakedness of Hyacinthus ("phullos" means a leaf in Greek and "phallos" is of course the penis) with the heat of desire kill him. He dies naked when the sun is highest in the sky. The ultimate image must go back to Sumer, where the young vegetation dies at the end of spring. Interestingly the Greek story suggests that Boreas, the god of the north wind, was perhaps involved (one version suggests that Boreas was himself attracted to Hyacinthus and caused the discus to go astray out of spite).[93] In the milder climate of Greece it is more likely that the early vegetation will be killed off by cold north winds rather than hot suns. Some Greek poet was making the myth more at home by including a cold-wind god.

We have only incomplete information on the cult of Melqart and Eshmun in the Syrian and Palestinian context; Melqart was worshiped in the sea-coast towns such as Tyre, where there was an annual ceremony reenacting the death by burning a wooden image of Melqart, who somehow returned to life again.[94] Eshmun was likewise well known and widely worshiped by the western Semites; as Melqart was god of Tyre, so Eshmun was the patron god of Sidon. The myth had it that one day Eshmun, a beautiful young god, was hunting in a sacred grove. He came upon Astarte, goddess of sex and love (equivalent of Ishtar), who attempted to force him to have sex with her. The young god fled from the goddess and in a sort of self-protection cut of his genitals with an ax and threw them at her.[95] A Greek myth probably reflecting a Semitic counterpart has Iolaos bringing Herakles back to life after he had been killed by the great serpent Typhon.[96] Since Iolaos was one of the boy-loves of Herakles, there was a parallel myth of Iolaos returning to life as well.[97]

The element of self-castration and mutilation that was part of this mythic paradigm in the Semitic context never was adopted in the Greek culture. The notion that young men should completely abstain from sexual excitement while engaging in sex with older men (who did not abstain) may be a faint shadow of this terrible ritual. Much more will be said on this matter in the discussion of homophobia in Plato.

By great good luck we can actually observe at first hand the transformation of a myth from its original archaic form to a myth that approves of pederasty. Pindar's "First Olympian Ode" was written in 476 BCE or shortly thereafter to celebrate the victory in the Olympic games of Hieron of Syracuse. The body of the ode deals with a retelling of the myth of Pelops, in whose memory the ancient Olympic Games were founded. In the original myth Pelops had been killed and roasted by Tantalos, his father, and served at a banquet to the gods; Demeter ate his shoulder. Obviously the myth remembered human sacrifice.[98] Pindar, however, will have none of it; human sacrifice and cannibalism are too evil to be attributed to the gods.

> It is proper for a man to speak well of the gods
> for less is the blame.
> Son of Tantalos, of you I shall say, contrary to my predecessors,
> That when your father invited the gods
> To his most orderly feast...
> giving them a banquet in return for theirs,
> Then it was that the Lord of the Splendid Trident seized you
> his mind overcome by desire, and with golden steeds
> conveyed you to the highest home of widely honored Zeus....[99]

Pelops had been abducted to Olympus by Poseidon, and spent some time there as the boy-love of the sea god. Later, returned to earth, Pelops, is seeking to marry the beautiful princess Hippodameia of Pisa; he must win a chariot race to succeed in his marriage plan. To be sure he wins, Pelops calls in some old favors:

> He approached the gray sea alone at night
> and called upon the deep-thundering
> Lord of the Fine Trident, who appeared
> right by his feet.
> He said to him, "If the loving gifts of Kypris
> count at all for gratitude, Poseidon,
> come! ...
> and speed me in the swiftest chariots....[100]

Poseidon does honor the memory of Pelops' "gifts of Kypris" ("Kypris" is a name for Aphrodite and this is a standard phrase for the act of cooperation in sex); he gives Pelops a golden chariot and winged horses to pull it. Pelops wins the race, wins Hippodameia and has six sons by her.

Pindar's new, revised myth of Pelops accomplishes a number of things at once. First it substitutes an ethically acceptable myth for one that had been horrible and blasphemous. Second, it puts the myth of Pelops securely in the mode of the vegetation myths: the young Pelops disappears for a while to live with Poseidon on Olympus, then returns to life. Last, it conforms admirably to the biological and anthropological model that Frank Muscarella and others have proposed to explain the genetic persistence of homosexual desire. Pelops succeeded biologically in winning a desirable woman because of the efforts of Pelops' older male lover. The overall survival of Pelops' genes was due to the fact of a genetic structure that admitted homosexual desire in the total structure of Pelops' and Poseidon's capacity for love, though at the same time, that same-sex desire was not exclusive. Seldom have mythology and biology so happily met.

The final piece in the puzzle of the formation of a ritualized and politicized pederasty in early historic Greece comes from history rather than mythology. About 635 BCE there was a failed coup in Athens, and the men who had tried and failed to overthrow the government claimed sanctuary in the Acropolis. In order to get them out the rulers of the city, the archons, promised them safe passage. The men came out, but an archon named Megakles of the Alkmaionid family had them executed. The result was that Athens was saved from a revolution, but by killing men who had been under the protection of Athena, it had also become terribly polluted. To cleanse itself of the pollution, the whole Alkmaionid family was sentenced to permanent exile; they went as strangers and exiles to Apollo's shrine at Delphi.[101]

How exactly the Alkmonids were received at Apollo's shrine is not a matter of historical record. We only know that they prospered there. The tradition of homosexuality is to receive the outcast, the "queer" who is out on the edges of society, and the priests of Apollo honored the tradition well. The fact that polluted exiles were welcomed implies a human equality was part of the intellectual climate at Delphi. The exiled family remained there for several generations, marrying and carrying on the family tradition. In 510 BCE, 125 years after their exile, Kleisthenes returned to Athens as the leader of the revolution that had been touched off by the murder of Hipparchos. There was a division between geographical areas in the reforming state. The men of the plain and the men of the hills had different economical interests and looked upon each other with distrust. Kleisthenes set about welcoming many new citizens into the bounds of citizenship.[102] Anthropologists have often observed that societies at odds with each other use homosexual relations to form bonds of trust; quite probably such was the case here. As we have said, the primary reason pederasty was valued among the Greeks of the classical era was as a civic institution, a support to the city.

Among Greek speakers on Cyprus and in the Aegean, Melqart and Eshmun are adopted and adapted to become Greek gods. Herakles and Iolaos, who had a shrine at Sparta, inherit the paired-lovers aspect most clearly; Herakles (called Ba'al in Thespiae in Greek Boetia) keeps the attribute of serpent killer and with his various descents into Hades, the aspect of dying, rising-again god. Hylas, another boy-love of Herakles, was associated with the late-spring lamentation for Tammuz,[103] while Apollo was the primary god for the initiation of youth into manhood.

At the about same time that Pythagoras was forging the Pythagorean movement in southern Italy, Kleisthenes and others of the exiles who returned to Athens after the fall of Hippias were creating the mythology of a democracy. "Democracy"[104] in the Athenian use of the word must be limited — only free, adult, native-born males were entitled to participate fully and on an equal basis in Athenian government. Democracy as we enjoy it in the United States today is Greek democracy extended much further than any Athenian is likely ever to have dreamed possible. Pederasty was made central to the new, revolutionary, free government. Theseus, who had been a minor hero in the legends of Athens, was remade into the equivalent of a boy-loving George Washington; and the Tyrant Slayers, who had acted according to Thucydides mostly out of jealousy and private animosity, were recast as patriots, the Minute Men of the movement. Kleisthenes, his family and the other new democrats had been resident for many years at Delos, the cult center of Apollo, the chief god of pederastic initiation, so the association may have a long history.

In his "Life of Theseus," written in the Imperial Roman age, Plutarch summarizes the career of Athens' patron hero briefly. Born to a royal family on Troezen, across the Saronic Gulf from Athens, Theseus came to Athens after performing a series of labors — defeating monstrous men, killing a fearsome sow, a huge bull, etc. He arrived in Athens to find it sending an annual tribute of young men and women to Minos, the king of Crete. Joining the group of victims, he went to Crete and there killed the half-man, half-bull Minotaur in the Labyrinth of Knossos, near Mt. Ida. Returning in triumph to Athens, he fought and won a desperate war against an army of invading Amazons — women warriors who had crossed from Asia. He formed a close friendship with a young man named Perithous.

Plutarch's story is itself a labyrinth of conflicting accounts, citing legends, poets and legend-mongering historians. One major thread remakes Theseus as the ideal of homosexual initiation, and the founder of Athenian democracy. One of the earliest pieces of evidence we have for the labors of Theseus is a fragment of painted pottery, dating about the time of Peisistratos, that shows Theseus before he entered Athens as an adult male, with a full beard. Later, during the era of freedom and democracy, the frequent depictions of Theseus performing his labors on the way to Athens always show him as a beardless youth.[105] A revision of the myth is clearly under way, like that performed later on the myth of Pelops by Pindar. Many of the democratic reforms known to have be introduced by Cleisthenes in the mid–sixth century were attributed to Theseus.[106] He is often shown in the pose of one or the other of the Tyrant Slayers[107] — the "fighting for democracy" pose we might say. Zenis of Chios in Hellenistic times says that Minos loved Theseus (Fragment 1); and Plutarch ("Life of Theseus," 17) citing Hellenikos of Lesbos, writing in the latter half of the fourth century BCE, says Minos especially selected Theseus to go back with him to Crete. Aristotle says the Cretans believed their laws came from Minos,[108] and it was widely believed in antiquity that pederasty began in Crete.[109] Minos was generally said to be the son of Zeus and an ideal lawgiver — his brother Rhadamanthos was sometimes said to be a judge of the dead. The relationship with Perithous places Theseus as the older lover and Perithous as a youth to be taught (Plutarch, "Life of Theseus," 30), just as the relationship with Minos has cast him as the young man who is loved.

Elsewhere in Greece homosexual love was also linked to the public world and the good of county and city though the institution of pederasty. Hieronymos, a follower of Aristotle, sums the matter up: pederasty was widespread "because it happened that the vigor of the young men joined to the mutual sympathy of their companionship brought many tyrannical governments to an end."[110] Freedom seems always to have been a Greek value, though it was expressed as democracy most distinctly in Athens, and in Athens we can most clearly trace the trajectory of the not-fully-sealed union of democracy and pederasty.

Elsewhere the independence of individual states was dependant on their armies and the armies were often composed of male lovers; the independence of the state, not of the individual within the state, was the motivating force in support of pederasty. When the vast army of the Persians invaded Greece 20 years after the fall of Hipparchos, it was smaller armies of

Greeks, composed largely of same-sex lovers, who stood in the forefront of the defense of the Greek world. We hear of the Sacred Bands, elite military units that relied on sexual love for coherency. Most famous of all is the Sacred Band of Sparta, led by King Leonidas.[111] The normal discipline of the Spartan army involved a shared meal,[112] where all the men ate together as equals, though as we have seen, choice of lovers does not seem to have been free in Sparta. Because they fought in a narrow mountain pass where only a tiny number could fight at any one time, Leontiadas' army of 300 lovers held back the vastly larger army of the invading Persians till the other Greek states could prepare themselves. Likewise, the Sacred Band of Thebes, led by Epameinondas, was composed of same-sex lovers. Both bands were destroyed — the Spartans dying to the last man.

> Go, stranger, tell them in Sparta we died
> Obedient to their laws.

So Simonides wrote for their tomb. Anyone who wished to suppress Greek freedom and patriotism would have had to suppress pederasty. On the fringes of this fifth and fourth century flowering of art, democracy and power stood the Pythagoreans, protesting against it all, their asceticism a radical challenge to the self-regard of the individual and the religion of the state.[113] It is to these Pythagoreans, hating homosexuality as much as they hated democracy, that we turn next.

2

Pythagorean Origins

CASSIO: O thou invisible spirit of wine, if thou hast no name to be known by, let us call thee devil!

....

IAGO: Come, come, wine is a good familiar creature if it be used well ... good lieutenant, I think you think I love you.

—*Othello* 2.3

An aged man, over 80, was invited to a wedding in Athens in 347 BCE. He had a wide forehead and a neat white beard combed to a point. Weddings could be rowdy events, and the old man politely asked if there was a quiet place he could go to do what he had done most of his life — write. The guest was given an upstairs room and furnished with pen and tablet to write with. Next morning, when the last sexy song had been sung at the chamber of the bride and groom, and the last flagon of wine had been drained, someone noticed that the old man had not come down. There was no answer at his door. The door was opened. The philosopher was slumped over a table, the lamp still burning in the dawn light. A pen lay by his cold hand. Plato was dead.

This is a beautiful legend, preserved by Cicero. In fact we know very little about the life of Plato. What we do know is that the very last book that he is said to have written is the very first homophobic document written in Europe. This chapter is a careful investigation of the intellectual background of Plato's thought. The *Laws*, said to be the very last work of Plato, is the source of the charge that homosexuality is "against nature." No charge has been more influential in the sorry history of homophobia. The most likely source for the extremely influential homophobia in the writings of Plato is the Pythagoreans.

What ideas Plato originated and what he inherited from philosophers before him was long a vexed question with no clear solution, because so little pre–Platonic Greek philosophy has survived. However, the discovery of a fragmentary papyrus scroll at Deverni that contained a clearly Pythagorean text more than a century older than Plato has finally put the matter beyond doubt: Plato took over and passed on ideas from the followers of Pythagoras, and it is nearly certain that homophobia was among those ideas. The body of this chapter will be an effort to locate the very earliest sources of homophobia in the obscure, mystical and elusive early Pythagoreans, beginning with Pythagoras himself.

The first philosophical statements of homophobia in the Greek world occur in or connected to the Orphic-Pythagorean tradition. No major intellectual movement among the Greeks seems more difficult to trace. To this day the relatively little scholarship on this subject is what the Germans call a *troddenplatz*, an area where scarcity of information has led to proliferation of interpretation not unlike a torn-up battlefield — indeed as one scholar pointed out, even in antiquity the vastly informed Aristotle knew little about the odd and secretive Pythagoreans.[1]

"Orphic-Pythagoreanism" is a term for what was a movement both philosophical, scientific and religious; it originated in the Greek world in the sixth century BCE, but most of the information we have that purports to deal with it comes from 400 years or more later and seems to be mixed with elements from the Platonic tradition. Many of the documents we have are certainly forgeries, and the question of authorship of others is in doubt. Finally, to complete the difficulties, much of the surviving material is a jumble of philosophy, fact, mysticism, the occult and the arcane. That we find it so is due, no doubt, in some degree to our modern sensibilities, for the Greeks made little or no distinction between science and philosophy, the mystic and the rational.

In the early sixth century BCE, roughly about the time Athens was throwing out its tyrants and establishing a democratic government where homosexual activity was channeled to the service of the state, a movement was beginning elsewhere in Greece that seems the very antithesis of the Athenian ideals. Absolutism, obscurantism and antidemocratic forms of government as well as homophobia all found shade in the wide, deep shadow of Pythagoras.

Pythagoras emerges from the context of sixth century Samos. Samos was a prosperous island in the sixth century BCE; trade down the Meander River on the Anatolian mainland poured past it and through it. About 535 BCE Polykrates overthrew the oligarchy and set himself up as tyrant. Arts and sciences flourished. Geometry was developed to the degree that a tunnel could be dug from the two sides of a mountain and meet in the middle only a few feet off. Famous poets like Ibykos and Anakreon came to sing in the court of Polykrates, and the island was famed for its gems and fine cups of gold.[2] A great temple, the Heraon, went up to the praise of the queen of the gods. Pythagoras was born on Samos probably about 570 BCE,[3] the son of a gem-cutter who had been attracted by the prosperity of the island to settle there. A late tradition, which is probably reliable, says that Polykrates gave the young Pythagoras a passport so that he could study in Egypt.[4] Certainly we know that Polykrates was till late in his reign on good terms with Pharoah Amasis.[5] Likewise we are told that Pythagoras gave fine gold cups to the high priests of Thebes and Memphis, gifts for their imparting of sacred knowledge, a statement made more likely by independent evidence that Samian craftsmen specialized in such cups.

Pythagoras seems to have returned to Samos, then gone, perhaps about 515 BCE,[6] to Italy. The reasons for his leaving Samos are said by our late source to be opposition to the tyranny of Polykrates, but as Berkert has pointed out, this is probably a late fiction intended to conceal a reputation for tyranny that Pythagoras himself had due to his activities in Italy.

Crotona was one of the great cities of the western Greek colonies, Magna Grecia; founded in 703 BCE in a wave of Greek colonialization, its famous temple of Hera overlooked a harbor on the gulf of Taranto (Tarentum), on the southwest side of the instep of the Italian boot. Livy was later to say that its walls were 12 miles around. Today an Italian village nearby carries the name, and a single column of the temple marks the acropolis of a ruin.

Crotona was a defeated, demoralized city when Pythagoras arrived — perhaps that was his reason for going there. The defeat of Crotona by the Lokrians about 535 BCE[7] had left a moral vacuum, and the philosopher of Samos intended to fill it. We are told that he revitalized the city in a few years by teaching virtue to the citizens.[8] He seems to have taken power by means of establishing *sunedia*, clubs of men dedicated to a single political aim — controlling the city in this case, though details of Pythagoras' political activity in Crotona are late and unreliable. The Pythagoran clubs were, at least in the heyday of their power, secret societies (no doubt with initiation rites) that engaged in religious practices as well as scientific research. How serious they were about secrecy may be gauged by the case of Hippasos, who is said to have divulged some secret (perhaps of a mathematical nature) from the club he belonged to. As a punishment he was drowned in the Gulf of Tarentum.[9] Ancient evidence is fairly clear, though, that the ascendancy of Pythagoras and his followers in Crotona was a tyranny.[10]

The one clearly historical event that can be attributed without doubt to Crotona under the sway of the Pythagoreans is the destruction of Sybaris, about 510 BCE. Sybaris was an even larger and richer Greek city north of Crotona on the Italian boot. Pythagoras himself helped stir up a war with Sybaris; and, when the city was defeated, the Crotonians wiped it off the map, so effectively that archeologists have only recently found traces of it. Walter Berkert calls the destruction "the worst atrocity wrought by Greeks against a Greek city in that era."[11]

Extremes promote extremes in the opposite direction. We hear of counterrevolutions in Crotona led by one Kylon. In the first of these Pythagoras himself seems to have been driven into exile to Metapontion in the north, above the Gulf of Toranto, where he died, perhaps about 510 BCE. Pythagoreanism as a political movement continued without its founder, and spread to many of the Greek colonies in southern Italy and in Sicily. In a second uprising against the Pythagoreans, about 50 years after the death of Pythagoras, there were revolts in many cities in Magna Grecia, and the leading Pythagoreans were murdered en masse in Cronona.[12] Only two of the major Pythagorean leaders are said to have escaped the slaughter — Philolaus and Lysis. Pythagorean political power was broken.

The details of Pythagorean thought in this era, both before and after the suppression of the movement about 450 BCE, are largely lost to us. It seems likely that, having once had power and having suddenly lost it, to find themselves fleeing and hiding contributed strongly to the many of the qualities of Pythagoreanism we know from later sources. The strong emphasis on producing families one finds in the Neo-Pythagorean texts may have grown up in the clubs of the defeated Pythagoreans as a survival method. Likewise the strong insistence on strict monogamy may arise partly from the need to keep peace and unity within small, threatened groups of Pythagoreans for whom any family disputes could weaken the group fatally.

With the exception of a few traces, there is no explicit homophobic statement in a purely Pythagorean context that can be traced to the early period of that movement. This is hardly surprising, considering the scarcity of information that we have. But since the Neo-Pythagoreans 400 years later were conspicuous for their homophobia, it should not surprise us if we find the deep roots of the homophobia that was to be rampant in much of Western civilization for 2,000 years in the Orphic-Pythagorean movement of the sixth and fifth centuries BCE.

What little we know of the early Pythagorean political theory suggests that it was totalitarianism, based on a highly trained intellectual elite — the Learners (*Mathematikoi*), who were educated in the clubs in an almost Machiavellian art of manipulation and who kept the second class of Pythagoreans, the Hearers (*Akousmatikoi*) in subjection, using among other things a mystery religion invented by Pythagoras himself and some of his colleagues, Orphism. There was for the Pythagoreans an inner and an outer truth, both revealed by Pythagoras himself.

The Hearers were expected to listen in silence as Pythagoras lectured behind a curtain (a *sundon*) to his advanced students.[13] What the Hearers heard were perhaps discussions of geometry illustrated by diagrams drawn in sand they could not see. They were also taught the *symbola*— more matter intended as much to intrigue and befuddle as enlighten. The *symbola*— Pythagorean "symbols"—were enigmatic sayings, often commands that the Hearers were expected to memorize and obey. Fifty-two of these have come down to us, some of them perhaps spoken originally by Pythagoras himself.[14]

> Sow mallows but never eat them.
> Wear not a narrow ring.
> Do not urinate in the sun.
> When it thunders, touch the ground.
> Do not leave the mark of the pot in the ashes.
> Do not eat fish whose tails are black.
> When the winds blow, adore Echo.
> Do not write in the snow.
> Never sing without harp accompaniment.
> Do not eat the heart.

And most famously:

> Do not eat beans.[15]

It seems that the Learners, when they graduated to that status in the Pythagorean hierarchy, were taught allegorical interpretations of these symbols. "Do not eat the heart" might be interpreted to mean "Do not grieve excessively," while the Hearers were left with the simple understanding that one should not eat the heart of an animal — without being told why not. We have many such interpretations of symbols, all from late sources and sometimes quite contradictory, so we cannot say what any particular *symbola* was said to mean by Pythagoras. Blind obedience is what the Hearers were taught. Through some selection process the details of which are lost to us, some few Hearers were given access to a more reasonable understanding of Pythagorean teaching, but not before they had ground long at the mills of obscurantism. Most interesting in this regard is the story of Milon of Crotona — than whom no athlete of his age was more famous; he won the wrestling contest an unprecedented six times at the Olympics as well as six times at the Pythian Games. He became a Pythagorean, and the Pythagoreans were supposed to avoid eating meat. Since it was not thought that a vegetarian could have the full strength an athlete like Milon required, it appears that Pythagoras gave him a sort of dispensation to eat meat — implying that there were perhaps two truths for the follower of the Sage of Samos.

Onomakritos, whom we have already seen at Athens, helping Peisistratos edit the text of Homer, lost his job and was forced into exile when his employer discovered that he had forged a book in the name of Orpheus,[16] part of the Pythagorean effort to create a new cult. About the same time a Pythagorean named Kerkropes[17] wrote a book, *The Songs of Orpheus*, also under the name of Orpheus.[18] Likewise we hear of an Orphic poem called *Souteria* by Timocles of Syracuse, and of one called *The Descent to Hades* by Orpheus of Camorina, and the anonymous *Crater*.[19] These later works were a major influence on the growth of the often highly homophobic Christian apocalyptic tradition. Moreover we are told on good authority that Pythagoras himself wrote a poem that was published under the name of Orpheus.[20] All these are lost, except for fragments. As with so much else in the fifth and fourth centuries, we must relay on scant pieces of these works, later testimonials and conjecture to fill out the shape of the early Orphic cult.

What Orphism amounts to is a new religion operating within the context of the Greek traditional religion.[21] Orphics could, and did, still pray to the gods of the Homeric pantheon, but the reforms they introduced in the understanding of the traditional theology were so radical that, whether it is called a cult, a religious reform or a new religion, Orphism is a brilliant and wholly new departure for Greek religious thought.

There seems to have been an Orpheus before Pythagoras and his colleagues began their work[22]— perhaps a Thracian culture hero who was credited with ending the practice of human sacrifice. This was the Orpheus of popular legend, which survived side by side with the Orphic-Pythagorean Orpheus. By the same token there was an ancient Dionysus—a god of fertility, of wine and of the joy of life. For him the bacchants danced themselves into a frenzy and tore living animals apart with their hands, eating them raw. Neither were any more homophobic than the other members of the Greek pantheon. Orpheus is said to have taken Kalais, a male lover, to console himself after he finally lost Euridyce in the underworld.[23] He is generally portrayed as a gentle singer, the opposite of the more common hypermasculine heroes of legend such as Achilles and Herakles. Dionysus was "worshiped as the incarnation of all natural life and vigor ... the enjoyment of life."[24] Dionysus is called "mad" by Homer,[25] and he is generally the god who breaks bounds and transgresses norms. Dionysus is likewise credited with same-sex erotic adventures (with Adonis, for example[26] and with Prosymnos[27]), and especially in Hellenistic times Dionysus is often portrayed as androgynous.[28]

The New Orphic-Pythagorean cult had its own mythology, including much that was common to the traditional mythology of Homer and Hesiod—but with a difference. Partly because the myth-system of Homer-Hesiod has been transmitted to us by textbooks in a conveniently simplified, standard version (far from the subtlety and complexity that one finds in, say, Pausanius), Orphic theology seems vastly complicated. The Orphic theologies pullulate with gods who fade into each other, change names, do odd things and change into allegories or abstractions with maddening frequency. Thankfully here we may deal with only those aspects of this new set of gods that led in some way to a change in the attitude of the classical world toward homosexuality.

The conventional Greek story of the origin of the world in Hesiod begins with a series of single deities that somehow produce one after another in succession:

> Chaos was first, then
> Gaia (Earth) with broad breasts
> ....
> From Chaos came black Nix [Night] and Erebos
> And Night then gave birth to Day and Space [Hesiod, *Theogony*, 116–17, 24, 25].

Earth produces Ouranos, mates with him and gives birth to Kronos and Rhea. Kronos and Rhea mate to produce Zeus, Hera and the older generation of the Olympians. The first Olympians then mate in various combinations to produce the 12 gods, various demigods and so on. In this theogony there is ultimately a single source for all, and two or more generations pass before dual, sexual reproduction begins. Essentially, though on a crude level, this is monism. Everything in existence goes back to one source and therefore must partake of the same nature.

By contrast the theogony put forward by Ononmakritos or one of his colleagues under the name of Orpheus is distinctly dualistic from the beginning.[29] The Orphic theogony begins with two, Earth and Water, not one.[30] Earth and Water mate to produce Chronos (serpent-like Time), and Adrastia (Necessity). That pair in turn produce Phanes. Phanes is the Orphic effort at unity, but it is not clear how this was arrived at. Phanes is androgynous; he has both male and female genitalia,[31] but he also has the heads of bulls, a serpent growing out of his body, etc. It is probably a mistake to see Phanes as hermaphroditic in the usual sense of the term—rather he is the god who contains everything and unites everything in himself—a *pantheos* and thus transcendent.[32] Phanes reproduced, but whether autonomously or by mating with another deity is not clear.[33]

After further generations of gods and goddesses that we may omit here, we arrive at Dionysus. In the Orphic theogony he is the son of Zeus by Persephone (Zeus' daughter by his sister, Demeter, rather than his wife, Hera) and born in Crete.[34] At this point the Orphics completely inverted the moral order of the original cult of wild Dionysus. They said that Zeus intended that his son Dionysus should succeed him as the ruler of the universe, and put him on the throne. However, the Titans, Dionysus' uncles, provoked perhaps by the jealousy of Hera, gave the child toys to distract him, and, while he looked in a mirror (the Mirror of Enitharmion), killed him, then boiled him in milk[35] and ate him. Zeus in anger burned up the Titans with thunderbolts. The human race was formed from the ashes that remained from this barbarous act and hence is predominantly made from the stuff of the evil Titans, but also contains something of the innocent divinity of Dionysus.[36] Athena saved the heart of Dionysus; Zeus swallowed it, then impregnated the mortal Semele by whom Dionysus was reborn in Thebes of Greece.[37]

This briefly is the *pathe tou Dionusou*, the Suffering of Dionysus. The effect was to criminalize the worship of wild Dionysus — the Bacchants who tore fawns and calves up to eat them raw were regarded as reenacting infanticide and cannibalism, and all humans inherit a sort of Original Sin by being descended from the Titans.[38] There were rumors in late antiquity that Bacchants did engage in human sacrifice.[39] Possibly this myth created by Onomakritos and the other sixth century Orphics is the source of the calumny so often hurled at groups of hated outsiders — that they kill children and eat them. We find the pagans accusing the Christians of this; then in the Middle Ages the Christians accuse the Jews, witches, etc. of the same enormity with resulting pogroms and witch burnings. The dangerous cult, one may say, is not a band of human monsters devouring infants, but the intolerance and superstition that have perpetuated such a lie.

Orphism was a dualistic mythology; it saw the world as split between good and evil — an innovation in Greek religious thought.[40] The criminalizing of the Bacchants is an essential denial of tragedy, in the fullest Classical sense of the word. Tragedy had originated somehow in the festival of the wild Dionysus, before the Orphic reform. At the heart of the Greek tragedies beats a sense of a divine world that is beyond human knowing, but perhaps good in a transcendent way — Oedipus is made to commit crimes against his will, blinds himself and is finally, in some sense as a balance for his agony, made a god. This cannot be rationally understood, but if one does not think in purely either-or, dualistic terms, it can be felt as essentially religious.

Pythagoreans had a similar dualism expressed in philosophic rather than mythic terms; Aristotle (*Metaphysics*, 986a 22) gives a list of Pythagorean dualities:

limit	unlimited
odd	even
one	plurality
right	left
male	female
at rest	moving
straight	crooked
good	bad
square	oblong

The dualism of the Orphic-Pythagoreans is the breeding ground for the concept of homophobia as we know it, whether expressed in the mythic origin of the universe from two entities or in a categorization of everything in terms of paired opposites. By a sort of irony, dualism leads to a more tidy, orderly view of reality than monism. The habit of mind that insists everything must fit perfectly into one of two categories without overlap or mixing leads inevitability to an insistence on a distinct maleness and a distinct femaleness — there is no place in the list that Aristotle quotes for the bisexual or any variant on male-female sexual relationships. Aristophon, a writer of the New Comedy (about 220 BCE), puts the following words into the mouth of a character in his *Puthagoriste* (*The Pythagorean*): "And so is it not right and fitting that Eros has been banished by the twelve gods from their company? For he used to upset them by the quarrels he provoked."[41] By contrast, the traditional Eros, who presided over both same-sex and opposite sex unions, was described by the Hellenistic dramatist Alexis (flourished about 356 BCE) as "neither male nor female; again neither god nor man, neither stupid nor yet wise but rather composed of elements from everywhere."[42] This suggests that the traditional Eros was what we would call an indeterminate being, capable of expression in many contexts.

There was a sort on monism in early Pythagoreanism which saw the One as a transcendent order of things. The One is "most likely the seed"[43] of Limit and the Unlimited. But this mystical One seems to be the Void, as Aristotle says: "The Pythagoreans too, held that void exists and that it enters the heaven itself, which as it were inhales it, from the infinite air. Further it is the void which distinguishes the nature of things, as if it were like what separates and distinguishes the terms of a series. This holds primarily in the numbers, for the void distinguishes their nature."[44] The later Pythagoreans had a bizarre and fantastic system of numerology in which numbers were regarded as divinities.

If Pythagoras did go to Egypt in the sixth century BCE to study the Egyptian religion, he found it in a period of deep decline and corruption. He is said to have visited Memphis and the priest of Zeus[45] (probably what later Greeks called Zeus-Amon, at Thebes). If he did visit Egyptian Thebes and was admitted to the "mysteries" of the temple he would have found corruption rampant and religion being used in the crudest of ways to support an absolute ruler.[46] The high priest of that temple was supposed to be a male, but the pharaoh had appointed his daughter to the position, almost certainly to be sure that the temple would be faithful to his political agenda. We hear in this period that statues of the gods were made with moveable jaws and hollow tubes inside them so that priests hidden behind or underneath could make them speak, giving out oracles that routinely supported the power elite.

Virtually the oldest reference we have to Pythagoras is a fragment of Heraclitos of Ephesos, a generation or so after the time of Pythagoras. Heraclitos calls Pythagoras *kapidon arkhegos*, "the chief of swindlers."[47] A curious series of evidence points to a link between what Henry Breasted called "priestly jugglery" in sixth century Egypt and Pythagoras' activities in Italy. Pythagoras' house in Crotona became a shrine of Demeter.[48] A legend recorded by Hermippos has Pythagoras going into seclusion in a chamber built under his house[49] and Iamblichus mentions that a man who later bought the house for his own use was prosecuted for sacrilege for selling the golden jaw of the image.[50] The image may have been a wooden statue, sheeted with metal (a common way to make large statues at the time), but it is curious that it was the jaw that came loose and was sold rather than say, a hand or foot that would have been more readily detachable — unless the jaw had originally been made moveable.

There is strong evidence that Pythagoras absorbed and later transmitted to his followers many Egyptian customs and concepts. Herodotus, who had very probably been in contact with early followers of Pythagoras at Thurii, tells us that they refused to wear wool because it was forbidden to the Egyptians on religious grounds.[51] There is abundant archeological evidence to confirm that the Egyptians avoided wool in such a context. Although it is not certain that the Egyptians had not been homophobic in all contexts through all their long history, it is certain that there was an homophobic strain in Egyptian culture.[52]

The link between Egyptian homophobia and Pythagorean is weak, but enticing. The Book of the Dead is a general name assigned to a collection of prayers, charms and magic formulae that never assumed a standard form. Written on tomb walls, on coffins or on scrolls buried with mummies, it was intended as a magical guide and protection to the soul in the afterworld.[53] One of the most interesting texts in the Book of the Dead for many reasons is the "Negative Confession." The soul in the Underworld is judged, standing before Osiris, and an array of 42 fearful deities (one each for the 42 divisions of Egypt) with names like Bone-Crusher and Eater-of-Souls[54] proclaim its innocence in negative terms, including "I have not had sexual relations with a male lover."[55]

Strictly speaking, the Book of the Dead is not a moralistic sacred text. The point is not that one should not do the things that can cause trouble at the judgment; rather, the Book of the Dead provides magic spells that get one safely past that crisis, regardless of how one has lived. On the other hand, this text can be cited as giving some idea of what the Egyptians believed the gods might be angry about. However, there is considerable evidence that the prohibition on homosexuality was confined to priests while actually in the temple area and later fell into the general text of the Book of the Dead.[56] If Pythagoras took this prohibition over and promulgated it as a universal rule, he was deliberately erasing the distinction made in the Egyptian context between sacred place and secular place, perhaps because, as a dualist, he could not be secure that the two were united.

The pharaoh was the supreme autocrat of Egypt, the son of the sun god, and the high priests of the various temples in Pythagoras' time held similar power over their subjects. This could not have escaped the notice of Pythagoras or any other curious traveler who spent any time inquiring about the religion of Egypt. Perhaps during his lifetime, certainly soon after his death, Pythagoras was credited with working miracles[57] and was called either the son of Apollo or Hyperborean Apollo himself.[58] Certainly there are major elements in Orphic-Pythagoreanism that have no counterpart in Egyptian thought — notably reincarnation. The earliest Egyptian deities were decidedly monistic, and often reproduced by spitting, masturbation, etc.,[59] but dualism was very common in Ancient Egyptian thought,[60] and Erik Hornung has written an extended discussion of Being and Non-Being, the Limited and the Unlimited in Egyptian thought[61] that bears a striking resemblance to such discussions in later Pythagorean texts. All and all, it seems that the Egyptian influence on Pythagorean thought was such as one very intelligent person might pick up during a few years spent in a fully developed alien culture.

The Orphic-Pythagorean movement was then essentially ascetic. Humans were seen as having a dual nature, a physical body that was bad, cursed from the beginning, and a spiritual soul completely distinct from the body that could be purified through many reincarnations till it joined its divine source.[62] The Orphic-Pythagorean movement was male-dominated, too, unlike the cult of wild Dionysus, where men and women mingled freely.[63] The thrust of the dualism in the list cited above puts the feminine on the side of evil, and a general misogyny is the result. Femininity was "immeasurable," not capable of exact definition, and therefore to be subjected to rational number. James A. Philip calls the distinguishing mark of the early Pythagoreans "a doctrine of the mathematical structure of reality, and of the soul that comprehends reality."[64]

This, before Plato and separate from the Judaic tradition, is the source of the puritan tradition in Western religion, and dualism in Western philosophy from the Neo-Platonists through Descartes. Before however, we proceed to Plato and other fourth century BCE thinkers, we must pause to inquire if there is any evidence of an explicit homophobia in sixth and fifth century Greek thought.

Tantalizing clues lead us in opposite directions, but no "smoking gun" evidence comes from those distant and obscure times. One of the most respected military leaders of ancient Greece was Epameinondas of Thebes. He was renowned not only as a strategist and general but for his honor and personal integrity. He is said to have been a pupil of Lysis,[65] one of the very last of the Learners, and a survivor of the massacre of Pythagoreans in the house of Milon in Cronona. Lysis is said to have taught the young Epameinondas to play the flute — which may sound trivial to us, though learning music in ancient Greece seems to have been more like what we might call a liberal education. At any rate, Epameinondas called Lysis his "father."

Epameinondas' great military standing came largely though his founding, or renewal, of the Sacred Band of Thebes,[66] an organization based on pairs of male lovers who fought side by side like the Sacred Band of Sparta. This was clearly an homoerotic organization. Furthermore, evidence suggests that Epameinondas himself was what we might call a Kinsey six — a male whose sexual orientation was completely directed toward other males. He never married, though there was strong social pressure on him to do so,[67] and Plutarch says that two of his lovers fought beside him at the Battle of Cunosephalae.[68]

On the face of it this would seem to indicate that Pythagoreans in the early period had no problem with homosexuality. However, this is not so clear. First of all, the evidence of Pythagorean influence in Epameinondas is late, and the Neo-Pythagoreans may have simply claimed as one of their own a man whose contact with the teachings of Pythagoras was slight. Moreover, there seems to have been two sets of ethics in the Orphic-Pythagorean worldview — the story of Milon suggests that what may have been forbidden to Hearers, was not to Learners. Quite possibly the massacre of the intellectual elite of the Pythagoreans about 450 BCE left only a less sophisticated following who knew only the ethics of the Hearers and passed them on to the Neo-Pythagoreans as the sole moral truth. Epameinondas may have been at the end of a secret tradition that died with him and with the freedom of Greece at a place called the Head of the Dog.

A second tantalizing bit of evidence comes from the fragments of Parmenides (born about 513 BCE). Parmenides seems in his youth to have been a Pythagorean. He had a mystical experience that led him out of a belief in Pythagorean duality and into a vision of oneness. The book that he wrote was divided into two parts, the first dealing with the Way of Truth (a unified world-view, that reality is "what is"), as opposed to the Way of Opinion (the Pythagorean fragmented world, the world of appearances). It is from this second part that we get a fragment that may have to do with homosexuality. Our fragments at this point come to us thirdhand. Cacaelius Aurelianus, a late Roman physician, discussed briefly what he considered the "disease" of desiring the passive role (that is, accepting the penis in the mouth or anus) in male-male sexual relations. Aurelianus in turn quotes Soranos of Ephesos, a Greek physician (about 100–50 CE), who was quoting from the second half of Parmenides' book. Three words of Greek are quoted in Aurelianus' Latin text, apparently from Parminides: "on the right, boys, on the left, girls" (fragment 17). The homophobic views of Aurelianus are typical of the educated Roman of his time. The source (Soranos/Parmenides) seems to be saying that the position that a couple assume in begetting a child determine the gender preference of that child. Parmenides is expounding what came to be call the doctrine of the double seed.[69] Because males have two testes and females have two ovaries, he is assuming that there are several possible combinations that shape the offspring. Apparently this is an early version of the argument that homosexuality is what we would call genetic. Parmenides (or his Pythagorean sources) may have believed that sexual union between a man and a woman with the man in the rear (the "doggy style" favored among ancient Greeks for heterosexual intercourse) aligned his testes with her ovaries (his right testicle on the same side as her right ovary, etc.). Since the list of opposites attributed by Aristotle to Pythagoras puts "male," "good" and "right side" in the same category, I suspect that the notion was that males were produced from the right testicle, and males produced by a conjuction of right testicle and right ovary were likely to be attracted to other males. However, males produced in the what came to be known as "missionary position," with the male on top, his face opposite her face, were thought likely to be heterosexual, since in that position his right testicle and her left ovary are on the same side.

The greatest dualism expressed by the Pythagoreans was certainly the dualism between self and the world. The fear of death as either annihilation or a shadow existence in the underworld, such as Homer described, seems to have led Pythagoras to separate himself from a body so obviously fated to die. Pythagoreanism is often called puritanical by modern writers; the term is perhaps an anachronism, but it carries a basic truth. Many of the ethical principles of the followers of Pythagoras were picked up by Christianity from the general Imperial culture of the first and second centuries of Christianity's existence and have reemerged again and again in the two millennia since. Fear and hatred of the body, of earth, and any sort of impurity, mark Pythagorean teaching from the beginning. Berkert says, "A Pythagorean acusma [saying] calls our birth a punishment. Such a puritanical attitude to life which sees our existence as a burden and a punishment can scarcely be called anything but Pythagorean."[70] Orphism-Pythagoreanism seems from its origins in the sixth century BCE to have represented the dark, solemn side of Greek thought and culture. When Greece itself fell into decline, Pythagoreanism found itself in its element.

3

Plato and the Tragedy
of Greece

Every nation is built on the blood of young men.
> — Oliver Wendell Holmes, Jr., lieutenant
> colonel, 20th Massachusetts Volunteers,
> War of the Rebellion

Power wrongly used defeats the oppressor and the oppressed.
> — Wally Lamb, *I Know This Much Is True*

The life of Plato, the son of Ariston, May 21, 428, to November 7, 348 BCE, spans the period of Athens' and Greece's greatness, and lasts well into its decline. He was old enough to have met old men who had fought at Marathon and had seen the sea at Salamis swim red with the corpses of Persians. Yet he lived long enough to correspond with Philip of Macedon, the king who would exterminate the freedom of Greece till modern times.

The glory of the victory of Greece over the invading Persians was such that Herodotus almost invented history to retell it; a small, disunified people had turned back the vast armies of the greatest empire of its time. That so many of the Greek armies, especially the elite corps such as the Sacred Band of Sparta, had been composed of same-sex lovers was not lost on the age that enjoyed the freedom so perilously won.

Arts flourished; Sophocles put same-sex lovers into his plays, and Pericles decked the new temple of Athena with the finest work of the greatest sculptors depicting young men in the bloom of their youth, naked in Pentalenic marble translucent to the light. But it cost money.

The roots of the decline of Greece are tangled and lost in its victory over the Persians. The Delian league had been formed, perhaps as early as 478 BCE, as an association of Greek city-states, centering on Athens to protect against and to harass the Persians, a perennial threat.[1] We need not name over the glorious names of Themistocles, Kimon, Pericles and the rest, who built the navy of Athens, warred on the Persians, and gradually turned the league that they headed into an Athenian empire. By 446 BCE law cases from the conquered Khalkis were being tried in Athenian courts.[2] Wealth flowed into the city, as it does into capitals of empires; the mines of Laurion, worked by slaves in unutterable misery, poured silver into the coffers of Pericles. What did not go to build more ships, fund more armies, Pericles diverted to the pockets of Iktinos and Kallikrates, the architects of the Parthenon, and Phidias its sculptor and a hundred other artists. Graceful beauty has its price, and Athens had the money

31

to buy it. The more cities Athens conquered, dominated, the larger its wealth and glory grew and the more beautiful it became. Plato's stepfather, Puralampos, was a political associate of Pericles, so it is likely the boy grew up very near to the springs of power. He saw too, heard, felt what a sensitive young man must have seen and heard, the disintegration of the very concept of freedom in the jingle of coins and the glamour of beauty.

Soon the Peloponnesian War began: powerful city-states such as Sparta and Thebes, outside Athens' hegemony, feared that city's growing power. Most of Greece was soon involved in a war of each against all. Plato was 12, a most impressionable age, when the armies of Athens overran Melos, an independent island-city in the Cyclides. Thucydides narrates the conversation (perhaps imaginary) between the Melians and the Athenians:

> MELIANS: How could it be just as good for us to be the slaves as for you to be the masters?
> ATHENIANS: You by giving in would save yourselves from disaster; we by not destroying you would be able to profit from you.
>
> ....
> MELIANS: Is that your subjects' idea of fair-play? ...
> ATHENIANS: So far as right and wrong are concerned, they think there is no difference.... By conquering you we shall increase not only the size but the security of our empire.... Our opinion of the gods and our knowledge of men lead us to conclude that it is a general and necessary law of nature to rule wherever one can.[3]

The Melians refused to surrender; the Athenians took the island, killed all the males, enslaved all the females. The appeal to raw power politics, what the Germans would later call *realpolitik*, seems to be new in the Greek context.

Athens' turn came soon enough. In 413 an enormous Athenian army was cut to pieces in Syracuse, and the following year Athens' empire revolted. In Athens there was a revolution, too, fueled by the too apparent failings of the democratic system. The oligarchs — men of wealth — seized the government and set up, in place of the democracy of Kleisthenes, a council of Four Hundred, selected by and owing their loyalty to a small body of the very rich who had long held ties to Sparta, as allies against the aggressive democracy of Athens. Democracy had lasted a century, half of it imperial. In the long sad story Thucydides tells, we may glimpse friends of Plato: Alkibiades had gone over to Sparta long before the fall of Athens. Plato is said by late biographers to have refused a career in politics; perhaps that decision saved him, as Wordsworth was to leave France on the eve of the Terror.

The Four Hundred lasted only a few months. An Athenian fleet with democratic leanings returned, the old democratic system was restored, and the war with Sparta went on.

At the end of summer in 405 BCE Lysander, navarch of Sparta, surprised and annihilated the Athenian fleet at a place called Aegosopotomi (Goat Rivers), and Athens was left defenseless. Xenophon, a disciple of Socrates less erratic than Alkibiades and less eloquent than Plato describes the fall for us; a single ship survived to return to Athens' harbor, Piraeus:

> It was at night that the *Parclos* arrived at Athens with tidings of the disaster and a sound of wailing ran from the Piraeus through the long walls to the city, one man passing the news to another, and through that night no one slept, all mourning, not for the loss alone, but more for their own selves, thinking they would suffer such treatment as they had vested on the Melians.[4]

The Spartans refused to destroy Athens, though their Corinthian allies wished it. The Comanche Indians have a saying: "If you pity a fallen enemy, you kill his heart." Probably nothing in its whole history to that point struck Athens more deeply than the mercy of its conquerors. Lysander set up a Council of Thirty to create an oligarchic government; it proved to be a reign of terror. Socrates was suborned by the Thirty to cooperate in the judicial murder of one Leon, which he refused to do. Sparta succeeded to the unstable condition of empire in Greece; then, in quick succession, Thebes dominated the Greeks. War followed war. The catalog of them, of the battles, of the thousands killed, is an *Ilias mallorum*, a thick book of sorrows that need not be repeated here.

Surely this hideous spectacle of a culture destroying itself led thoughtful persons to think seriously about the institution of pederasty. Armies cause wars just as wars cause armies. The institutionalized form of homosexuality had worked well; it was producing hundreds of thousands of young men, brave and efficient at war. One would be surprised if many of them did not wish for a war, so that they could prove themselves in the all-important eyes of their beloved.

When one begins to write about Plato, one is daunted by the complexity of the task. Like Homer before him, Plato is shy of using the first person singular pronoun; and, like Homer, he sets the tone for an age of the world. The canon of works that may be safely attributed to Plato is far from securely settled, and there are two distinct sorts of Platonic dialogues — the Socratic and what German scholars in the nineteenth century decided were "late dialogues." Moreover, there travel with the Platonic corpus 13 letters, also attributed to the Silver Swan of Athens, though most probably all are forgeries; and there are a few short poems that have come to us in the Greek Anthology that are attributed to Plato. Furthermore there is the issue of glamour. Because he is so great a writer, elegant, lively, calm and persuasive, it is difficult not to love Plato and accept with the worshiping ardor of a lover everything he wrote as both simple and true. A similar mystique gathers round, and easily clouds, the works of Homer, Dante, Shakespeare and a very few others.

The author of this study cannot settle questions that generations of scholars have labored over arriving at no clear conclusions. Here we shall assume that all the commonly accepted dialogues, with the exception of *The Laws* (about which much must be said) are by Plato; the authorship question to the extent that it involves authority is irrelevant here; date of composition is however of major importance, since that affects the understanding of the historic interrelations of ideas.

Individuals and ages have, as we shall see, interpreted the works of Plato by their own lights and come up with images of those works that others, later and with different interpretive techniques, find amazingly wrong-headed. Similarly, it is unlikely that the view of Plato taken here is beyond the reach of all mere systems, or that the "thing in itself" that is the real — we may say "ideal" — Plato is known to this generation as to none before. Modernism, which even at this writing is fading into postmodernism, is an ironic, self-aware way of dealing with texts; and deconstructionism takes this attitude to the point of absurdity. Joyce and Beckett cast long shadows, and exactly what those crabbed Greek texts mean in those shadows is difficult for us now to say.

First, and informing any discussion of Plato, is the question of dogma. No genuine work of Plato, not even so much as an epigram, survives that is not a dialogue. To say that here or there we have Plato saying this or that is like saying that in the "To be or not to be" monologue Shakespeare expresses his own ideas on suicide. Plato, like Homer, remains completely anonymous. I think Plato teaches — indeed he is one of the great teachers in all history — but what he teaches is not this or that specific insight, not dogma, but rather philosophy as ongoing dialectic. Here and there characters in the dialogues, usually Socrates, arrive at positions on some issue that they seem to recognize as "truth"; but they never transcend the dialogic framework, and the reasoning that they use to get to those points is sometimes so shaky as to call attention to itself. In other words the "truths" are quite possibly ironic; Dyson Clay and others have given us good reason to believe that the rationally constructed government outlined in the *Republic* is best read not as a utopia but as a dystopia. Plato is taking ideas of a perfect state, perhaps such as the Pythagoreans in his time were advocating, and showing their very absurdity by taking them to a logical extreme. The problem is we are apt to read the *Republic* as the *Communist Manifesto*, not as *Animal Farm*, to which latter it is closer in spirit.

What we find regarding homosexuality when we turn to Plato is at best puzzling, at worst homophobic. Throughout the genuine works pederasty is taken for granted, as almost any Athenian in that age would have taken it; the praise of same-sex love in the *Symposium* is both lavish and profound. Yet in other works of Plato a curious, semihomophobic twist is put on male-male sexual relations. This is approximately what has come to be known as "Platonic Love"—the notion that male lovers ought to desire each other, touch, kiss, do everything that lovers do except achieve climax.

This is, of course, an interdialogic teaching: Plato does not teach this as a dogma to his readers, but Socrates teaches it to his listeners, and seems to take it as a profound truth. The image that Socrates presents, as we shall see, in the *Phaedrus*, of male lovers lying beside each other with erections but having no climax, is so absurd a reader might take it for one huge joke, though considerations both within the dialogues and outside them seem to preclude that ironic reading. However absurd it may strike us, one suspects that the Socrates of the dialogues and the Plato who created him took the idea in all dead earnest. It is a slippery slope from there down to the blatant homophobia of the (perhaps pseudo–Platonic) dialogue the *Laws*. One feels one enters the world of magic so subtly as to hardly realize the fact.

He began well, but Plato contradicts himself. Any effort to hold that the statements about homosexuality in the *Symposium* do not contradict those about it in the *Phaedrus* and the *Republic* is doomed to failure. The truth of the matter seems to be, as Thomas Gould points out, that Plato's basic concept of the human's soul and its relationship to the world changed, the crux being in the *Phaedrus*.[5] The turn in Plato's thought seems to be externally induced; it comes from his contact with Pythagorean teachings. About 390 BCE, ten years after the death of Socrates, Plato went on a prolonged trip to Sicily and Italy and returned with much Pythagorean lore. Phrases like *phasi d' hoi saphoi* ("certain wise men say...") begin to appear in his dialogues introducing Pythagorean dogmas.[6] If we knew the exact date of the writing of the *Phaedrus*, then we might be able to pinpoint the momentous movement of the greatest mind of classical Greece away from the tradition of freedom and reason in which he and his generation had been nourished, backward toward magic and authoritarianism. It was a turn that the whole classical world made; and a dark age closed down, within a century of Plato's death, that was to last for two millennia.

Essentially then there are two Platos: the homosexuality-friendly Plato of the *Symposium*, who valued same-sex love as the bottom rung on the great ladder that leads up to God, and the homophobic Plato of the *Laws*, who forbade homosexuality for the first time in the history of Greek thought. As we shall see, scholars though antiquity wrestled with the inherent contradiction in these two positions.

It will be well to look at Plato's initial attitude toward homosexuality. In the *Symposium* (generally considered an early work) Plato thinks of sexual love as divine, initiatory and equalizing, whether male-female or male-male. It was perhaps Plato's desire, as Robinson Jeffers thought in his "Prescription of Painful Ends,"

> To gather the insights of the age summit against future loss
> ... Plato smiling carves dreams, bright cells
> Of incorruptible wax to hive the Greek honey.

The *Symposium* of Plato stands as the monument and in some ways the terminus marker of the golden age of pederasty in the Greek tradition. For a century and more after the Tyrant Slayers, Greek men had loved each other and freedom with it. Plato sums up half a dozen generations of love and desire and thought, and perhaps he sees in the dialogue some end in the "misted landscape" of its future.

The scene is an all-male drinking party, a symposium. These were common among the ancient Greeks, though one suspects the intellectual atmosphere was seldom as refined as Plato's narrative might make us assume.[7] As a sort of contest the guests take turn seeing who can praise Love (*eros*, here always same-sex love) in the most exalted terms. The speech of Pausanius is perhaps the finest encomium of same-sex love anywhere. The speech put in the mouth of Aristophanes offers a fantastic myth of the origins of love and mentions lesbian love for the first time outside of Sappho. It is simply the female parallel of male-male love. One searches in vain for a trace of patriarchy here.

But the speech of Socrates, who alone seems not to have gotten drunk, seems to be the authoritative voice on the subject. Plato makes Socrates tell of the teaching he received from a woman, Diotima. Perhaps Plato introduced her to add to the ambisexual nature of much of the dialogue.[8] Half-playfully, Love is said not to be a god at all (as both the commonly received mythology and the Orphic said he was); rather Love is a sort of demigod, halfway between the divine and the human.[9] Diotima has taught Socrates that love is experienced alike by males and females: "The conjunction of man and woman is a begetting [*tokos*] for both. It is a divine affair ... an immortal element in the creature that is mortal."[10] Furthermore the sexual imagery is obvious: a man experiencing sexual arousal is pregnant, "hence it is that when the pregnant approaches the beautiful it becomes not only gracious, but so exhilarate that it flows over with begetting and bringing forth, though when it meets the ugly it shrinks and curls up [*suspeiratai* and *aneilletai*] in a sullen dismay."[11] In Plato's Greece females were debarred from any participation in politics (though not in his ideal state). The noblest natures desire to bring forth the noblest offspring — a well-regulated city, and a man who is pregnant with this desire seeks a beautiful soul in a beautiful body. In the company of his beloved man, "he bears and brings forth his long-felt conception ... so that men in this condition enjoy a far fuller community with each other than that which comes with children."[12] The ultimate foundation of Kallipolis, the beautiful city, is in the *Symposium* the relation of two male lovers. From that community, rather than the biological family, truly beautiful human relations begin. The persistence of the image of sexual arousal seems to preclude any interpretation of this as a conventionally "Platonic" — that is sexless — relationship. Love, Socrates maintains in the *Symposium*, is the principle that gives energy to the soul. "That is the essence of the Platonic theory of love and it did offer an explanation of how the Good and therefore Intelligence functioned in the world."[13] Immortality in the *Symposium* is at best a philosophical sort of thing. Love is the lowest rung on the *klimax*, the ladder that goes up to the Ideas. Like Spinoza's Intellectual Love of God, the philosophical lover moves up from the love of one beautiful man, to a love of all beauty, to the everlasting idea of Beauty itself. To behold beauty itself is to share its timelessness — this is *theoria*, when the mortal looking upon the immortal with philosophical eyes becomes immortal for an instant.

But there are problems. The dialogue ends on a sour note. A drunken Alkibiades, crowned with vine leaves, as Dionysus was generally pictured, enters the party. He seems to be Eros personified, as Orphics understood that god.[14] Eros in the general understanding of the Greeks could be a baleful god, a bringer of discord and destruction, especially as he was portrayed in tragedy,[15] and this is a banquet celebrating Agathon's victory in writing tragedy. Alkibiades in real life had, as a young man, been in love with Socrates,[16] but as an adult he had proven a traitor to Athens. Brilliant, physically beautiful, erratic and unstable, yet the pupil of Socrates, the drunken Alkibiades may be taken as a critique of pederastic love. In the *Symposium*, Socrates refuses to have sex with him, though he tries his best to seduce the philosopher, literally crawling under his cloak. Socrates resists him and spends the night with him as chastely as a father would his son. Some have read Socrates' refusal to have sex with Alkibiades as a repudiation of Eros as pederastic love,[17] while others have seen the refusal not as a repudiation of Eros, but of Alkibiades, who was unworthy of love because he didn't understand it as a dialectic.[18]

The nearest this writer can come to an interpretation of the matter involves the image of the hollow Silenus that Alkibiades refers to. Our attention is focused at the climax of the *Symposium* on an unlikely pair of lovers, Socrates and Alkibiades, and lovers we have been told complement each other. Socrates and Alkibiades stand as a pair of lovers that are both in some way in disguise, mirror images of images with images in them. Alkibiades' speech at 215A compares Socrates to a hollow image of Marsyas, the satyr who was skinned alive for competing with Apollo: open the image of the horribly ugly flayed satyr and inside is a beautiful statue of a god. Yet the lover of Socrates who says this is himself in the costume of a beautiful god — Dionysus. Alkibiades admits his own failings; open the beautiful Dionysus/Alkibiades and you "see such black and grained spots / as will not leave their tinct."[19] His corruption lies in neglecting his soul for the sake of a political life (in Athens, in that age, the pursuit of power), and he admires Pericles' oratory. If we read this with an Orphic handbook near by, we see Alkibiades' Dionysian costume as the image of the conventional Eros — Eros the disrupter. But Eros in Orphic theology is a different god altogether — he is a form of both Phanes and Dionysus — the supreme and transcendent god who is in some way all things. Alkibiades disrupts the feast and ends as fine a bit of conversation as you will find anywhere. The only hope for redemption of this wild reveler is to really follow Socrates; his attraction to Socrates is Eros, sexual desire. There are three layers to Alkibiades — Eros, Dionysus and the inner man. His soul is, to borrow from another dialogue we must soon look at, tripartite. Only one of these is attracted to Socrates — Eros. His tragedy is that this is not enough. Plato elsewhere (*Gorgias*, 515B) can speak very harshly indeed about the leadership of Pericles.[20] If we take Anderson's surmise about Diotima seriously, then the confrontation of Socrates as private citizen and philosopher against Alkibiades as public man and corrupt individual — both, like Pericles and Aspasia, lovers — may be seen as a rejection, not of homosexual love, but of the kind of greed that in Pericles made Athens the capital of an empire and denied its highest ideals.

The basis of sexual thought in the *Symposium* is heterosexual, generative activity; Plato offers for consideration a male-male Eros that is, like male-female lovemaking, generative. Two related Orphic-Pythagorean interpretations suggest themselves. First, the dualistic thought implicit in Orphism must have demanded an ideal double to biologically reproductive sex — a "spiritually" reproductive sexuality that parallels and reduplicates the world of biological generation. Such an interpretation would, one suspects, arise spontaneously in anyone of a creative and philosophical bent who was habituated to think in dualities, so that we need not suppose any specific Pythagorean teaching with regard to homosexuality is being echoed here. Secondly, and more intimately Orphic, is the possibility that Plato is attempting to overcome the Orphic dogma of inherited sin. Everyone born of the union of a male and female the Orphics saw as inheriting in their material body a "Titanic nature," an inclination to violence and arrogant pride that was derived from the Titans, who murdered and ate Dionysus because humans are made from the ashes of those Titans. The new children that are born in lovers' eyes, ideal selves, are not from the earth, and so free from the taint of "that ancient grief."

Plato's *Republic* is a book-long dialogue that attempts to define and exemplify justice with a Just City, Kallipolis, as an example. Much of the dialogue is concerned with a detailed plan for the social organization of Kallipolis. Modern readings of the *Republic* almost inevitably read it as Karl Popper did, in the light of World War II and the absolute states that have so troubled the middle part of the twentieth century. It seems inescapable that something of the impulse of both the Fascists and Marxists comes from Plato, and from the *Republic* particularly — how could it not, when so much of Western thought for good or ill derives from the same source? Partly, one suspects, in order to rescue Plato from implication in Auschwitz and the gulags, some modern readers have read the *Republic* ironically and seen it as an antiutopia, "an antidote to the utopian spirit."[21] Certainly the philosopher-kings in the *Republic* look like Pythagoreans, and the work may be read as a satire on that "Dorian absolutism" and greed that had brought on the Peloponnesian War and as a critique of Pythagorean anti-intellectualism in the banning of poets.[22] This would be clear enough if Plato had written only the *Republic*, but there are other works. Diskin Clay has argued that the *Republic* is "the only Platonic dialogue which displays *within* itself the possible dialogues the argument of any Platonic dialogue can and should provoke — the argument that it is ironic."[23] John Randall, Jr., has argued[24] essentially the same point. If we turn to the *Republic* on the topic of same-sex love we find hints of the curious abstention that we will discuss at length in the *Phaedrus*. The following passage from the third book of the *Republic* sounds serious:

"Then," said I, "when there is a coincidence of a beautiful disposition and corresponding and harmonious beauties of the same type in the bodily form — is not this the fairest spectacle for one who is capable of its contemplation?"

"Far the fairest."

"And surely the fairest is the most loveable?"

"Of course."

"The true musician would love persons of this sort; but if there were disharmony, he would not love this."

"No," he said, "not if there were a defect in the soul; but if it were in the body he would bear with it and still be willing to bestow his love."

"I understand," I said, "that you have had favorites [*paidika*, more explicitly boy-loves] of this sort and I grant you your distinction. But tell me this, can there be any communion between soberness and extravagant pleasure?"

"How could there be," he said, "since such pleasure puts a man beside himself [*ekphrona*] with pleasure no less than pain?"

"Or between it and virtue [*arete*] generally?"

"By no means."

"But is there between pleasure and insolence and license [*hubrei te kai akolasia*]?"

"Most assuredly."

"Do you know a keener pleasure than that associated with Aphrodite [more literally, with sex]?"

"I don't," he said, "nor yet of any more insane."

"But is not the right love a sober and harmonious love of the orderly and beautiful?"

"It is indeed," said he.

"Then nothing of madness [*manikon*], nothing akin to license [*akolasias*— unpruned, unchecked, not disciplined, nor punished or cut back, hence licentious] must be allowed to come nigh the right love [*ortho eroti*]?"

"No."

"Then this kind of pleasure may not come nigh, nor may lover and beloved [*eraste te kai paidikois*, older male lover and boy-love] who rightly love and are loved have anything to do with it?"

"No, by Zeus, Socrates," he said, "it must not come nigh them."

"Thus then as it seems you will lay down the law in the city that we are founding that the lover [*erastein*] may kiss [*philein*] and pass time with and touch the beloved [*paidikon*] as he would a son, for honorable reasons, if he persuade him [*ton kalon kharin, ean peithe*]. But otherwise he must so associate with the objects of his care, that there should never be any suspicion of any thing further, on penalty of being stigmatized for want of taste and true musical culture."

"Even so," he said [The *Republic*, Book III, 403A–C].

The whole sense of the passage turns on the subjunctive.[25] *Hubris* is a more serious word. It is a relationship of hubris that is forbidden here — where the boy is not persuaded to accept the man, and the man is forcing himself on the boy. If the boy will not accept the man, then the man must act toward him as a father does. But if the boy accepts they may become lovers, and the lover may touch his beloved — but no more than that. Thus they avoid any possibility of hubris, the sort of arrogant pride that made free states seize others out of greed and a lust for power. That the relationship of man and boy here is to be defined like that between a father and a son is yet another point to which we must return. The *Republic*'s tone when it refers to same-sex love is unmistakably light. Those who win a prize of valor in war are to be rewarded not only with crowns:

> "But I presume you wouldn't go as far as this?" "What?" "That he should kiss and be kissed by everyone?" "By all means," he said, "and I add to the law the provision that during the campaign none whom he wishes to kiss be allowed to refuse, so that if one is in love with anyone, male or female, he may be more eager to win the prize."[26]

It is hard to miss the humor here, either in the pretended shock of or Socrates' response that tends to make war a kissing game. Even the homophobic Paul Shorey[27] can call this "deplorable facetiousness."[28] Taken seriously, and there is that level too, the frequent references to harmony in this passage show that Pythagorean thought is in the background, not very far away.[29] Aristotle in his *Politics* is puzzled by the attitude toward homosexuality in the *Republic*. He admits that there might be some problem in Plato's ideal state of fathers and sons becoming lovers (since parents would not know their children) — the Greeks were always deeply troubled by any suggestion of incest — but Aristotle cannot understand why homosexual love was found "objectionable" by Plato.[30] The *Republic* seems at best a satire whose point is often missed, but it requires more definite statements of homophobia from Plato to read it as sincerely homophobic.

The *Phaedrus* is Plato's examination of the irrational nature of love and the rhetoric related to love and seduction. It is probably later than the *Symposium*,[31] and it takes its name from the beautiful lad who was so admired in that dialogue. Socrates and Phaedrus meet while walking outside Athens in the beautiful countryside. The two are alone; it's a perfect place for a seduction; there are bushes everywhere, and any one of them might serve to conceal two lovers performing the rites of Eros. Socrates cannot hide that he is attracted to young Phaedrus; the drama of the dialogue is Socrates resisting his urges to seduce with rhetoric the younger man[32]; thus the action of the dialogue imitates one of its themes — sexless love. The younger man has a copy of a speech on Love by Lysis. He reads it, and the related topics of love and rhetorical seduction are opened up. To talk about love, we must first talk about the human soul; Socrates tells us: "Every soul is immortal. For the ever-moving is never dying.

But that which moves something else or is moved by something else when it stops dies."[33] Thus, in a few sentences, the psychology of the *Symposium* is revoked. The soul is no longer seen as moved by the beloved but moves itself eternally. The endless circling of souls about the world is led by Zeus; and the chariots of the lesser gods, demigods and human souls follow. Soul can rule the world when it is perfect, but when a soul falls it becomes incarnated in a human or other animal.[34] The rule of destiny[35] is that some souls, because of unruly horses or unskilled drivers, are "filled with forgetfulness and evil and so grow heavy," and fall from the heavens and become mortals. Those who have seem the most of truth before the fall become philosophers and so begin to mount back up to the heavens, but there are eight lesser categories, each farther from heaven:

1. The first category, already mentioned
2. Lawful kings
3. Politicians and businessmen
4. Gymnasts and those concerned with the care of the body
5. Prophets or mystagogues
6. Poets and artists
7. Crafters, farmers
8. Sophists, demagogues
9. Tyrants.[36]

Of these the philosophical will return to the skies and follow the endless procession again after 3,000 years and numerous reincarnations. The metaphor of the charioteer is resumed; now the charioteer approaches his beloved boy. The dark horse becomes wild and unruly, wishing to do something evil to the beloved; but the charioteer after a long and painful struggle subdues the wild horse:

And as this intimacy continues and the lover comes near and touches the beloved in the gymnasia and in their general intercourse [*homilias*— nonsexual intercourse], then the fountain of that stream which Zeus, when he was in love with Ganymede, called "desire" flows copiously upon the lover [*erasten*— the older male] ... the stream of beauty passes back into the beautiful one through the eyes, the natural inlet to the soul... [255B–C]. Now as they lie together [*sugkoimmesei*— literally to lie side by side, though it has about the same sexual implication in Greek as in English] the unruly horse of the lover [*erastou*] has something to say to the charioteer and demands a little in compensation of his many pains; and the unruly horse of the boy says nothing, but swelling and not knowing what to do, throws himself upon the older man and kisses him, violently as his most welcome well-wisher. When they lie burning side by side [*sugkatakeontai*] he would not refuse the older man his share if he asked it, but the other horse and the charioteer oppose all this with modesty and reason. If the better elements of the mind, which lead to a well ordered life and to philosophy, prevail, they lead a life of happiness and harmony, self controlled and orderly, enslaving [*doulosamenoi*] that which causes evil in the soul.... If however they live a life less noble and without philosophy, but yet ruled by the love of honor, probably when they have been drinking or in some other moment of carelessness, the two unruly horses, taking the souls off their guard, will bring them together and seize upon and accomplish that which is by the many accounted blissful; and when this has once been done, they continue the practice, but infrequently, since what they are doing is not approved by the whole mind. So these two pass through life as friends [*philo*].... At last when they depart from the body ... shall live a happy life in the light as they journey together [256A–D].

Now he who is not newly initiated, or has been corrupted, does not quickly rise from this world to absolute beauty when he see its namesake here, and so does not revere it when he looks upon it, but gives himself up to pleasure, but like a four-legged animal attempts to go upon [*bainein*—literally to go upon, used by Herodotus 1, 192 of the mating of horses] and begetting children [*paidosporein*—literally sowing the seed of babies]; he makes arrogance [*hubrei*] his companion and is not afraid or ashamed to pursue pleasure against nature [*para phusin*] [250D].

The traditional interpretation of these passage from the *Symposium*, the *Republic*, and the *Phaedrus* is that Plato was talking about unconsummated homosexual love consistently throughout the three dialogues. This is difficult to believe, especially when he describes a fully consummated sex act between two men literally enough to verge on pornography. The passage at 250D is the crux of the puzzle. Sex, some sort of sex, is being condemned as *para phusin*, "against nature." This sex is like the mating of horses and involves *paidosporein*—a word that is almost identical to the English term "making babies." That homosexual activity is "against nature" is perhaps the most common charge used to condemn it (though hardly the most reasonable) and the central point of condemnation in the *Laws*. Yet here the term is applied to what horses do, as well as, it seems, to what heterosexual humans do in the act of reproducing. Gregory Vlastos reads this as condemning homosexuality exclusively.[37] Kenneth J. Dover reads the same passage as referring to heterosexual intercourse.[38] There is some considerable doubt posed at the beginning of the Second Speech as to how seriously we should take it,[39] but both scholars may be right. The passage condemns sex without reference to the gender of the participants. Sex, regardless of the genders of the participants, is likely to lead to *hubris*, to turn into arrogant pride. The desire for pleasure can cause humans to do terrible things. Such arrogant pride is no essentially different from the rhetoric of Pericles that sent the armies of Athens marching over Melos and anyone else that opposed them. Metaphorically, the wrong kind of rhetoric is rape.

Socrates here seems to recommend that the most passionate desire be carried through to the very brink of consummation—but not beyond. The consequences of "going all the way," though, are not too dire. Only philosophers have wings that can carry them back to the heavenly procession without many incarnations; those who give way and actually have sex with their boys have their wings fall off. It seems to be taken for granted that the nonphilosophical will have sex routinely. At the same time it is clear that homosexual desire is what causes wings to grow [255D], in the philosophical, at any rate. One rather suspects that here "to grow wings" means to become sexually aggressive—like Zeus who became an eagle to rape Ganymede. After 3,000 years, even the unwinged will return to the procession. A very close parallel is the Hindu concept of *tapas*. By refraining from indulgence in sensory pleasure (including all forms of sex) the ascetic gains a sort of spiritual power, *tapas*, that can be used for everything from gaining enlightenment to working magic.[40]

This seems to one reader very un–Platonic. It is, Socrates admits, a *mythos*, a story told to illustrate a point. The point is both philosophical and political. Eros brings men together in love, and that is good—so love may well be called a god. But Eros can change its character: once the possibility of consummation enters the picture, so does possessiveness, greed, willfulness—in short, *hubris*. If we keep in mind the political background of the Melian dialogue, as well as Plato's recurring image of homosexuality as generative sex from the *Symposium*, then a little-known passage from the Platonic tradition can explain why the lovers in the *Phaedrus* are expected to have unconsummated love. Socrates, who is working hard at not having sex with Phaedrus, calls himself elsewhere a "midwife" to ideas.[41] Midwives are, of course, female and do not impregnate women — rather they help to pull out what is already in them. Plutarch, more than 400 years after Plato, applies this idea to the question of Platonic dogma. Plutarch says "begetting" (*genan*) is inimical to the practice of judgment.[42] Plutarch holds, as many modern scholars do, that Socrates did not teach a dogma. Socrates "maintained nothing."[43] It is widely held that homosexual acts between older men and younger in ancient Greece were an effort to transfer to the younger the manly traits of the elder through the semen; by depositing his semen, his metaphorical manhood, on or in a younger man, the older male impregnated him with *arete*— virtue in the older sense of the term. The evidence of Plutarch implies that this metaphor was extended to philosophical teaching. To dogmatize, to teach specific doctrines as true is to impregnate with ideas. This Socrates refused to do. Like the Diotima of the *Symposium*, he was female to the young men he taught, remaining outside them and with a relentless criticism of casual opinion, urging them to give birth, rather than impregnating them. This, to take Plutarch's word for it, seems to have been the understanding of the followers of Plato as late as the second century CE. With this in mind we may look back at not only the *Phaedrus* but the passages in the *Republic* that imply that homosexual desire was good and to be encouraged (the lovers lying side by side on fire with desire); but operating within the metaphorical understanding of philosophy as sex act, we can also understand why the sex act was spoken of as unconsummated. The teaching of opinion, the use of false rhetoric to persuade young men to accept penetration, was all too like the invasion of Mellos — and act of *hubris* that must be avoided.

Xenophon in his *Symposium* has Socrates say much the same sort of thing — that pederastic union must go without physical climax. Xenophon was a disciple of Socrates as well, and it is possible he heard the latter say something to that effect; however, it is fairly clear that Xenophon's work is derived from Plato's *Symposium*, written somewhat earlier.[44] Xenophon is not the philosopher that Plato was, nor the writer, though his *Symposium* is probably his best work. When the subject of same-sex lovers comes up Socrates is vehement. Referring to Pausianius' speech in Plato's *Symposium*, Socrates says:

> Pausanius says of those who wallow in lasciviousness [*akrasia*] that the most valiant army would be composed of lovers and their boys. For these in his opinion would be least likely to desert one another. A remarkable statement! For persons accustomed to censure and shameless acts toward one another should be induced to act by fear of shame! And he added as evidence that this was the policy of both the Thebes and Ellis. Anyway he said that though they shared the beds of [*sunkatheudontas*] their boys, nevertheless they put them by their sides in battle. This is what he said, but the two cannot be compared because use of boys is an acquired custom among those people, but with us it is a matter for the greatest reproach [*Symposium*, 8.32–34].

Xenophon contradicts himself, however; earlier in his *Symposium* Socrates asks the Syracusan if he sleeps with his boy, and the Syracusan replies:

> "Of course, all night, every night."
> "By Hera!" said Socrates, "you are fortunate that your flesh alone does not corrupt [*diaphtheirein*] those who sleep with you" [*Symposium*, 4.53–54].

All in all Xenophon's attitude toward pederasty is inconsistent, here as in his other writings, and his facts are impossible to reconcile with each other.[45]

If sexual intercourse (clearly implied by "sleep with" in English as in Greek) were so shameful at Athens, it hardly seems likely that the Syracusan guest would have admitted to it with such gusto. Furthermore, Socrates regards homosexual coitus as inevitably corrupting, though he also regards it as only a matter of local custom, right in one place, evil in another.

The often commented upon conjunction of flirtatious sexuality and abstruse discussion of the ethics of rhetoric in the *Phaedrus* becomes then much more understandable; what is "unnatural" about sex—whether homosexual or heterosexual—(the word Plato uses is more often concerned with heterosexual coupling) is the disastrous arrogance that it can produce. Only if we see this in metaphorical terms—sex = teaching, dogma = rape—does it begin to make something like sense. And that sense stands out boldly against the politics of Plato's time.

To put it in readily understandable if vulgar modern terms, Athens had thoroughly fucked the Melians and the other states in its empire. The persuasive power of Periclean oratory had seduced the state to its arrogant pride, and eventually Athens would pay the price. There was a sort of folk belief current in Athens at this time that the Spartans, though they practiced boy love, did not actually have sex with the boys.[46] Is Sparta's merciful dealing with conquered Athens somewhere in the back of Plato's mind when he writes this?

There is, however, another context in which we may consider the tripartite soul in the *Phaedrus*; Plato is mystical-religious. This three-part soul belongs to the world of Orphism, not the common religion of Plato's time; the immortality vouchsafed by the image of the procession is a much more literal one than that of the *Symposium*, implying a continuation of the personality throughout endless time, while that in the earlier work is an abstract participation in eternity. A close parallel to the myth in the *Phaedrus* is the myth of Er near the end of the *Republic*, which also includes the descent of the guilty soul and reincarnation; this is not a unique expression, but a part of Platonic thought. Is Plato addressing the common, unphilosophical multitude with a homely parable? The highly sophisticated reasoning about rhetoric that much of the *Phaedrus* is concerned with makes that seem far-fetched.

Reluctantly we must admit as a likely fact that the Silver Swan of Athens, at some point, perhaps late in his life, embraced the teachings of Orphic-Pythagoreanism. One is saddened to say it, yet the evidence is conclusive, both internally and externally, that Plato knew and used Pythagorean teachings in at least his later dialogues. Olympiadorus, who knew Orphism better than we ever can, tells us Plato was "full of echoes of Orpheus,"[47] and a modern researcher, Jane Harrison, finds Plato "deep dyed in Orphism."[48] Plato went to Sicily, first perhaps about 390 BCE. Diogenes Laertius says the first trip was made with the goal of observing lava from Mt. Aetna (though this sort of scientific concern with physical phenomenon sounds uncharacteristic of Plato). While he was there he became involved in perhaps the two greatest disasters of his life—the affair with Dion and Pythagorean philosophy. The second of these is of paramount importance to our present study.

Why Pythagoreanism, and why Plato? Perhaps Plato's contact with Pythagoreanism came earlier than his trip to Italy about 390 BCE. Aristophanes' *Clouds* (first version produced in 423 BCE when Socrates was 45) parodies the Orphic initiations, with Socrates being initiated (lines 250 and following).[49] Any answer must, of course, be speculative. We know little about the development of Plato's mind; but the historical context does offer, if not a justification, at least a rationalization of Plato's affinity for the Pythagorean teaching. Eric Dodds reminds us that "Plato's thought was historically conditioned."[50] A brilliant and sensitive young man, Plato had grown up in the shadow of fallen greatness. Greece, especially Athens, had, in the wake of the victory over the Persians, experienced a golden age without parallel in human history. The very names of Pericles, Sophocles, Aristophanes, Phidias and Socrates suggest heights seldom matched let alone surpassed in politics, drama, art and philosophy. But by the time the young man Plato had cut his hair and taken his first lover, it was all beginning to fall apart. The democracy of Athens, built, legend said, on the blood of two martyred lovers, had turned to an empire, feeding ruthlessly on its weaker neighbors. The city ruled by reason and measure, guided by such godlike men, had betrayed its own ideals, and by the time Plato was in his maturity, had paid the price in blood, treasure and humiliation. If the truly Beautiful City was ever to be built, it must have seemed to Plato that it would have to be built on some basis other than what he had known, seen with his own eyes, of the City of Reasonable Men. The Peloponnesian War brought into severe question the ability of mere humans to govern themselves successfully. The democrats of Athens had proven themselves to be tyrants to the Melians and others who stood in their way to power. Pythagoreanism held out the offer of a transcendence of human nature. It proposed to create, through ascetic discipline and the revealed wisdom of a divine sage, a new, superhuman nature — the nature of the sage. Only a few humans could become true sages, but only a few were needed if they could be put in absolute power to save the rest of humanity from themselves.[51] Surely to Plato and to many another in his time, and since, Pythagoreanism seemed the last, best hope of a tragically flawed, self-doomed humanity.

Not that Plato swallowed Pythagoreanism whole; the *Republic* is as much a criticism and satire on Pythagorean ideals as it is an exposition of them, but while granting a deeply ironic mindset in Plato, and the ability to play with ideas that are to some fraction embraced, we must conclude with some sadness that Plato looked upon the Pythagorean corpus of ideas as it existed in his time, with no small admiration and desire to implement. The desire for wealth and power had led Athens astray from its democratic principles; the desire of one young man for another had formed the discipline of the armies that had crushed Melos and a hundred other innocent places. The powerless, money-despising Socrates had been killed by the democratic, pederastic state. It was time to try asceticism. This is the central disaster of classical civilization and the birth of homophobia almost at the same instant.

It is important then that we look at Plato's indebtedness to his Pythagorean context to understand how that later such a document as the *Laws* could be attributed to Plato. Moreover, the Neo-Platonic tradition, which was distinctly homophobic, results largely from an unholy union of Pythagorean thought and Platonic. That later generations of scholars were so readily able to see the two schools of thought as compatible is in no small way due to the Pythagorean element already implicit here and there in Plato. One rotten apple spoils a barrel, as they say.

We have no direct evidence regarding the pre–Platonic thought of the Pythagoreans on homosexuality, as we have already said. In the *Phaedo* Socrates is made to discuss the immortality of the soul with two Pythagoreans, Simmias and Kebes. Indeed, as Dodds has pointed out, the abstracted states of thought that Socrates is said to have gone into suggest that he was, or was being portrayed by Plato as, a shaman in the tradition of Pythagoras.[52] It is said that on his first trip to Italy Plato sought admission to the Pythagorean brotherhood, which had survived there, but was refused; Cicero records what may be an oral Latin tradition that Plato met Archytas of Tarentum, famed general, political leader and Pythagorean.[53] Theopompos, the pupil of Isocrates, says that Plato borrowed from the teaching of Bryson, a Pythagorean.[54]

Then there is the famous matter of the Pythagorean book. Early accounts say that Plato, perhaps at great expense, perhaps through the intervention of Dionysus of Syracuse, obtained a book or books of Pythagorean teachings — the *hupermnemata* of Philolaos, or another Pythagorean. This story goes back to Timon of Phlios the sillographer (320–230 BCE), a writer of satires. That Plato had such a book by some Pythagorean and used it in the *Timaeus* seems certain.[55] A handful of fragments attributed to Philolaos have survived, and a small river of ink has been spilled over the question of which, if any, are genuine; happily the fragments only concern cosmology and mathematics and may be ignored here. The story that Plato obtained such a book is not unlikely; about 390 most of the original members of Pythagoras' secret society were dead or about to die; apparently some of the few who knew the esoteric inner teachings chose to put them in writing rather than let them die utterly. Probably the first Pythagorean books appeared about this time, and it is not unlikely that a man like Plato would have been anxious to get one.[56]

More convincing, more damning, if you will, is the testimony of Aristotle that Plato knew and used Pythagorean ideas about the One and the metaphysical nature of number — though, says Aristotle, he approached them with dialectic, not as the Pythagoreans did, as dogma.[57] The metaphysics of the *Timaeus* reflect an essential problem that was to vex Neo-Platonism to its very end — dualism versus monism. Plato, in what is perhaps his last genuine dialogue,[58] sees the world as created by a single source, God, but the manner of creation is dualistic. God creates a lesser god, the demiurogos, who then creates the soul of the world by combining opposites into duples, quadruples, etc., then according to harmonic ratios.[59] The ever-circling sun, moon and planets are the visible soul of the universe, just as the human soul in the *Phaedrus* is the circling soul of the individual. The smell of Pythagoras is everywhere in that cosmology, yet tempered by monism. The result is perhaps the most monumental confusion anywhere: everything is One, yet everything is Two. The One and the Two would lie side by side in philosophical thought for a long age of the world, more restless, surely, than any unconsummated lovers.

Something must be said, though little can be said, of Plato's famous speech "On the Good"; the tradition has it that sometime late in his life Plato gave a long lecture on this topic before the assembled Academy. The speech was about the One and the Two, the good and God understood as numbers — in short a sort of Pythagorean-Platonic lecture. He spoke without notes, and all we know of the speech is what is reported of it by those who heard it; it seems to have been long, esoteric and utterly confusing. One tradition has it that no one stayed to the end of the speech except Aristotle[60] — "audience enough," said Cicero, grandly.

If we believe the late and unreliable biographical tradition, Plato had hopes of saving his world more directly, through a young prince of Syracuse he was in love with, Dion. Dion was a younger son of Dionysus II, the tyrant of Syracuse. When Dion's father died, Plato is said to have advised the young man on ways of coming to power by disposing of his older, unphilosophical brother, who took the throne. The idea apparently was to create a philosopher-king, a brilliant young man trained by Plato in the pederastic tradition and fit to save, if not the world, a great city at least. Of course the plan failed. Dion was no more worthy of his teacher than Alkibiades had been of his. If the story is true (and in rough outline it probably is), then this was the high-water mark of pederasty, and the point at which it irrefutably begins its last decline. Perhaps the sad, last word is that Plato himself never succeeded in fitting all the pieces together, the rational tradition and the mystic — what had created Greece and what he hoped would save it.

Plato certainly used Pythagorean ideas on politics and the art of rulership; we have seen that the evidence suggest the early Pythagoreans favored absolute government, and absolutism, from the time of Hippias onward, looked on pederasty as prodemocratic and its natural enemy. The Guardians of the *Republic* resemble Pythagorean initiates, as we have said, and their rule was absolute. The notion is that a sort of super race of humans may be selected and trained by an ascetic discipline in such a way as to transcend the normal human passions. Dodds calls them "shamans." These were the inner circle of the Pythagoreans, and Plato makes them the Guardians of his perfect state.[61] The general advice on statecraft that Plato gives in his *Politicus* (also translated as the *Statesman*) strongly resembles the teachings *Concerning Kingdom* of Diotogenes, Ekphantos of Syracuse and Sthenidas of Locri (Neo-Pythagoreans all), suggesting that Plato and those later authors all drew on some common source of Pythagorean statecraft.[62] The point in *Politikcos* (2297 E 4) that puts the king above the law is thought to be an echo of Archytas the Pythagorean, whose rule in Tarentum was extra-legal.[63]

As to Plato's position on the politics of his time, the record is contradictory but not encouraging. He is said in a tradition that goes back to the late third century BCE to have been a lover of Aster, who died fighting against Philip II of Macedon,[64] yet a later tradition has him sending friendly advice to that destroyer of Greek freedom. One suspects that the tradition of Plato's aid to Philip is, like the letter that narrates it, a later forgery. Theopompos of Khios, who seems to have been a consistently anti–Pythagorean writer, calls Plato's disciples "tyrannical and diabolical."[65] Perhaps his prejudice was showing; however, history does say, reliably, that a large percentage of Plato's disciples became tyrants.[66] This fact is indisputable, but context does soften it; the generation that followed Plato had an atmosphere where tyranny thrived, and the example of Socrates and Alkibiades reminds us that the disciple does not always reflect the teacher.

But it is through a sort of constellation of ideas that we may come nearest to understanding the Pythagorean sources of Plato's doctrine of homosexual restraint. In the *Phaedrus* it occurs in conjunction with the doctrine of the tripartite soul. That idea, that the soul has an irrational part, a rational part and a spiritual part, which is expressed more than once in Plato, is Pythagorean.[67] Related in the Platonic context is the image of the soul circling forever; this occurs long before Plato's time in the writings of Alkmaeon of Croton[68] and is picked up in later Pythagorean writings. That its most characteristic expression occurs in a passage that also expresses most fully the concept of unconsummated sex between male lovers suggests strongly that this may have been a Pythagorean idea too, one that was traveling in company with the idea of the tripartite soul. Xeneophon puts the same idea in the mouth of Socrates. That Plato put these ideas forward together suggests that both were Pythagorean, though to what extent he modified them cannot be known. The mind of Plato was nothing if it was not creative, ironic and subtle. It is absurd to think of him embracing without question or modification any dogma; Pythagoreanism interested him, and he clearly went to some lengths to inform himself on what must have been almost as obscure a topic to him as it is to us. That Plato was interested at all in it is probably the highest praise that can be lavished upon early Pythagoreanism. He played with it, changed it, and no doubt deepened whatever of it he touched. Finally we can say that it is there in the works of Plato, but we can never say exactly what is there, in regard to homosexuality or any other topic; Pythagoras haunts Plato elusively and, through Plato, the rest of Western thought.

The death of Plato in 347 BCE will, conveniently for us, mark the end of an epoch. If we pass in review the public status of homosexuality in the Greek word in that year we find it still flourishing, though now shadowed. Aristophanes could still write of it with approval, Plato could attribute to homosexual desire the growth of philosophical wings, but a ruler who was both an adherent of Orphism and publicly homophobic was on the throne of Macedon and beginning to menace all of Greece. Philip II of Macedon was already looking to pick up the pieces of the Greek city-states that had shattered themselves in more than a century of war; democracy that had institutionalized male homosexuality to support itself was in deep peril. Demosthenes' "First Philippic," a ringing speech denouncing the tyrant of Macedon, was delivered four years before Plato died.

4

Macedonian Imperialism and the Hellenistic Age

THE POLITICAL SCENE

> History is the story of hobnail boots climbing up stairs and silk slippers
> padding down.
>
> — Voltaire

On a day in August of 338 BCE the last battle for the freedom of ancient Greece was fought and lost. The opponents were apt leaders for what they represented — almost living symbols: Philip and Demosthenes. Thebes was the leader of a shaky alliance of free city-states including Athens and Corinth, held together by little more than the ringing oratory of Demosthenes, who was himself in the Athenian contingent of the battle. Beside him, in the center of the allies' battle line on the plain near the little town of Chaeronea, stood the Sacred Band of Thebes, 300 male lovers, the elite troops of all Greece.

Three miles long the battle line stretched, to the River Cephisos. Against the Thebans and their allies stood Philip II, King of Macedon. A stout man, with a scar in place of his right eye, he was by religion an Orphic, and he was homophobic, the first distinctly homophobic man we know of in Greek history. He was also a brilliant tactician. Philip had arranged his foot soldiers in great squares, defended in front against cavalry charges by men carrying long pikes — the famous Macedonian phalanx.

When the battle joined, the center of the Macedonian line consisted of cavalry led by Philip's son, Alexander, then 22 years old and a promising young man. His horsemen broke the Theban line. Philip turned his foot soldiers against the Athenians. Many died; the rest fled. Demosthenes fled, throwing behind him his shield with the Greek word for "luck" painted on it. Hopeless, the 300 men of the Sacred Band fought on, dying to the last man, as the Sacred Band of Sparta had died, saving Greece.[1]

It was not a holy war for the Macedonians; Philip's interest was power. The fact that the men he cut down like ripe wheat in the summer sun were same-sex lovers was largely irrelevant to the king of Macedon; perhaps it meant more to his son, Alexander. Alexander, forever to be remembered as Alexander the Great, was the first example we know of anywhere of a "closet case," a person raised to repress his or her homosexuality. What it meant to this young man as he triumphed across the field, killing pair after pair of lovers, who in desperation fought back to back like the statues of the Tyranacides in Athens, we may only speculate — perhaps he thought it was something in himself he killed, again and again, something his father called a weakness, a womanliness.

When the heavy red sun set on the seventh of the month of Metageitnion, Philip II of Macedon was absolute king, not only of Macedon but of all of Greece. The freedom that the Greeks had maintained at battles like Thermopylae and Salamis, and in insurrections like that of the Tyranacides, they had frittered away in endless wars among themselves — first the series of wars relating to the Athenian empire, its growth and destruction, then in wars among the victors over Athens. Now, bled white and led by incompetents like the Athenian Kares, they fell to what they regarded as outside forces — the semibarbaric Macedonians.

The Macedonians were a Greek tribe who settled on the seacoast in the northwestern fringes of the Greek world in times beyond the reach of history. From there they extended their power inland, over a period of centuries, conquering and intermarrying with the wild tribes of Anatolian, Illyrian and Thracian peoples that occupied the woody valleys north and west of Mount Olympus. By the time we can glimpse them historically, the Macedonians spoke a language distinct from Greek and worshiped a pantheon of deities parallel to but distinct from those of the Hellenic peoples of the south. Dionysus, whom they called Sabazios, was particularly popular. They retained a form of government identical to that in Homeric times — an absolute monarchy,[2] and their long experience with the inland tribes had made them inveterate imperialists.

By the mid–fourth century BCE Macedon was a powerful kingdom, ruled by a dynasty that claimed descent from Herakles, hence related to the royal houses of Sparta and other surviving monarchies[3] (presumably they acknowledged Herakles' relations with Iolos, as well as other young men). For centuries the royal court at Pella had imported culture wholesale from the south; Greek was the official language of royal administration.[4] The very little we know of native Macedonian sexual mores suggests that they had no more aversion to homosexuality per se than did their Greek neighbors. King Archelaus of Macedon was assassinated by a conspiracy of two of his lovers, Krateias and Hellenokrates, about 400 BCE; Aristotle tells us that Hellenokrates joined the plot because he concluded that Archelaus had been his lover out of willful arrogance, rather than passionate love.[5] The remark is telling: The death of Archelaus occurred just at the point when Macedon was emerging from a backwater of Greek culture to a leading position in the scramble for power that the decline of Athens prompted. Homosexuality at just the same point was turning from an exchange of pleasures, knowledge, and perhaps wisdom to a miniature of power politics. Theopompos of Chios in the next century tells us the men of the court in Macedon were "he-whores" (*hetairai*), and the common men of Macedon would readily offer their rears to all comers.[6] Worse yet, says our historian, the men shaved their bodies, and adult men had sex with adult men[7] — body hair was considered quite a sexual turn-off by then, among the Greeks. In *Philip*, a satirical comedy of the time by Mnesimakhos, we hear of more homosexual goings on among the soldiers of Philip II. The erotic content in this soldier's bragging about how tough they are cannot be missed:

> Our sort make their dinner
> Off honed up swords, and swallow blazing torches
> For a savory snack....[8]

Again, this goes against common sexual practice among the Greeks, who disdained fellatio. One is reminded of nineteenth century Americans looking with horror on the debauchery of the French. Theopompos was anti–Macedonian, so we may take his pronouncements with a grain of salt—Attic salt, of course—but mercenaries have never been distinguished for their high sexual morals. We do not hear of any pederasty, though, among the Macedonians; all that Theopompos refers to seems to be casual homosexual activity. We must analyze it more closely when all the evidence is on the table; for now suffice it to say that homophobia was an introduction of Philip II. He enforced it in his family if he did not concern himself with the mores of his mercenary troops—desperate men recruited from all over Macedon, Greece and wherever men would fight for money.

Philip II was born in 382 BCE, the son of Amyntas II of Macedon and Euridyce, the daughter of Sirras, king of Lyncestae.[9] The royal line of Lyncestae were Bacchiad—they claimed descent from Dionysus himself. When and how Philip fell into the Orphic orbit is not certain; as a boy he lived for three years as a political hostage in Thebes, under Epameinondas, the pupil of Lysis, a high-ranking Pythagorean; it is likely that Philip absorbed the Pythagoreanism readily.[10] There also may have been an Orphic-Pythagorean influence at the Macedonian court before Philip's time—tomb paintings in the royal Macedonian tombs at Aegeae show scenes from Orphic mythology and date from Philip's childhood.[11] Indeed Orphism seems to have been fairly common in Macedon in the fourth century BCE.[12] One of the curious footnotes to history suggests that some sort of Orphic conversions at the court of Macedon may have occurred about the time Philip came to the throne. Queen Euridyce, Philip's mother, learned to read in her middle age.[13] In that age of the world a Greek woman (and Euridyce was very much a Greek, not a Macedonian),[14] even a queen, was not expected to know how to read. Like her more famous daughter-in-law, Olympias, Euridyce was not a woman to stay in doors and weave shrouds for the men; her hand was everywhere in the politics of Macedon in the early to mid–fourth century BCE. She didn't need to read to practice power politics, though. It seems quite likely that the reason that Philip II's mother went to the trouble to acquire literacy in midlife was religious. The Orphics believed that anyone could purify his or her soul by merely reading aloud from one or another of the Orphic holy books that narrated the sufferings and restoration to life of Dionysus. Pythagoreanism was a religion that attempted to interiorize the order and life of the universe by thought and observation, not by eating as the ancient followers of Dionysus had in eating the fawn who represented the god. She had a lot of reading to do, for rumor implicates her in the murders of both her husband and her oldest son. We know that Euridyce dedicated statues to the Muses,[15] who were associated with literacy and were favorite deities of the Pythagoreans. Did her son convert her after his return from Thebes? Or did the Orphism at the Macedonian court come from some other source, perhaps an ancient Rasputin lost to history? A good candidate for just such a gray eminence is Euphreios of Oreos, the court philosopher to Philip's brother and predecessor, King Perdikkas. He came from Oreos in Euboea, on the Mallian Gulf; *Suda* calls him a disciple of Plato. Karystios of Pergamon says that Euphreios was in charge of Perdikkas' elite guard, the Companions, and that he would let no one among them eat at the common table unless he knew geometry.[16] Most of Plato's disciples are gravely suspected of Pythagoreanism, and the grim insistence on geometry by Euphreios makes it more likely that he was more a Pythagorean than a Socratic Platonist. Was Euphreios hired on the recommendation of Philip, already steeped in Pythagoreanism? Did Euphreios think as Pythagoreans thought later, that here was a chance to regain the power they had lost in the debacle of about 450? Our sources are too thin to answer these questions, but the possibility cannot be dismissed either. The most likely case is that a native form of the cults of Orpheus and Wild Dionysus, untouched by the reforms of Pythagoras and Onomakritos, was known to Philip from the folk tradition of his homeland, and this was drastically altered for him by contact with Reformed Orphism in Thebes. Philip at an impressionable age learned the shocking "truth" about Dionysus and the orgiastic bacchants — that they were reenacting the great and cosmic crime of killing a god.

Philip's homophobia is likewise well attested. We shall see how he responded to his homosexual son. Meanwhile there is the question of Philip's own sexuality. The evidence suggests a thoroughly heterosexual man, with one possible exception. He married numerous times, "withouten other compaignye in youthe"—all female.[17] The joke in antiquity was that he married a new wife with each campaign he undertook[18]—and "he made many wars." Ancient sources accuse him of a single homosexual liaison: with Alexander of Mollosia. This Alexander was the son of Neoptolemos, king of a small city-state that happened to be in Philip's way. About 350 BCE Philip took Alexander of Mollosia hostage to guarantee the cooperation of his father. The boy was 12 years old and lived for a while in the court of Philip. In Athens Demosthenes publicly charged that Philip was having sex with the boy, and Theopompos, who was at the court of Philip eight years later, repeats the charge.[19] It seems unlikely. In the turnings of politics, Philip released the boy, who became his ally and king of Mollosia; Philip then married Alexander's sister, the famous Olympias, mother of Alexander the Great. Finally, Philip gave his daughter (by Olympias) to Alexander of Mollosia for his wife. It is true that "politics makes strange bed-fellows," but this seems too strange an interchange on the part of a rapist and his victim. Demosthenes' use of the allegation was clearly political— he was saying anything he could to make Philip look bad (of course the scandal was not the charge of homosexuality but that the boy was under age, and a hostage entitled to Philip's protection). Theopompos, too, as we have said, was anti–Macedonian. Finally, even if we believe the charge, many a man has been opposed to homosexuality in principle who has practiced it in fact. Philip was not the last, if he was perhaps the first. In a survey on the battlefield at Chaeroneia, he came to where the bodies of the Theban Sacred Band lay, "mingled with each other," says Plutarch, in the very image of love and death. Philip wept and said, "A bad death to anyone who says these did anything shameful [*aiskhron*] or suffered [*paskhein*] anything shameful."[20] The gerund here translated as "suffered" is related to the noun commonly used in Greek, *paskhones*, meaning "a male who receives penetration." Perhaps the king was weeping, as Plutarch says, but he was also making a grim joke. The point is he admired the courage of the Sacred Band, and their sexual conduct did not detract from that admiration, though he disapproved of their sexual relations. Likely too, those were crocodile tears, for that night Philip got drunk and paraded though the captive Greeks, mocking them and singing lewd songs.

A curious court-judgment of Philip II also suggests homophobia. Our only source is late and telling the story for the sake of a bon mot, though more than a poor joke peeks through the text. Plutarch tells the story: "Being called upon to decide a suit between two knaves [*ponaron*], he ordered the one to flee from Macedonia and the other to pursue him."[21] The word translated here as "knaves" simply means persons who work hard at doing evil; it need have no sexual connotation. However, the fact that these men were somehow paired and that Philip's sentence of exile demands that one be behind the other both suggest that in fact the two men were lovers and that Philip's decidedly wicked sense of humor was coming into play. He was, in other words, making their punishment fit the crime.

Olympias, Philip's most famous wife and the mother of his only famous son, was no quiet, obedient woman in the mold of classical antiquity. What we know of her suggests she was a curious, perhaps unstable, mixture: when her young son Alexander would go out on long military training expeditions, she would hide honey cakes in his baggage as a treat for him[22]; on the other hand, she was involved in a number of political murders, including perhaps her husband's, and more certainly a child's. She must have had the personality of

Kali-Durga with a bit of June Cleaver thrown in. In some ways she was quite the match for her conquering husband. Plutarch tells us she was "addicted to the Orphica"[23] and seems to have used her religion to manipulate her husband. When she did not wish to have sex with him, she put a huge snake in the bed beside her and let Philip believe it was Zeus Ammon; later she was to tell Alexander that his real father was not Philip, but Zeus Ammon.[24] Of course this divine serpent was a manifestation of Phanes-Dionysus.[25] There was a well-established cult of Zeus Ammon in Greece going back to the time of Pindar, with shrines to that god in Athens and Thebes.[26] Originally the Egyptian god Amen, the Greeks assimilated him to their supreme god. It was Amen that Akhenaton had worshiped as the One God, in an abortive attempt to establish monotheism in Egypt. Perhaps Pythagoras had picked up some echoes of this while in Egypt and afforded Amen-Ammon-Zeus a special place in Orphic thought.[27] If she was taking it seriously, Olympias was winding the serpent around her belly to create the Divine Serpent coiled about the World Egg in the hope that she too would give birth to a manifestation of Phanes-Dionysus, who would rule the world.

If Philip disapproved of homosexuality, he disapproved, too, of his son, Alexander. Alexander III, called with no exaggeration the Great, was born in 356 BCE. He seems to have had a strong genetic predisposition to homosexuality. His maternal uncle, and namesake, Alexander of Mollosia, was distinctly gay. Modern geneticists believe they have established a genetic inheritance pattern whereby a predisposition to male homosexuality is passed on the female side, mother to son. Possibly this was the case with Alexander. The first portrait busts we have of Alexander show him as feminine[28]—indeed the Athens bust of Alexander at about 14 can be identified as the work of the sculptor Leochares because it resembles his sculpture of Ganymede, the boy abducted by Zeus.[29] When he reached puberty, Alexander showed no sexual interest in women. Fearing that he was a *gunnis* (weakling, or womanlike man), both Olympias and Philip procured a prostitute named Callixeina, hoping she would make a man of him. Alexander would have nothing to do with her.[30] Just at this time Alexander, a 13-year-old, was put to school in the royally sponsored School for Pages at Mieza, a seacoast town famed for its scenery. Philip had hired no less a teacher than Aristotle, but it is likely that Alexander remembered the place more because he had met the love of his life there than because he cared about lessons in dialectic and the dissection of mollusks. The young man who became the lifelong lover of Alexander was named Hephastion, and we know amazingly little about him though his name is all over the biographies of Alexander.

We do not even know his age. Hephastion was a Macedonian noble, and the fact that he was at the School at Mieza with Alexander suggests the two were about the same age.[31] When Alexander came to power, Hephastion was steadily and swiftly promoted though the ranks, becoming eventually "chillarch"—second in command only to Alexander himself. He served well and was consistently loyal to his friend. The Cynic philosophers, who were proud of saying things no one else would say, claimed that Alexander was only defeated once, and that was by the thighs of Hephastion.[32] We know little of his personality otherwise—he argued often with other commanders. He had been, as we say, a pupil of Aristotle, and Xenocrates dedicated a book to him.[33] Alexander and Hephastion remained together until Hephastion's death, about 17 years after they met.

Meanwhile, outside the budding grove, the world moved on. Philip dealt leniently with conquered Athens; the Corinthian League, dominated by Macedon, left the "school of Greece" with its internal forms of government intact. The Athenians put up a statue of Philip,[34] and plenty of Athenians were found who were all too willing to cooperate with the conqueror, most notably for our purposes Lycurgos of Athens. Lycurgos was probably something of a Pythagorean himself by both disposition and opinion, but his building of a temple to Ammon-

Zeus[35] was sure to be favored by the court of Macedon; he coated in gold the altar of Apollo as well.[36] He had been a pupil of Plato and was a friend of Xenocrates,[37] the Pythagorizing third head of the Academy. Lycurgos was a cold and calculating man — his principle title was head of finances for 12 years (337–325 BCE). He was perhaps more than a "traitorous hireling of Philip,"[38] but he acted always with an eye toward the conqueror; he began by killing off a goodly number of opponents — always with a pretext of justice — men who had fought Philip at Charoneia.[39] One ancient source says, "Against wrong doers his pen was dipped in death, not ink,"[40] and his personal life was austere.[41] Pederasty was abolished in the Athenian military by Lycurgos of Athens. That form of institutionalized homosexuality had been the standard form of military training for centuries. That it produced brave and efficient warriors, even Philip acknowledged; but the massed squares of fighting men, trained to act not as paired individuals but as a unit had proven superior on the field. Lycurgos set up a system in Athens that trained young men en masse with machine-like efficiency, very similar to the military organization recommended in the *Laws*, attributed to Plato.[42]

Homosexuality was no longer a factor in military training, in Athens or elsewhere, and the state-sponsored homosexuality that had been at the center of public life in the Greek city-states came to a permanent end. The bluff and pragmatic character of Philip suggests that this change was purely practical. There was an old and widely held opinion that tyranny and pederasty were inimical; pederasty was now militarily outmoded as well. The end of male same-sex unions as a means to maintain the military, and through that the freedom of the state, was the gravest single blow suffered by homosexuality in the ancient world. In the exuberant freedom of Greece following the victory over the invading Persians, pederasty was almost a sacrament. In the Macedonian world it became solely a matter of individual taste. Some philosophers, most noticeably the Stoics, and also the early Academy, continued to use pederasty a means to train their disciples, and it is likely that it lingered in the military context more or less clandestinely for some centuries. But the brave new world of the Macedonian kings had no place for it.

A parallel case to Greece under the Macedonians may be offered from Chinese history. Homosexuality had been both common and accepted in China as far back as the Han dynasty (202 BCE–220 CE); Li Po, the greatest of Chinese poets, wrote love poetry to a younger man. Generally relationships were between a younger and an older man, though there is no sign of formal pederasty on the Greek model. Lesbianism is scarcely heard of[43] until the Ming dynasty, when it was looked on with tolerance by male writers.[44] The last great flowering of Chinese art, literature and philosophy under purely native rule was during the Ming dynasty; the accomplishments of that age would fill a thick and beautiful book. Homosexuality was common in the literature of the period and not disparaged.[45] Homosexual relations among males were called the Love of the Cut Sleeve — the story went that a Ming emperor's male lover fell asleep once lying on the emperor's long, elaborate sleeve. The emperor was called to attend to some important matter of state; and, rather than disturb his lover, the emperor cut the sleeve off and left it there. The philosopher Wang Yangmin (1472–1528) and his follower, He Xinyin, declared "emotional desires and sensual appetites are rooted in human nature ... to give [them] free reign is to give full expression to human nature."[46] The Jesuit Mateo Ricci was in Beijing in 1583 and found male homosexuality common and approved.[47]

All this, and much more, came to a sudden and disastrous end with the invasion of the Mongols; Beijing fell in 1644 to the armies of the Manchus. In ways analogous to the Macedonians when they conquered Greece, the Manchus began to rule China with an iron hand. A narrow, legalistic form of Confucianism was made the law of the land, officially in 1646; and in 1740 sodomy was outlawed.[48] The Mongol dynasty, the Qing, were soon suppressing homosexuality, and the art and literature of homosexuality, saying it was the result of demonic possession.[49] We hear of Cawing Hi (Kang XI 1662–1722), the second Manchurian emperor, executing men suspected of being his son's lovers, and having himself certified "pure" of homo-erotic activity[50] — a real witch hunt. The lesson is clear: Anyone who would lord it over a sub-ject people must begin his dominance in the bedroom. No one is so controlled as when his/her sexuality is controlled; sheer practicality prevents a ban on heterosexuality, but homosexual-ity has always offered tyrants a convenient handle on the souls of their subjects. None knew this better than Philip II of Macedon.

If, like Shakespeare's Richard II, we "sit upon the ground and tell sad stories of the death of kings," few are more tragic than the death of Philip II. It occurred too late for the great dramatists of Athens to put it on the stage, but the story is worthy of a Euripides, at the least. Pausanios of Orestis[51] was a page in the court of Philip; the king was fond of Pausan-ios because Pausanios' good looks contributed to the atmosphere of the court — we probably should not see Philip's interest in him as sexual.[52] However, a second Pausanios appeared among the pages, and Philip was more fond of him than the first. Out of jealousy, Pausan-ios of Orestis addressed the second Pausanios "with abusive language accusing him of being an effeminate male [*androgonon* man-woman] and prompt to accept the amorous [*erotas*] advances of any who wished." In response to this, the second Pausanios confided in a friend [*philos*] of his, Atollos, Philip II's prospective father-in-law. Then in a battle against the Illyrians, the second Pausanios leapt in front of the king, taking the blows intended for Philip, and so died. Clearly he was trying to prove his manhood. The understanding of male sexuality that was maintained in the Macedonian court equated homosexuality with femi-ninity and both with cowardliness. Quite possibly the same attitude led to Philip's marriage with Cleopatra, the niece of Atollos — he had given up hope that Alexander, his son by his first royal wife, was "man enough" to succeed him, since Alexander was proving incurably homosexual.

Atollos did not forget the death of his friend. Seeing the proper occasion, he got Pau-sanios of Orestis drunk and turned him over to the royal mule drivers, who raped him repeat-edly. The revenge has a certain quality of poetic justice to it. Sobered and outraged at his treatment, Pausanios of Orestis appealed to Philip for revenge. Philip did not wish to alien-ate Atollos, so he refused to do anything about it, perhaps even making a cruel joke of it.[53] This was salt in a wound, a wound in a most intimate place, and Pausanios decided he would have vengeance — not on Atollos, but on Philip, who was protecting him. We should prob-ably suspect in Pausanios the jealous lover — whether Philip had ever returned his love or not. Perhaps he was suborned by Olympias, who was both jealous that Philip was marrying another woman and anxious for her own position and that of her son, Alexander, who could be super-seded by a son of Philip and Cleopatra. Gossip whispered to the end of antiquity says she did urge the assassin on, and similar gossip attaches to Alexander as well.[54] At any rate, at a splen-did festival at Aegae, with golden statues of the 12 gods and Philip's golden statue making a thirteenth,[55] Pausanios of Orestis found Philip alone for a moment and stabbed him to death.

Philip II was the first homophobe who can be documented by name in history; if we believe Demosthenes' "Second Olynthian,"[56] he was also a crude, brutish man; power came to him by his military genius and by the circumstances of the world into which he was born. He sets a type for the domineering hypermasculine father with a disdain for everything not immediately tangible and with a sensitive, gay son. Both were real, flesh-and-blood historic persons, but they seem almost archetypical in the familiar ritual they act out. What Philip did to that young man, Alexander, his son, and what that young man did to the world is the next subject we take up.

THE QUEEN OF THE WORLD

It is not our purpose here to give an account of the full career of Alexander the Great; any number of single-volume accounts of his meteoric career are available, dating from antiquity down to the present. Those who want to know more about this remarkable man from ancient sources will find Plutarch's short "Life of Alexander" an excellent starting place. For those who wish a more modern treatment, Green's *Alexander the Great* is probably as clear and balanced an account as one will find in a single volume. Enough may be said of his career in the opening of the Book of Maccabees:

> And it happened after that Alexander, son of Philip, the Macedonian, who came out of the land of Kittim, had smitten Darius king of the Persians and Medes, that he reigned in his stead, first over Greece, and made many wars, and won many strongholds, and slew the kings of the earth and went through the ends of the earth, and took spoils of many nations, insomuch that the world was quiet before him; whereupon he was exalted, and his heart was lifted up. And he ruled over countries and nations and kings, who became tributaries unto him [I Macc. 1: 1–3 (King James Version)].

It is not Alexander the conqueror who extended and diffused Greek culture throughout what had been the Persian Empire that we are concerned with, but rather Alexander the repressed homosexual. His repression furnishes up further proof that Philip II and Olympias were homophobic and also serves as a sort of example of the beginnings of the Hellenistic world and the closet cases that occur in it. We begin by looking at the man and his gender identity.

Alexander's appearance was, as one commentator has said, "altogether scary."[57] A modern sensibility conditioned by nineteenth century Romanticism might find him intriguing, not to say romantic, because, like Coleridge's Spirit of Life in Death, Alexander contained in himself contradictions. He was of average height, shorter than Hephastion, and handsome. He had physical attributes that Greek physiognomists would say were signs of the male who sought penetration by other males; Alexander was pale, his neck drooped, and his head was crooked to one side. He was always smooth-shaven in an age when adult males regularly wore beards. His eyes were large and "melting."[58] Theophrastos, who had known him in his teens, said that he was almost impotent.[59] Still, with all these physical attributes of the effeminate male, Alexander in some ways affected the hypermasculine in matters of choice: he always spoke in a loud voice, and he held his head high — both conventional signs of the manly man in the time and place.[60]

As an adult, Alexander would only pose for one sculptor, Lysippos of Sikyon[61]; the choice is telling, for Lysippos, the greatest sculptor of that age, was the master of an art of unease. Fifth century sculptors had idealized humans with a godlike calm, a sense of both flesh and marble at once. The fifth century sculptors showed us persons fully at ease with themselves, at rest, unified, calm and inward-looking. In the following century, Lysippos, by manipulating the planes of his figures, created an art of the moment, one that suggests a frenzied movement, unsteady, anxious and unbalanced, in contrast to the already classical past.[62] The best portrait we have of Alexander by Lysippos (the Azara herm) is only a Roman copy; but still, ravaged by time as it is, Alexander looks thoroughly haunted and evanescent, a man destined to see much and die young.

It seems, though, that his attitude toward his own effeminacy never quite recovered from the bitter reproach of his parents. It is probably not an exaggeration to say that his entire adult life was spent in one long, desperate attempt to "prove that he was a man." Of course we cannot tease out into separate strands what in him was a desperate overcompensation for his threatened "manhood" and what was part of the drive of history and caused by such factors as greed and the will to power; but it seems clear that many of his actions were caused by nothing more than overcompensation. Philip had certainly intended to invade the Persian Empire; but he may have planned to only "liberate" for his own empire the Ionic Greek cities still under the control of Persia. Alexander took the conquest much farther, not only to the heart of Persia but also deep into India, and then only turned back because his army mutinied. No one can read a life of Alexander without perceiving a man driven.

By the time he had conquered Persia, he was occasionally cross-dressing in public, sometimes wearing the clothes of the goddess Artemis when he was riding his chariot.[63] Cross-dressing was not unknown in Greece, but the examples we have are in the context of heterosexual relationships,[64] or in the *kinades*. The choice of Artemis means that Alexander chose not only to cross-dress, but to do it in the clothes of the goddess who presided over female homosexuality, as Apollo did over male homosexuality.[65]

Cross-dressing and suchlike feminine behavior on the part of males has been analyzed by Richard Isay in terms of a sort of homosexual Oedipal complex. Isay takes it for granted that some males are born with an inherent inclination to develop homosexual desire. Such males develop a sexual desire for their fathers, in the same way that inherently heterosexual males desire their mothers. In a context where there is a sharp dividing line between "homosexual" and "heterosexual," young homosexual men see their fathers lavishing affection on the boy's mothers and assume that adult men are attracted by whatever distinguishes females in that society—feminine clothes, activities, etc. So those boys who inherently desire affection from adult males attempt to adopt the feminine accouterments that they perceive their mothers as using.[66]

If we apply Isay's model to Alexander, the fit is remarkable. The essential element we find in what we know of Alexander's parents is a dualistic view of sex. Alexander certainly saw his father lavishing affection on women (his mother among them) and probably not on men. In the classic pederastic environment, males and females lived apart, and the young men saw only affection between their fathers and their fathers' lovers. The human environment that homophobia creates changes subtly the manifestation of homosexuality, and that in turn intensifies homophobia in a pattern of great complexity. To many "straight" men (the word only has its full meaning in a homophobic context) effeminate men are a bad joke. Obviously the effeminate male still has a male body, and to both males that desire sexually activity with females and males who desire it with other males the incongruity is sometimes unsettling. Perhaps this explains much of Philip's hostility to Alexander; Isay believes that straight fathers of gay sons are often hostile to their sons because the former find some rejected parts of themselves reflected in the sons.

All in all, Alexander seems to have been what is called a "Kinsey number six"—that is, a male homosexual who has little or no sexual interest in females. He simply could not conform to the expectations of his father and mother and their expectations in regards to his sex life. He seems to have been more or less "in the closet" during Philip's life; he peeks out once he becomes absolute ruler of most of the known world, but his denial was deeply, deeply ingrained, and in his brief life he never seems to have fully come to terms with what he was.

Essential to the coming-out process for any homosexual is acquiring a positive image of homosexuals as a group.[67] To the degree that Alexander "came out," he acknowledged at least to himself that he was what he was due to his education, specifically one book. Perhaps never in history have absolute genius and absolute power come quite so close as when Aristotle strolled in the quiet groves of Mieza, instructing Alexander. We know surprisingly little of what he taught the boy; probably he could teach him little. We do know that the one book that Alexander cherished was a carefully annotated copy of Homer's *Iliad* that Aristotle had given him. He believed himself descended from Achilles on his mother's side.[68] When he had conquered Persia, a brilliantly made golden chest was found among the treasures of Darius; the question arose what should be put in it; and, after the sort of debate that he must have learned from Aristotle, Alexander chose to use it as a carrying box for his *Iliad*.[69] The choice speaks volumes.

Most young persons who "come out" do so when they are first on their own, away from censorious parents, and making their own way. Alexander was no different. He was well away from Olympias before he publicly acknowledged his relationship with Hephastion. In 334 BCE he had crossed into Ionia, the region of Greek cities that rounded the coast of what is now Turkey; these had remained under the control of the Persians after their invasion, and Alexander was conquering them one by one. Early on he came to the site of Troy. When he came to the tombs outside Troy that were said to contain the remains of Achilles and Patroklus, Alexander placed a crown on the tomb of Achilles, while Hephastion crowned the tomb of Patroklus.[70] This was seen by contemporaries as clear proof that Alexander was "passionate for boys."[71] This incident is as near as he ever came to "coming out," to publicly declaring himself to be something his parents had taught him was evil. Any educated Greek knew what it meant for two men to be like Patroklus and Achilles. Yet he never says more than this; only in the Homeric context where two same-sex lovers were perfect examples of manhood could Alexander define himself and his relation to the only other person besides his mother that he ever loved. Olympias responded with one or more angry letters; we do not have Alexander's reply, but part of a reply by Hephastion has come down to us. "Stop quarreling with me," he wrote to Alexander's mother; "not that I much care. You know that Alexander means more to me than anyone."[72] The emotion was reciprocal. A year later, flushed with the victory of Issos that had put the Persian empire at his feet, Alexander told a Persian that he and Hephastion were the same person.[73] Alexander, who has a streak of hero worship in him,[74] found in the *Iliad* a model for his life, a breathing space, some field of the world that would let him be what he was; he once said that Aristotle had taught him how to live well.[75]

He was, in an odd way, the first classicist; A.E. Housman would own him as a brother; and so would a long list of gay man and lesbians down to our own times who found in the classical image of the homosexual role models they could live by. Philip and Olympias had tried to make something of Alexander he was not; but in terms of the *Iliad* he could live, he could be himself. The models for his life that he found in Homer were the restless search for fame and the relationship of Achilles and Patroklus. Achilles, whom he believed to be his ancestor, was a great warrior — the greatest warrior in the greatest epic ever written — and a homosexual man much in touch with his feminine side. In the epic tradition, the young Achilles had disguised himself as a woman — Polygonotos had painted the cross-dressed Achilles in a famous work in Athens in the fifth century,[76] and Euripides (a dramatist Alexander must have known well)[77] wrote a drama about the incident.[78] In Homer there is no doubt that Achilles and Patroklus were lovers, though their relationship does not conform to the established norm of a pederastic union — Achilles is the greater warrior, yet he is younger than Patroklus.[79] That they were lovers was a commonplace in Greek literature[80] — probably Alexander heard it first from Aristotle.

In the *Epic of Gilgamesh*, the hero is a king who is given a sort of double, Enkidu; the two men become lovers. The great goddess Ishtar offers Gilgamesh immortality if he will become her lover, but he refuses. When Enkidu dies, Gilgamesh, convinced of his own mortality, seeks immortality, adventuring to the world's end. Like Gilgamesh in the *Epic of Gilgamesh* and Achilles in the *Iliad*, Alexander saw himself as having two ways to become immortal: he could surrender to the great goddess and beget children who would live after him, or he could reject the goddess and perform great deeds that would always be remembered. Achilles makes the same choice in Homer; he could have left the Trojan war, gone home to "deep soiled Pthia," had a family, a modestly good life, a straw death, and been forgotten. Or he could fight on at Troy with his lover, Patroklus, win immortal fame and die young.[81] When Alexander had completed his career, buried his Hephastion and died at 31, a Babylonian poet recognized his similarity to the legendary Gilgamesh and wrote an epic of Alexander that had him seeking the Well of Life at the farthest end of the world, as Gilgamesh had sought the Plant of Life in mythic realms.[82]

The Orphics and Pythagoreans deeply disapproved of Homer.[83] Alexander, as soon as he could be his own man, completely cast off Orphism and worshiped the standard deities of the Greeks. When he had led the poor remnants of his troops out of the Gedrosian Desert to the fertile and grape-abounding land of Camarina, Alexander staged a magnificent Bacchic orgy — he himself lying on a sort of altar to Dionysus — drinking and feasting for days,[84] in a manner that would have profoundly offended the Orphics, who saw Dionysus in a sober light.

There seems to be a sort of conspiracy of silence by the historians with regard to Alexander and Hephastion as lovers; the evidence is clear and given in the surviving Greek sources, but no Greek historian explicitly calls them lovers.[85] Latin authors, on the other hand, make it explicit. Only a few fragments of histories written by contemporaries of Alexander survive; we are almost entirely reliant on later sources. It is possible that the later Greek historians said nothing explicit about Alexander and Hephastion as lovers because they did not understand it. It was not a pederastic relationship on the model that had been set in the sixth century; neither was it a casual pleasure-based relationship like that of Polykrates and Bathyllos. Lifelong commitments of same-sex persons having the same age and similar status was a thing almost unthinkable in the homophobic climate of the age. Homosexuality, like heterosexuality, had ceased to be thought of as a reciprocal relationship. Rather it was thought of as a matter of dominance. When Alexander called his lover "a second Alexander," he may have praised Hephastion as highly as he was able; but he also succeeded in confusing the world.

The Latin texts term the relationship of Alexander and Hephastion explicitly sexual — Hephastion was Alexander's "*delecti*." The word is a general term that we may translate as "beloved." It carries a clear sexual implication, though a Roman would have thought of it as properly applied to a pretty slave-boy, kept for his master's pleasure. In other words, the Romans explicitly state that the relationship was sexual but also convey the idea in their own terms, which had to also imply that it was a power-based one.

Alexander's attitude toward women sexually was that of utter indifference.[86] When he was about to leave Europe for the conquest of Persia, his best advisors strongly recommended that he marry and beget an heir to leave behind, ensuring a stable succession; the most marriageable young man in the world, he refused.[87] Soon, the harem of Darius was available to him, including some of the most alluring women in the world; he would have nothing to do with them.[88] He did eventually marry, once only,[89] at 27, to the Persian princess Roxane, daughter of the satrap (Persian governor) of a district he needed to pacify.[90] Aelian, a contemporary painter, made a famous painting of the event called "the Wedding Night of Alexander." He showed a reluctant Alexander being tugged by this purple cloak toward Roxane by the god of love (the purple cloak was the Macedonian symbol of royalty). To put it less allegorically, Aelian understood then, as most historians have since, that the marriage was a matter of politics, not desire. Oddly, Aelian painted Hephastion watching this scene.[91] Interestingly, Roxane's only pregnancy began four years later, a month after Hephastion died.[92]

On the other hand, where sex was not involved, Alexander was for the times unusually courteous to women, especially older women, and was violently hostile to any man known to have raped a woman.[93] One expects this indicates a sympathy for those who are sexually penetrated that may have originated very close to home in Alexander.

The bravado continued. One need only open Arrian or Plutarch at random to find Alexander performing some spectacular feat of derring-do. In India, when his army was besieging a town called Malli, Alexander climbed a siege ladder alone, armed only with sword and shield, fought on the wall, then, still alone, jumped down into the hostile city. He was followed by three of his best soldiers, but the number of soldiers trying to follow him broke the ladders and Alexander and the three others were left alone, fighting hand-to-hand in the city, until his horrified troops could batter the gates in and rescue him. By then he had taken an arrow in the chest, just above the lung, and almost died.[94]

Often "closet queens"—homosexual persons who try to maintain a false identity as exclusively heterosexual—are more vehemently homophobic in their public acts than more securely heterosexual persons.[95] Depending on the self-realization of such persons, acts against homosexuality may be a smoke screen intended purely to deceive the public, or more drastically, an effort to deceive one's self. Some of the strangest, darkest acts of Alexander the Great seem to fall under this latter category. He was absolute ruler of most of the world he knew of. Homophobia seems not to have been deeply imbued in the attitude of his soldiers. Alexander's strange and sometimes violent acts against homosexuals can best be attributed to internalized homophobia striking out at that quality in other persons that Alexander most hated in himself.

After he had conquered Halicarnassus, a Greek city on the coast of what is now Turkey, Alexander is said to have banished all the *kinades* (cross-dressing males) to the island of Arkonessos off the coast and renamed it Kinadiopolis ("Drag-queen City" in a free translation).[96] The story is told only in a late source that is not a history. It becomes comprehensible in the context of what had happened at Halicarnassus. Alexander the Mollosian, Alexander the Great's uncle, had gone this far with him as a commander of cavalry; he was openly gay. Word reached Alexander the Great that the older Alexander had been offered a bribe to kill him; and, following a premonitory dream, Alexander the Great had the Mollosian arrested.[97] What we know about the Mollosian suggests he may have had an entourage of *kinades*, and they were the ones Alexander had sent into exile. It appears that the exile of the cross-dressers of Halicarnassus following the arrest of Alexander of Mollosia may have been part of a witch hunt—a persecution of every openly homosexual person, based on the sudden and somewhat superstitious distrust of a single gay male.

Then there is the matter of Bagoas. He was a beautiful young eunuch who had been used by Darius; when he was given to Alexander as part of the booty, Alexander seems to have fallen for him.[98] The practice of castrating beautiful young men so that they would retain their youthful and feminine appearance was old among the Persians. Herodotus tells us that when the Persians were looting Greece, whole villages were stripped of their young men; the young men were castrated and given to Persian nobles as spoils of war. Though he has a Persian name, Bagoas seems to have been an Ionian Greek by birth, since we are told he performed excellently, singing and dancing in a Greek chorus for Alexander—he kissed the boy as a reward[99] and soon promoted him to the level of governor. By contrast, when one of his other governors offered him "an incomparable Ionian boy in the fairest prime of youth," Alexander responded with an angry letter, protesting he never used boys; he called such practice "evil."[100] The obvious difference is that Bagoas was a eunuch, while the Ionian boy was not. One suspects that Alexander's relation to Hephastion was as the passive partner, so

Alexander would have no use for another pretty boy who would be likewise passive. An ancient source says explicitly that Bagoas was "used sexually the way women are."[101] Apparently Alexander in some curious way, having to do, one suspects, with power relationships, found a eunuch acceptable.

How Hephastion viewed Bagoas we are not privy to know; we hear of Alexander publicly arguing with Hephastion toward the end.[102] A very late source has Alexander and Hephastion drinking "at the house of Bogoas,"[103] but our source does not tell us whether it was Bagoas the eunuch or another Bagoas, the son of Pharnuches, who was also in that circle. Perhaps the three men came to an understanding, with Hephastion and Bagoas each ministering to the needs of Alexander in different ways.

After winning the battle of Issos, Alexander turned westward toward Egypt, solidifying the half of Darius' empire he had already won before the climactic confrontation. It was in Egypt that one of the most puzzling and dramatic events of his career occurred. He went to visit Ammon. Good explanations can be offered for most of Alexander's actions, but the six weeks he took off to visit the oracular shrine of Ammon at Siwah in the remote desert west of the Nile are difficult to account for. Darius was behind him, building his army steadily; Alexander needed to consolidate Egypt quickly and get on with it. But he visited Ammon at Siwah.

The god whom the Greeks referred to as Ammon, the Egyptians called Amun or Amen, though they usually combined the name with the names of one or more other gods — Amun-Re, Min-Amun, etc. From the earliest glimpses we have of him, Amun was a god associated with aggression and dominance. When the fifth dynasty of Egypt collapsed in disorder, a Semitic people, the Hyksos, invaded Egypt and maintained rule there for centuries. Then about 1530 BCE the Egyptians revolted against their Hyksos overlords and, led by the rulers of the obscure town of Thebes, drove the Hyksos out of Egypt, followed them into Palestine and established Egypt's first and only empire there. These vigorous kings cultivated a personal image of the wasp-waisted athlete, hypermasculine and aggressive, and they worshiped Amun, making him the supreme god of Egypt and Thebes his capital.

Amun was originally an obscure god of an obscure town. As Amon-Kamutef ("Amun the bull of his mother") he was believed to have created himself by impregnating his sky-goddess mother.[104] When we first glimpse him in the eleventh dynasty, he has absorbed the qualities of the fertility god of Koptos, Min; and, as Amun-Min, he has the eternal erection of that god. Occasionally he was represented as a serpent.[105] Assimilated to the sun god of the empire, he adds Re to his kit of names. It was to Amun that the victorious pharaohs of the eighteenth dynasty used to sacrifice prisoners of war, clubbing them to death in his temple.[106] On an even more sinister note, we hear of a battle against Libyans in which the Egyptians believed that Amun had given them the victory. They cut off the penises of their slain enemies and carried them to the temple of Amun as a tribute.[107] Min, as late as the Ptolemaic period, was the god *par excellence* who dominated sexually his enemies.[108] Clearly here we have a god of aggressive male sexuality, asserted by his prominent erection and his dominance and castration of those who dare oppose him.

Perhaps not surprisingly we find Amun occasionally sodomizing his male worshipers. The widespread notion in early societies that semen deposited in the anus confers strength and magic qualities was common in ancient Egypt. Whether semen is expressly intended or not, we hear of gods who have a "magnetic fluid" that could be conveyed to worshipers. It was exclusively a right of the pharaoh to receive the "magnetic fluid" of the god in an embrace, or more than an embrace, of the deity. We hear of Amun as well as other male gods who so embraced the king. One text says of Geb, the earth god, "His phallus is between the buttocks of his son and heir."[109]

The pharaohs of the eighteenth dynasty made the high priest of Amun the head of all priests in Egypt, whatever god or goddess they served.[110] The elaborate hierarchy assigned each person a role in a divine scheme; the pharaoh was king because Amun, through the high priest, owned him as son and subject. Various pharaohs claimed that they were the son, in a literal fashion, of Amun, who sometimes appeared as a serpent (as he had to Olympias) to impregnate a queen. The Orphic-Pythagorean interest in Amun probably goes back to Pherekydes of Syros, the teacher of Pythagoras, who was apparently influenced by the Egyptian cult of Amun.[111]

On a day late in January, 331 BCE, Alexander, while planning the city of Alexandria, was seized by a *pothos*, a strong desire, to go to the oracle of Amum at Siwah.[112] The word *pothos* often occurs in the narratives concerning Alexander — sometimes he seems to have used it to explain actions whose real motives he preferred to keep secret.[113] In fact the motives for going to Siwah remain obscure. The journey was difficult — 600 miles, first along the seacoast, then due south through desert, dry and treacherous. At one point Alexander's party was lost in a sandstorm. Birds are said to have guided them on the last leg, a not improbable story, since the pass in the hills on the way to the Oasis of Siwah is called to this day the Pass of the Crow.[114]

Arriving in the five-mile-long fertile valley that is the Oasis of Siwah, Alexander was greeted by the high priest of the oracle as the son of Ammon (or as some versions have it, of Zeus).[115] After the appropriate ceremonies, Alexander went alone with the high priest into the dark, windowless holiest of holies of the temple. Surely then the priest opened the shrine and showed Alexander by candle light the blue standing image of the god, with its erection standing out toward him.[116] Alexander is said to have received some sort of private communication from the god. The exact nature of this message we will never know, for Alexander would tell no one what had happened in the holy of holies,[117] though we are told that the priest "acted the part of Zeus" (*ton Dia hupokrinamenou*), and that the oracle was delivered mainly by gesture (*neumasi kai sybolois*),[118] nods (bendings down) and signs.

Did the high priest of Amon sodomize Alexander, either ritually or literally? David Greenberg, whose knowledge of Egyptian homosexuality is extensive and whose judgment is sound, believes the possibility that pharaohs in the earlier ages of Egypt were sodomized.[119] An eighteenth dynasty sculpture shows Amon making magical passes over Queen Mutemwiya, who was said to have become pregnant by that god.[120] Modern explorers who have visited the Oasis of Siwah report that male homosexuality there is common and institutionalized.[121] The Persians, who had conquered Egypt 200 years before Alexander arrived, had persecuted the Egyptian religion and had suffered from continual revolts by the Egyptians; but the Greeks, beginning with Alexander, had little in the way of rebellion among the conquered. Perhaps the Greeks because of a similar attitude toward homosexuality were able to conform more readily than the Persians, who, as we have said, regarded receptive male homosexuals as contemptible. However, the only explicit statement (outside of legend) that Alexander was crowned pharaoh is a sculpture on wall of the Sanctuary of Ipet Resyt at Luxor, which shows Alexander wearing the phaoronic crown, in front of and below Amun-Kamutef, whose erect penis points at Alexander.[122]

With Egypt secured, Alexander turned back toward Persia and Darius. After sending Hephastion ahead to bridge the Tigris, he met Darius in a fateful battle, at Arbela on the first of October, 331 BCE. Alexander's generalship was daring, exact, flawless. As Shelby Foote has said of another general, he was to war what Keats was to poetry. As he had before, Darius turned and fled. Later he, styled like his ancestors the King of Kings, would be killed by his own troops at a lonely watering hole. The Greeks won a complete victory over enormous odds and Alexander now ruled the greatest empire the world had ever seen.

The darkest, most terrible facet of Alexander's lifelong denial is his occasional murder of young men in a sexual context. Two reliable sources tell the story.[123] Athenophanes, the master of Alexander's bath, employed a certain young man named Stephanos as a singer to amuse the king. Stephanos was remarkably homely and apparently was only there for his voice. One day Athenophanes proposed an experiment in the presence of Alexander; Stephanos was drenched with naphtha (a naturally occurring form of petroleum and extremely flammable) in order to determine if fire (as a metaphor for sexual desire) would "catch" on the homely Stephanos. The whole "experiment" was based on a poor pun: Plutarch uses the word *hapsatai*, from *hapto*, which can mean both "to seize upon" and "to catch fire." Alexander ordered a burning lamp to be touched to Stephanos, and of course the young man burst into flame. Attendants threw water on him immediately, though the young man was seriously burned. Alexander is said to have been properly terrified by the experiment. What Alexander was terrified of seems to be not naphtha, but sexual desire; a similar story reported by a very late source[124] suggests that it was in some terribly perverse way a pathological acting out of his own self-hatred — his own burning with a desire he could neither extinguish nor accept — in burning men alive.

Alexander was almost king of the world. "It was now that Alexander gave public reign to his passions and turned ... to dissipation"; so wrote a Roman historian.[125] Mostly he turned to wine. Alcoholism is all too well known as a symptom of homosexuals in denial,[126] and Alexander and Hephastion both showed signs of what we would today call advanced alcoholism by the time they were in their late twenties. It seems fairly clear that Hephastion had drunk himself to death by the time he was about 30.[127] When the royal friend died, after a drinking binge, the king lay on Hephastion's body for a day and a night before he was pulled away. Alexander had the Greek physician who was tending Hephastion crucified, and staged what may have been the most spectacular funeral in the world. The sober Plutarch reports Alexander performed what amounted to human sacrifice to the ghost of Hephastion,[128] as Homer said that Achilles did for the ghost of Patroklus. Alexander planned an ornate, huge and rather tasteless tomb for Hephastion; probably he expected to be buried in it himself (as Achilles was buried with Patroklus).[129] The general plans for this edifice survive, and the dominant motif is suggestive: an eagle in sculpture, looking downward at a serpent[130]; the eagle was certainly a royal symbol — the serpent perhaps is too obvious to need explanation. But work was never begun on the monument; within a year Alexander, too, was dead, advanced alcoholism at least a contributing factor.[131] Grief, presumably, should be added. His last words were: "Take me to Ammon."[132]

Probably the noblest thing Alexander ever said was at Opis, in the farthest reaches of the Indian desert. Making a speech to his rebellious army, he waved briefly the banner of his new world order —"We are family," he said.[133] He certainly transcended Aristotle in that speech — the world has not yet quite caught up to him yet.

If we have dwelt little upon a chronological retelling of Alexander's life, we need say less about his death and his successors; he was 32 when

> he fell sick and perceived that he should die. Wherefore he called his servants, such as were honorable, and had been brought up with him from his youth, and parted his kingdom among them, while he was yet alive. So Alexander reigned twelve years and then died. And his servants bare rule every one in his place. And after his death they all put crowns upon themselves; so did their sons after them many years: and evils were multiplied in the earth [I Macc. 1, 5–9 (King James Version)].

Alexander is pivotal not only in the political history of the ancient world, but in its sexual history. His personality and his relation to his father are paradigmatic of the relationships of homophobic fathers and gay sons for 22 and more centuries to come. Yet the deepest irony is Alexander's own attitude to power. In his love for Hephastion and his awe for Amon, Alexander, conqueror of his world, showed a lust for power turned against itself, a desire in the most intimate reaches of his soul and body to be conquered.

5

The Hellenic Twilight

THE ARGUMENT FROM NATURE

> Reason and arguments are incapable of combating certain formulas.
> They are uttered with solemnity in the presence of crowds, and as soon
> as they have been pronounced an expression of respect is visible on
> every countenance, and all heads are bowed ... they evoke grandiose and
> vague images in men's minds, but this very vagueness wraps them in
> obscurity and augments their mysterious power.
> — Gustave Le Bon, *The Crowd*

One of the great lies in the history of philosophy, if not of the world, was uttered by a man in his late middle age, on an autumn day in 348 BCE. Speusippos, delivering an oration at the funeral of his uncle (whose considerable property he had just inherited) announced that Plato had been begotten by the god Apollo.[1]

He certainly knew better, though apparently he claimed to have gotten the story from magi, Persian priests who happened to be in Athens at the time.[2] He was about 60 at the time, 20 years younger than his famous uncle, so it is likely that he had known his grandmother, who was Plato's mother, well. The Greeks had plenty of myths about amorous gods and goddesses who seduced or more often forced themselves upon mortals, homosexually or heterosexually, but by Plato's time these were thought of as pious fables that might have actually happened in the remote past, but certainly not in the present. Especially in the philosophical school of Socrates these stories were discounted, not only because they blurred the distinction between the divine and the human, but because they did the gods little credit. No single sentence perhaps says more than Speusippos' lie to signal that the brief, bright and golden age of freedom in thought and politics in which homosexuality was not only tolerated but valued was over.

Speusippos' lie can be understood somewhat in context. In the north Philip II, homophobic and Pythagorean, had ruled Macedonia for ten years; he was consolidating his power in the northern tribes and few doubted where he would turn next; other democratic city-states were falling to him.[3] The Macedonians had kept the concept of divine kingship from ancient times (many of Homer's aristocrats are offsprings of gods and goddesses, and most of the rest get the epithet *dias* applied to them), and Philip was all too willing to exploit the idea to support his throne.[4] It is likely that the Orphics agreed with him. The story that Pythagoras himself had been begotten by Apollo was very widespread in late antiquity, but we can trace it no farther back than about the time of Speusippos, and it is uncertain whether the Pythagoreans were imitating Speusippos or the other way around.[5] It is certain that divine kingship became a pillar of Macedonian imperialism; and, as a son of Apollo, Plato was half-brother to Alexander and his successors.

We know that at this time Philip II was saying some very unpleasant things about Plato, and Speusippos was trying to protect his inheritance.[6] Perhaps the one-eyed king of Macedon had read the *Republic* as a satire against militarism (as we know it was read at the time)[7] and was thinking of a preemptive strike against his philosophical enemies as well as against his more literal ones. Courting the Macedonians for protection against the unruly Athenians, Speusippos chose to read the *Republic* literally, as a militaristic document.[8] He had property to protect. The Academy, which had begun as a crowd of young men gathering around Socrates on the streets of Athens and in private homes, was now an institution with grounds, buildings, probably a library. It was property, something to own and protect. Philosophy had come a long way from the poverty and freedom of Socrates, and it is said that Speusippos was greedy.[9]

Dogma, too, was born. Whether it was born in Plato or was developed after his time is a question antiquity wondered over[10] and one which we are not likely to settle. Almost literally over Plato's dead body the Academy filled the general demand for dogma; thus was produced, as Cicero said, "something that Socrates had habitually reprobated entirely, a science of philosophy."[11] The wondering, wandering, searching, questioning that began the Socratic endeavor began to freeze up into an orthodoxy.

Pythagoreanism was, as we have seen, a strong influence on Plato, perhaps more so as he grew old. In Speusippos and his successors, it "captures" the Academy, as Victorino Tejera has said.[12] In his metaphysics and mathematics, Speusippos was a Pythagorean, according to Aristotle.[13] He embraced a curious Pythagorean set of concepts that Plato had toyed with that identified numbers with physical entities, persons and moral ideas. Metaphor becomes fact.[14] The world is ruled by the Dyad, the "Two-ness," an inherent duality in all things under heaven. "The Dyad, female and mother of the gods bears sway in this lower world," Speusippos said.[15] Of course the Pythagoreans maintained that the female was evil.

The Academy was organized much like what we know of the Pythagorean clubs; there was an inner circle that practiced philosophy, and an outer circle of politicians and rhetoricians[16]; perhaps like the Pythagoreans the inner circle maintained an esoteric doctrine, different from what the more practical members were told, or what they in turn told the public. It is likely that the story of Plato's miraculous birth was an "outer circle" story intended to move the common people. Our late source adds to that story that Ariston was told to abstain from sexual relations with his wife after she had been impregnated by Apollo, so that Plato would be born pure of the taint of mortal sexuality. This certainly fits in well with what we know of Speusippos' philosophy.

It is said that Speusippos "held faithfully to Plato's dogmas,"[17] which implies that Plato was being regarded as a producer of a set of principles regarded as true—not as a spur to independent thought, as Socrates seems to have consistently done. Speusippos was vehemently against pleasure,[18] claiming it could not be good under any circumstance[19]; only a passionless middle ground between pleasure and pain was the proper way to live—a teaching common to Aristotle and the Old Academy in general.[20] In Plato's *Philebus*, Socrates seems to arrive at the conclusion that a rational human would enjoy moderate, rationally chosen pleasures; pleasures and reason should be mixed like wine and honey in a bowl (*Philebus*, 61 D–E)—though Plato has more pure and philosophical pleasures in mind[21] than the metheglin of Aphrodite. We may wonder how far the nephew of Plato adhered to his own philosophy; Speusippos was denounced in a letter from Dionysus of Sicily for his drinking, his greed and his fondness for one of the female students at the Academy, Lastheneia.[22] When Speusippos' fellow student in the Academy, Lycurgos, came to power in Athens and reformed the army in a way that eliminated pederasty, homosexuality was left as a private concern in the eyes of the state, as simply pleasure. That Speusippos was homophobic is shown by one of the few anecdotes about him that survive: To a rich man who was in love with another man who was homely, Speusippos said: "For a large sum of money I will find you a better looking bride."[23] The philosopher was saying that a bought bride was better than a free relationship with a man who might or might not be willing — though that latter love was not based on physical attraction.

Happiness, Speusippos argued, was "the complete achievement of things which are conformed to nature," meaning "nature" in a partly Platonic sense.[24] The Greek word *phusis* readily translates as the English "nature," and it has the same slippery quality in Greek as English. Originally the Greek word seems to have meant the "stuff" of which anything is made, and hence its "makeup" or general character.[25] The word in Greek can sometimes mean what we might call supernatural, as well; in Epicurus and Democritus the gods are thought of as part of "nature,"[26] though one would not expect a follower of Plato to agree. Anaximander of Miletos (611–586 BCE, according to Apollodorus) implied that nature was ruled by justice, time being the great equalizer.[27]

Gays and lesbians were to be the unfortunate heirs of a discussion that arose in a context apart from that of sex. The whole question of the meaning and nature of "nature" as it affects human conduct — the roots of the concept of "natural law" — arose in fifth century BCE Greece in response to the growing prestige of the newly wealthy. The old oligarchy maintained that its *arete*, its particular virtues or excellences, were inborn and passed from parents to children — *arete* was a function of *phusis*. A school of teachers, the Sophists, arose, claiming they could teach anyone, whether the offspring of virtuous parents or not, how to be virtuous.[28] Of course the Sophists found customers among those who were making money, not those who had inherited it. Traditional Greek education had already an established tradition of pederasty; in so far as that education aimed at imparting *arete* to all students, it was a leveling force. If an education (involving homosexual activity) could make the son of a midwife as good as the son of Pericles, then it is likely that the oligarches looked upon such education with no little suspicion. The discovery of a long papyrus fragment has enabled us to read in some detail the thoughts of Antiphon, a Sophist and contemporary of Socrates, on nature: Antiphon saw nature (*phusis*) as truth itself and as the inherent way a thing develops. Opposed to and irreconcilable with nature (*phusis*) was law (*nomos*); law consists of the customs and legal enactments of cities, and these could never be in any way natural.[29] "Law" is simply a social convention. Euripides, as he did so often, summed up the controversy in a line from one of his plays: "Nature desires it which cares nothing for law."[30]

Antiphon and others would add that the individual could decide when to act in terms of law, or when to act in terms of nature.[31] Aeschines and Euripides, among others in the classical age, recognized that "nature" could compel homosexual acts and that these could be either lawful or unlawful; Xenophon has the tyrant Hieron of Syracuse say of a beautiful young man: "My passion for Dailkhos is for what human nature perhaps compels us to want from the beautiful, but I have a very strong desire to attain the object of my passion only with his love and consent."[32] Justice, which might control the passions of even tyrants, the Sophists thought to be neither a natural quality nor one always found in human law, but above both.[33] However, in the fourth century BCE the argument from nature was generally that nature says that the more powerful are right.[34]

Plato, on the other hand, had viewed "nature" as only a part of the whole; in the *Lysis* he has Socrates quote with approval those wise men (probably Pythagoreans) who wrote about "nature [*phusis*] and the All,"[35] implying the world of ideas separate from the tangible world, the two constituting all that exists. Plato's *Timaeus* is an elaborate discussion of how the physical world came to be made according to ideal plans, but imperfectly constructed by an artificer who mediates between the physical and the realm of the forms. All this (which has its roots in Empedocles among others) leads up the concept of a great overmind that establishes the physical and the moral order of the universe.[36] To extract a consistent doctrine of nature from Plato is, of course, to assume that he had one, and that scattered throughout the large body of his writings that doctrine may be found and assembled like a shattered stature fallen from the Parthenon. In the *Gorgias* Plato argues against Kallicles' amoral superman, whose guiding principles are cleverness (*phronesis*) and manliness (*andreia*); against this Plato recommends wisdom (*sophrosune*) and justice (*diakosune*). Plato (or his mouthpiece, Socrates) invokes (508 A) certain "wise men" as saying that the order of the "whole" (*holon*) aught to be imitated — obviously these "wise men" are Pythagoreans.[37] The invocation of "nature" does little in terms of logical argument beyond adding a sort of glamour to the worthy, if unexciting, virtues of fairness and self-control.[38] That the soul should be ordered to conform to the order of the universe can only be understood if one believes (as the Pythagoreans did) that both the universe and the soul are made of numbers.[39]

Plato does not explicitly state the argument for a physical universe and a soul both made of numbers — apparently Speusippos did, but that doctrine is essential to make sense of the argument from nature. Plato may have thought the concept as absurd as many do today. Certainly enough simple animism survived among the people of Plato's time that the concept had an immediate appeal, without the subtleties of Pythagorean metaphysics. Nevertheless, without explanation attached, the doctrine has traveled far. A modern writer on Plato, John Wild, has attempted to state clearly Plato's thought on the subject of natural ethics; the following is a summary of Wild's work on this difficult topic: Plato uses *phusis* in three or four senses (hence much confusion): For Plato nature is:

1. the whole world order of mutually supporting forces and tendencies.
2. the form or *eidos* of a thing — a sense which implies imperfection, since it is only a participation in the Good, which is beyond them.
3. this striving toward good itself.

Something may be in Plato's usual term *kata phusin* ("according to nature"). In this sense (the human equivalent of number three above) humans must act according to their own nature toward the Good.[40]

The opposite of this, of course, is *para phusin*, "against nature."

"Nature" in Speusippos and his immediate successors in the Academy is conceived in a way very remote from our current scientific understanding of the physical world. A kind of order was assumed intuitively to exist in the world that had ethical meaning for humans. As F.W. Russell has put it, "An Ethical category is hastily imposed on phenomenon by a religious and inward assurance ... which ... is quite incommunicable to sober and prosaic inquiries."[41] With this in mind we may understand what Lycurgos of Athens meant when he said that adultery was a crime against nature,[42] and we can somewhat understand later when we find homosexuality denounced as *para phusin*, "against nature." Speusippos' remark to the man in love implies a simplistic, utilitarian view of sex — as much as to say, "You want sex? Buy a woman." The man largely and the woman entirely are regarded as abstractions, without rights or emotions. This is (to put the best face upon it) hasty generalization; at worst it is philosophic totalitarianism, though it does agree with much else in Speusippos' philosophy. He was a monarchist,[43] a fact that must have endeared him to Philip. For Speusippos, as for Hegel in nineteenth century Germany, the state was all; the individual was not moved by any inner life, but by the needs of the whole.[44]

To return to John Wild, he sees the modern theory of natural law as derived from Plato through the Stoics, Locke, and others in the following terms:

1. Though the world has "divergent tendencies," on the whole they support one another.
2. Each individual in a species has an essential structure that it shares with other members of that species.
3. This essential structure determines the "basic existential tendencies of the species."
4. "Natural Law" is the realization of those tendencies "without distortion or frustration." Human nature is by nature free. The essential structure of the human species is the same for all humans. Virtues or moral obligations must be pursued in order to avoid frustration of the full expression of human nature, and "the good for man is the activation of his nature, the most complete and intensive living of a human life."[45]

If we take the understanding of human sexuality that Plato puts in the mouth of Aristophanes in the *Symposium* at all seriously, it is difficult to see that Plato could have regarded homosexual acts as inherently "against nature." Plato's Aristophanes, half-playful, half serious (as the plays suggest the real Aristophanes was), tells a myth about humans as once having two faces and four arms and four legs (*Symposium*, 190 B–193 E). Zeus in anger split these original humans in two (rather as the aggressive Spartans cut the territory of Arcadia in two). The result is humans who go about seeking their lost other halves. Purely male beings, having been split, become boy lovers; purely female beings become *tribades*—lesbians; and the persons who seek lovers of the opposite sex come from hermaphrodites that have been split. Aristophanes continues:

> Whenever the lover of boys — or any other person for that matter — has the good fortune to encounter his own actual other half, affection and kinship and love combined inspire him with an emotion which is quite overwhelming, and such a pair will refuse ever to be separated even for a moment.... No one can suppose it is mere physical enjoyment which causes the one to take such delight in the company of the other.... everybody would regard it as the exact expression of the desire which he had long felt but had been unable to formulate, that he should melt into his beloved and that hence forth they should be one instead of two.[46]

The form, the nature, as we may say, of human sexuality is the same, whether the object is a person of the same gender or the opposite gender. This is surprisingly in accord with the growing understanding in the modern science of sexuality, as well as the Western liberal tradition of politics — humans are free. Sex is more than genitalia and procreation. Humans are in some way inherently bisexual, though most prefer one gender or another as objects of sexual desire. A fully free human may choose to express his or her sexuality with a person of the same gender — and this is no less a fulfilling of human nature than sex with the opposite gender. Other than in the *Laws*, Plato's view of nature seems not to preclude homosexuality as a part of human nature, and therefore does not see it as inherently in conflict with any other part of the totality of nature.

There is simply not enough of the work of Speusippos surviving for us to be able to say exactly how came about the transition from the positive view of homosexuality in the

Symposium (and arguably Plato overall) to the narrowed, mechanistically oriented view of sexuality that the surviving fragments of his work suggest. The evidence we have indicates a particularly noxious combination of Pythagorean arithmeticism and Macedonian totalitarianism. Whether one sees this change as originating in Plato depends largely on whether one believes the text of the *Laws* to be wholly by Plato or partly by a later hand. Perhaps an esoteric doctrine survived in the Academy that was more humane; if it did, we have no trace of it.

We do not need to say much about Xenocrates, Speusippos' successor, as the third "scholarch" or president of the Academy. Xenocrates repeated the dictum "live according to nature" of his predecessor.[47] Among the fragments of his work we have something of an explanation of this: the first principle of living according to nature was, he said, self-preservation[48]; this sounds encouraging, since it is a real, observable trait, not an ideal. He also seems to have done a bit of backward mythologizing, teaching the Pythagorean doctrine that animals should not be eaten by attributing it to the legendary Athenian hero Triptolimos,[49] though he also knew and repeated the Orphic teaching that humans are born sharing the guilt of the Titans who killed Dionysus, and hence should abstain from eating flesh.[50] Politically Xenocrates is said to have been asked by Alexander the Great for a book on how a king should rule[51]; Alexander probably would not have even asked if he had not known what sort of work he would have gotten. It is clear that by the end of the fourth century BCE the Academy founded by Plato had been taken over by an ascetic, totalitarian philosophy that was opposed to the democratic tradition of Athens and to the tolerance and moderation one so easily finds in the early dialogues of Plato. Speusippos was heavily influenced by the Pythagorean Plato, less by the Socratic. Much of this doctrinaire attitude can be found here and there in Plato's works as well, but it was these followers of Plato that to a large degree in antiquity established the way Plato should be read. The philosophy of Speusippos and his immediate successors tended to form a sort of lens through which the future looked back at the writings of Plato.

We may also mention in passing, as an indicator of the intellectual atmosphere of the Old Academy, Heraclides of Pontus (about 390–310 BCE). He is perhaps the most distinctly Pythagorean of the group. Plato is said to have had a large collection of Orphic books, and Heraclides read much in them.[52] He represents the Pythagorean side of Platonism and the irrational side of Pythagoreanism, filling his books "with childish tales" of miracles and signs, as Cicero said.[53] He was much interested in the shamanistic tradition, especially in tales of travelers from the Realms Beyond — we hear of a man who fell from the moon and reported that it was an inhabited world which only looked empty because it was covered by clouds constantly.[54] When a terrible earthquake destroyed Helike, Aristotle looked for natural explanations, while Heraclides speculated on why the gods were angry.[55]

Something must be said about Aristotle, though he deserves little mention in the history of homophobia. Born in Stagria, just south of Macedonia, he was the son of the court physician to Philip II's predecessor. At 17, Aristotle came to the Academy and remained there off and on till Plato's death. After a brief stint tutoring Alexander, Aristotle opened his own school in Athens, though he had never fully broken with Plato in philosophy.[56] Aristotle's lost early work, the *Protrepticus*, is said the be a bridge between Plato's ideas and Aristotle's independent thought[57] and heavily influenced by Pythagoreanism; it influenced Cicero, and through him St. Augustine, and all of medieval thought.[58] Generally in his mature work Aristotle found Orphism and Pythagoreanism absurd,[59] though he labored conscientiously to explain and controvert them.

Aristotle's major work on human conduct, the *Nicomachean Ethics*, is essentially a treatise on *philia*— friendship or love in the most general possible sense; *philia* defines or should define the relationships of lovers to each other, of citizens within a state, of rulers to the ruled, etc. Homosexual relationships are mentioned, quite in passing, in this discussion:

> Lovers and beloved [*Eraste kai eromeno*] do not take pleasure in the same things, the lover [*erastes*] in seeing the beloved, the other in receiving attentions from his lover, and when the bloom of youth is passing, the friendship sometimes passes too ... but many lovers, on the other hand, remain lovers, if familiarity has led them to love each other's characters, these being alike. But those who exchange not pleasure but utility in their amour are both less truly friends and less constant ... they were lovers not of each other but of profit [*Nicomachean Ethics*, 8, 4, 1157 A].

Diogenes Laertius mentions that Aristotle divided friendship (*philia*) into three sorts: the friendship of blood relatives, "that of lovers [*erotiken*, with the same implication as "erotic" has in English], and that of host and guest.... The wise man would fall in love ... [and also] marry."[60]

Elsewhere in the *Nicomachean Ethics* Aristotle discusses how pleasure can result from unusual sources; some pleasures, he says can arise by nature, others by habit, and still others by bad natures. There are the

> morbid states [*theriodeis*, morbid or malignant][61] resulting from custom, for example plucking out the hair, or gnawing the fingernails, or eating charcoal or earth, and in addition to these sex with males; for these arise in some by nature and in others, as in those who were raped as boys, from habit. No one can describe as lacking in self-control those for whom the cause is nature, any more than women can be blamed because they do not mount, but are mounted [*Nicomachean Ethics*, 7, 5, 1148 B 25–31].

Any passage that links together the rape of children and nail-biting is bound to be problematic. John Boswell and Kenneth Dover both interpret this difficult passage as implying condemnation of those males who are habitually passive ("bottoms") in same-sex acts.[62] I take it to refer to two sorts of homosexuality — in those who are homosexual "by nature" and those child molesters who are prey to the compulsion to rape young boys, which often occurs in those men who were themselves raped as children.

Aristotle's definition of *phusis*, nature, is fairly close to what a modern thinker might give. In his *Physics* he distinguishes between what exists by nature (animals, the elements) from things that are made by art (a bed, a coat). The term *kata phusin*, "by nature," describes what a thing does of itself; for example smoke rises by nature. Undifferentiated substance does not exist except for argument's sake — it may be earth or a bone, but it is always something. The form inheres in, rather than being different from, the thing in question,[63] as some followers of Plato might hold. The fullest definition of nature in Aristotle is in his *Metaphysics*; Robert Grant has summarized Aristotle's "nature" there in the following terms: Nature is

1. the genesis or growth of growing things,
2. the part from which growth begins, probably the seed,
3. the internal principle of movement in natural objects,
4. the unformed and unchanging matter from which natural objects are produced,
5. the essence or form of natural objects,
6. the essence or form in general,
7. the essence of things that have a principle of movement in themselves.

Things come into being, according to Aristotle, in three ways: by nature, as a man or animal is born (such happens only with a purpose); by art, as a man builds a house; by chance. This last is most problematic, for accidents happen. Freaks of nature (*teras*) occur, yet are "contrary not to the whole of nature, but to nature as it generally is."[64] We have no example in the voluminous writings of Aristotle that he ever saw all homosexual acts as "against nature" or inherently evil.

On a personal level, the man whom St. Thomas Aquinas called simply "the philosopher" seems to have been by and large heterosexual in his personality. The will of Aristotle that Diogenes Laertius preserves speaks with reverence of his late wife and his mistress, as well as his son, Nichomachos[65]; however, the gossip of antiquity tells us that at one point he was "overcome" by the beauty of one of his male students, Pharselis (alias Theodektos).[66] A tradition of pederasty seems to have continued in the Lyceum. Lycon (who died in 225 BCE), the third head of the school after Aristotle, seems never to have married; in his will he leaves his property to his nephew, who had lived with him for a long time and "was like a son."[67]

In any dealing with the origins of homophobia in the pre–Christian West, there is no more influential and problematic text than Plato's *Laws*. It is appropriate to place the discussion of that document after the discussion of Plato because it is in a number of respects vastly different from the rest of Plato's works and because there is good reason to suspect that at least part of it is a forgery by a later writer — or writers. Of course authorship of any work can never be proven, though forgery sometimes can. The question of Platonic authorship had better be discussed first; its importance, though, is not because of any authority that the name of Plato has; rather an understanding of the *Laws* depends on its intellectual context.

Plato certainly wrote a work called the *Laws*. Aristotle, who was in Athens in the last years of Plato's life, devotes a good deal of the second book of his *Politics* (1264B, 26–1266A 31) to a discussion of Plato's *Laws* (which he calls [1264B 26] a "later work" than the *Republic*). When Speusippos died, we are told that Aristotle bought his library,[68] so that we can be certain that he owned as full a copy of the *Laws* as existed; he may well have had a copy in Plato's handwriting. A reference to the assassination of Philip II at 1311A shows that the *Politics* was being worked on as late as 336 BCE, at least three years after Speusippos' death and 17 years after Plato's. The following two points in Aristotle's discussion are relevant here: (1) Socrates was a speaker in the *Laws* (1265A, 10–16); (2) For the "most part" the *Laws* is a collection of laws (1265A, 1–5).

Socrates is not a speaker in the existing *Laws* at all. In fact only about a third of the text of the *Laws* that we have today is laws; the rest is *pronomia*, introductions in which the purpose of the various laws are discussed.[69] All of Aristotle's comments on the *Laws* cover only books three to seven — which leaves out entirely the passages in books one and eight, which forbid homosexual activity. Is this merely a coincidence?

The second major piece of external evidence regarding the authorship of the *Laws* is from Diogenes Laertius; in his "Life of Plato" from perhaps the second century CE Laertius writes, "Some say that Philip of Opos copied out the *Laws* which was left in wax [*metegrapsen ontas einai*]" (3, 37).

"Left in wax" is no more clear in Greek than in English; it can mean either "left written on wooden tablets coated with wax," which was the ancient way of making rough drafts or notes, because papyrus or parchment were too expensive, or it can refer to *cere predu*, the ancient manner (still used) of making bronze sculpture: a model is made of wax, which is then coated with clay; when the clay is dry, the wax is melted out and molten bronze poured into the hollow left by the wax. The sculptor then breaks the clay away and finishes the resulting work by filing and adding bits where the bronze did not fill. A sculpture that is not finished in bronze may be said to be "in wax."

With regard to the first explanation, Wilmowitz-Moellendorff may have been the first to notice (in his *Platon*, published in 1920) that a work the size of our present text of the *Laws* would be extremely unwieldy on what would have been many hundreds of wax tablets.[70] The second possible reading has even less to recommend it, since it would imply that Plato left the work in a highly unfinished state. If we assume the latter then we may well believe that parts that were lacking in the original were filled in by Philip of Opos, who was distinctly Pythagorean in his philosophy.

Aristotle is not likely to have been so careless as to say that Socrates was a speaker in the *Laws* if he was not. It is unthinkable that Socrates could ever have been part of this work as we know it — the Athenian Stranger is a most superbly anti–Socratic sort of a character, as several have noted.[71] G. Ryle in *Plato's Progress* attempts to argue that Aristotle saw a draft of the *Laws* during Plato's lifetime and that Plato changed the work before he died. However, the date of writing of the *Politics* shows it to be well after Plato's death; and any draft of the *Laws* that resembled our present text, but had Socrates as the major speaker, is absurd to contemplate unless the super-authoritarian state the *Laws* outlines was the object of Socratic criticism.

The first dateable reference to the *Laws* after Aristotle is in the records of a law case in Athens in the early summer of 306 BCE. One Philon, a follower of Aristotle, tried to found a new school of philosophy; certain laws enacted by Demetrius Poliocetes were invoked by Sophocles of Sunium to prevent the founding of a new school. Philon appealed on the grounds that free speech (*parrhesia*) was a longstanding tradition in Athens; on the other side, Demochares speaking for Sophocles of Sunium argued that philosophy was not a good idea to promote in a state because pupils of Plato had behaved badly and were "a fine product of the beautiful *Republic* and the lawless *Laws*."[72] Philon won the case, and philosophy went on in Athens.[73] "Beautiful Republic" is a swipe at Kallipolis, and "Lawless *Laws*" must be a denunciation of Plato's other ideal city — though how one could call the text of the *Laws,* as we have it, "lawless" is beyond the possibility of (all but Socratic) irony. Does the remark imply that a satiric, Socratic work existed, called the *Laws* and attributed to Plato, but radically different from the text we now have? About this same time or a bit earlier Dikaiarkhos of Messene, a writer on Macedonian political theory about the end of the fourth century BCE, rebuked Plato for favoring homosexual love,[74] which Dikaiarkhos (who was surely familiar with all the political thought of his time) hardly would have done if he had known our text of the *Laws*. The inference is that between the time of Dikaiarkhos' writing and the law case of Philon, the text of the *Laws* as we know it came into being. Posidonius, a Stoic philosopher and historian (c. 135–50 BCE), is quoted thus by Seneca: "I do not approve that Plato's *Laws* have had preambles added to them."[75] Posidonius was, with Varro, one of the most learned men of his age[76] and, as a Stoic, would have had no particular Academic ax to grind. Cicero mentions that the *Laws* of Plato with their preambles resemble the *Laws* of Zaleucus of Charondas[77]; however, the work of Zaleucus that was known to Cicero was certainly a late forgery, of neo–Pythagorean origin.[78]

The difference of language between the rest of Plato's work and the *Laws* is likewise troubling; works like the *Symposium* or the *Phaedrus* are standards for clarity and graceful beauty in Attic prose, while the *Laws* is, as Victorino Tejera says, "clumsy and ungrammatical."[79] Writers sometimes do change their opinions as they grow older and the quality of their work may decline (e.g. Wordsworth); however the problem with the *Laws* is not just that the language is occasionally baroque, not to say grotesque; rather, the grammar is occasionally defective.[80] Wordsworth's late work, *The Holy Sonnets*, for example, certainly represents a different intellectual atmosphere than, say, "Intimations of Immortality"; but the grammar in the later work is no less standard English than in the earlier; age and experience do not generally cause one to unlearn grammar or to neglect a perfectly developed style. A.Q. Morton and A.D. Winspear in *It's Greek to the Computer* attempted a stylometric test on the *Laws* by feeding portions of Plato's earlier work into a computer, which compared the linguistic structure to that of the *Laws*; the computer came to the conclusion that the text of books five and six are by another hand. Morton and Winspear suggested Speusippos.[81]

Something must be said about the editions of Plato's work that were made in antiquity. The last edition we know of before the Renaissance was made in the first century CE by Thrasyllus, the court astrologer to the Emperor Tiberius. Thrasyllus was strongly Pythagorean, ambitious and political,[82] and his position at the imperial court gave him vast prestige and influence. We know that a passage was added by a Pythagorean to the text of the *Timaeus* some time after the death of Cicero,[83] and the text of the *Republic* was altered between 50 BCE and 200 CE,[84] and so was the *Meno*.[85] The Pythagorean Eudoros added his own words to Aristotle's text to make it agree with him.[86] There is good evidence that Thrasyllus inserted his own words into Epistle Seven (attributed to Plato), and also that he tinkered with the text of the Platonic "Epistles" Two and Eight.[87] Curiously Plato — or whoever wrote "Epistle" 3 — goes somewhat out of his way to note that he, "Plato," added prologues to his *Laws*; Joseph Souilhe found this quite suspicious.[88] Thrasyllus stands at the beginning of a line of Neo-Pythagorean philosophers who called themselves Platonists[89]; a doctrine particularly favored by him was that God is *ton holon higemon theos*: "the leader of the procession of the gods."[90] We have seen this doctrine in *Phaedrus*, 246E, associated with the curious notion of unconsummated homosexual desire; it also occurs in our text of the *Laws*, but this had better be discussed in the context of that book. Is this another interpolation of Thrasyllus, using one of his favorite themes? We simply do not know.

In conclusion then, before we turn to the actual text of the *Laws*, we may say that there is considerable and weighty evidence that what we have today as the text of Plato's *Laws* is not fully what Plato wrote; suspicion falls most heavily upon the prologues, which are exactly the passages in the *Laws* that contain homophobic material. The comment in Aristotle's *Politics* that Plato forbad pederasty in his *Republic*[91] assures us that that text is reliable; however, he does not mention the matter in his discussion of Plato's *Laws*. There does not seem to be any reference to Book One of the *Laws* earlier than the Pythagorizing Platonist of the first century BCE, Eudoros of Alexandria.[92] Further, the concept of nature as a source for morals is not sufficiently developed in the other works of Plato to explain its invocation with regard to homosexuality in the *Laws*. It seems unlikely that an audience in Plato's lifetime would have fully understood the concept, since it was not fully developed until about two generations after Plato's death. It was in the century that followed Plato's death that nature as a source for ethical principle was most fully worked out, and the homophobic passages we are about to consider seem to belong to that later age. It is in the context of Stoic thought that we will look at these passages, fully and in detail, putting them in the context of the large book they come from.

The Laws is the longest work (20 pages or so longer than the *Republic*, though it seems far more) that has reached us under the name of Plato. It has come down to us from a single medieval manuscript. Like the *Republic*, it is a plan for a perfect city, "Magnesia" here as against the Kallipolis of the *Republic*. The speakers in the dialogue are three old men, Klinias of Crete, Megillos[93] of Sparta and the Athenian Stranger. They are trudging toward the sacred cave of Dactyean Zeus on Mount Ida overlooking Knossos on the island of Crete. It was said that Minos visited his father, Zeus, in that cave every eight years, receiving laws from him there.[94] Likewise Epimenides, the *gonos*, had received his prophetic powers from sleeping for 57 years in the Cave of the Dactyls on the Cretan Mount Ida; he is reported to have written a treatise on the laws of the Cretans.[95] Pythagoras is likewise said to have undergone such "incubation" in a cave or underground chamber[96] in order to gain divine wisdom. To discuss law on the way to Mount Ida is to bear coals to Newcastle. The three old men discuss a new city that is to be built on Crete — or rather the Athenian Stranger discusses it, for Megillos and Klinias are little more than yes-men — on what must have been a very long summer day.

If there is any humor in the work, it is difficult to detect. The old men remind one reader of nothing in Greek literature so much as Nestor in Homer — an old man who loves to talk and takes the fullest possible advantage of the Greeks' customary respect for the old to do so. The *Laws* is hardly a dialogue at all; really, it is a rambling treatise on statecraft interrupted here and there by speakers who say little more than "yes." Transitions are choppy or lacking altogether, and the Stranger has a peculiar habit of speech — he likes to use the same word in several different senses or grammatical forms — that becomes wearing very quickly. More than any other work under Plato's name, the *Laws* breathes the atmosphere of formal religion, rather than the deep mysticism of Socrates facing death in prison or the absorption of the self in contemplation of divine order in the *Timaeus*.

The Athenian Stranger, who speaks so prominently in the *Laws*, is fully aware of the problem in framing a universal law code: Aiming probably at the opinions of Archelaus,[97] he denounces the notion that the gods exist by social convention (*tekne*, art, something made by humans), not nature:

> They assert, moreover, that there is one class beautiful by nature and another class beautiful by convention; while as to things just, they do not exist at all by nature, but men are constantly in dispute about them and continually altering them, and whatever alteration they make at any time is at that time authoritative, though it owes its existence to art and the laws and not in any way to nature [*Laws*, 889D].

As an alternative to this ethical relativism, the Stranger proposes the concept of Mind (*nous*). Nature and art are not opposites; they are the same thing; the Stranger maintains that "design is prior both in time and importance to chance, since it came first and the whole universe is rationally planned," to quote Guthrie on this point.[98] We may just as well quote Alexander Pope:

> All nature is but art unknown to thee;
> All chance direction which thou canst not see [*Essay on Man*, 1. 267–68].

Essentially the argument for the existence of God (or gods) is from design in, or behind, nature. Design implies reason, and this moves in a constant circle (898A–B). Of course the problem of evil immediately arises. To explain the contradictions in the universe, the Stranger resorts to a dualism — there are two souls in control of the universe, a good one and a bad one. Plato explicitly denied this idea in *Politicus* (270A), but here the Athenian Stranger has all but invented the devil. Evil is the opposite of intelligence, not part of a divine plan that will come round right in the end; rather evil is the result of the weakness of God; it is random and originates in *psyche*, in soul.[99] Many have seen this idea as coming to Plato from Zoroastrian sources,[100] but a more immediate source is possible in Pherekydes of Syros, who seems to have held there were two souls in individuals — a warm, divine one and a cold, earthly one.[101] The concession of a permanent evil coexisting with good in the world "put an end to the hope that the world could be explained with any clarity as a product of love."[102] Ultimately the dualism in the theology of the *Laws* renounces the optimism of the *Symposium*, and the legislation that follows would put an end to the sort of love that the *Symposium* embraced.

In typical style, the Athenian Stranger asks himself what the "first law" (*proton nomon*) of a city should be, then answers his own question; the lawgiver (*nomothetes*) will follow the order of nature (*kata phusin*) and regulate the first starting point (*arkhe*) of generation in states — the sexual union and partnership of marriage (*ton gamon summixis kai koinonia*). Men must be obliged by law to marry between the ages of 30 and 35; those who do not are to be fined annually until they do marry.[103] It is by marrying and producing children that humans become immortal, and nature has implanted in us a "sharp desire" for immortality (*Laws* 720D–721D). This physical immortality, through biologically producing children, is not quite in keeping with other Platonic concepts of immortality.

We have pointed out earlier that the Greeks thought of their cities as having been founded and given their essential quality by pairs of same-sex lovers — Herakles and Iolaos in Sparta, Laios and Chysippos in Thebes, Athena and Britomartis in Athens — an idea that may be as old as the city of Erech in Sumer. Here, Athenian Stranger is insisting that the foundation of his perfect city is to be placed not in same-sex unions, but in male-female marriages. The choice is inevitable, given the completely absolutist character of Magnesia; same-sex unions were thought of as essentially democratic in character; Eros was the great equalizer; heterosexual marriage, on the other hand, was universally thought of in antiquity as an unequal relationship: the husband completely and permanently dominated his wife. In a city such as the Stranger is planning the latter union, dominance and submission, is a perfect *arkhe*, a perfect foundation.

For precedent in this sort of foundation we may, in a unique instance, go back earlier than Pythagoras, to the man who was said to have been Pythagoras' teacher; again we meet Pherekydes of Syros. He flourished on the island of Syros in the Cyclides about 544 BCE[104]; he is said to have had an observatory there, hence to have been interested in astronomy or astrology.[105] A treatise by him circulated in antiquity that proposed a sort of theogony with Zeus marrying the Earth[106]; as with the Orphics, the creation of the world "is put in the language of seminal conception and embriology."[107] This, along with a theory of a dual soul, he passed on to Pythagoras.[108] The concept of a River of Rebirth that Plato used in *Phaedo* (112A) seems to have originated with Pherekydes, who was possibly influenced by the theology of the Egyptian cult of Ammon.[109] Ammonism in Pythagorean thought was assimilated into the theory of both sexuality and law. God is the sun, or symbolized by the sun, and the regular movement of the sun is a metaphor for law. The female aspect of reality is the dark earth, disorderly and chaotic; the ideal is the dominance of the ordering principle (law, the sun, the male) on the chthonic world of female desire and matter. Homosexuality, by blurring the dualistic distinction between male and female, threatens the world order of Pythagorean thought; it goes radically against their concept of "nature." Here again we may quote from the *Laws*:

"Friends" we say to them, "God, as the old tradition declares, holding in His hand the beginning, middle, and end of all that is, travels according to His nature [*kata phusin*] in a straight line towards the accomplishment of His end. Justice always accompanies Him, and is the punisher of those who fall short of the divine law. To justice, he who would be happy [*eudaimonesin*] holds fast, and follows in her company with all humility and order; but he who is lifted up with pride, or elated by wealth or rank, or beauty, who is young and foolish, and has a soul hot with insolence, and thinks that he has no need of any guide or ruler, but is able himself to be the guide of others, he, I say, is left deserted of God; and being thus deserted, he takes to him others who are like himself, and dances about, throwing all things into confusion, and many think that he is a great man, but in a short time he pays a penalty which justice cannot but approve, and is utterly destroyed, and his family and city with him" [716 A–B1].

The proverb quoted at the beginning of this passage is thought to be Orphic.[110] The reference to the arrogant man who can lead himself and lead others probably glances at pederasty. In fact, in Magnesia no one leads, all follow:

> We ought in times of peace from youth upwards to practice this habit of commanding others and being commanded by others; anarchy should have no place in the life of man or of the beasts [Laws, 942 B–C].

Pederasty was certainly at home in Crete, where the *Laws* is set; it was believed to have originated there.[111] We have seen how Minos and the Cave of the Dactyls on Mount Ida overlooking the ruins of Knossos figured into the official Athenian institution of pederasty, so the choice of setting has many overtones. Mention also might be made of the "Watching from the Wall" passage in the *Iliad*, where the old men of Troy murmur together like cicadas and agree that, beautiful though she is, Helen should leave Troy (*Iliad*, 3.154 ff). So the old men in the *Laws* trudge though a hot summer's day up the mountain of Law, murmuring that desire must be exiled.

The Athenian Stranger says:

> Now the gymnasia and common meals do a great deal of good, and yet they are a source of evil in civil troubles; as is shown in the case of the Milesian, and Boeotian, and Thurian youth, among whom these institutions seem always to have had a tendency to degrade the ancient and natural custom of love natural [*kata phusin*] to humans and animals. The charge may be fairly brought against your cities above all others, and is true also of most other states which especially cultivate the use of gymnasia [the traditional meeting places of men and boys for erotic encounters]. Whether such matters are to be regarded jestingly or seriously, I think that the pleasure is to be deemed natural which arises out of the intercourse between men and women [*kata phusin apodedosthai dokei*]; but that the intercourse of men with men, or of women with women, is contrary to nature [*para phusin*], and that the bold attempt was originally due to unbridled lust. The Cretans are always accused of having invented the story of Ganymede and Zeus because they wanted to justify themselves in the enjoyment of unnatural pleasures by the practice of the god whom they believe to have been their lawgiver. Leaving the story, we may observe that any speculation about laws turns almost entirely on pleasure and pain, both in states and in individuals: these are two fountains which nature lets flow [*metheintai phusei rein*], and he who draws from them where and when, and as much as he ought, is happy; and this holds of men and animals — of individuals as well as states; and he who indulges in them ignorantly and at the wrong time, is the reverse of happy [Laws 636 A–E].

We shall return at some length to the point that the Stranger makes about pleasure being due to nature; the statement is important for the dating and context of the *Laws*. The Stranger seems confused about pleasure and its relation to nature. Pleasure is present in homosexual acts as well as heterosexual, therefore the presence of pleasure in homosexual acts is "natural." Yet to avoid disaster, we must use pleasure in the right way; however, the Stranger seems to assume there is no right way to use homosexual pleasure. But to continue: The next mention of homosexuality is much later, after the Stranger has outlined those sports that are to be used for the military training of young men.

> ATHENIAN STRANGER: In many ways Crete and Lacedaemon furnish a great help to those who make peculiar laws; but in the matter of sexual love, as we are alone, I must confess that they are quite against us. For if any one following nature should lay down the law

which existed before the days of Laius,[112] saying we should not have the same kind of sex with men and with boys as with women [*to ton arrenonkai neon e koionein kathaper theleion*], and denounce these lusts as contrary to nature [*dia to me phusei*], citing the animals as a proof that such unions were monstrous, he might prove his point, but he would be wholly at variance with the custom of your states. Further, they are repugnant to a principle which we say that a legislator should always observe; for we are always enquiring which of our enactments tends to virtue [*areten*] and which not. And suppose we grant that these loves are accounted by law to be honorable, or at least not disgraceful, in what degree will they contribute to virtue [*areten*]? Will it make many the character of him whose thigh is rubbed on [*ti meros hemin xumballoit' an pors reten*]?[113] or in the soul of the seducer produce the principle of temperance [*sophronos*]? Who will ever believe this?— or rather, who will not blame the cowardliness of him who yields to pleasures and is unable to hold out against them? Will not all men censure as womanly him who imitates the woman [*eis mimesin tou theleos iontos ten eikonos homooitera ar' ou mempsetai*]? And who would ever think of establishing such a practice by law? Certainly no one who had in his mind the image of true law. [837] How can we prove that what I am saying is true? He who would rightly consider these matters must see the nature of friendship and desire, and of these so-called loves [*ton legomenon eroton phusin*], for they are of two kinds, and out of the two arises a third kind, having the same name; and this similarity of name causes all the difficulty and obscurity.

CLEINIAS: How is that?

ATHENIAN STRANGER: Dear [*philon*] is the like in virtue to the like, and the equal to the equal; dear also, though unlike, is he who has abundance to him who is in want. And when either of these friendships becomes excessive, we term the excess love.

CLEINIAS: Very true.

ATHENIAN STRANGER: The friendship which arises from contraries is horrible and fierce, and has often not mutual; but that which arises from likeness is gentle, and it return lasts through life. As to the mixed sort which is made up of them both, there is, first of all, a difficulty in determining what he who is possessed by this third love desires; moreover, he is drawn different ways, and is in doubt between the two principles; the one exhorting him to enjoy the beauty of youth, and the other forbidding him. For the one is a lover of the body, and hungers after beauty, like ripe fruit, and would fain satisfy himself without any regard to the character of the beloved [*eromenou*]; the other holds the desire of the body to be a secondary matter, and looking [*horon*] rather than loving [*eron*] and with his soul lusting [*epitethuekos*] for the soul of the other in a becoming manner, regards the satisfaction of the bodily love as wantonness; he reverences and respects temperance and courage and magnanimity and wisdom, and wishes to live chastely with the chaste object of his affection. Now the sort of love which is made up of the other two is that which we have described as the third. Seeing then that there are these three sorts of love, ought the law to prohibit and forbid them all to exist among us? Is it not rather clear that we should wish to have in the state the love which is of virtue and which desires the beloved youth to be the best possible; and the other two, if possible, we should hinder? What do you say, friend Megillos?

MEGILLOS: I think, Stranger, that you are perfectly right in what you have been now saying [Laws VIII 836A].[114]

The solution here, to the problem of passion, seems to be "Platonic love," essentially the sort recommended in the *Phaedrus*, where homosexual desire is not suppressed until it reaches near physical consummation. Notable is the statement that homosexual love lacks an object, that it aims at nothing, while the sex between men and women aims at procreation. However, the

Stranger goes on to propose a system of repressing not homosexual acts, but homosexual desire itself—a system that has a remarkably modern ring to it:

ATHENIAN STRANGER: We are all aware that most men, in spite of their lawless natures, are very strictly and precisely restrained from intercourse [*sunousias*[115]] with the fair, and this is not at all against their will, but entirely with their will.

MEGILLOS: When do you mean?

ATHENIAN STRANGER: When any one has a brother or sister who is fair; and about a son or daughter the same unwritten law holds, and is a most perfect safeguard to prevent having sex with them [*sugkatheudonta*], so that no open or secret connection ever takes place between them. Nor does the thought of such a thing ever enter at all into the minds of most of them.

MEGILLOS: Very true.

ATHENIAN STRANGER: The reason of this is that incestuous connections have ever been deemed infamous.

Does not a little word extinguish all pleasures of that sort?

MEGILLOS: What word?

ATHENIAN STRANGER: The declaration that they are unholy, hated of God, and most infamous; and is not the reason of this that no one has ever said the opposite, but every one from his earliest childhood has heard men speaking in the same manner about them always and everywhere, whether in comedy or in the graver language of tragedy? The legislator who wants to master any of the passions which master man may easily know how to subdue them? He will consecrate the tradition of their evil character among all, slaves and freemen, women and children, throughout the city:—that will be the surest foundation of the law which he can make.

MEGILLOS: Yes; but will he ever succeed in making all mankind use the same language about them?

ATHENIAN STRANGER: A good objection; but was I not just now saying that I had a way to make men use natural love and abstain from [839] unnatural, not intentionally destroying the seeds of human increase, or sowing them in stony places, in which they will take no root; and that I would command them to abstain too from any female field of increase in which that which is sown is not likely to grow? Now if a law to this effect could only be made perpetual, and gain an authority such as already prevents intercourse of parents and children—such a law, extending to other sensual desires, and conquering them, would be the source of ten thousand blessings. For, in the first place, moderation follows nature, and deters men from all frenzy and madness of love, and from all adulteries [*moikheion*][116] and immoderate use of meats and drinks, and makes them good friends to their own wives. And innumerable other benefits would result if such a law could only be enforced.... The ordinance once consecrated would enslave [*doulosesthai*] the soul of every man, and terrify him into obedience.

[Exercise is recommended to control passions in the young, the Athenian Stranger then says.]

The principle of piety, the love of honor, and the desire of beauty, not in the body but in the soul. These are, perhaps, romantic aspirations; but they are the noblest of aspirations, if they could only be realized in all states, and, God willing, in the matter of love we may be able to enforce one of two things—either that no one shall venture to touch any person of the freeborn or noble class except his wedded wife, or sow the unconsecrated and bastard seed in female prostitutes, or barren seed in males [*mede agona arrenon para phusin*]; or at least we may abolish altogether the connection of men with men [*arrenon*]; and as to women, if any man has to do with any but those who come into his house duly married by sacred rites, whether they be bought or acquired in any other way, and he offends publicly in the face of all mankind, we shall be right in enacting that he be deprived of civic honours and privileges, and be deemed to be, as he truly is, a stranger [Laws, VIII, 838A–341E].

That homosexuality must be put an end to by laws that will create internal repression in the individual similar to the manner in which incest is repressed is in its way a brilliant understanding of the psychomechanics of internalized homophobia. It raises interesting questions about both the consistency of the Athenian Stranger's thought, and the date of the *Laws*; the latter will be discussed under Stoicism, the former may be dealt with here. The *Phaedrus* clearly, as well as the *Laws* a few pages above, values or at least does not look down upon homosexual desire. Plato and any other informed Greek of this age must have known that incest was common and accepted among the Egyptians and Persians; it was, as any reader of Sophocles knows, the ultimate taboo among the Greeks. It seems likely that whoever wrote this passage was familiar with internalized homophobia in practice, though the Stranger has said that society as a whole would be amazed to hear that homosexuality was being forbidden in Magnesia. Quite possibly the author of this passage came from a deviant group that forbade homosexuality within its bounds. The sophistication of the author suggests a firsthand knowledge of homosexual repression. If so, surely the group in which homosexuality was repressed were the Pythagorean-Orphics.

The reasons put forward for forbidding homosexual acts in the *Laws* are essentially four: (1) It makes young men unruly and may lead to civil insurrection. (2) Because it involves one man assuming a passive (womanly) role, it makes men cowardly. (3) Because it involves pleasure, it causes young men to give way to luxurious living. (4) It is against nature — not even animals do it.

The first of these we have seen before — the argument of tyranny, going back to the murder of Harmodios and Aristogeiton. The second seems to have its roots in the dualism of Pythagoreanism, which insisted that male and female roles were distinct and the latter inferior. The third — that passion must be controlled — is very broadly based in classical ethical thought, but is here for the first time applied to homosexuality. Virtue again and again in classical writers is identified with self-control. One may enjoy pleasure, but to give way to it is to invite vice. Finally we note (as the Stranger does not) that it seems contradictory to assume that what makes young men unruly and a danger to the state also makes them weak and cowardly. To examine the last point, certainly the most important one for the history of homophobia, we must return to the context of Greek thought a generation and more after Plato.

THE ACADEMY AFTER SPEUSIPPOS: THE RETURN OF PHILOSOPHICAL HOMOSEXUALITY

When Xenocrates died at the age of 82 in 314 BCE, Polemon, the son of Philostratos, was elected head of the Academy at the age of 35, the first young man to head that institution.[117] Diogenes Laertius tells us that Polemon had been an alcoholic before his conversion to philosophy; meeting philosophy in the person of Xenocrates, he sobered up, his wife divorced him and he became the lover of one of his male fellow students.[118] It sounds as though Polemon had what we may call a "coming out" experience; in a homophobic environment he had denied his basic nature, then when philosophy made him question social conventions he found himself and lost his old life. In a larger sense, a change may be detected in the atmosphere of thought and behavior in what comes to be called the Old Academy. Diogenes Laertius speaks of Polemon as "generous and refined," and a lover of the poetry of Sophocles and especially of Homer.[119] The fact alone that he admired Homer marks him as no Orphic-Pythagorean, since they disliked Homer's work as too much "this worldly." Polemon's thought was mostly ethical and his ethics, like those of Speusippos and Xenocrates, were based around the dictum "live according to nature." He seems to have regarded this, like Xenocrates, as implying self-preservation and, perhaps, in addition to Xenocrates, self-love, based on the observation that "every living creature loves itself." According to Cicero, he taught the doctrine of *Oikeiotes*—that the world is a household where humans should live together in harmony, friendship and kindness—which was later taken over and slightly modified by the Stoics.[120] *Oikeiotes* can also be translated as "marriage," and it appears that Polemon may have been quite serious about this, for we are told that he and his pupil Crates were lifelong lovers. "They were so attached to each other that they not only shared the same pursuits in life but grew more alike to their last breath, and dying shared the same tomb."[121] It is said on less authority that Polemon had been the boy-lover to Xenocrates.[122] He is thought to have written the dialogue called the *Rivals* (once attributed to Plato), which portrays the philosopher as the Great Lover.[123] He had a statue added to the grounds of the Academy showing Prometheus, the bringer of divine fire to humans, as an old man passing a flaming torch to a young man, Hephaestos.[124] "Love," he said, "is provided by the gods for the good of the young."[125] Crates succeeded his lover as head of the Academy in 276 BCE. "They did not side with the popular party," Diogenes Laertius says,[126] and as so often with that writer, we wish he would be more clear. Perhaps the sentence reflects a break in the Academy between old-line Orphic-Pythagorean Academics, followers of Speusippos and homophobic, and the younger men who were reinstating the acceptance of homosexuality and pederasty that had been part of the tradition of Greece for centuries. Numenius, a Pythagorean in the Imperial Age, speaks of a break in the Academy in the time of Polemon but attributes it to Archisilaus and Krantor (both of whom he accuses of homosexuality)[127] and of course Zeno, all pupils of Polemon. Numenius does not explicitly mention homosexuality as an issue, but one expects it must have been at the very least "the elephant in the room that no one speaks of." If we take Laertius' "popular party" to mean a homophobic element in Athenian society, then in remarkably little time homophobia and Orphism had become the accepted norm in common Greek society.

STOICISM AND HOMOSEXUALITY

In 312 BCE a new spirit entered an Athens that was still chewing over the ideas of Plato and Aristotle. Twenty years old, he was named Zeno; a tall, thin man, with a dark complexion and a head persistently held to one side, he was led to Athens by the reputation of that city for philosophy. Born on the island of Cyprus (Kittium) two years after it passed into the empire of Alexander, his father had given him books about Socrates and he wanted to meet such a man.[128] Theophrastos, the successor of Aristotle, was lecturing to 2,000 every morning; and his school was offering lectures in all branches of knowledge. Zeno, like his hero Socrates, was more interested in learning how to live, so he chose Crates the Cynic as a teacher, then went to Polemon in the Academy; we also hear of him studying logic under Diodorus Kronos.[129] Soon he broke from his teachers and eventually founded his own school: the Stoics. The importance of Zeno and the early Stoics for this work is that they maintained a distinctly positive attitude toward homosexuality.[130] It will be useful to compare the position of Zeno with that of his teachers, especially those in the Academy, since that debate is a crucial point in the development of homophobia out of a gay-positive culture.

Zeno's view of nature may be called pantheism: that nature and God are the same.[131] He was staunchly anti-idealistic and resisted formal logic in favor of what Giovanni Reale calls "intuitionism," a blunt denial of the existence of the incorporeal.[132] His system was also materialistic in the sense that it held that everything, even the mind, is made of the same physical substance. Nature to Zeno was what holds the world together, what causes things on earth to grow (*phousan*). Nature is a force that moves itself, producing and maintaining its offspring by "seminal principles" (*spermatikous logous*), "semen" meaning that which is able to generate offspring like the parent.[133] The aims of nature are both use and pleasure.[134] "Nature" for the Stoics implied both matter and the "intrinsic agent principle"; meaning it is both matter and God.[135] Zeno began all his discourses with a reference to the order of the world.[136]

In his *Republic* (lost except for fragments) Zeno held that there should be no nations each with differing law codes, but "one way of life and one order, like that of a single flock of sheep on a common pasture feeding together under a common law"[137]—a much clearer statement of a "law of nature" than anything in Plato. However, Zeno does not appeal to *ho nomos koinos*, the common law of nature, in any specific instance of ethics, nor do the other early Stoics.[138] "To live according to nature is to live according to reason.... God is the perfection of reason. But because Man is not God, he cannot embrace all things. Common law ... does not offer any criteria to help his choosing."[139] Reason (*logos*) is the active principle of the world; Heraclitos had defined nature as fire, and the Stoics went on to call the fire of nature "a craftsman like fire,"[140] reversing the metaphor — nature is a fire that constructs, rather than destroying. In that sense nature has purpose; nature has made us what we are — self-loving, social[141] and at least capable of reason.

"Self-love," *oikeiosis*, in Stoic thought is not selfishness, but rather a generalizing process that starts with the notion that every one, even an animal, seeks self-preservation. This principle is then extended outward to the "household"— the root of the word *oikeiosis* means "house." The child loves its family, the adult man or woman loves the city, or nation, and the true sage loves all humanity,[142] based, it would seem, on the recognition that others are like one's self. Sexual love the Stoics called "an impulse prior to an impulse," *epibole*,[143] and all such impulses were, they maintained, chosen. Josiah B. Gould illustrates this with the story of the love affair of Jason and Medea, which ended disastrously. When Medea met Jason, he appeared to her to be a handsome and desirable young man. At some instant she made the decision that to fall in love with him would be a good thing. Love is the judgment that something that is not yet present will be good. Such a judgment may be correct or incorrect, depending on how solidly based it is in reason. After she fell in love with him, it was probably impossible for Medea to change her mind — once strong emotions come into play, it becomes nearly impossible to change them; as a Stoic wrote, "For when emotions are aroused, they repel reasoning and things which appear differently [from that which they wish] and thrust violently forward to actions contrary [to reason]." What is unnatural is what is unreasonable — uncontrolled passion, regardless of the object.[144] Jason treated Medea abominably; her mistake was that she did not look before she leapt. A love affair with a truly good man could have been a genuinely good thing; humans have, the Stoics said, "from nature inclinations to discover what is appropriate and stabilize ... impulses and stand firm."[145]

The sage, the ideally wise person envisaged by the Stoics, will "make sexual advances" to young men in their prime and will have "sexual intercourse with those who are worthy of [true] sexual love [i.e.] those who are well-born and endowed with natural ability.[146] The Stoic sage, says a source from late antiquity, acts with good sense and dialectically and ... erotically, but the erotic man is so called in two senses, the one who is virtuous, and the other who gets his quality from vice — a sort of sex-fiend ... and being worthy of sexual love means the same as being worthy of friendship and not the same as being worthy of being enjoyed, for he who is worthy of virtuous sexual love is [properly] worthy of sexual love. They [the Stoics] understand virtue exercised at a symposium as similar to virtue in sexual matters ... to hunt for talented young boys, which encourages them to virtuous knowledge; and in general proper knowledge of sexual activity. That is why they say that the sensible man will engage in sexual activity. And sexual activity just by itself is indifferent, since at times it occurs among base men. But sexual love is not desire, nor is it directed at any base object, but is an effort to gain friendship resulting from the appearance of beauty.[147] ... Passion is impulse which is excessive and disobedient to the dictates of reason, or a movement of the soul which is irrational and contrary to nature.... Irrational is equivalent to disobedient to reason ... since people in states of passion see that it is not suitable to do thus, but are carried away by the intensity as by a disobedient horse ... the sense "contrary to nature" [*para phusin*] ... is of something that happens contrary to the right [*orthon*] and natural reason [*kai kata phusin logon*].[148]

Love's sole end is making friends, and it depends upon respect of the beloved, the Stoics held, and cited the case of a man who had a woman he loved in his power but did not rape her, because she disliked him.[149] Zeno regarded Eros as exclusively the god of friendship and concord; in his *Republic* he called Eros "the god which contributes to the security of the city."[150] Zeno himself never had sex with a woman (as perhaps became a wry-necked man), but only with men; and said one should keep his boy-love till the latter was 28[151] — long after many Greek men would have thought the lad too old to be attractive.

The contrast of Stoic erotics with that of Plato and his followers is illuminating. In the *Symposium* it is always assumed that the soul is drawn upward by the beauty of the beloved's soul *and body*. Homely young men, though their souls were as beautiful as that of Socrates, might find themselves quite unbeloved. Zeno and his immediate followers attempt to concentrate on the potential excellence of the young man, rather than that as only one requirement. The objection that sex between equals (of the same gender) was more passionate than that between unequals (e.g. men and women), the Stoics overcame by separating the concept of "pleasure" and an act that may be pleasant. Pleasure, for a Stoic, is *epigennema*, supervenient or parasitic on an act.[152] The sage will control his passions, regardless of their degree of intensity, by recognizing that the act is the important thing, not the pleasure involved. A Stoic, at least in theory, did not look for the beautiful mind in the beautiful body to breed a perfect community as Plato had recommended in the *Symposium*. Rather the Stoic sought to make a young man who might have all the faults of youth — arrogance, impatience, selfishness — into a sage using erotic desire on the young man's part while he (the Stoic) had delinked pleasure and action and was safe from acting purely on desire, which might be reckless.[153]

The notion that genitalia exclusively determine sexuality and that therefore the end or proper use of the genitals is making babies has not survived in any explicit expression from this age. However, Zeno's insistence that homosexual love has an end in making friends *rather than reproduction* suggests that the idea may have come up in some work of the Academy lost to us and is being refuted by Zeno. The concept of Eros as benefiting the community by linking man to man is not new in the Greek world; however, that the Early Stoics found it necessary to state it explicitly suggests that it was under attack. Because there is some considerable doubt as to when the homophobic portions of the *Laws* were written, it is not clear whether Zeno is responding to the Athenian Stranger or the other way around, though the insistence on ends and things being according to nature or against nature strongly points to the fuller development of Natural Ethics in the Stoics, 50 years or more after Plato's death.

OTHER SCHOOLS OF PHILOSOPHY

We need say little about the other schools of philosophy that were founded after the Academy and Lyceum. The Cynics will be discussed later, where their context is more directly relevant. Epicurus, founder of the Epicureans, held pleasure to be the highest good and did not exclude the pleasure one might have with members of the same gender. He lived under the Second Democracy, so to speak — in the time of Antigonos Gannets — and did not hesitate to say how much he disliked the Macedonians.[154] There is a certain pessimism in Epicurus' attitude toward sex:

> You tell me that the stimulus of the flesh makes you too prone to the pleasures of love. Provided that you do not break the laws or good customs and do not distress any of your neighbors or do harm to your body or squander your pittance, you may indulge your inclination as you please. Yet it is impossible not to come up against one or other of these barriers: for the pleasures of love never profited a man and he is lucky if they do him no harm.[155]

One would like to know exactly what those "laws or good customs" were. Likewise the Cynic school did not object to homosexuality. Demetrius, the Cynic who had the nerve to practice free speech and vituperate Vespasian to his face, openly preached "the gospel of Diogenes,"[156] which almost certainly included the traditional Cynic approval of homosexuality. Much more must be said about this topic later in this work, however.

The Pythagoreans remain as obscure to us in the third and second centuries BCE as they were before the time of Plato. Modern theories have varied as to what happened to them.[157] Morals seldom leave traces archaeologists can unearth, but temples from the Hellenistic era have been found in what was Macedonia with numbers engraved on their walls, suggesting that some form of Pythagorean arithmeticism was embodied in the Macedonian state religion. Unfortunately details are lacking; it is probable that if any prohibition on homosexual activity was enforced by the Macedonians, they did not bother to impose it on the conquered peoples with any rigor. The inner circle of the Pythagoreans, the Mathematikoi, seems to have disappeared. Aristoxenos of Taras in the early third century says that he knew "the last of the Pythagoreans"; he probably means by this his inner circle teacher, Xenophilos specifically, and in general he is trying to distance the inner circle teachings from those of the unwashed commoners, the Acusmatics.[158] Most likely the inner circle was absorbed into the other schools of philosophy in this age. The Acusmatics, the outer circle of less sophisticated, religiously oriented Pythagoreans, survived long enough for Plutarch to meet one at a party in the second century CE[159] and for Justin Martyr to study under one before he became a Christian.[160] In the Hellenistic era, we catch glimpses of Acusmatics as stock characters in the New Comedy, where they appear as street philosophers. They wear dirty white robes and do not drink wine or eat meat. They move from town to town, making a bare living by casting horoscopes and performing brief rituals that guaranteed the forgiveness of sins to those who participate. Probably it was these Acusmatics whom Antigonos of Karustos called "sham philosophers." They denounced as effeminates (*kinaidous*) those who dressed softly and used a bit of perfume. Zeno the Stoic in turn accused them of doing much more along that line.[161]

THE POLITICAL SCENE

The story of Athens' fate after the death of Alexander, and that of Greece, is sad but not generally relevant here. Omitting the ups and downs of dynasties and the fates of kings, something must be said of the constitutional history of the time because this relates to homosexuality.

Dikaiarkhos of Massene gave his name to the form of government that prevailed in Greece from 322 BCE onwards — the *genos Dikaiarkhon* — the Species of Dikaiarkhos. Dikaiarkhos did not invent the system; he merely codified in a treatise what had been the governmental procedure hammered out in practice by Philip and Alexander the Great. As we have seen, Dikaiarkhos objected to the prohomosexual statements in the writings of Plato. Possibly the objection to homosexuality went all the way back to Philip II; Alexander, when he spoke before the Council of Corinth shortly after taking the throne, declared that "the king has changed in name only"[162] — meaning that he intended to implement the same principles and laws as his father. Very likely his exiling the homosexuals of Hallicarnassus was in compliance with Philip's rules. On the twenty-second of the month Boedromion (about August) 322, Antipatros stationed a unit of Macedonian troops in the Munichia fortress to guard the loyalty of Athens.[163] The oldest of Alexander's generals, and something of a power behind his throne, he had staked out Greece and Macedonia for his own following Alexander's death. Soon a Macedonian hegemony was established over Athens, as over the rest of Greece (except for Sparta). Like Alexander before him, and Demetrius of Phalerium after, Antipatros was worshiped as a god.[164] Rather than any constitutional system, the Macedonians held the king as supreme — law incarnate.[165] After Anitpater's death in 319, Polyperkhon was appointed regent for his son, Kassander, and issued a decree in the name of Philip II and Alexander,[166] since technically he was regent for a regent and the king was Alexander's posthumous son, Alexander Aigos.

In Athens election by lot was ended, and power was put firmly in the hands of the oligarchy, the wealthy class; the voting privilege was reduced to 12,000 citizens — about four-sevenths of the citizen population.[167] Gradually the economic position of the middle and poorer classes declined, while that of the oligarchy was maintained.[168] When Demetrius of Phalerium came to the governorship of Athens he set up a strict puritanical authority, including a *gynaiekonomi*, an office of "women-watchers" who were in charge of seeing that no free woman appeared outside her house without a veil and accompanying attendants.[169] The antifeminine tone of his legislation reflects the machismo of a conqueror; to Demetrius Athens was a woman he was all too willing to rape; he called the city "a gruel guzzling old slattern in slippers."[170] Not one to follow his own laws, he was personally addicted to cross-dressing, and Dioginis, his boy-love, had to compete with crowds of male prostitutes, and hired women as well.[171] Though an old law forbade it, he had his statue set up in the Agora beside those of Harmodios and Aristogeiton.[172] The "Harmodios Melody" was still being sung at drinking parties, but Antiphanes says it was becoming old-fashioned.[173] Pederasty was dead, along with freedom.

The poor no longer had their wages paid on theater days, so their patronage of comedy — which had been the art *par excellence* of the lower and middle classes in the golden days of Aristophanes — virtually ceased. The New Comedy reflected the mores of the oligarchy,[174] and homosexuality was absent from the it,[175] as indeed were all direct references to sex. Aristotle lived long enough to describe the differences:

> The well-bred man's jesting differs from that of a vulgar man, and the joking of an educated man from that of an uneducated. You can see the difference if you compare the Old with the

New Comedy. The masters of the Old Comedy thought obscenity was amusing; the masters of the New prefer innuendo, which is a great improvement from the point of view of decency [*Nichomachean Ethics*, 4, 8, 1128 A, 20–25].

In short wealth demands repression; the very word "vulgar" in English comes from the Latin for "common people," but it has come to mean "referring to sex, and other bodily functions, foul-mouthed." Sexual repression clearly has a class element. It belongs predominantly to the upper class, and is found in the lower only when they are trying to imitate the mores of their "betters." Likewise the political invective that was such a prominent feature of the Old Comedy ceased — we hear of nothing like Aristophanes' scathing denunciations of corrupt politicians — in fact we hear nothing in the New Comedy of any happenings in the real world. As Werner Jaeger recognized, the rise and fall of political comedy coincided with that of Athenian democracy.[176]

The typical plot of a New Comedy work depicts a young man of good social position who falls in love with a young woman who (apparently) has none. Everything turns upon the young woman's lack of status. Such works reflect, in Theodore Momsen's words, "the dreadful desolation of life ... the fearfully prosaic atmosphere ... above all the unmoral morality."[177] Money, not love nor the desire to establish a family, motivates the plot. The free-wheeling criticism of all public officials that had been a main feature of the Old Comedy is gone too. The homophobic wealthy class of Athens were having their values reflected back to them in a comforting manner, without criticism or divergence.

About 311 BCE a change comes over the position of the homosexual in Greece. The regent Kassander decided to put an end to the sham that he was ruling in the name of Alexander Aigos, the teenage son of Alexander the Great; perhaps the boy was showing the initiative and charisma of his father. At any rate, Kassander had the luckless young man killed, along with his mother, the Persian princess Roxanne, and their bodies thrown down a well.[178] The dynasty of Philip II, along with the laws and policies against homosexuality it had enacted, came to an end after 27 years. Some greater measure of democracy was restored in Athens in August, 307,[179] a date that coincides with Polemon's "coming out" and taking the presidency of Plato's Academy. About the same time Zeno of Kittium was founding his own school of philosophy in Athens, one that was, as we have seen, distinctly gay-friendly — a homosexual renaissance. Antigonos Gonates, one of the major players in the power struggles of the third century, was a friend and patron of Zeno,[180] and gay-friendly Stoicism became the court philosophy of the later Macedonians.[181] Generally this reflected a more democratic strategy on the part of the Macedonian conquerors,[182] who were after a few generations being absorbed into the culture of the country they had conquered.

Many writers have noticed the emergence of the feminine in Greek art in the Hellenistic period.[183] Women were generally better educated in the Hellenistic period than they were earlier; and they came out of confinement in the houses, and moved more freely in public.[184] The female body likewise came out in the arts — while male sculpture had routinely been nude; it was only in the Hellenistic era that the nude female body began to be portrayed — often it came as quite a shock, too. Most interestingly, the effeminate male becomes a commonplace in Greek sculpture, ranging from true hermaphrodites with both male and female genitals, to sculptures that show graceful, slender, smooth and feminine males,[185] in sharp contrast to the beefy, angular, distinctly male sculptures of the classical age. Likewise literature and history more frequently refer to male cross-dressing and gender-bending in the Hellenistic age.

We have already cited the theory of Richard Isay regarding homosexuality and effeminate behavior in our discussion of Alexander the Great. To briefly recapitulate: in his *Being*

Gay, Isay holds that basic gender identity is inborn. Young boys who are born gay are attracted to their fathers in the same way that heterosexual males are attracted to their mothers and undergo an Oedipal stage. If the gay boy sees his mother receiving affection from his father, he will try to take on the characteristics that distinguish his mother in order to win love from his father — hence cross-dressing and effeminate behavior.[186] It appears that the same process that occurred on the individual level in Alexander was occurring on a much wider level in Hellenistic Greece. In order to test this in a historical context, in what Montesque called the "laboratory of history," we turn briefly to premodern Japan.

In the Tokugawa period in Japan (1603–1868 CE) homosexuality (*nanshoku*) was very common, especially in an institutionalized form called among the Samurai *shudo*. *Shudo* originated in the Buddhist monasteries in homosexual attachments (which were not forbidden in Japanese Buddhism) between monks and novices. In the warrior context it is remarkably similar to pederasty among the Greeks; young boys became attached emotionally and sexually to Samurai warriors and learned Bashido, the art of war, from their older lovers; then went on to become warriors themselves in turn.[187] In the same period, women had no noticeable part in public life.[188] However, as women become more prominent in the social life of Japan toward the Meiji period,[189] we correspondingly find the boy-beloved becoming increasingly effeminate.[190]

The parallel in the Greek context is remarkable and probably accounts for a good deal of unfocused homophobia in the Hellenistic period and following because effeminate males are often stigmatized by more heterosexual males as well as by many straight-acting gay men. *Kinaidos* (Latin *cinaedus*, hence the English cinedus), the Greek word for a male who is effeminate or given to cross-dressing, was a term of insult as far back as the time of Aristophanes[191] (who was not opposed to pederasty), and to the degree that such males became more common, homosexuality became more disparaged. Here for example is a poem from the *Greek Anthology* by Murnos in the first century CE:

> When Time was about to drag down to the underworld
> Statullios, the effeminate [*androgunon*, literally man-woman] old oaken stump of Aphrodite,
> His summer dress dyed red and crimson,
> His wig dripping with spikenard,
> The white shoes that set off his well-turned ankles,
> The chest where he kept all his finest clothes
> And his flute that breathed so sweetly
> In the revels of the prostitutes,
> All he dedicated to Priapos at the temple door [Book 6, poem 254].

If we turn to poetry for insight into the nature and position of homosexuality in the Hellenistic age, we must chiefly turn to the *Greek Anthology*. That anthology of over 10,000 short poems contains the only collection of homoerotic poetry per se that has come down to us. The twelfth book, called the *Mesa Puerile* — the Muse of Boys, is an anthology in itself, compiled perhaps in the second century CE, but containing work from much earlier times.

Poets of the anthology tend generally to repeat themes and motifs over and over again — the emphasis is on careful and gracious versification, not originality in subject matter. There are for example, any number of "gather ye rosebuds while ye may" poems, warning boys to enjoy sex with men before hair grows on their legs and around their butt-holes, making them undesirable.[192] There is nothing that can be called homophobic in this work, but a disturbing pattern does emerge. Poets use very frequently three themes in regard to male-male love that suggest a sadomasochistic undercurrent in the homoerotic tradition in Hellenistic times.

Bondage, burning and piercing occur quite frequently in erotic poems addressed by men to men, but rarely if at all in such poems addressed by men (sometimes the same men) to women. These themes are new in the Hellenist age; the surviving fragments of pederastic love-poetry from the classical era lack such themes generally. Admittedly, of course, these are literary conventions, used often in a playful or psychological sense, but, especially in the burning theme, one is too often reminded of Alexander the Great's habit of literally setting fire to young men. Perhaps some court poet of his whose work is lost started the convention.

One poem conveniently (and uncomfortably) sums up the three conventions; Possidippos in the third century BCE wrote: "Love [*Pothos*, Desire] tying down the Muses' cicada [the poet's soul] on a bed of thorns, would lull it there, holding fire under its sides. But the Soul, sore tired of old amid books, makes light of other pain, yet upbraids the ruthless god"[193] (12, 98).

Bondage, often involving the soul as bird caught in bird-lime, occurs in the following poems: book 5, poem 96; book 12, poems 50, 84, 89, 112, 132, 142, 146, 149, 160, and 256 (in the last two the term Master, *despotin* is used); book 16, poems 195–199.

Burning, usually spoken of as an internal, emotional fire that threatens to consume to poet, occurs in book 5, poem 117; book 12, poems 17, 63, 72, 74, 79–83, 87, 89, 91, 98, 99, 109, 122, 132, 166, 177, and 196; and in a rare heterosexual context, Book 5, poems 87, and 209.

Piercing, usually the arrows of love that penetrate the poet's heart, is found in book 12, poems 45, 48, 50, 76, 83, 98, and 109; and a subcategory of scratching in 126 and 166.

How much serious and enjoyably painful activity lies behind these conventions we do not know. The scarcity of these themes in the abundant heterosexual love poetry of the same period suggests that such sadomasochistic activity was largely thought of as a particularly homosexual activity. As such it almost certainly contributed to the general air of disapproval of homosexuality that we encounter in later antiquity: persons who did not on an emotional or literal level understand the nature of sadomasochism thought that gay men simply enjoyed hurting other men for sexual thrills. Probably some did.

On a lighter note, we may mention some subtle, hidden homophobia in the great Hellenistic epic, the *Argonautica* of Apollonius Rhodius. We have no firmer date for him than the likely story that he was appointed librarian at Alexandria in 196 BCE. The focus of the book is the heterosexual love affair of Jason and Media, which ends disastrously. In the first book of the *Argonautica*, Herakles and his boy-love Hylas are fairly minor characters. We read of Heracles' effort to get himself an oar to row the ship Argo; he finds a pine tree in the forest and "with his legs wide apart and one broad shoulder pressed against the tree, he seized it low down with both hands and, gripping hard, he tore it out."[194]

While Herakles is thus giving a rather suggestive demonstration of his strength and size, his boy-love is wandering the woods too, and meets a stream with a nymph in it: "But as Hylas leant over to one side to dip his ewer in ... with her right hand she drew his elbow down and plunged him in midstream."[195]

Hylas remains with the beautiful nymph in her watery den, and Herakles searches in vain for the boy, frightening the woods with his loud laments. The joke is rather obvious. We hardly need to explain why Hylas seems to find being pulled into the water by a young goddess perhaps more pleasant than contemplating the prodigious strength of Herakles and his huge oar.

For explicit homophobia in a religious context we may turn to a temple inscription from Lydia (in what is now Turkey). Temple inscriptions are fairly common all over the Greek world, warning potential worshipers not to enter the temple or shrine if they have incurred certain pollution, usually ritual, for example: "You must not enter within three days of eating goat's flesh, one day of eating cheese, forty days of abortion...."[196] Likewise, one might not enter certain temples if one had been to a barber within the last three days or had walked in a funeral procession. Usually such were simple purity taboos, though a few relate to moral cleanliness.[197] In Lydia we find monuments set up relating that such and such a person had violated such taboos and suffered the wrath of the god or goddess of the shine: "I did ... and the goddess punished me with...." The text of one such taboo inscription needs quoting at length. On the entrance of a private shine in Philadelphia, Lydia, about 100 BCE devoted to the goddess Agdistis and other deities:

> Let men and women, slave and free as they come in this shrine swear by all the gods that they will not knowingly devise any evil.... No man shall have intercourse with any woman other than his wife, neither free nor slave, nor with any boy, nor with any virgin.... To those who obey the gods will be propitious ... if any transgress, they will hate them and will inflict great punishments on them.[198]

This seems particularly odd in a shrine devoted primarily to Agdistis. She was a hermaphrodite creature, daughter of the Great Goddess. The Great Goddess we are told was manifest as a rock, Agdos, and Zeus copulated with her. From this union was born Agdistis, originally male and terribly violent. To curb Agdistis' violence, the gods castrated him making a female deity, Agdistis; from his/her blood sprang a tree that produced Attis, the self-castrating god of the Galli. Agdistis was worshiped as a mother-goddess.[199] Otto Weinreich thinks the origin of these prohibitions was Neo-Pythagorean, imposed on a Lydian context without much attention to the mythic background.[200]

Before we turn to the Imperial Age and look at homophobia in a Roman context, a brief summary of Hellenistic homophobia may be in order. The sources for our knowledge of Hellenism are scarce. The works of the historians who first wrote about this era, such as Theopompos and Antigonos of Karustos, survive only in fragments; but enough has survived to demonstrate that a sort of sexuality of dominance was growing up in the Greek world. At the same time a philosophical and religious movement, Orphic-Pythagoreanism, arose and exerted a wide influence. Its political thought favored authoritarian government, and its ethical thought forbade homosexuality. It heavily influenced two of the most powerful men of the end of classicism: Plato and Philip II. The opening decades of the Hellenistic era saw what appears to be the first government-backed campaign of repression of homosexuality. That campaign was brief, but it left a lasting effect. The courts of Philip, Alexander and those of the immediate successors set the form for the policies of caesars, emperors, kaisers, kings and tyrants for two millennia to come.

6

Roman Domination:
The Origins of Modern Homophobia

[The Romans were] the great carnivores of the ancient world.
— Carlin A. Burton

Where Liberty cannot be hoped for, and power can, power becomes the
grand object of desire.
— John Stuart Mill, *On the*
Subjugation of Women

The homophobic tradition that has dominated morals in the West for more than 2,000 years has been far more an inheritance from Rome than directly from Greece. The origins of Roman homophobia are, like Greek homophobia, half hidden in the "dark and backward of time"; and, also like Greek homophobia, there is strong evidence for a Pythagorean source in the Roman strain. As we have in the Greek context, we find in the Roman a vicious constellation of three elements: Pythagorean thought, an addiction to power and authoritarianism, and homophobia. In the Roman context these elements are far more clearly developed; and rather than having to tease out a few homophobic texts that in the Greek context were largely isolated, in the Roman world the wealth of evidence on homophobia forces us to choose what to mention rather than magnifying what we must. The interplay between a declining culture that had not fully lost its esteem for homosexuality with a growing one that never seems to have had any honorable place for homosexuality is the subject of this chapter. In many ways the Greeks educated the Romans, but the Romans, surely one of the most tenacious and ferocious cultures ever to come into being, stubbornly remained to the end Romans.

We may begin with a love story, a bittersweet one, one conducted in a closet, perhaps a tragic one — a Roman love story as Romantic as any nineteenth century novel. Meet a young man whose string of names is as impressive as his short career: Publius Cornelius Scipio Aemelianius Africanus Numantius, more conveniently known as Scipio the Younger. Born about 185 BCE, he was the offspring of one of Rome's oldest, most distinguished families, the Aemilii, who traced their lineage back to Aemilius Mamercus, the son of Pythagoras.[1] Scipio was the younger son of Aemilius Paulus, a harsh man and cruel.[2] He divorced his wife, Scipio's mother, when Scipio was three or four, though the son remained close to his mother.[3] Aemilius Paulus, like his putative ancestor, claimed prophetic powers — when a dog named Perseus died, he declared it an omen that his enemy, Perseus the king of Macedonia, was doomed.[4] Omen or not, the last king of Macedonia was conquered by Aemilius' legions and

Greece was "liberated" to become part of the growing Roman Empire. Scipio, then 17, was with his father at the fateful battle and accompanied him on a sort of victory tour to the most famous religious sites of Greece in 168 BCE. The father had both his sons thoroughly educated in Greek, as became Roman gentlemen. It was on that tour that Scipio met Polybius.[5]

Polybius, the son of Lucortas, was an older man, in his early thirties when they met, and much a man of the world.[6] He was born in Megalopolis, a small town (despite its name) in Arcadia, old-fashioned, in the quiet backwaters of Greece,[7] where it is all but certain that the tradition of pederasty still lingered.[8] He had risen in the ranks to the level of general in the Achaean league; and, with the Macedonians defeated, the Romans now turned a wary eye on the Greeks under their thumb. Kallikrates, a minor quisling, denounced a thousand of his fellow Greeks to the Romans, and Polybius was one of the leaders taken hostage.[9]

Of course they were all gentlemen; perhaps because of his superior education, Polybius was housed more like a guest than a prisoner, in the house with Scipio. There the Roman lad in his late teens and the Greek general fell in love.

It was a vastly profitable relationship for the younger man. Scipio seemed destined for obscurity and a life of shame when he met Polybius. There was a weakness about him that made it difficult for him to conform to the norms of the upper-class Roman male of his time; he thought himself unworthy of his famous ancestors.[10] He was not good at the violent public oratory that marked the public man.[11] He was thought "soft" (*mallakos*), a word that was beginning to take on the sense of "effeminate" among Greek-speaking Romans. He had a fondness for the theater, writing poetry,[12] and for Greek books. It was this latter habit that brought him and Polybius together. One day, walking away from the Forum, Scipio asked Polybius for help "in a quiet and gentle tone and blushing slightly." The older man in response, he tells us, "was somewhat taken aback" and offered his services to Scipio. Scipio exuberantly "seized his right hand in both his own and, pressing it affectionately, he said, 'I only wish that I will see the day when you will give me the first claim on your attention and join your life to mine.'"[13] The two obviously had become lovers. They spent much of the rest of their lives together, Polybius acting as the political[14] and probably military advisor to his younger friend. There is repeatedly in the fragmentary account we have of the education of Scipio an almost Machiavellian quality to the narrative — even the best things that Scipio did, he seems to have done on instruction and for the sake of political advantage rather than principle. Following Scipio's early death, Polybius became his biographer in a monumental history of the rise of the Roman empire.

We do not know if the love affair of the General and his Historian was "platonic" in the sense of physically unconsummated; Scipio's concern over living up to the expectations of his ancestors has a distinctly Pythagorean ring to it. He probably expected to meet those ancestors in the underworld.[15] In this world, Scipio as a boy had almost certainly worn the *bulla*, a golden seal, on a string round his neck; to the Romans this was a sign that he was freeborn; to the Greeks a sign that he was off limits for pederastic activity.[16] Polybius, in the (quite considerable) fragments of his history, nowhere explicitly states that he and Scipio were lovers, but that is surely an effort to conceal from Roman eyes a relationship that they would have found disgraceful. Appian, writing 300 years later, calls Polybius Scipio's "boy-love" (*eromenou*),[17] ignoring the fact that Polybios was old enough to have been Scipio's father. It would have been a very dangerous love, if it did find physical expression. Valerius Maximus tells us that in 317 BCE and again in 280, men were executed for having seduced freeborn youths.[18] In fact Scipio seems to have had a lifelong fondness for older men; the handsome and older Terrence (famed as a playwright) is linked to his name erotically by Cornelius Nepos, though another historian, Fenestella in the age of Augustus, tried to rearrange the chronology and maintain that Terrence was younger than he actually was.[19] The irony is deep that Polybius, one of the last of the ancient Greeks to, however briefly, assert his freedom, became the *erastes* to one of the last great Romans of the Republic; the two are in fact the last pederastic couple we know of in the ancient world. Polybius' deepest philosophical-religious belief was that the universe is ruled by Tukhe — Fortuna in Latin and Lady Luck in English.[20] Luck had turned against the Greeks, and it took no great historian to see that the future belonged to Rome. By guiding, training, teaching a promising Roman youth, Polybius perhaps hoped to save some Greek values and transmit them through this lad. In however ambiguous a circumstance, the torch was passed.

Under Polybius' tutelage, Scipio began to build for himself a public image that would be popular among the Romans, spending himself into near poverty to get a reputation for generosity, risking his life hunting wild game in Macedonia.[21] He served in the army under Cato the Censor and won praise from him — a man no more generous with praise than anything else.[22] By 142 BCE Scipio was in the political arena, denouncing the maladministration of the Roman forces in Spain; he denounced his political enemies in ringing terms and like old Cato positioned himself as a defender of the *mos maiorum*, the Ways of the Ancestors[23] — including denunciations of those who behaved like *homini delicato* ("effeminate men"). The following is from one of his speeches against a political opponent, Publius Sulpicius Gallus:

> For one who daintily perfumes himself, and dresses before a mirror, whose eyebrows are trimmed, who walks abroad with beard plucked out and thighs made smooth, who at banquets, though a young man, has reclined in a long-sleeved tunic on the inner side of the couch with a lover [*cum amatore*], who is fond not only of wine, but of men [*qui non modo vinosus, sed virosus quoque sit*] — does anyone doubt that he does what wantons [*cinaedi*] do?[24]

Elsewhere he expressed horror that young men and women of the nobility should go to dancing classes and there mix with *cinaedi*.[25] The cinaedi were the "submissive partners" in homosexual acts — the ones penetrated (usually slaves, and generally young ones). This was quite perfectly in line with Roman homophobia — a sort of half-homophobia that regarded the male penetrated with hatred and loathing, but had no objection to the one penetrating. On another occasion, in the field, he expelled from his army all "foul-mouthed men"[26]; of course by this we should not understand men who used scurrilous language, rather men who "defiled" their mouths by performing oral sex on other men. Any sort of contact, especially by mouth, with the genitalia of another was seen by the Romans as horribly filthy.[27] Scipio's hypocrisy is palpable.

Of course he got ahead. He married a woman named Semphronia; she was, Astin tells us, "unattractive, unloved, unloving"[28] — but wealthy. His victories in the Third Punic War (culminating with the burning of the helpless Carthage) assured Rome the control of the known world. We need not follow Scipio's political and military career in any detail here, but some notice of his philosophical interests is pertinent. In his thirties Scipio became acquainted (almost certainly through Polybius) with one of the most famous philosophers of that era, Panaetius of Rhodes.[29]

Modern physics cannot fully describe the gravitational interaction of three bodies in space; so much less do we, at this distance in time and with only fragments and Latin translations to depend on, hope to fully describe the intellectual interrelations of Polybius, the historian; Scipio, the general; and Panaetius, the philosopher. What came out of that decade and more of conversation (beginning about 140 BCE) was the essence of Roman Stoicism, a specifically homophobic form of what had begun as a homosexuality-positive school of philosophy. Roman Stoicism in Panaetius is the nobility of Zeno conceding to power, wealth and luxury. The *Republic* of Zeno, surely one of the most ethically radical documents ever written, was conveniently considered to be a likely forgery in these philosophical circles[30] (indeed an effort had been made to falsify the text of Zeno's *Republic* by Isodore, the head librarian of the famous library of Pergamos).[31] Zeno had proclaimed the equality of all humans[32]; Panaetius, taking the idea, perhaps from Aristotle, says that some humans are naturally slavish, and therefore the more powerful, energetic and wise are justified in enslaving them; slavery is natural.[33] Coming from Rhodes, which was a center of the Hellenistic slave trade,[34] such an opinion may be truly natural to Panaetius. Wealth and power, which the old Stoics had considered indifferent, were in Panaetius proclaimed as things of value.[35] Likewise in government, Panaetius considered monarchy the best and the Roman senate an embodiment of monarchy.[36] He was, we might add, influenced by the text attributed to Timaeus of Locri that had appeared just at that time, in Neo-Pythagorean circles.[37]

Might made right. Rome was proving better than the Greeks; therefore, Rome had the right to dominate them, Panaetius maintained.[38] The familiar "live according to nature" was still an axiom of Panaetius,[39] but the understanding of human nature differs in this Rhodian philosopher. Panaetius maintained that the desire to dominate is as much a natural part of human nature as the self-love (*oikeiosis*) and gregariousness of earlier Stoics.[40] The argument from natural law developed by the old Stoics gave the individual an appeal to reason against superior power; in the Roman context (especially in Cicero, who derives from Panaetius), still within circles who considered themselves Stoics, the appeal to nature becomes a scarcely concealed appeal to naked power. For Roman aristocrats, enjoying the pleasure that power gave them, it was very easy to believe that the world was a good, orderly entity; nature was the earliest father in the patriarchy and anyone who questioned or tried to take their power away was obviously going against nature. Simply put, whatever went against custom and civil practice was to be avoided.[41] For these philosophers, the law of nature was scarcely distinguishable from what we may call totalitarianism.[42] So Scipio watched Carthage burn, acting on the orders of the senate, but still weeping, for, he told Polybius, who was at his side, Rome's turn would come.

Panaetius disagreed with the Old Stoics on the nature of sex itself and homosexuality. Zeno and his immediate followers saw sex (homosexual or heterosexual) as one of the powers or aspects of the soul. The soul, they believed, sat in the middle of the body (probably in the heart) like a great octopus with seven arms. These "arms of the soul" were its activities, sex being one of them. Beyond and apart from the soul was the natural aspect, including growth that humans share with plants and simple organisms.[43] Panaetius rearranged his view of human nature, downgrading sex from a function of the soul to a part of *phusis*, a part of the bodily nature which occurs spontaneously.[44] Thus sex was removed from the realm of choice and degraded to the level of the growth of the nails. Panaetius saw homosexuality in terms of the dichotomy of power—powerlessness, slave and master. A reflection of his attitude toward homosexuality comes from a remark preserved in Seneca. A young man asked Panaetius if the Stoic's ideal, the sage, would be a lover (obviously referring to the Stoic tradition of pederasty, so a lover of boys). "As for the sage," Panaetius replied, "We shall see. Your task and mine, who are a great distance from the sage, is not to fall into a state which is disturbed, powerless and subservient to another."[45] This attitude toward homosexuality is quite distant from the that of the founders of Stoicism. Since he was an admirer of Plato,[46] the nearest source that can be suggested for it is the *Laws* which, as we have seen, spoke of the boy as becoming womanlike because of being the source of the man's pleasure. That the position of women was inferior and in a position analogous to slaves was the common understanding throughout classical antiquity, though Plato denied it, and so did the early Stoics.

Panaetius' specific objection to homosexuality seems to come under the heading of propriety or decorum (*to prepon* in Greek; *decorum* in Latin needs no translation). The Old Stoics had had a doctrine of propriety, a sub-virtue to wisdom (*sophrosune*),[47] but in Cicero (who is again likely to be following Panaetius) decorum in speech involves refraining from the "effeminate": "In these matters we must avoid especially the two extremes. Our conduct and speech should not be effeminate and over nice" (*effeminatum aut molle*).[48] The same regard for decorum leads to a condemnation of "the manners of the palaestra" (*palaestrici motus*),[49] meaning the Greek gymnasia, which were still associated with pederasty. Cicero is probably following the lost work of Panaetius throughout when he condemns any sort of un–Roman behavior (nudity for example) as "unnatural": "to beget children in wedlock is indeed morally right; to speak of it is indecent [*nomine obscenum*].... But let us follow Nature and shun everything that is offensive to our eyes and our ears."[50] Again, this habit of considering anything culturally alien to be against nature becomes a major source for ethical thought in the Middle Ages and a major source as well of homophobia.

All in all, it seems most likely that Panaetius was simply repeating the sentiments of most of his Roman audience. How much of this was a sincerely held philosophical position and how much mere bids for popularity is more than we can say at this distance in time. Mention may also be made of the Stoic philosopher Boethos of Sidon, a pupil of Diogenes of Babylon, who introduced dualism into Stoicism — a heavenly godhead opposed to earthly matter.[51] The dualism of the latter Stoics makes them almost indistinguishable from the Neo-Platonists and Neo-Pythagoreans, both seeing a world part good, part evil, rather than a seamless universe of god and nature. Cicero's Platonism was dualistic; in the *Tusculum Disputations* he says that Pherecydes taught the immortality of the soul to Pythagoras and he to Plato (120, 80).[52]

Scipio died fairly young and under a cloud. He was involved in the question of land reform, where the Gracchi became so famous; one night he went home after an inflammatory speech, intending to make another speech the following day, and was found dead in bed in the morning. Scipio's friends used their power to prevent any official investigation of his death, apparently fearing the result would be a scandal.[53] Polybius survived him by more than a decade and died by falling off a horse at 80.

HOW THE ROMANS GOT THAT WAY

The early history of Italy in the Mediterranean world resembles in its way the history of the Americas in the larger sea. As early as 1500 BCE, Italiot peoples were inhabiting the central boot of Italy, speaking languages ancestral to Latin. They were a simple folk as far as we can know from archeology, bronze-working farmers with tightly knit, patriarchal families. What archeology does not tell us is what attitudes they held toward homosexuality. The fact that most Latin words having to do with homosexuality were borrowed at a late date from Greek suggests that among the early Latin peoples homosexuality was not commonly spoken about; certainly there was no well-established institution like Greek pederasty among the early Latins,[54] though a bit of evidence suggests Mars may once have been associated with homosexuality among young men.[55] However, with regard to some of their later neighbors, the case is different.

About 700 BCE bands of invaders began to colonize the coasts of Italy. They called themselves the Rascenna, but history knows them better by the name the Romans used for them, Etruscans. Tradition has these first named invaders of Italy coming from Lydia, though the accuracy of that has been doubted.[56] They arrive in Italy with a tradition of urbanism, a technology advanced to the use of iron (over the bronze that the Italians were working so well), a propensity for trade and adapting the art forms of other peoples, a sinister, revealed religion — and a fondness for boys.

The Etruscans had an archaic form of government — even for the age. Their kings, called *lucomones*, ruled by divine sanction, impersonating gods[57]; under them was a small class of aristocrats, each attended by numerous slaves and vast numbers of serfs; a middle class hardly existed.[58] Their culture was superior, both in social organization and technology, to the Italic peoples, and soon the natives of Italy were furnishing the Etruscans with forced labor to till their land and build their walled cities. Quite possibly for the first time in their history the Italian peoples began to think in terms of "in group" and "out group," one of the major factors in colonialism. Such thought inherently dehumanizes the out-group.[59] Sexual aggression was one of the major factors in the somewhat later Greek colonial expansion in Italy. We read that, when the Greek colonists of Tarentum conquered the indigenous Iapygians of Calabria, they publicly raped the women and boys of the conquered.[60] Perhaps for centuries the Romans regarded themselves as the out-group while the godlike kings of the Etruscan walled towns were what sociologists today call a "reference group,"[61] one looked upon with a mixture of envy and hatred and emulation.

Homosexuality was common among the Etruscans; Theopompos, who has already furnished us with so much information on the subject of homosexuality, says of them, "The Etruscans like women, but they prefer boys and young men [*paisi kai meirakiois*], for in their country these latter are very good looking because they live in luxury and keep their bodies smooth by means of depilatories."[62]

The reference to "living in luxury" and the use of depilatories strongly suggest that homosexuality among the Etruscans was mostly viewed in terms of effeminacy. Hair was removed from the legs and pubic area of boys to suggest pubescent girls. Women were very prominent in Etruscan society,[63] and we have seen that the presence of women in public tends to make homosexuality particularly likely to be involved in effeminacy. The oldest works of Latin literature that have come down to us complete, the plays of Plautus, abound in boy slaves who are sexual toys for their masters — the *pueri delicati* ("pretty boys").[64] The boys were not being trained in manhood on the Greek model but were slaves maintained in idleness as trophyboys for the Etruscan lords. Having a pretty boy or a stable of them was another sign of the aggressive power of an Etruscan noble.

Possibly the Etruscans entered Italy with a written language; certainly a wealth of inscriptions show they were literate from an early date.[65] They never achieved a literature or bothered much with their own history, but they were famous to the end of antiquity for the *Disiplina Etrusca*, a vast sort of encyclopedia of the dark arts — divination, theurgy, ritual magic, etc. The early Romans often sent their sons to Etruscan teachers in Cerveteri to be educated.[66]

Many an attractive Roman lad must have learned more than his ABCs from an Etruscan teacher. Homosexuality was already thought of in terms of dominance and submission by the Etruscan colonizers: a mirror image of it grew up in the minds of the subject people. Countless thousands of acts of rape must have been perpetrated by the colonial masters on their Italian subjects, male and female; for the first time in history it becomes possible to discern the formation of that richly poisonous soup of homosexuality and the politics of submission-dominance that resulted in a homophobia that has lasted to this day. As colonialized peoples do so often, the Romans had a love-hate relationship with the Etruscans: the Romans loved and admired their power, their lordly dominance, but at the same time they hated like the gates of death to be the subjects of that lordship. The result, once we factor in a Pythagorean dualism, is the abiding hatred of the Romans for "submissive" homosexuality — the position of the one penetrated — along with no aversion at all to the penetrator.

Likewise and even more surely lost to history are the origins of the strong vein of misogyny in the Romans. Women are always the most immediate caregivers and milk-givers to children; in times of stress, when food or protection is scarce, women are sometimes forced to make compromises with those in power for the sake of their own offspring. Surely many a Roman woman was more than friendly to an Etruscan lord. The Rape of Lucrece is a typical (though not likely a historical) incident, and the male historians who have transmitted the tale surely omitted many of the circumstances. Because from time to time the native Roman women went over to the enemy, we may surmise one of the major causes of the distrust and fear of women and those who were judged to act like women among the Romans.

Latin gave us the word; and the Romans, from the earliest knowledge we have of them, exemplified patriarchy. The patriarch, the oldest living male in a family, was the unquestioned head of that family; no son, at whatever age, came into full citizenship if there was a older male in his family.[67] For a young male to have a free and equal relationship with another person would take him out of the patriarchal chain of command. Women were legally the possession of the husband, though in fact they had considerable authority and were generally freer than in classical Athens.[68]

The little mud-streeted village on the Tiber that was to rule the known world enters its history dominated by its Etruscan neighbors; copper deposits and rich, volcanic soil drew the Etruscans farther inland. Three great Etruscan cities — Tarquinii, Caere, and Veii —flourished within 30 miles of Rome in the middle of the seventh century BCE. They traded with Greece, Corinth especially, and Greek myths characterize much of the distinctly Etruscan art of this era. The first monument of Rome, the Great Sewer, dates from this era, built almost certainly under Etruscan influence, with engineering techniques brought ultimately from Mesopotamia.[69] It drained the muck from the Forum Boarium, the first major building in Rome, a cattle market that doubtless furnished the tables of the Etruscan cities to the north and west.

Soon Etruscan kings ruled in Rome. The tradition of Roman law (eventually there were to be laws forbidding homosexuality) begins in the kingly context — the laws were issued by the priest-king as sacred law; the root of the Latin word *jus* (right, law, justice) means sacred, mystical,[70] for those Roman kings, like their Etruscan counterparts, paraded themselves as Jupiter Best and Greatest on earth.[71] The famous Roman law has its deepest roots in the revealed religion of the Etruscans. Later Roman "history" speaks of the first kings of Rome as Latin, but in the realm of reliable facts, Rome enters history with Etruscan kings, the last of them Tarquin the Proud.[72]

Pride, they say, goes before a fall. Fall Tarquin did, in a series of events that are no ways clear to the modern historian. The date given for the expulsion of the last king, an Etruscan, from Rome is 510 BCE—a date that must live in suspicion, because it is the same as the traditional date of the expulsion of the tyrants from Athens.[73] The expulsion of Tarquin seems to have been helped along by the defeat of the Etruscans by Aristodemos, the tyrant of the Greek city of Cumae; no trust can be put in the later legend that has Tarquin fleeing for help to the court of Aristodemos.[74]

At any rate the Etruscans were expelled from Rome, and Rome and the Latins begin the development of a national consciousness; Jerome Carcopino has demonstrated that from the very beginning the national consciousness of the Romans was essentially Pythagorean.[75] Rome at this earliest stage in its history was in close contact with Metapontum and Locri — both

Pythagorean centers.[76] Just at the time the kings fell in Rome, Pythagoras himself had conquered the great and rich Greek city of Croton, destroying it to the very foundations and building his ideal communities near the ruin; Rome was born in an Italy already dominated by the thought of Pythagoras and suckled on that thought. As we shall see, there were at least two "revivals" of Pythagoreanism in subsequent Roman history, but the deep base note of its original Pythagorean foundations never really ceased to sound.

Early Roman religion was fertile ground for homophobia. There was no ancient Roman deity who paralleled Eros, the god in Greece who primarily presided over homosexual relations.[77] The earliest form of Roman religion that we can discern involved deities that were little more than abstractions, with little or no mythologies attached; each deity had a very limited, very specific area of concern. For example, cutting firewood involved four gods, one for the felling of the tree, one for cutting it up and so on.[78] Compartmentalization and regimentation in the Roman religion stand in stark contrast to the humane quality of Greek mythology, where every god and goddess had a long and complicated biography and the full range of human desires. We do hear of a goddess called Frutis among the most ancient Romans; she presided over gardens and fruit trees, and her name is an Etruscan mispronunciation of "Aphrodite."[79] Only quite late in the Republican era was Aphrodite proper introduced among the Romans; after a disastrous battle in 217 BCE, it was decided that the Aphrodite of the Greek Sicilian town of Erycina would be drafted, as it were, to fight for the Romans (it was said that Aeneas was her son). However, Venus of Erycina was not allowed to bring her traditional retinue of cult prostitutes into the city with her[80]; Rome wanted only power, not love.

And Rome needed power. About 385 BCE Celtic tribes from the north swarmed down the Italian boot and took Rome after a siege, burning the city to the ground.[81] Life was tenuous for the Romans; they must constantly have thought of themselves as under siege or about to be besieged. To insure that the city would not be taken again, Greek architects were hired and, with the use of stone (and probably slaves) from the recently conquered Etruscan city of Veii, a massive wall was built round the Seven Hills[82]; much of it remaining to this day, a monument of survival and self-protection.

Such a wall implies strong central authority to plan and build it as well as a deep sense of insecurity to need it. It appears that already, by the early fourth century BCE, the Romans had responded to the violence and threats of the time and place with the kind of authoritarianism they became so justly famous for; the desire on the individual level for power and the willingness to yield readily to authoritarian and totalitarian governments on the societal level are both well recognized forms of response to threats and violence.[83] Stanley Milgram has shown that persons who feel they are following an authority are considerably more capable of cruelty and violence against others.[84] Theodore Adorno in the late 1940s devised what is called the "F- Scale" (for Fascist scale) to describe the authoritarian personality. To a remarkable degree that scale can describe the Ancient Romans as well as it can Mussolini and his followers, who looked back with such adoration on them.

The Romans passed through a long age (most of it lost to detailed inspection) of ambivalence and confusion over values and culture complicated by several external threats from Etruscans, Celts and finally Carthaginians. Ervin Staub has written, regarding such periods of threat and confusion, that "an ancient way of coping with such threat is to create a group to blame." Even small distinctions between persons can serve to increase the sense of value in the in-group,[85] and difficult life conditions tend to intensify the process of social dichotomization.[86] Turning once again to Theodore Adorno's "F-Scale" we find that it can describe the Romans' authoritarian practices:

1. Conventionalism.
2. Submission to authority and the idealized morality of the in-group.
3. Aggression in the name of the conventions of the in-group and an urge to condemn and punish those who violate those norms.
4. A distaste for the subjective, the imaginative and all tender-mindedness.
5. Superstition, belief in fate. A habit of thinking in rigid categories.
6. A love of power, admiration of powerful figures, of toughness and strength.
7. A cynicism and nihilism, a need to destroy and a loathing of humans.
8. A tendency to project wild, violent and destructive thoughts on the world, seeing it as a chaotic, dangerous place.
9. A preoccupation with sex, a suspicious attitude toward others' sexual activity.[87]

It is hard to say, in fact, whether this is a better description of the Ancient Roman personality, the Neo-Pythagorean philosophy, or both. Probably a clear and fair statement would be that the Roman personality and Pythagorean thought grew together, each modifying and reinforcing the other. As we have seen, there is no sound proof that Pythagoras or his immediate followers were homophobic. No undoubted statement of homophobia in the classical context exists before Plato's *Laws* (about 389 BCE); but, if we assume that the homophobia so common in Neo-Pythagorean documents existed in Pythagoreanism in the fifth century BCE, then Pythagorean homophobia is surely the nucleus around which it grew. The force that so magnified — till it could dominate a culture — what was originally a fairly minor religio-philosophical movement was the adversity the early Romans faced from wave after wave of invaders, colonizers, and sackers of cities. That very ancient Roman pain sought and found scapegoats, traitors within the walls, in the feminine — whether in the bodies of men or women. Conventionalism, authoritarianism and superstition led to the ready acceptance of the Pythagorean texts and their homophobic statements as natural, as stating the obvious. Homosexuality from the earliest times existed in the Roman context without a direct and defined relationship to the society as a whole. Two men or two women who became lovers did not contribute children to society, and the fascist mind-set refused to perceive or grant worth to tenderness, emotional satisfaction or any of the subtle benefits of love. Moreover, linked to effeminacy, homosexual males were perceived as loathsome by those who worshiped nothing naked but power. Finally, the Roman taste for cruelty set the stage for what has been a slow, smoldering genocide in the Western world: the pervasive, two-millennia-long hunting out and killing of gays and lesbians.

About 300 BCE we arrive at a state of knowledge that we may not disdain to call history — though history from sources written centuries later and with a particular set of nationalistic biases in mind. Therefore the patient reader will understand if we skip a couple of centuries of legendary history and look at certain documents dating from about 200 BCE, which, if they tell us little reliable about the facts of early Rome, tell us much about the mind-set of the Romans in the early Republic who wrote them.

History at Rome begins in crisis. The great struggle that determined not only the fate of Rome but also of the Western world was the series of wars with Carthage — the Punic Wars, caused ultimately, Michael Grant has said, by the Roman fear of foreigners.[88] Every schoolchild knows that Hannibal of Carthage brought war elephants over the Alps to invade Italy and almost destroyed Rome itself. Great battles with great loss of Roman life were fought — 15,000 fell at Tharasimene, 70,000 at Cannae; the old order of the Roman aristocracy was decimated, and slaves had to be inducted into the army; the countryside was devastated, and fearful citizens crowded into Rome — it was, as George Dumezil has said, "a breeding ground for psychosis."[89] Breed it did.

While Hannibal was besieging Tarentum in 212 BCE, a kind of religious revolution threatened in Rome. Petty priests and crowds of women filled the streets, practicing what Livy calls "unaccustomed rites." These petty priests had books of prayers and rituals they read out of. Alarmed, the senate ordered the praetor, Marcus Atilius, to confiscate the books.[90] Livy is disdainful of these superstitious folk and gives us few details, but one suspects there were many Orphics among those women publicly sacrificing. If the women were reading, it is even more likely. However, when Atilius read one of the confiscated books, he found what seemed to be a prediction of the disastrous Battle of Cannae four years earlier in a book attributed to Ancus Marcius, the legendary fourth king of Rome; the senate suddenly reversed itself and ordered that the book of Marcius be followed.[91] Almost certainly the book was a forgery, written after Cannae and intended to give prestige to its author; both Jerome Carcopino and A. Dellate have seen this as the beginning of a secret conspiracy by a Pythagorean group to seize the government of Rome, though George Dumezil disagrees.[92] It hardly seems necessary that there have been a conspiracy, so widespread and influential were Pythagorean ideas; Scipio the Elder, who was ultimately to defeat Hannibal, often claimed that his decisions were divinely inspired. He meditated alone in the Temple of Jupiter and, like Alexander the Great, was rumored to have been begotten by Jupiter in the form of a snake[93] — a motif we have seen that originates in Orphism.

The one factor that seems to have been crucial in the relationship between Romans and Pythagoreanism is the shedding of animal blood. As we have seen, the objection to the sacrifice of animals to the deities and the eating of the flesh of animals was a major factor in the early Pythagorean teaching and remained so to the end. But the killing of animals both for food and as offerings was too deeply ingrained in Roman culture to be given up, so that absolute Pythagoreanism and Romanism remained in a state of tension, the Pythagoreans never being quite able to get the Romans just as they wanted them. A classic example of this struggle is recorded in Seneca the Younger's *Epistles*. That philosopher, who was tutor to Nero, tells us that in his youth he was taught by the Pythagorean Sotion to avoid eating meat, since any animal he ate might have had a human soul, even the soul of one of Seneca's dead relatives. The young man duly became a vegetarian. However, during the reign of Tiberius a wave of anti–Jewish sentiment made vegetarianism unpopular in the upper classes of Rome; and Seneca, without it seems too much struggle of conscience, gave up his vegetarianism.[94] The Way of the Ancestors had triumphed again.

When the first real Roman historian, Fabius Pictor, wrote his *Annales*, Rome was under a double threat. Externally the Republic was deep in the first Punic war, fighting for its life against Carthage; at the same time and more subtly Rome was fighting for its soul against the intellectual threat of Greek hegemony. Little need be said here about the Second Punic War. By 218 Hannibal was riding round and round the besieged city on his great black horse.[95] The city survived by the skin of its teeth and the sword of Scipio Africanus the Elder (adoptive grandfather of the Scipio discussed above). The Greek threat was more pervasive — Fabius Pictor wrote in Greek. Greek art and Greek thought had been pouring into Rome since before the expulsion of the kings.[96] Rome was importing grain from the Greek colonies in Sicily as early as 486 BCE[97] and Greek gods about the same time (a temple of Diana stood on the Aventine in the fifth century BCE[98]); the conquests of Alexander the Great had given Hellenistic culture immense prestige in the view of the more practical and military minded Romans. The temptation to adopt Greek culture wholesale must have been almost irresistible.

One of the major stumbling blocks was pederasty. The custom of initiating boys into manhood by men having sexual relations with them was deeply imbedded in Greek culture and just as deeply abhorrent to Roman. Boy-love had been one of the primary signs of

Etruscan domination. The Greeks thought of pederasty as a rite of passage for citizens of a free state; the Romans had a taste for absolutism that made such training of boys in freedom disagreeable to them. Little wonder then that, when we turn to the earliest documents available to us from a Roman context, we find a studied effort to position Rome both in and separate from Hellenistic culture.

Quintus Fabius Pictor was born about 254 BCE to a distinguished and ancient Roman family. He fulfilled the ideal life of a Roman writer: military service to the state so that he might not be suspected of Greek softness, then as a sort of second career, writing. First he fought to subjugate the Gauls in northern Italy and later to prevail against the Carthaginians at Cannae. Elected a tribune and recognized as an expert in religious matters, he was sent by the senate to consult the Delphic oracle during the Second Punic War.[99] Returning, he wrote, apparently in haste, perhaps on orders from the senate, the *Annales*, the first Roman history.[100] The purpose was more propaganda than scholarship; in the middle of a desperate struggle against Carthage, Pictor tried to give, as Alfoldi has said, "a political and judicial documentation of the growth of Roman power, as being in accordance with the will of the gods, pointing from the hour of its birth towards greatness."[101] His intended audience seems to have been both Greeks and Romans, since he wrote in Greek and provided dates in both the Roman system and the archon dates of Athens.[102]

Pictor began with the story of Aeneas. Aeneas had escaped the fall of Troy and settled in Italy; almost certainly the original story started with the Greeks of Magna Grecia, perhaps Stesikhoros, the epic poet who wrote a continuation of Homer[103]; Timaeus the Historian (315–260 BCE), working probably from Roman sources, made Aeneas found a city in Italy.[104] The story was well established among the Etruscans (who claimed Aeneas as their ancestor),[105] who probably took it from the Greek epic tradition that they so greatly admired.[106] Overall the legend was originally Greek and used by the Greek colonists as a justification of their aggression; in Roman hands it became an instrument of a sort of reverse cultural imperialism. It allowed the Romans to claim that they too were Hellenic, a part of the tradition that went back to Homer, and properly masters of Italy, yet at the same time by claiming descent from the Trojans they were Hellenic with a difference; it defined them very precisely as Hellenic non–Greeks.[107] Moreover, the legend placed them securely outside the Greek tradition of pederasty. Achilles and Patroculos were the archetypal Greek lovers in Homer and both were Achaeans. Homer never hints at homosexuality among the Trojans — indeed, quite the opposite, since the paramount Trojan hero is the happily married Hector, whose love for Andromache is a centerpiece in Homer's characterization of the Trojans. By claiming descent from Aeneas, Pictor was claiming his people were a different breed of Hellenes, ones apart from the pederastic tradition.

We know from Aristotle that early Pythagoreans placed women on the evil side of their charts of dualism; a fear and distrust of women and of the feminine in general is one of the hallmarks of Pythagorean thought, and we find it likewise in the early Roman historians. Pictor had a strong interest in women,[108] often a misogynistic one: he picked up female characters from the romantic Hellenistic literature of his time and turned them into "historical" characters — often very negative characters, willful, violent women or alternatively demure, chaste virgins or noble Roman matrons.[109] It is not clear whether Pictor or his younger contemporary, Naevius (a poet with a strong Pythagorean bent)[110] brought together Aeneas and Dido.[111] We do know that, when the cities conquered by the Carthagenians in the First Punic War brought out a coin with a picture of Dido on it, the Romans responded in a sort of numismatic battle of goddesses with a coin carrying the image of Ilia, the female personification of Rome (based on the Trojan legend).[112] The effort was to counter threatening goddess with threatening goddess. Dido, called Deido by Timaeus the Historian, was the Carthaginian Elissa (perhaps the Punic Eli-shat, a divinity). In the form of the story known to the oldest historians, Elissa was about to be married to Hiarbas but chose rather to burn herself on a pyre. Performing an act of self-sacrifice in order to win in a crisis was a Carthaginian custom — when the younger Scipio took Carthage in the spring of 146 BCE, the wife of Hasdrubal threw herself in a fire.[113] This was uncomfortably close to the Roman tradition of *devotio* — an offering of one's life to the gods in exchange for a desired end (P. Dacius Mus voluntarily died in battle in 340 BCE, offering his life to the gods in exchange for victory).[114] To the Romans such *devotio* was the supreme act of self-will,[115] and therefore fearful in the extreme in a woman. Traditional interpretations of Elissa's name have it meaning "the virile woman," "virago" or "husband murderer."[116]

The fear and distrust, not to say hatred, of women is a major theme of Pictor and the general tradition of legendary Roman history. The Rape of the Sabine Women, in Pictor, positions women in Roman society as essentially foreigners, inspiring distrust.[117] Rome began in Pictor's view as a city of men, ruled by Romullus (whose name means merely "man of Rome"); women enter the story only as foreigners, taken by force into the city and divided in their loyalties.[118] However, his treatment of the expulsion of the kings is perhaps the most telling episode for our purposes. The year he assigns to that event, identical to the year of the expulsion of the tyrants from Athens, certainly implies a comparison. It was well known that the tyrants were expelled from Athens as a result of a homosexual love affair. In his heterosexualizing of the legendary history of Rome, Pictor makes it a heterosexual rape — of the chaste Lucretia (the very ideal of a Roman matron) instead of a boy. To further distance the Romans from Greek homosexuality, Pictor uses a deliberate forgery of historical fact to draw a homosexual Greek tyrant into the tale and place him on the anti–Roman side.

As far as can be discerned regarding the events that surrounded the expulsion of the kings from Rome, the key event was the weakening of Etruscan power in the region by the tyrant of the Greek city of Cumae, Aristodemos, who turned back an Etruscan attack on his city in 524 BCE.[119] These events were narrated in Greek by the Cumaeian historian Hyperchorus, in his *Kumaika* (lost except for fragments). Since Aristodemos and the Greeks in general were enemies of the Etruscans, it seems extremely odd that Tarquin, the deposed Etruscan king of Rome, should flee to the court of Aristodemos and that Aristodemos should offer him help in regaining the throne of Rome — yet that is exactly what Pictor says happened. In fact Pictor was working from a forged version of the *Kumaika* of Hyperchorus[120] — a version revised to appeal to the patriotic tastes of Romans. In this forged version (and hence in Pictor) Aristodemos is portrayed as the archetypal Roman image of the tyrant — an aggressive homosexual who forces boys to cross-dress and wear their hair long[121]; we are told further that as the ultimate insult Aristodemos was assassinated by his own mistress, Xenokrite.[122] Aristodemos and Tarquin the Proud are both examples of the haughty, effeminate and enslaving tyrant, whom the Romans saw as their divinely established duty to overthrow.[123] The only reason that Pictor chose to use (indeed perhaps he created) a forged text of Hyperchorus' work is that it gives him an opportunity to set up an aggressively boy-loving tyrant as the enemy of the virtuous, straight Romans.

It was probably some annalist of the time of Pictor who invented the famous priest-king of Rome, Numa Pompilius. The story is well known that Numa was lover (or husband) to a nymph. He slept with her in a cave, and she gave him the earliest laws Rome knew. The parallel is obvious with the shamanistic stories that gathered around Pythagoras, who, as we have seen, is said to have gone into a pit underground to commune with the gods. So many of the laws attributed to Numa were identical to those attributed to Pythagoras that it was very frequent in antiquity to say that Numa was a disciple of Pythagoras,[124] though wiser heads knew that accurate chronology placed Numa a century and more earlier than Pythagoras of Samos.[125] It appears that the character of Numa became a sort of dumping ground for all the Pythagorean elements that had crept into the Roman constitution; possibly he was an historical character, though much of his so-called legislation dates from a later era.[126] Likewise, prominent Pythagoreans were cited as lawgivers in other Italian cities: Zaleucos, who is said to have written the laws of Locri, was given Roman citizenship; and Charondas, who is said to have written laws for the Chalcidian cities, is reported to have been a disciple of Pythagoras.[127]

We may deal briefly with a few of Fabius Pictor's contemporaries — all known to us only in fragments. Ennius, the poet, was said by St. Jerome to have been born in Tarentum[128] — an error, but the association of this poet with that Italian center of Pythagoreanism is telling.[129] Cato the Censor found him in Sardinia and brought the poet to Rome, the most valuable of prizes, Nepos says.[130] He wrote an epic history called, like Pictor's work, *Annales*, in 28 books, the first seven dealing with the founding of Rome. The Pythagorean character of the work is clearly indicated by the beginning — the poet dreamed he went to Mount Parnassus, where Homer told him that he, Ennius, was his reincarnation and that his soul had passed through a peacock at some point.[131] Ennius' work on Epicharmus, the Sicilian playwright, featured a conversation with the soul of Pythagoras in the underworld.[132] One of the first and certainly most influential poets of ancient Rome was a Pythagorean.

Cato the Censor

It was however a pupil of Ennius who was most instrumental in the revival of Pythagorean ideas at Rome — Cato the Censor, who learned Greek from Ennius when he (Cato) was about 30.[133] Marcus Porcius Cato (234–149 BCE), "energetic, obstinate, brave and miserly,"[134] cruel to his slaves, savage to his opponents in debate, anti-intellectual and all in all one of the great curmudgeons of history, was a "new man," one of a class of men who filled the power vacuum when many of the old aristocracy were killed in a series of disastrous battles early in the struggle with Carthage. His influence was great in his long life; and, as a writer and a symbol of the purest Roman ideal, his prestige was even more significant after his death; he was a conduit through which a new wave of Pythagorean thought was introduced to Rome, just at the point when that city was about to dominate its world.

We may pick up Cato's career when he was a young soldier in the army of Fabius Maximus, besieging Tarentum . A Greek city and once an ally of Rome, Tarentum had gone over to the Carthaginian side. When the Romans retook the city in 209 BCE, there was indiscriminate, or nearly indiscriminate, slaughter and looting.[135] Almost certainly a certain Pythagorean philosopher and his house were spared the fury of Rome; his name was Nearchus, and he seems to have quite willingly cooperated with the Romans. We have seen that the Pythagoreans had an especial fondness for absolutist power, so Nearchus probably felt no pinch of conscience. Cato was billeted in his spared house, and there the philosopher introduced the practical-headed young Roman to a new sort of Pythagorean thought.[136] Nearchus claimed to have the notebooks of Archytas of Tarentum, a Pythagorean philosopher and general of the time of Plato. They were forgeries, almost certainly, but Cato was delighted to have them and probably thought them genuine. This "Archytas" denounced pleasure as the greatest incentive to evil in life: "The body was the chief detriment to the soul and the soul can only escape and purify itself by reasonings that wean it away from bodily sensations."[137] Cato rejoiced that he had found a truly "Italian philosophy"[138] that he could oppose to what he perceived as the dangerous taste for luxury coming in with the loot of Greek cities and the philosophy being taught by Greek slaves to Roman boys.

There seems no doubt that Cato the Elder embraced the Pythagoreanism that Nearchus had handed him. The only complete book by Cato to come down to us is the *De re rustica*, a treatise on farm life. The work is an amazing hodgepodge of instructions on planting, cooking, religious offerings to the farm gods, and soon. Cato's distrust of Greek physicians led him to turn to a sort of medical regimen that has one foot in Pythagorean lore and the other in most ancient folk-remedies. He seems to think that the major cause of disease is impurities in the body, and he recommends the purgative qualities of cabbage, especially "the cabbage of Pythagoras" (*bressica Pythagorea*) as a cure-all.[139] In his recommended treatment for a sick ox (chapter 70), he says one should administer every ingredient in threes, clearly based in Pythagorean numerology.[140]

Cato represents the high-water mark of "Romanitas" — a strong nationalistic and ethnocentric effort to reclaim what was perceived as the true essence of the Roman character, then in danger from Greek culture. He had a virulent hatred of all things Greek,[141] though he was quite well-read in Greek.[142] Socrates he esteemed a mere babbler and, worse yet, one whose reasoning could dangerously undermine law; about Socrates only his home life had been admirable, Cato said.[143] He was likewise uncomfortable with the feminine; female violence threatened the "liberty" of the Romans, he claimed.[144] The good Roman woman, Cato wrote, would stay at home, visiting only the neighboring women and that seldom — her true duties never went beyond cleaning and cooking. "Make sure" he advised husbands, "that she stand in awe of you" (*ea te metuat facito*).[145] He seems to have shared, probably before he was given the books of "Archytas," the Pythagorean distrust of the feminine as an irrational element, opposed to order and the "natural" dominance of men. Obviously by extension any man who "played the woman" in bed with another man was not just sleeping with the enemy, but really sleeping as the enemy.

Cato became quite alarmed in 155 BCE when Athens sent as ambassadors Carneades, the head of the Academy, and Diogenes, the Stoic. Both men lingered in Rome, teaching their philosophies, until Cato — so "distressed," Plutarch tells us, "when this zeal for discussion came pouring in"[146] — appealed to the senate and had the philosophers sent home as quickly as possible. "We ought to decide one way or the other ... that these men may return to their schools and hold dialogue with the boys of Greece."[147] He is said to have been troubled in particular by Carneades, who would eloquently argue on one side of an issue one day and just as eloquently on the other the next; he brought into question the hierarchical understanding of the order of the universe. Carneades was revealing the philosophical flaws of Panaetius' justification of Roman dominance; their "justice" was no more than a self-serving prudence.[148] That Cato used the power of that state to silence a critic he could not refute should hardly surprise us. That the old censor wanted the head of Plato's Academy dismissed so he could "hold dialogue with the boys of Greece" (*dialegontai pasin Hellenon*) is an obvious dig at the pederastic tradition. The Pythagorean texts that Cato knew and loved offered no rational justifications for their teachings — on homophobia or the desirability of absolutist government. Carneades was long remembered as a "formidable controversialist."[149] Cato could not confute Carneades. When ideas unfavorable to power cannot be logically refuted, they will, if at all possible, be silenced.

The most explicit statement in Cato's surviving work is from a speech of his called "On the Property of Florus." Cato refers to "the case of a man who had openly sold himself in prostitution, or hired himself to a pimp; even if he had had a bad reputation [*famosus*] or been suspected [*suspiciosus*], they decided it was unlawful to use second hand information against a free man."[150] Cato was citing common usage in his day rather than his own opinion, suggesting one of the earliest examples we know of men who were suspected of performing certain homosexual acts being regarded as a special class of persons and a class, at that, who were the object of strong social disapproval — the *cinaedi*, or men who chose to be sexually penetrated.[151]

Cato is on record as denouncing the reciting of poetry at banquets, calling the men who did so *grassotores*, a word linked by a latter lexicographer with sexual immorality.[152] One suspects that the sort of songs he had in mind were Greek *skolia*, drinking songs that praised the beauty and worthiness of boys; perhaps even the *Melos Harmodios*, the praises of the Tyrant Slayers, a song long out of fashion in Greece, had a vogue in Roman banquets, turning the stomachs of Cato and the other conservatives. Perhaps Cato even looked askance at the food. He suspected that Roman physicians were in a conspiracy to poison their Greek masters — which indicates not just a climate of thought but outright paranoia.[153]

The Greek habit of men exercising and bathing together nude disconcerted Cato; he complained that the Romans got from the Greeks the "deplorable habit of appearing nude" in public, and he himself never appeared nude even before his own sons.[154] Roman male modesty seems to be very old; one of the numerous prohibitions under which the Flamen Dialis, the high priest of Jupiter, labored was that he could not undress except in an enclosed space "lest Jove see him."[155] Male nudity was associated by the Romans with Greek pederasty.[156] Probably the idea comes both from the association of the gymnasium with homosexual meeting and from a Stoic notion called *epibole*; an *epibole* is "an impulse prior to an impulse," they said, and cited sexual love as an example: "beginning a friendship [with a beautiful boy] is caused by a presentation of beauty."[157] The Old Stoics were attempting to define (and for purposes of ethics, disrupt) what happens at the moment of sexual attraction. This seems to have been just too much for practical-minded Romans to fully grasp; and, prejudiced against Greek pederasty, they assumed the Stoics were saying "Seeing naked boys makes one lust after them." Cicero has an amazing discussion on avoiding nudity; he says:

> Nature seems to have a wonderful plan in the construction of our bodies. Our face and our figure generally, in so far as it has a comely appearance she has placed in sight; but the parts of the body that are given us only to serve the needs of Nature and that would present an unsightly and unpleasant appearance she has covered up and concealed from view. Man's modesty has followed this careful contrivance of Nature; all right-minded people keep out of sight what Nature has hidden.[158]

One would imagine that Romans were born in their togas.

The penis was believed by the Romans to have magical properties; the Latin word that we translate as "bewitch"—"fascination," means to entrap in magic by the sight of the penis, and one could cause evil to another by singing *fescennine* songs, songs about the penis[159]; as an apotropaic charm, many Romans wore about their necks little golden penises intended to repel black magic directed at them. "Casting the evil eye" in classical time could mean no more than looking at someone with sexual desire; this it was believed could harm or even kill the person looked at, and looking at the genitals was particularly deadly since they were so tender — as the eye was.[160] The Greek gymnasia, literally the "places of nakedness," had been the primary place for men and boys to meet both for athletics and more romantic endeavors, as we have mentioned. When Marcellus took Syracuse in 211 BCE and sent to Rome fabulous booty including statues, Cato was appalled to find that many of those statues showed gods quite naked.[161] The Romans invented the use of the fig leaf in sculpture to hide the "naughty parts." Except for copies of Greek works, collected by connoisseurs, Romans had no taste for male nudity in art[162]; and caesars and generals have come down to us without exception in full battle armor, or toga.[163]

The themes of male dread of nudity and male dread of sexual penetration cross at per-haps the single most typical symbol of ancient Roman attitudes, the gladiator. Men, usually slaves, were forced to fight to the death in the arena. The earliest information we have on the gladiatorial tradition is a painting from Samnite territory which shows two gladiators fight-ing. Their garments are too short to hide the genitals: one man is fighting with a spear through his leg, bleeding profusely.[164] Essentially the gladiator was a man who consented to be pene-trated, both by the eyes of the spectators, metaphorically, and by sword and spear, literally; and the gladiator was, like the mime (a milder form of popular entertainment in Roman times), the most despised of humans.[165] Generally the image of the gladiator can be seen as a dramatic enactment of the *cinaedus*, the male who consented to be sexually penetrated and was violently despised for it.

We have some incidents from the Republican era in Rome that further suggest the strength of the bias against homosexuality: Livy tells the story of a freeborn young man who was forced by debt to become a slave. When his master made sexual advances to him, the young man killed his master. For a slave to kill a master would normally be for Romans as horrible a crime as could be imagined.[166] However, since the young man was freeborn and defending his masculinity, he was acclaimed a hero, freed and his debts paid.[167] Even more famous was the case in 102 BCE of Trebonicus. A centurion, Trebonicus' own nephew, serving under him tried to seduce Trebonicus[168]; the nephew, Caius Lucius, was probably trying to establish what would in Greece have been a perfectly honorable pederastic relationship with the centurion; however, Trebonicus killed the younger man. Marius the Dictator, then leading an army against the Germans invading northern Italy, praised and rewarded Trebonicus for his Roman manliness, executed the offending soldier, and the case became a standard example in ora-tory for centuries.[169]

We cannot depart from the old Censor without noting an extremely important book that he wrote, one that has influenced deeply the course of Western civilization. Cato's book on the education of children has not survived, but its message has — picked up by Musonius Rufus and passed on to the Christian tradition though Clement of Alexandria. The warning against Greek education of boys[170] — certainly pederasty included — has become one of the major cornerstones of the homophobic tradition.

Undoubtedly this Pythagorean teaching struck so pleasant a chord in Cato's heart because Romans were already Pythagorean in a loose, traditional way. Cato, a "new man," descended from peasants (his name, Porcius, indicates his ancestors were hog farmers); but joining the depleted ranks of the ancient Roman aristocracy he would be expected, if anything, to over-compensate in his desire to be a pure Roman of the Romans; and Neo-Pythagoreanism had a ready appeal to him. The introduction of a revived Pythagoreanism to Rome is a movement that occurred over the next two centuries; but it began here, with the vastly influential Cato the Censor pouring over a forged book in the house of a Turrentine quisling. It is to the con-tent of those books and others like them that we turn next.

Neo-Pythagorean Texts

The Pythagoreans seem to disappear, or nearly so, from history after the time of Plato. The cause may be as much the thinness of our historical information in this era as a cessation of Pythagorean activity. Aristotle and a number of philosophers after him were interested enough to write books (all lost) on the Pythagoreans. Then suddenly about 180 BCE the movement scholars have termed Neo-Pythagoreanism surfaced. Because a very considerable amount of material has survived, we are in a good position to say a great deal about these new Pythagoreans; the one thing that we cannot say with a great deal of assurance is just how they are connected to the Pythagoreans that Plato and the generation or two before him knew. Probably Holgar Thesleff is right in saying that the organized Pythagorean communities, the brotherhoods that were instruments of political domination in southern Italy, vanished by about 300 BCE; while a form of Pythagoreanism survived, heavily influenced by Orphism, among wandering teachers.[171] It seems likely that some small brotherhoods may have survived in secret among a few families in Magna Grecia, nurturing secret doctrines and remembering the glorious days when they ruled cities. Certainly the suppression of the bacchants and the affair of Numa's coffin referred to below suggest that some small, secret societies may have been at work trying to manipulate Roman society toward their agenda.

The affair of the bacchants disturbed Rome in 186 BCE. There was a furious round of persecution for participating in the rites of Wild Dionysus, and a significant part of the charges against the worshipers of Dionysus was homosexual acts. The worship of Dionysus had come to Italy first though the Etruscans, who adopted him under the wonderful name of Fuflans.[172] Later, more direct contact with Hellenistic culture brought in the establishment of the cult of Dionysus on an official basis in 496 BCE.[173] Certainly there were gender-bending aspects to the cult; Diodorus Siculus tells us that the orgiastic worshipers of Dionysus "responded to the feminine principle of nature ... in opposition to the Olympian deities."[174] In the Mysteries of Wild Dionysus, worshipers reenacted Dionysus' descent to the underworld in search of his mortal mother, Semele; this was, in fact, a search for the feminine.[175] How such a cult managed to survive in homophobic Rome for over 300 years is obscure. We are fortunate to have not only the account of Livy but also a partial version of an inscription detailing the edict of the senate. The story told in the thirty-ninth book of Livy is no doubt "embellished by romantic and exaggerated details,"[176] as Livy often did; but the basic facts certainly occurred. The trouble began with a Greek, says Livy, a "hedge-priest," who set up outdoor rites performed at night, where we are told, "Men and women, those of tender age with their seniors ... had pleasures at hand to satisfy the lust he was most prone to [*ad id quisque, quo natura pronioris*]."[177] Worse yet, "more impurity [*stupra*] was wrought by men with men than with women. Whoever would not submit to defilement, or shrank from defiling others was sacrificed as a victim."[178] This seems doubtful in the extreme, since there was no compulsion upon anyone to participate in sexual acts in the context of the Greek rites of Wild Dionysus.[179] Moreover, the notion of the orgiastic rites being so suddenly introduced by a single individual likewise has the flavor of propaganda, the sort of propaganda that can fuel witch hunts. The rites were denounced by a young woman to the senate and severely repressed. Noteworthy is the dual role women play in Livy's account: both as instigators of the rites and as a noble, "true Roman" woman who betrayed them to officials. As many as 7,000 were implicated. Many were executed, or imprisoned; many killed themselves, or fled into to exile. Women who were involved were regularly turned over to their guardians for punishment; women who had no guardians were publicly executed.[180] The rites were severely cut back by the senate. A century and a half later Julius Caesar officially reinstated the bacchant rites, but in a very sedate indoor version, popular among the wealthy.[181] This repression of the rites of Dionysus is the first "witch hunt" of gay and lesbian persons we know of in history. The rites of Wild Dionysus were particularly opposed by Orphics and Pythagoreans; one suspects that Pythagoreans were in some way involved in setting on this persecution.

Then there is the suspicious matter of the stone coffins. According to Livy,[182] some workers were digging on the Janiculum Hill in 181 BCE on property belonging to Lucius Petilius, a professional scribe (*scriba publicus*).[183] They unearthed two stone coffins, both sealed with lead. One was inscribed with the name of Numa, and was found to be completely empty; the other carried an inscription saying it contained the books of Numa. Inside the second coffin were found two bundles of books, seven volumes in Latin on pontifical law, seven in Greek on Pythagorean philosophy[184]; all the books looked perfectly new (*recentissima specie*). When the senate saw what the books contained, it moved promptly to buy them from Petilius (who wished not to sell but was forced to) and had them publicly burned. They regarded them as subversive; probably they feared the individualistic quality of mysticism involved[185]; the forced sale was clearly unconstitutional.[186] The empty coffin with Numa's name on it presumably was to demonstrate Numa's immortality — he had left his coffin. Of course, the books were forgeries (though neither the senate nor Livy seemed suspicious of that fact); someone, perhaps Petilius himself, had gone to great pains to prepare them and conceal them where they would soon be found, hoping they would be received as genuine and authoritative. Farther details are lacking, but the story as we have it proves a Pythagorean secret movement was afoot, readily willing to use forgery to influence Roman public opinion.

With the prestige of Cato the Censor, "as great in the City as he was on the battlefield," as Livy says, Neo-Pythagoreanism became the dominant religio-philosophical movement in Rome in the late Republican age. Though written in Greek and representing an essentially Greek thought, the surviving works of the Neo-Pythagorean philosophy are distinctly and explicitly homophobic. Some considerable attention must be paid now to these books.

What has come down to us is a body of writing a bit shorter than the *Republic* of Plato and called loosely the Neo-Pythagorean texts. Many are fragments of what must have been much larger works, and no doubt the whole collection represents a tiny percentage of what must have been a large body of material, now lost. This collection represents fragments of many works, allegedly by various writers close to the time of Pythagoras. All are forgeries. The actual authors of none of these works are known, though one suspects that Cato's host, Nearchus, may have been the author of some. They fall into two categories: the older ones (from about the time of Cato) are attributed to Pythagoras and his immediate family. These abound in asceticism, number mysticism and Orphic religiosity.[187] They are written in a transparently false form of literary Doric Greek.[188] Fifty years or so later, about 120 BCE, a second wave of Neo-Pythagorean documents appears, also from the same geographical area (southern and southeastern Italy), pretending to be from a later generation of Pythagorean teachers (Okkelos, Charondas, etc.) along with the "Letters of Plato"— all forged, all intended to make Pythagorean philosophy accepted at Rome[189]— which was rather to carry coals to Newcastle.

This material is not philosophy at all, in the common sense of the term. It makes no effort to reason, define or explain. Rather, it is a collection of quasireligious instructions, oracular and admonitory, rather than rational. "The treatises are bald and didactic, without attempts at proof, and aimed at an audience which, it would seem, was prepared to substitute faith for reason," says John Dillon.[190] Though written in Doric Greek, it breathes none of the classical Greek air of free speculation and spacious-mindedness. One suspects that it was written for an audience of practical-minded Romans. Rome in the second century BCE was undergoing a deep shaking of its ethical roots, due to the influx of Greek thought and the luxury empires create. Romans needed to be told that there was a solid cultural basis for their attitudes; "culture" at the time was virtually synonymous with "Greek." The prestige of Greek learning was vast; no well-to-do Roman family thought its wealth was complete without a Greek teacher among its slaves, yet that same status symbol could bring into question all the rest of the culture. The Neo-Pythagorean movement addressed a real need in its time — it allowed Romans who didn't think much to at least think they were following the tradition of the deepest, oldest Greek culture — and gave them permission to despise all the rest as innovation and corruption. Small wonder we have so much Pythagorean material, and almost nothing from, say, Carneades.

We may well begin with the "Life of Pythagoras"[191] cobbled together by Iamblichus in the fourth century CE out of a farrago of materials much older. Only a vague outline of fact can be discerned by modern scholars, but the point is not what the historic Pythagoras thought and did, but rather what he was believed to have taught and done at the revival of Pythagoreanism in the second century BCE. The "long hair of Samos," as Pythagoras was called, was born to a woman named Parthenis, the wife of Mnesarchos. His father was Apollo; and, when Pythagoras was born, Mnesarchos changed his wife's name to Pythia.[192] "Parthinis" means "virgin," and it seems likely that Iamblichus or whatever Pythagorean document he had before him tried to hide an original story that had Pythagoras not only the son of Apollo, but also conceived by a virgin. Iamblichus was a furious opponent of Christianity and certainly must have been familiar with the doctrine of the virgin birth of Jesus; perhaps he had denounced that doctrine as irrational and found it impossible thereafter to accept it even in the biography of his hero.

Pythagoras not only went to Egypt, where he studied all the lore of the priests of Memphis, Iamblichus tells us, but he also traveled to Sidon, where he studied under the disciples of Moskhos.[193] Porphyry adds at this point that what he studied was Hebrew and dream interpretation.[194] (Moskhos seems to be a rendering of "Moses," and the matter of dream interpretation is probably derived from a Greek romance based on the story of Joseph and the pharaoh's dreams.) Afterwards he was captured by the army of Cambyses, king of Persia, and taken to Babylon, where he absorbed all the lore of the Babylonian priests and the magi.[195] Next, after observing governments in Crete and Sparta, he took over a cave on Samos and meditated in the dark.[196] Here his followers came to be called *koinnobioi*— the word that comes over into English as "cenobites" and means that they had all things in common.[197]

Before we continue with Iamblichus' summary of Neo-Pythagorean materials, let us pause and look at the legendary wanderings of the sage. The most ancient strata that we can observe in classical mystery religions is a reconciliation with the Great Mother, the earth goddess. As classical civilization broke down and individuals lost control of their fate with the loss of the polis, people began to see themselves not as beloved offsprings of the earth, but as fallen beings, lost under the rule of what Luther Martin calls "the unfavorable feminine," Tukhe, Lady Luck, who may as well destroy as nourish.[198] The myth of the wandering sage is the myth of the exile seeking home, lost in a hostile universe governed by *heimarmene*, oppressive Fate. Pythagoras' followers did not think of themselves as of the earth, earthy, but as originating in a transcendent realm and fallen by sin into a world where they must wander in search of return to the realm of the pure masculine, antithetical to the evil world of Lady Luck.[199] Hence, the misogyny of all the Neo-Pythagorean texts — the feminine is evil because the world of matter is evil; evil must be avoided at all costs, and to practice homosexuality is welcome the enemy within one's inmost gates.

Returning to Iamblichus, we are told that arriving in Italy, Pythagoras made a speech to 2,000 disciples, and "they took their laws and ordinances from Pythagoras as if they were divine commands ... some called him Apollo."[200] He "liberated" a number of cities and established in them the laws of Zaleucos and Charondas. Everywhere his political power extended, "divergence of opinion he utterly abolished."[201] Obviously neither freedom of speech nor any form of a pluralistic society was compatible with the Pythagorean ideal. At Croton, one of the rules he established was that men "should be resolved that they would know only their own wives"[202]—"know" meaning "have sex with." This simple axiom, which utterly eliminates male homosexuality, was later taken up by the Christian church as the "Alexandrian Rule."

Iamblichus quotes at length from a document he says was the teaching of Lysis, the teacher of Epameinondas—more, obviously, of the Neo-Pythagorean pseudepigrapha and probably from what Thesleff calls "Class II"—dating to the first century BCE. "Lysis" warns severely against false teachers who, "working for no good, entrap young men."[203] The denunciation is clearly against pederasty. Boys, we are told elsewhere, "should be brought up not to look for sexual intercourse before the age of 20; and, when they do reach that age, their experiences should be few."[204] Pythagoras had warned against all self-indulgence, and Lysis adds that from self-indulgence springs "unnatural pleasures and passionate desires."[205] The appeal to absolutism is unswerving: "In general a human being should never be allowed to do as he likes. There should always be a government, a lawful and decorous authority to which every citizen is subject."[206]

Seldom have such rigorous political absolutism, puritanism and homophobia come together in a single, brief document. We may remind our readers, as Giovanni Reale has pointed out, that this Pythagorean material is not in fact philosophy at all; rather it is dogma: "Pythagoras for the Pythagoreans became what Christ is for the Christians, the son of God in human form and his philosophy became a divine revelation."[207]

The matter did not end with the Neo-Pythagorean revival of 180 BCE or so. A third wave of Pythagorean texts swept across the classical world in the first century BCE, producing more, and somewhat different, texts. As the uncertainty and tumult of the Punic wars broke ground for the first revival, so the upheavals of the cycle of civil wars that brought down the Roman Republic may be looked to as a factor in turning Romans again towards a source of alleged certainty. The names associated with this third wave are far more obscure than Cato the Censor. Few remember Alexander Polyhistor or Pius Nigdius Figulus, and fewer still read the texts that passed though their hands, but the third wave of Neo-Pythagorean texts helped to set a final pattern of homophobia that would last two millennia.

Alexander Polyhistor was a Greek of Ephesos by birth; in his eastern campaign Sulla, the Roman dictator, picked up Alexander more or less as a piece of booty and took him to Rome as a slave. Freed in 82 BCE, he took the Latin name of Cornelius and wrote "books without number."[208] We are principally interested in him here for one reason: he made public Pythagorean notebooks he claimed to have discovered. As for these *hupomnemata*, notebooks, we have no information as to where they came from. W.K.C. Guthrie thinks it unlikely that Alexander Cornelius forged them himself since "he seems to have been an unoriginal and industrious collector of facts, free from the fantasy that characterizes ... later Neopythagorean notebooks."[209] Probably it was this industrious scholar that provided the Roman world with works attributed to Okkelos Lukanos, Archytas, Charondas, and others; and these in turn provided Eudorus of Alexandria with a basis for his Pythagorean Platonism.[210] Through Eudorus the torch of Neo-Pythagorean–Neo-Platonic thought passed to Philo Judaeus and into the Church Fathers. On the Roman and predictably practical side of the matter Alexander Cornelius's texts provided Figulus with intellectual underpinnings (however shaky) for his efforts to further revive a moribund Pythagoreanism.

Publius Nigidius Figulus (O felicitous name!), 98–45 BCE, was a contemporary and friend of Cicero in the first century BCE; Cicero calls him the "most learned of Romans" after Varro, and Aulius Gellius repeats the compliment. Little has survived of that great learning—Gellius preserves the titles of several of Figulus' books: *On Sacrificial Meats, On Private Augury, On Animals*[211] — all suggest that he was much concerned with the occult, religious ritual and reincarnation in animal form. Cicero tells us that Figulus "revived the order of Pythagoras,"[212] which is generally taken to mean that he tried to resuscitate the more or less defunct Pythagorean brotherhoods[213] that had been powerful units for antidemocratic reforms in Italy four centuries earlier. He probably succeeded to a considerable extent; archaeologists tell us that just about this time Pythagorean symbols begin to appear in Rome.[214]

Eudorus of Alexandria took this new (he no doubt believed ancient and genuine) Pythagorean material very seriously. We have already seen he was much interested in the first book of Plato's *Laws*[215]; his influence was probably far more wide ranging than he could have dreamed, for his pupil Arius Dydimus became the friend of Macaenas and the teacher and court-philosopher to the Emperor Augustus. He wrote a book, *On Pythagorean Philosophy*, the fragments of which still exist, deriving his information from Thesleff's Class I documents.[216] One suspects that Arius Dydimus' Pythagorean fingerprints were all over the puritanical laws that Augustus passed — for example the *lex Julia de adulteriis coercindus*, passed in 18 BCE, which severely curtailed the sexual freedom of the Romans. It made adultery a matter of criminal rather than private concern and subjected it to grave punishment.[217] However, lest this discussion turn into a dry (or even dryer) succession of the philosophers, let us turn to the texts that Alexander Cornelius Polyhistor (or someone near his time) published.

Among the surviving fragments attributed to Archytas (it is impossible to say if this is a work by Cato, or some later forgery), we find the following:

> The laws of the wicked and atheists are opposed by the unwritten laws of the Gods ... which have developed the unwritten laws and maxims given to men.... Law must conform to nature.[218]

From a work called "On the Nature of the Universe" (*Pari tes tou pantos phuseos*) and attributed to Okellus Lukanos (Ocellus Lucanus, in Latin — not known to have been a historic personage, but said to be a follower of Pythagoras):

> The following laws should be taught in the Grecian cities: that connection with a mother, or a daughter, or a sister whether in temples or in public place should be forbidden, for it would be well to employ numerous impediments to this energy [this passage seems to confirm the suspicion of modern scholars that women participating in the secret rites of various goddesses sometimes engaged in Lesbian activity].... For those who are not entirely connected with each other for the sake of begetting children injure the most honorable system of convention.... All unnatural connections should be prevented, especially those attended with wanton insolence. But such as harmonize with nature should be encouraged.[219]

From the "Preface to the Laws of Charondas of Katane [*Pronooimia nomon*]" (a historic lawgiver, whose work — certainly not this — was known to Aristotle):

> Let everyone dearly love his lawful wife and beget children by her. But let none sow the seed due his children into any other person. For nature produced the seed for the sake of producing children, and not for the sake of lust.[220]

Moving from such learned statecraft to the art of cookery (the Pythagoreans overlooked few details), we may say something about the most famous of the Pythagorean "symbols" — the injunction to abstain from eating beans. Aulius Gellius (about 123–170 CE) tells us from some Pythagorean source that the injunction is really a pun; that in "*Kai kuamon kheiras ekhein*," "Hold back from beans," we should read *kuamous* for *kuamon*. Since *kuamous* means the testicles, the real meaning of Pythagoras was, Gellius tells us, that males should abstain from sex with other males.[221] This sort of rather fanciful playing with words is common in late antiquity (as any casual reader of Isidore of Savile is all too aware), but here it provides one more bit of evidence that Pythagoreanism is the major, if not unique, source for Roman homophobic thought.

A late Orphic source, used by Dio of Prusa (about 40–120 CE), suggests a possible explanation for both the Neo-Pythagorean texts' insistence on large families and their disapproval of homosexuality. The words are put in the mouth of one Charidemos (perhaps a fictitious character), but they seem to represent Dio's own early philosophic schooling, and clearly are Orphic-Pythagorean.[222] The world, Charidemos says, is a terrible prison where humans suffer all sorts of torture and deprivation.[223] After a long and somewhat gruesome account of the human condition, Charidemos adds:

> Such then are the tortures, and so numerous, by which men are afflicted while they remain in this prison and dungeon, each for his appointed time and the majority do not get out until they produce another person from their own loins and leave him to succeed to the punishment in their stead, some leaving one and others even more.[224]

Behind this text is the doctrine of the arrogance of the Titans who killed Dionysus and were burnt to ashes for it by Zeus. From their ashes, humans were made, as we have seen earlier, in the discussion of Orphism above, and the suffering of the human race is a manifestation of the continued wrath of Zeus on the very substance of the Titans. By Dio's time and probably a good deal earlier, this concept of an inherited curse was applied with a sort of odd legalism to the individual. Anyone who escapes the prison of the world should be careful to leave behind one or more offspring to take on the suffering. Otherwise that escaped soul might have suffer in the next world as well or be reborn to suffer fully in this world. A further implication seems to be that the Titanic substance is passed on in the act of generation. A man who ejaculates into a woman is planting Titanic material in her that may produce a new child-prisoner. Presumably a man who ejaculates into another man leaves the Titanic material there, and the receiving partner in a male homosexual acts builds up the very substance of Zeus' curse in his body. Hence another aspect of the contempt that fell particularly on the receiving partner.[225]

One suspects that in the second century BCE such Pythagoreanism as actually survived in the Greek cities of Italy and Sicily was largely impoverished for ideas, for it was found necessary to steal them wholesale. A major effort in all the Neo-Pythagorean material is the effort to claim for Pythagoras and his immediate followers all the basic tenets of the nonmaterialistic tradition in Greek philosophy. The work ascribed to Timaeus of Locri is nothing more than a simplistic summary of Plato's *Timaeus*; works attributed to Pempelos derive from Plato's *Laws*[226]; Occellos repeats the Categories of Aristotle. The claim put forth is that Pythagoras originated these ideas, and Plato and Aristotle were only writing down and publishing what they had found in Pythagorean documents written long before their time. At least in Pythagorean circles, the effort succeeded, too. For the rest of antiquity with numbing regularity, we find writer after writer in the Pythagorean tradition saying that Plato and less often Aristotle were nothing but minor disciples of Pythagoras, and the true and pure representations of concepts like the Forms and the Categories are not in Plato and Aristotle, but in what was said to be earlier works — these pseudepigrapha.

Primarily the notion seems to have been aimed at Romans and those sympathetic with the Roman world-view. The basis for all Roman ethics was the *mos maiorem*, the Way of the Ancestors. Any aristocracy is naturally conservative — once the power is gotten, the object is to keep it. Every respectable Roman tried to live and conduct himself as his ancestors had. Ennius' ringing line summed up the entire ethical system: "*Moribus antiquis res stat Romana virisque* [On the manners of the olden men stands the Roman state].[227]

The entire aristocracy of Rome, as Donald Earl has written, "had a vested interest in maintaining the present state. Its whole power and position was founded on custom and precedent."[228] Anything intruding from without, even the slightest innovation, could upset a very great apple cart indeed. It was only by representing Pythagoreanism as a source for both Rome and Greece that men like Nearchus and Alexander Polyhistor could hope to get a sympathetic hearing from their intended audiences of Roman aristocrats. Pythagoreanism was put forward as the original philosophy, the source of all that was great and worthy in Greek thought as well as Roman culture. Was not Numa a disciple of Pythagoras?—and so were Plato and Aristotle. Therefore, the argument ran, by studying Greek philosophy, the Romans were only doing what their revered ancestors had done. No doubt the hoard of Neo-Pythagorean documents that flooded the Roman world were intended to make Pythagorean ideas acceptable to Romans (indeed, those Roman ancestors probably were Pythagorean), but they also made a broader world of Greek learning appear a bit less alien to the suspicious Roman nobility.

With all the Pythagorean insistence on law and written codes of conduct, it is inevitable that laws against homosexuality came into being. It is obvious from what we have already said that sexual activity by any male with another male who was freeborn was regarded with great horror and rage by the Romans from as early as records are available. However, that rage and horror were not expressed in law until much later; in the early Republic, sexual matters were considered wholly private within the family. The patriarch, the *pater familiaris*, enforced the traditional rules among all the members of his own family—no matter how old his sons and daughters might be. A young free man, or indeed any free male, who willingly accepted penetration by another male might expect to be harshly punished—killed perhaps—by his father, grandfather or whoever was head of the family. Of course the same is true of an unmarried female. Sometime between 227 and 149 BCE the *Lex Scantinia* was created. This was the first actual law enforced by a state in the Western tradition to punish homosexual acts. Unfortunately we know rather little about the details of this law, other than it forbade with a stiff fine *stuperum cum puero*—defilement with a boy.[229] We should not be surprised to find that only a fine was imposed; under the Republic aristocrats could only be punished by the law courts with fines or exile.[230] The details of Roman law on homosexuality before the time of Justinian are at best obscure. Perhaps the best witness we have is Sextus Empiricus, who wrote in Greek between 200 and 250 CE: "Among us for instance, homosexual sex is shameful—or rather has actually been deemed illegal."[231]

We then may briefly sum up the Roman attitude toward homosexuality at the end of the Republic—an attitude that continued in full force well into the Empire. The often quoted lines of Plautus (died 184 BCE) in his *Curculio* say it briefly:

> No one prohibits you from going down the public way
> as long as you don't make a path through posted land—
> as long as you hold off from a bride, a single woman, a virgin,
> young men [*iuventute*] and free boys [*pueris liberis*], love anybody you please
> [lines 35–38].[232]

Sexual relations with slaves, male or female, were permitted without either moral disapproval or legal censure to all freeborn Roman men.[233] Of course in homosexual relations with male slaves it was assumed that the Roman aristocrat was the penetrating partner; to be penetrated "shames by its very subordinancy," as Amy Richlin has said.[234] There were then three classes of males who might engage in homosexual relations among the Romans: slaves who were routinely forced to receive penetration from their masters; the masters themselves who penetrated their slaves; and those free males who, laboring under severe social disapproval, sought to be penetrated. As for mutually reciprocal, free sexual associations between persons of the same gender, they hardly seemed to have existed in the Roman world, and have left only the slightest evidence where they did. We will examine each of these groups in turn.

Under Roman law slaves were nonpersons; they had no rights, and a master could rape, torture or kill a slave with complete impunity.[235] Ulpian of Tyre (died 228 CE), one of the greatest of late Roman jurists, maintained that slavery was against the law of nature, though, since it was universally permitted by the *jus gentium*, the common law of the nations, it was therefore permissible.[236] To be orally or anally raped by their masters was routine for young male slaves.[237] Female slaves were protected often from their masters, being under the authority of the master's wife, the *matrona*,[238] though there is some indication that a parallel custom existed in which female slaves were forced into sexual relations with their mistresses.[239] Indeed the rape of male slaves seems to have been not merely an act of sexual desire on the part of the masters, but (as heterosexual rape usually is) an effort to "put the slave in his place"—demonstrate the absolute dominance of the master over the male slave, who would be called "*puer*," "boy," all his life.[240] Obviously the masters of slaves were placed in a difficult and contradictory position: it was virtually mandatory that they penetrate their male slaves,[241] an act that would be consummated privately; but at the same time they must not be suspected themselves of being penetrated by the slave (who seems magically to become a human being under Roman law when he becomes a sexual being). We hear derisively of a master who maintains a male slave who is "a girl in the dining room, a man in the bedroom,"[242] implying that the master had the slave dress in a feminine manner before his guests, but received penetration from his slave in private.

Hence, the use of the most horrible single aspect of Roman homophobia, the eunuch. The practice of castrating boys to make or maintain them longer as sex objects is very old; Herodotus tells us that the invading Persians sometimes enslaved all the handsome boys of entire villages, castrated them and sent them as catamites to Persian nobles.[243] We have already met a Persian eunuch, Bagoas. The Greeks seem to have had no use for the custom, but the Romans revived it,[244] and we hear often of eunuchs among them—e.g., Earinos, the cupbearer to the Emperor Domitian. Festus, the consul of Asia in the time of the Emperor Valens (364–78 CE) earned himself the nickname Echetus after a tyrant in Homer, who habitually castrated men.[245] As we said, the ostensible reason for this practice was to keep boys looking younger for a longer time and to prevent the growth of body hair, particularly around the anus (which the Romans found an erotic turn-off).[246] However, one suspects that a strong motive was the desire of the Roman masters to be above suspicion of penetration in their sexual relations. Likewise we hear of the infibulation of males among the Romans—the foreskin of boys was fastened closed over the glans with a needle to prevent copulation.[247] If the young man one took to one's bedroom was physically incapable of an erection, or perhaps had no penis, then no one could suspect that the master was being penetrated.

Amid this moral squalor, love nevertheless pitched his tent. Occasionally real affection developed between slave boy and Roman master. Inscriptions occasionally tell us that masters were remarkably generous to their freed slaves and the slaves' families, suggesting a kindness that may have had a sexual origin.[248] Cicero wrote an erotic poem about his slave-boy Tiro[249]; but, when the latter fell sick in April of 53 BCE near Rome, the philosopher-statesman at Cumae shot off a series of letters to Tiro and those caring for him full of affectionate concern and promising Tiro his freedom if he recovered.[250] In the works of Statius (61–96 CE) we hear of Melior's careful affection for Glaucias, his boy slave, and of the sorrow of Flavius Ursus when his boy died.[251] When a conspiracy against the Emperor Commodus went wrong in 189 CE, Julius Alexander, one of the conspirators, chose to stay behind with his boy (who could run no more) and die.[252]

Men who chose to be penetrated anally or orally by other men were recognized as a distinct category of humans (or subhumans) by the Romans. This discrimination is the first known in history of a class of persons isolated and ostracized for homosexual acts; contempt for *cinaedi* can be shown to go back at least to the time of Cato the Elder and makes the *cinaedi* in some ways similar to the modern "homosexual" in the fully prejudicial sense of the term.[253] Amy Richlin has pointed out that "*cinaedus*" and a number of other terms applied to males who chose to be penetrated are not words those persons applied to themselves, but rather are terms of insult applied by the larger culture[254] — like "faggot." Richlin has found clear evidence for the existence of a subculture of males who sought penetration by other males. Like many gays and lesbians today, the *cinaedi* of ancient Rome dressed in a way and used gesture so as to be recognized by other members of the subculture —"lisping, putting the hand on the hip," wearing light green or light blue, or using other signals.[255] Such persons were considered at least "sick" by the Romans and vile criminals at worst.[256] Likewise, women who engaged in same-sex activity were regarded as "monstrous" by Roman males. Iphis, a female in the *Metamorphosis* of Ovid (43 BCE–18 CE), falls in love with another woman, Ianthe. Devastated by internalized homophobia, Iphis prays to the goddess Isis to be delivered from a state so unheard of, so monstrous (*prodigiosa*); she would greatly prefer, she says, to have a natural evil, or one according to custom (*naturale malum ... et de more*); Isis answers the prayer and changes Iphis into a boy, so she can marry Ianthe and live happily ever after.[257]

We hear little of free and mutually reciprocal same-sex unions in the ancient Roman world. Juvenal mentions marriages taking place among men in the underworld of the *cinaedi*, but for that satirist (and no doubt most of his readers) this is the very height of depravity.[258] Probably it was only in that despised underworld of slaves and the impoverished free that really equal sexual unions — heterosexual or homosexual — could take place. Not much evidence has come down to us from those classes of society that could not write and patronized only the simplest arts. In the greatest Roman novel, Petronius' *Satyricon*, Encolpius and Giton are clearly lovers, clearly in a (usually) stable relationship but at the very bottom of the social ladder.[259] Likewise in fiction, Lucian of Samosata (second century CE) tells of a female prostitute named Megilla who is married to a woman from Corinth, which another speaker in the work regards as "bizarre."[260] A few funeral inscriptions may suggest "love in a hut" existed among Ancient Romans of the same sex. "Psamante, Furia's hairdresser, lived nineteen years. Mithrodates, the baker of Flaccus Thorius, put up this tombstone."[261]

We hear more about lesbian activity in the surviving Roman sources than in the Greek, but all we have is written by men and very unfavorable to lesbianism. Seneca the Younger tells us of a man who found his wife in the sex act with another woman and killed the other woman in a rage. He then appealed to the ancient Roman custom that allowed a husband to kill a man he found in his wife's bed.[262] Martial, the epigrammatist (about 40–104 CE), addresses three of his epigrams to the subject of "tribades," which he despises.[263] Generally we find the same distancing of homosexuality in regard to lesbian acts as we have observed in male-on-male sexual acts; the Romans generally chose to pretend that such things were uniquely Greek and belonged to the remote, non–Roman past.[264]

In instances where the word "marriage" occurs, the married persons of the same sex are almost always of very different classes, and the relationship is at least as much one of power as love. We hear of the emperor Nero marrying Sporus, though not before he had had Sporus castrated. It is worth noting that the marriage of Sporus and Nero took place while the emperor was on his tour of Greece,[265] and to some extent it is an aspect of the Emperor's well-known love of all things Greek (very unseemly for a Roman).[266] Tacitus says this marriage was one of the causes for the revolution that deposed Nero,[267] and rumor had it that Sporus was the one who finally betrayed Nero to his enemies, in revenge for what the emperor had done to him.[268] Curio the Younger (died 48 BCE is said by Cicero to have had a marriage-like relationship with a man named Antoninus,[269] though Curio later married Fulvia, who went on to marry Mark Anthony. We need not speak of the marriage-like relationship of the Emperor Elagabalus and the athlete Hierocles,[270] which was thought of as the same sort of moral monstrosity as that of Nero and his male spouses.

The singling out and stigmatizing of the *cinaedi* represents the second major step in the growth of homophobia in the ancient world. The first was the stigmatizing of homosexual acts, which had already occurred in Plato's *Laws*— in fact the statement in the *Laws* that homosexual acts make boys effeminate is a close approach to the "disease" stereotype. Furthermore, in Roman the only acceptable male sex-objects for those men who desired such objects were slaves or prostitutes (almost always slaves as well); passive homosexuality was identified with slavery, with a class of beings physically identical to their masters but not thought of as really human. The very thought of receiving anal or oral penetration caused a typical male Roman to think of himself as less than a full man — rather in the way that the thought of being descended from apes so disturbed the Victorians.

The process of stereotyping and creating out-groups is one of the most common and ancient of human practices. Some think that stereotyping is genetically motivated[271]; others see it as implicit in thought and language[272]— the very words "us" and "them" lend a positive glamour to us good people in the in-group and a corresponding negativity to those wicked out-group persons. "Just defining persons results in devaluing them," as Ervin Staub has said.[273] However, we should not think of such stereotypes as simply mistaken ideas — as one who had never been to Louisiana might think New Orleans was the state capital. Rather, stereotypes held against racial, religious or sexual minorities are deeply embedded in the minds and personalities of prejudiced persons and cannot be changed with a mere assertion of fact. Once a strong negative stereotype is formed, the reaction against it partakes of the nature of the "flight or fight" response in an animal that feels itself in danger, a knee-jerk reaction that involves little clear thought. A typical Roman male who felt that he was likely to be the object of another male's sexual desire reacted very much as though a bow were drawn and a poisoned arrow aimed right at him. If he did not flee, he tried mightily to kill the bowman. The Roman prejudice against passive homosexuality has lasted in the culture that succeeded the Roman Empire to this day.

Walter Lipmann, who pioneered much modern thought on stereotyping and the origins of prejudice, saw the stereotype as a defense:

> It is the guarantee of our self-respect; it is the projection upon the world of our own sense of our own value, our own position and our own rights. The stereotypes therefore are highly charged with feelings that are attached to them.[274]

Milton Kleg calls such stereotypes "concept prototypes," ideal mental pictures of the world that are used to fit new information into categories[275]— an idea strongly reminiscent of Plato's Forms. These stereotypes are inherently aggressive, changing everything that they encounter in the objective world till it occupies a place in the paradigm that is almost the soul of the observer. These "concept prototypes" change how the prejudiced person sees reality, and they change reality as well — they make the in-group different as well as the out-group.[276] The process feeds on itself: the homosexual out-group becomes more distinct as it is separated from the in-group and internalizes some of the stereotypes of the in-group; and, to the degree that the stereotyped out-group is distanced from the in-group, the latter group has its prejudice intensified. Once perceived and stigmatized as an out-group by most Romans, *cinaedi* in a sense came into being where they had not existed before.

Most human beings are inherently bisexual. Research in the homophobic United States in the 1950s found that a large percentage of adults had had homosexual experience despite the heavy legal and religious prohibitions against such activity. In a heavily homophobic society many, perhaps most, persons repress their homoerotic desire and live with varying degrees of comfort the sort of sex lives society expects of them. Roman society permitted homosexual release freely to males who could afford attractive male slaves or the price of male prostitutes on the condition that the Roman master be the penetrator. Nevertheless it is clear that the desire to be penetrated by another man was too strong in some few Romans; such persons sought sex in defiance of both the state and the state's religion — the first queers.

When Scipio the Younger used the prejudices of his time as a convenient stick to beat his political opponent's head, Scipio himself probably enunciated his Latin a bit more carefully if that queer outgroup was thought to lisp. Senators standing to hear the speech may have half-consciously removed their hands from their hips. Perhaps the sale of light-blue togas declined ever so slightly. Of course Scipio was promoting prejudice — and the Roman ideal at the same time. Like the gladiator who chose to fight and die in the arena, and the audience that cheered as he did, Scipio, by destroying Gellius, was also condemning himself to the closet and winning the cheers of those who heard his speech.

7

Double Edged Homophobia: The Final Shape of the Classical Heritage

Two Christians, bishops in fact, were tried before the emperor; we know their names: Alexander of Diosopolis in Thrace and Isaiah of Rhodes. They were found guilty; no surprise. There were no accusers, and any witnesses against them would have been tortured into giving evidence, but there were no witnesses. The emperor had his reasons to want these men out of the way and that was enough; the *quaestor* and the officials under him received all the property of the victims.[1] The punishment was severe: mutilation. Alexander's genitals were sliced off with the short Roman battle sword, the *gladio*. Sharpened spikes were driven into Isaiah's anus. Then the two men, naked and bleeding, were dragged though the streets, where the crowd jeered at them. Many in the crowd were Christians, but they jeered too, jeered perhaps even louder in a certain nervous sort of way. Above the bloody spectacle, calm in the sun, a statue of the emperor as Achilles overlooked the scene.[2] The emperor seemed satisfied. The persons he wished to impress had no doubt been impressed; some people had learned their lesson. He had, as befitted an emperor who was the representative of divinity on earth, accomplished what should be done. As the crowd dispersed and a calm evening settled on the great city, the Emperor Justinian went in. The two pederasts were dead or dying. In a few days the emperor would be officiating at the great cathedral, at Hagia Sophia, calling himself the Thirteenth Apostle.[3] The Patriarch would put bread into his hands, telling the emperor it was the body of Jesus Christ, a Jewish peasant who had been nailed to a cross some 500 years earlier.

Why did Justinian want these men tortured in so horrible and public a manner? Probably as scapegoats. The "Thirteenth Apostle" had had a stormy relationship with the Church. Monophysitism, a much disputed theological problem in defining the nature of Christ, had troubled his reign. Justinian had barely survived a popular revolt, the Nika Riots in 532, aided by a brilliant general and an equally brilliant if unscrupulous wife, Theodora. In 541 bubonic plague hit the city; by 548 Theodora, still young, was dead of cancer. Moreover, the huge church Justinian had had thrown up in the space of five years, Hagia Sophia, had had half its great dome destroyed by an earthquake in 558.[4] Constantinople was built on the Anatolian Fault, one of the most earthquake prone parts of the world; but, to Byzantines in the sixth century, an earthquake was more likely to be attributed to the anger of God[5]; and this earthquake had affected the emperor's showpiece church. *Novella 77*, part of Justinian's personal addition to the monumental compilation of Roman law, the *Panedects* he had sponsored, specifically attributed famine, plague and earthquakes to homosexual "crimes."[6] With the need to blame someone for the disasters of his reign, homosexuals were a convenient target. Executing two bishops no doubt helped remind churchmen just who was in authority. Procopius, a contemporary historian, who portrays Justinian as "malicious, tyrannical, mischievous, malevolent, gullible, fatuous, flattery prone, greedy, hypocritical and actually demonic,"[7] tells us that Theodora often used unfounded accusations of homosexuality to eliminate her enemies.[8]

Justinian is a difficult man to like. By his own lights he saw himself as an almost god-like savior to the Roman people — a savior from themselves as much as from any barbarians. He stands at the very end of the classical age and the beginning of the Middle Ages. Looking back through the lens of Justinian's soul, we see the Besieged City — Rome threatened by barbarians without and paranoid about secret monsters within. Looking forward, we see already coming into birth the Medieval Synthesis; "already the concept of the heretic, the religious dissenter, not only as an enemy of Divine Truth, but as social menace and political traitor ... had clearly taken shape." Jews, Samaritans, homosexuals and pagans all suffered under the despotism of Justinian.[9] The vague, fuzzy image of a horribly unclean, dangerous, secretive sort of subhuman was brought to a perfection by Justinian and would haunt Western civilization for 1,500 years. However harshly we may judge the emperor, he no doubt believed in the righteousness of his acts,[10] even if they were motivated by a certain convenience. In his personal life, he was austere, hardworking and disdainful of all pleasures[11]; his only failing was an inability to distinguish his own will from that of God.

History is full of strange turns, ironies, sometimes of complete reversals. A thousand years earlier two male lovers, Harmodios and Aristogeiton, were acclaimed heros and martyrs in the name of freedom and democracy in the leading city of Greece. They were looked up to as almost divine, like Achilles and Patroklus, or Zeus and Ganymede; and their fame would be sung at a thousand symposiums. They were thought of as the new founders of Athens, as Gilgamesh and Enkidu had founded Erech in the dim dawn of legendary history. Now two men, bishops of the church, in Constantinople, the Greek-speaking capital of the Roman Empire, accused of doing the same thing between themselves,[12] were tortured to death by a Greek-speaking man who was surely one of the most thoroughgoing autocrats and tyrants who ever lived, an emperor who claimed to be the successor on earth of Jesus Prince of Peace, who may have had a male lover himself and who was executed under the authority of Justinian's distant predecessor, the Emperor Tiberius. For a long age of the world, the tyrants had won.

This chapter will look at the opening of the final stage in the growth and elaboration of homophobia in the classical world. Homophobia had originated in a theory in Greece, while the Romans on quite separate grounds had instituted a sort of half-homophobia, stigmatizing one partner only of the male-to-male sex act. By the time of the Emperor Justinian (527–565 CE) homophobia had taken on a form that was to survive though the twentieth century, regarding with horror all persons who engaged in same-sex acts. This new, full-blown homophobia was enshrined in Roman law and enforced with the full rigor of an absolute state that claimed to speak for God as well as humans. Isaiah and Alexander are the first victims of this homophobia whose names are known, though they would not be by any means the last.

Roman law, Roman style of government and the sheer prestige of Roman power were to dominate Europe east and west for more than a thousand years. The code of law enacted by Justinian became the model for European law down to today. The last monarchs claiming to be in some ways successors to Justinian died or were deposed in the First World War. How many persons were imprisoned, mutilated, or burned at the stake for homosexual acts cannot be known, but the number is vast. The number of persons who led lives crippled by fear, self-repression and denial is probably much greater. The last days of the Roman Empire inaugurated a slow, quiet, age-long genocide of homosexuals that has not yet ended.

In the last chapter we outlined a one-way homophobia, an attitude that condemned the receiving partner in the same-sex act, but not the penetrating one. The final form that homophobia took, the one Justinian embodied in his law code, was double-edged. Both the receiver and the penetrator were condemned, though the ethics of earlier Rome lingered to the extent that the receiving partner was regarded generally with greater contempt. Homophobia in its fullest sense, the form known today, has its origins in the Jewish tradition, mediated though Christianity, and is a synthesis of the philosophical and moral traditions of the latter Roman Empire. Following the death of Nero in 68 CE, a change began to come over Roman ethical thought. Its progress was slow and irregular. Although in many ways the later ethical thought of the Romans was a great improvement over the imperialist philosophy of Panaetius, one of its most distressing aspects is a complete homophobia. Most of the ideas behind this new, fully developed homophobia were not new; they had existed in Greek philosophy since Pythagoras, and in the Jewish tradition perhaps as long; however, it was in the context of the dominant culture of the late Roman era that these elements came together and were accepted as the general view of Western civilization. Without the sanction of Greco-Roman culture, it is unlikely that homophobia would have survived in the West as more than a curious idea mentioned in some ancient texts. So it is with the Greco-Roman culture that we begin.

Gaius Musonius Rufus (born about 30 CE) typifies many of the trends of his time; and, with his popularity and wide influence, he must be regarded as a major factor in the beginning of the trend toward full homophobia. An Etruscan by birth, he taught Greek in Rome, for the empire that had been a collection of nations held together by raw power was gradually melting into one culture.

Musonius Rufus entered the world stage in the reign of the last Julio-Claudian, Nero. The Conspiracy of Piso (67 CE) to assassinate Nero had been masterminded by philosophers or Roman aristocrats deeply influenced by philosophy. Seneca, the philosopher, and Lucan, the poet, were among the conspirators to die; and Nero exiled all the surviving philosophers from Rome. Musonius was recalled to Rome, perhaps by the short-lived Emperor Galba,[13] arriving in time to come between the soldiers of two more competing would-be emperors and prevent war in the city.[14] Vespasian, the winning emperor, befriended Musonius; and he and his disciples (especially Euphrates and Dio of Prusa) were prominent in the reign of Vespasian's son Titus.[15]

After the Jewish War, Titus, who had taken Jerusalem and burned the Temple, took Bernice, the daughter of Herod Agrippa, the last king of Judea, as his mistress. Apparently he was intending to marry her. This set off a sort of constitutional crisis in the Roman government: not only was Bernice not a Roman, but also the prospect of Titus marrying and having children threatened a new dynasty, not unlike the Julio-Claudians, who had ruled for more than a century (often disastrously) and certainly were holding power that the Senate still claimed. Although we do not have the details, there was a bitter confrontation over Titus' marriage in the senate, Vespasian emerging in tears and vowing that his son would succeed him. The essential issue was the choice between absolute monarchy vested in a Caesar and passing to his biological heirs, however qualified, and absolute power vested in the senate. The relevance for the growth of opposition to homosexuality in the Roman Empire is the argument between senate and emperor, which had a parallel on the philosophic level; and

Musonius Rufus was homophobic. Caesars like Domitian might indulge in forced homosexuality: the enemies of Caesar were generally homophobic. The question is the division we have mentioned earlier in Stoic philosophy. Panaetius and Cicero, his Roman follower, had remained at least in name Stoic, while renouncing the radical elements of Zeno's *Republic*, along with Zeno's approval of Greek pederasty. We have little information on the anti–Imperial Stoics in the Flavian era, though Tacitus does tell us that the philosophic Rubellius Plautus was accused of something like sympathy with "tyrannicides"[16] in the time of Nero. Probably we should see this as following Panaetius' view that the monarchy (which Stoics generally favored, if the monarch was a sage) was wisely vested in the senate.[17] Vespasian exiled all the philosophers from Rome, as Nero had done, excepting only Musonius Rufus, who was openly pro-monarchy — a king, he said, "is Law incarnate, the contriver of good government and harmony, the emulator of god and as He is, the father of his subjects."[18] Perhaps Musonius applied this to Vespasian personally, or as Edward Vernon Arnold speculates, refrained from political statements altogether[19] in the reign of an insecure, touchy emperor. Domitian, the second son of Vespasian, is known to have kept boys for his pleasure (we have mentioned Earinos, his cup-bearer) as Titus had, though he too persecuted the Stoics.[20] Musonius found himself in a difficult law case, though in general his persecution and that of other Stoicism advocates like Arulenus Rusticus seems to have been exclusively on the grounds of opposition to the tyranny of the rulers, not specifically their homosexual acts.

Musonius Rufus' philosophy survives in large fragments. The 21 short essays that have come down to us, written down by one of his pupils, Lucius,[21] read like more graceful versions of the Neo-Pythagorean tracts we have discussed earlier, in that they are not abstract philosophy, in the manner of, say, Aristotle, but practical treatises intended to tell his audience how better to live. Much of his advice seems today commonplace and unexceptionable. He follows the old Stoics in regarding women as equal to men,[22] since "they have the same parts of the body"[23] as men. The best life is that of a farmer, tilling the soil by hand, taught by a good man:

> Now I know perfectly well that few will be willing to learn in this way, yet it would be better if the majority of young men who say they are studying philosophy did not go near a philosopher. I mean the spoiled and effeminate [*malakoi*] fellows by whose presence the name of philosophy is spoiled.[24]

As in other Greek writings about this time the word *malakos* seems to have sexual overtones; the usual English translation, "effeminate," however, implies perhaps more than the Greek supports. We will return to the meaning of this word later. Here suffice it to say that this is a slap at the more traditional Stoic philosophers, who practiced pederasty with their students. The homophobia is far more explicit in Musonius' essay "Sexual Indulgence":

> Not the least significant part of the life of luxury [*turphes*] and sexual indulgence lies also in the use of boys [*paidikon*]. Such a life craves a variety of loves, not only female but male, not only lawful but unlawful. Sometimes they pursue one love, sometimes another; and not being satisfied with those who are available, pursue those which are rare and inaccessible, and invent shameful intimacies [*askhemonas zetountes*], all of which constitute a grave indictment of manhood. Men who are not wanton or immoral are bound to consider sexual intercourse justified only when it occurs in marriage and for the purpose of begetting children, since that is lawful, but unjust and unlawful when it is mere pleasure seeking, even in marriage. But of all sexual relations, those involving adultery [*moikheias*] are most unlawful; and no more tolerable are those of men with men because it is a monstrous thing against nature

[*hoti para phusin to tolmema*].... All intercourse with women without lawful character is shameful and is practiced from lack of self-restraint ... like [a] swine reproducing in his own vileness.

But what of the monster who has sexual relations with a female slave? What if his wife had sex with a male slave? ... One will not expect men to be less moral than women, nor less capable of disciplining their desires thereby revealing the stronger in judgment inferior to the weaker, the ruler to the ruled.... What need is there to say it is an act of licentiousness and nothing less for a master to have relations with a [female] slave. Everyone knows that.[25]

Finally, from Musonius' essay "What Is the Chief End of Marriage," we learn perhaps with no surprise that the chief end of marriage is producing children, but also "perfect companionship and mutual love in health and sickness and under all conditions ... each striving to outdo the other in devotion, marriage is the ideal and worthy of envy, for such a union is beautiful."[26]

Besides the above surviving works, there was an essay by Musonius called *peri paideis*, "On Education," now lost,[27] though since the Christian Clement of Alexandria drew many of his violently negative ideas about pederasty from this work, we may confidently surmise that Musonius' opinions on the subject were as negative as his opinions were of homosexuality in other contexts.

Little of this is new. The condemnation of homosexuality as against nature and leading to woman-like qualities in a man is ultimately from Plato's *Laws*, though one suspects that in the Stoic Musonius there is at least one earlier level of transmission, perhaps Panaetius.[28] More original here is the linking of homosexuality to uncontrolled pleasure-seeking, which is in turn condemned, both in the heterosexual and homosexual contexts. One suspects Pythagoreanism at this point, since the production of children gave pleasure an object to aim at, while pleasure for its own sake was related to the *aparon*, the evil Unlimited, opposed in Pythagorean thought to existence itself. Even sexual relations with one's wife are immoral if the object is not to produce children. Furthermore this must be seen in the context of the all but universal distrust of pleasure among moralists of every sort in the classical world; even good Epicureans took their pleasure in such careful doses that they were hardly less than ascetics. Yet, with a certain inconsistency, Musonius praises married life beautifully, in language that surely influenced the wedding vows developed in the Church many centuries later. He also restated what in the Christian context came to be called the "Alexandrian Rule"—that all sexual relations outside of marriage are immoral, though this again was foreshadowed in Plato's *Laws*. Of course same-sex love can produce the same sort of bonding, mutual care and companionship. However, such relationships were remote from the lives of most of Musonius' audience, who knew homosexuality almost entirely in the master-slave relationship. Free love requires free humans, and such were scarce indeed in the Late Roman Empire.

Most novel and most admirable here is the strong condemnation of sexual relations with female slaves. Although the connection is never made in the extant fraction of Musonius' works that we have, one strongly suspects that the hidden agenda in the condemnation of homosexuality is a humanitarian respect for male slaves as well as females. Musonius came the nearest of any writer we have from antiquity, Christian or pagan, to advocating the abolition of slavery.[29] Perhaps the source is the laws of Solon that protected male slaves from their masters' desire, though by the early second century CE the laws of Solon and the democracy they created were fast fading from human memory. As we shall shortly see, Musonius Rufus' disciple Dio of Prusa shared his teacher's homophobia and is far more explicit in his opposition to slavery.

The great importance of Musonius Rufus in the history of homophobia is not the originality of his thought, but its diffusion. He was admired by the great and preached to the common people. Origin of Antioch says he was ranked as equal to Socrates and that they were the two best men who had ever lived.[30] Like the unknown authors of the Neo-Pythagorean tracts, he was essentially a popularizer. His disciples were as famous or more famous than he: Aulius Gellius,[31] Artemidorus, Fundanius, Euphrates of Tyre, Athenodotus, Lucius, Pollio, and the greatest of all, Epictetus.[32]

Perhaps more famous in his time than his teacher was Dio of Prusa (about 40–117 CE), called *Chrysostom*, Goldenmouth, for his eloquence. He had begun as a Cynic, but converted under the preaching of Musonius to Stoicism; he wore the single, poor cloak of the Cynics nevertheless.[33] When Domitian was assassinated, he helped keep the army from revolting, earning the respect of Nerva and later the patronage of Trajan. At the same time Plutarch was advising the surviving aristocracy of Greece to calmly accept and live with Roman rule. There were riots in Alexandria, strife in Tarsus and unrest in Bithynia and Palestine; the speeches of Dio, of Plutarch the Platonist and others were often addressed to these situations; it is no understatement to say that in the early second century CE philosophers as much as soldiers and statesmen were holding the Roman empire together,[34] a fact that gave them great prestige.

In fact a new constitution for the empire was adopted, under general public pressure[35] at the death of Domitian, that represented the triumph of Cynic and Stoic ideas on the nature of kingship; the secession ceased to be hereditary, and became adoptive — the best man was adopted by an emperor from among the senatorial ranks and succeeded his adopted father.[36] Such filial adoptions were based on principles deeply embedded in Roman law; the man adopted became the son of the one adopting.[37] It implied no sexual relation, unlike the brother- making procedures discussed by John Boswell in *Same Sex Unions in Premodern Europe*. However, as we shall see, erotic considerations came to disturb the process before it ended when Marcus Aurelius could not bear to disinherit his unworthy son. Interestingly, though, Dio preached homophobia as passionately as Musonius had; while denouncing keepers of houses of prostitution, he argued that customers of such establishments (staffed with slaves) were a danger to the free population. He denounced homosexuality by implication while denouncing prostitution and adultery: "[Brothel keepers do not respect the gods, not even] Aphrodite whose name stands for that union according to nature of man and woman."[38] This "adultery committed with outcasts" (*atimous kai moikheias*) paves the way for assaults secretly on "women and boys of good families"[39]: "Bored with harlots, he seduces well-bred girls and married women; and, when that becomes too tedious, because it is easy, he turns in his last state of degeneracy to seducing boys."[40]

The moral concern here is not for the prostitutes (who were slaves and had no choice of profession), but for the upper classes who might be infected disastrously by the lust bred in the brothels. Further, homosexuality is again seen as an excess of lust. Sexual desire pitched at its normal level was thought to be naturally heterosexual; only when it had been excited to extremes did it veer off course toward males.

Pederasty still existed among the Greeks in Dio's time, evidently, for he makes a slighting remark toward it. A man may be "a pitiable victim of the desire for boys [*ho pros paidas athios ekhon*]."[41] Trajan, who commissioned him to preach around the empire, is known to have had a harem of boy-loves.[42] That Trajan abided by the constitutional arrangements set up by philosophers opposed to homosexuality and yet had many boy-loves may be more than simple human hypocrisy. The new constitution recognized that the emperor must preferably have no son or pass over an unworthy son who would remain as a threat to the adopted heir.

Quite possibly it was understood that emperors would be allowed slave-boys because the emperor could not safely indulge in sex with his wife. No fully safe method of birth control was known to the Romans, and the birth of a son could (as the birth of a son to James II did in England) upset a carefully balanced government. For a while the philosophers looked the other way.

Trajan adopted a distant relative of his, Hadrian, to be his successor. The relationship between Hadrian and his boy-love Antinous remains one of the great and tragic love stories in history, and is one that also changed subtly the course of attitudes toward homosexuality in the latter Roman Empire. Hadrian seems to have been completely homosexual in his tastes: he was married quite against his will to Trajan's niece, Sabina,[43] a marriage that seems to have been purely one of convenience, for Sabina hated Hadrian, and he hardly thought better of her.[44] Soon Hadrian was having affairs with the boys in Trajan's court, and there was a mild unpleasantness about this[45]— perhaps this is one of the reasons Hadrian was sent to Athens, where he was much at home (he met among others Epictetus).[46] When Trajan died in 117 CE, Hadrian succeeded as emperor. Information on the private life of Hadrian is scarce: we do not know just where or when he met the young man whose name is forever linked to his. Antinous was born in Claudiopolis, Bithynia, November 27, in either 110 or 112 CE— at least 34 years later than Hadrian.[47] Antinous' parents were lower-middle-class Greeks; he was an intelligent young man and well educated, probably in the school for pages in Rome.[48] Perhaps Hadrian met Antinous when the former was in Bithynia in June 123 CE[49] and sent the boy to Rome to complete his education.[50] The first mention we have of Antinous is 130 CE, when he was at least 18, on a lion hunt in Egypt with Hadrian.[51] Then, suddenly, Antinous died. Not enough evidence exists to establish the facts of Antinous' death beyond doubt; Royston Lambert has filtered and weighed the existing evidence as carefully as seems humanly possible and reaches the conclusion that Antinous sacrificed himself in an Egyptian magic rite for Hadrian.[52] Hadrian's health had been poor for some time, and it appears that an Egyptian seer told him or Antinous that Hadrian was dying and that the gods would accept another man in Hadrian's place. Antinous drowned himself in the Nile. The *Historia Augusta* says succinctly that Hadrian "wept like a woman.[53]

There was already scandal about the relationship of Hadrian and Antinous.[54] To those who held the old Roman ethics about homosexuality, Antinous was suspiciously old for the emperor; a sculpture of Antinous about 130 CE shows him growing a beard[55]; young men with beards are capable of erections and penetration. Almost certainly the traditionalists had begun to suspect that the two men's relationship had become reciprocal, which would have degraded Hadrian profoundly in their eyes. Furthermore, to those who hold the more modern view advocated by Musonius and other philosophers of his school, any homosexual relationship was disgraceful, regardless of the details of who is penetrated. Either way, Hadrian was becoming an object of scorn. We may add that there is slender evidence that suggests that Hadrian's wife, Sabina, was involved in a lesbian relationship with Julia Balbilia, a Greek princess, whom she had met about 109 CE[56]— the only real lesbian relationship in antiquity since Sappho where the names of both women are known to us. The Roman attitude toward female homo-erotic activity was more one of denial than of condemnation — it was thought of as something alien, bizarre and Greek, though there was no differentiation in the Roman view between active and passive lesbian behavior.[57]

The dead Antinous was immediately deified by Hadrian, without the usual consent of the senate, and the boy from Bithynia became the god Osiris-Antinous the Just.[58] Hadrian created a cult to honor Antinous, with images, temples, priests, and sacrifices throughout the whole empire; in Egypt the small village near which Antinous had drowned was converted into a Romanized city with a central temple to Osiris-Antinous where a hollow image deliv-ered oracles in the usual manner.[59] Among the Greeks and Romans he was worshiped as a manifestation of Dionysus in his suffering and death.[60] By virtue of his *kalokagathon*, beauty of body and of soul, he was a god of the dead and of resurrection,[61] not unlike the ancient Semitic Eshmun. The emperor's grief was, as Lambert has said, "flamboyantly histrionic and calculatingly political."[62] Politically the point was to effect a unifying link within the empire as a whole[63]— a Roman-sponsored god with an Egyptian name and central temple, and a Greek image and status, that recalled the glorious days of a free Greece when pederasty flourished at the center of Hellenic culture.

Apparently Antinous' mummified body was brought to Rome and buried by Hadrian in his own villa. Within a generation the tomb was deliberately desecrated, perhaps as a gesture of contempt for what Antinous represented, though more likely for reasons of simple greed.[64]

The last years of Hadrian were not pretty. His repression of the revolt of Bar Kochba in Palestine and his outlawing of circumcision both speak of a man with an "obsessive cultural mission" to establish Hellenism at whatever cost in the blood of others.[65] But in Roman eyes the events of the last six months of his reign were even worse. His health declining, he adopted as his heir a man in many ways inappropriate, Lucius Ceionius. Lucius was physically ill, the father of a young son,[66] Etruscan in background and effeminate. The only reason for the adoption seems to have been an erotic bond between him and Hadrian.[67] The young Caesar was widely unpopular.[68] Then on December 31, 137 CE, Ceionius suddenly died, it is said of a drug overdose.[69] Having for the second time in his life lost the only person in the world he loved, Hadrian went bloody-mad. In a six-month reign of terror, many prominent senators were killed by imperial order, and more went into hiding. In a moment of lucidity before his death, July 10, 138 CE, Hadrian adopted a seasoned, mild and highly competent senator, Antoninus Pius, as his heir, along with a 15-year-old distant cousin to be Antoninus' heir— Marcus Aurelius.[70]

Politically, Hadrian had left the empire in good hands, but the relationship with Anti-nous (who was probably expected to be the heir adoptive), followed by the adoption on erotic grounds of a man hardly suited to be emperor surely must have put homosexuality in even deeper disfavor than the harangues of Musonius and Dio. Many Romans during the blood-bath of Hadrian's last half-year must have recalled (as they had in the reign of Nero) the leg-endary history of Aristodemos, the boy-seducing Greek tyrant who had almost destroyed Rome in its very beginnings; the link between homosexual desire and deadly tyrannical power was deeply rooted in the essential Roman myth, and Hadrian's allowing love to cloud his judg-ment till murder was the order of the day only repeated what Fabius Pictor and the other old historians had said, and confirmed the popular Stoics' admonitions.

Marcus Aurelius succeeded to the throne on the death of Antoninus (161 CE). His *Med-itations*, like no other book in the classical canon, lets us into the mind of the strange, sad man who presided over the Indian summer of the empire. The *Meditations* begins with a sort of litany of persons Aurelius is thankful for because they helped to form his good character. Included in the list is his "father"— that is his adoptive father, Antoninus, who *"to pausa ta peri tous erotas ton meirakion"* (put a stop to the love of large boys).[71] The specific word "large boys" here almost certainly glances back at the relationship of Hadrian and Antinous,[72] but it is not quite clear in this passage whether Aurelius meant that Antoninus opposed all homo-sexual acts, or only those, like Hadrian's relationship with Antinous, that put the older man in the awkward situation of looking openly like a *cinaedus*.[73] Later in the first book a bit of self- revelation casts a bit more light on the matter. Marcus is thankful that he "did not play the man before my time, but even delayed longer ... that I did not touch Benedicta or

Theodotus, but even in later years when I experienced the passion of love I was cured."[74] We do not know anything further about this Theodotus, but it is clear that Aurelius had felt sexual desire for him and repressed that desire. The clearest and most interesting piece of homophobia in the *Meditations* is in the third book:

> To receive impressions through the senses is not denied even to cattle; to be puppets pulled by the strings of desire is common to wild animals and to men-women [*androgunon*] and to a Phalaris and a Nero. Yet to have the intelligence as a guide to what they consider their duty is an attribute of those who do not believe the gods ... who do their acts behind closed doors.[75]

Aurelius extends, one might say reverses, the conventional Roman image of the tyrant who was said to make other men into women by using them sexually, declaring that Nero had made himself into a woman. He could hardly have said the same about Hadrian, even if (as is quite likely) he believed it was true. He owed his throne to Hadrian. He brackets men-women with those who do not believe the gods, suggesting a deep religious prejudice against homosexuality, probably Orphic, though the emperor was deeply imbued with Stoicism. One suspects that the religion of his family was Orphic, while a compromised Stoicism was the official philosophy of his dynasty. Aurelius himself, if not his teachers, syncretized the beliefs of both systems on the issue of homosexuality, probably on the hasty assumption that it was "against nature." The final irony is that those persons whom the emperor denounced for acts behind closed doors are identified as the Christians.

Certainly there must have been more intellectual temptation for Aurelius; his teacher of Greek oratory was Herodes Atticus,[76] famed for his pederasty in the Greek manner. Cornelius Fronto, who taught the young emperor-to-be Latin oratory, was one of his favorite teachers (he asked the senate to honor Fronto with a statue).[77] Fronto wrote a number of letters to his pupil that are full of stylized, often light-hearted flirtation, calling him "lover" and wanting to kiss him (Aurelius was 25 at the time). Yet at the same time Fronto warns Aurelius against men who write love poems to boys and used magic philters to gain their love.[78] Hadrian, too, was in close contact with the young Aurelius.[79] All in all, it seems we must accept the statement at full value and conclude that the scruples against homosexuality originated in Antoninus, probably both out of personal taste (Antoninus is not recorded to have had any boy-loves), religion and political expediency. Hadrian, in trying to harmonize the Greek Eastern Empire with the Latin West, had revived Greek ideals of equality, which were linked to pederasty. In some ways Antoninus continued the policies of Hadrian; but, aristocratic and rather old-fashioned senator that he was, he was not about to let the ideas of equality get out of hand. Yet Epictetus, pupil of Musonius Rufus, "spoke of homosexual and heterosexual attraction in terms of complete equality"[80]; and Philostratus of Lemnos wrote in its praise, about 200 CE, a beautiful collection of letters, many of them addressed to a young man, that stand as the last masterpiece in the history of Greek pederasty. The picture we get at the end of the second century, both at the court and in intellectual circles, is mixed with regard to the acceptance of homosexuality.

Yet Aurelius did not abide by the constitution that his beloved philosophers had devised. Boys were out of the question for him, and he was married to Antoninus' daughter, Faustina. They had a son, Commodus, born after he took the throne. In theory it was Aurelius' duty to remain biologically sonless as his seven immediate predecessors had, and hand the empire over to some worthy adopted successor. But Faustina was very beautiful,[81] and Aurelius was not the perfect sage of the Stoics, who was to be above all passion. Almost certainly Antoninus, in marrying his daughter to Aurelius, foresaw that his biological grandson would inherit the throne. Probably the succession of Commodus, with which Gibbon begins *The Decline and Fall of the Roman Empire*, was a triumph not so much of sexual desire over prudence as of patriarchy over philosophy.

There is much to admire in the teachings of the New Stoics, as there is in the Neo-Pythagorean writers — and that made them all the more dangerous for their vehement denouncing of homosexuality. Certainly Musonius' antislavery speeches led to legislation that improved the lot of slaves. Hadrian decreed that no slave might be arbitrarily tortured, mutilated, killed or used as a prostitute[82]; and Antoninus "was inexorably against any master who killed a slave. Anyone who killed, starved or otherwise misused a slave was deprived of him."[83] Marcus Aurelius, for all his philosophizing about free speech, democracy and equality, was very conservative in maintaining the distinction between the free and the slave.[84] Musonius Rufus and his followers left a dual homophobia deeply embedded in the minds of a great many ordinary citizens of the Roman Empire, and it remained for Christianity to take up those ideas, make them universal, and, in the person of Constantine, take them to the throne.

Of Commodus, the son who succeeded Aurelius, there is little to be said. He came to the throne at 18. After making a hasty peace with the invaders his father had died while fighting, Commodus rode in triumph into Rome, turning often to kiss the boy who held a golden wreath above his head.[85] The philosophers were gone who might have said that a more worthy man should have been adopted, instead of this chance of biology. Wishing to show off his athletic ability and to imitate the glory of Hadrian, who had killed a lion that was attacking Antinous, Commodus had a lion brought to the amphitheater, and killed it before the people[86] — an act that rather than glorifying him, reduced him to the level of a gladiator. Secure in power after killing his sister, who had conspired to depose him, he left the government of the empire to one of the prefects of the Praetorian Guard, Perrinis, and amused himself with a harem of 300 boys and 300 girls.[87] We have no gauge of how this more subtle indication of his athletic ability was regarded by the Roman people, but the drain on the treasury was unpopular,[88] and his indiscriminate adoption of foreign religions was even less popular with the Roman people.[89] This bringing in of non–Roman cults seems to be a feeble imitation of Hadrian again and a recognition that the empire lacked a central cult that could unite it under some banner other than the naked power of armies.

We hear little from pagan writers about homosexuality in the Roman context after Commodus. In a dizzying cycle of civil wars, emperor succeeded emperor purely on the basis of who won a battle or offered a larger bribe to the Praetorian Guard. We may mention Septimus Severus (193–211 CE), who outlawed the forcing of male slaves into prostitution. Trying again, the emperor Philip the Arab (235–48 CE), who is said by Aurelius Victor to have seen female organs in a sacrificed boar and seen a male prostitute who resembled his son; perceiving this as an oracle, he outlawed male prostitution.[90] The law seems to have had little effect, but the occasion of its enactment says much about the intellectual climate of the era. Both laws seem to have had their focus on a humanitarian regard for the rights of slaves rather than homophobic prejudice. Probably far more significant in the extension of homophobia was the law of Caracalla, Severus' son, enacted in 212 CE, that made practically all free persons in the Roman Empire full Roman citizens.[91] The result was that any Greeks who had not already adopted the *mores* of the Romans with regard to homosexuality were now legally compelled to do so.

UNOFFICIAL PHILOSOPHY

If we turn to philosophers more distant from the throne than Musonius and Dio, Plutarch of Chaeronea (about 46–120 CE) presents us with a somewhat mixed picture. He had been initiated in the mysteries of Dionysus, and taught for some time in Rome. Hadrian is said in medieval legend to have been his pupil. Late in life he retired to his home town and wrote extensively.[92] Plutarch's "Erotic Dialogue" (*Erotikos*) is the sole surviving example of what seems to have been a genre of philosophic writing in ancient Greece (and even Plutarch's *Erotikos* has survived though a single, damaged manuscript). The scene is probably chosen to remind its readers of Plato's two outdoor dialogues: the *Phaedrus* and the *Laws*, the one dealing favorably, the other less so, with homosexual desire. The speakers are at the shrine of the Muses on Mount Helikon, glancing at the Athenian Stranger on his way to Mount Ida, and suggesting we should expect a harmonious reconciliation at the end of this dialogue. The dialogue begins with a troubling question: a young man known to the speakers is about to be married to a rich widow; is it not likely that the situation of being younger and financially inferior to his wife will impair his manhood (753 C)?

The case of the young man marrying a widow turns into an argument over the worth of heterosexual married love compared to homosexual love. Protogenes claims idealistically, if not Platonically, that

> since it is necessary for producing children, there is no harm in singing its [Eros'] praises to the muses. But genuine love has nothing to do with women's quarters.... There is only one genuine love, the love of boys.... You see it in the schools of philosophy or perhaps in the gymnasia.... Love in fact attaches itself to a young and talented soul and through friendship brings it to a state of virtue [*areten*], but the opposite for women has for net gain only an accrual of pleasure and the enjoyment of a body [*somatos*].[93]

A speaker has some harsh things to say about men who approach boys pretending to be philosophers wishing to teach them, but are really only interested in sex. "They assume the outward airs of the learned ... so as to be safe from the law."[94] We would like to know what law is referred to. The opening of this paragraph refers vaguely to "many things that have happened in Greece," so Plutarch may be veiling a reference to some law imposed by foreign powers (Macedonian or Roman) that limited homosexual activity. A good guess would be the adoption of some form of Augustus' pro-family legislation by the "free" Athenians as a gesture of flattery toward Rome—but evidence is lacking.

There may be irony in Protogenes' justification of married love, since we are not sure if the rich widow is young enough to bear children to her young husband. Plutarch's father gives a long historical collection of examples of men who have been dominated by their wives and have thereby become "weak and effeminate [*heauton kai malakian*]."[95]

The fragmented state of the work does not always allow us to be sure who is speaking, but the opponent of pederasty states a familiar argument: The love between males is against nature (*para phusin*) while opposite sex love is "natural and normal [*te phusei khromenon*]."[96]

Later we read:

> Who can be patient when men revile Aphrodite [sex, especially physical] claiming that when she joins and accompanies Love [*Eros*] it is impossible for friendship [*philian*] to exist. Now of the union of male with male [*pros arren arrenos homilian*] it is rather not a union but a lascivious assault[;] it would be right to say[,] This is the work of Hubris, not of Cypris.
>
> That is why we class those who enjoy the passive part [*hedomenous to paskhein*] as belonging to the lowest depth of vice and allow them not the least degree of confidence or friendship.[97]

The language here offers a possible reconciliation with the remarkably positive assessment of pederastic couples in history that comes near the end of the dialogue. The word that

Helmbold translates as "those who enjoy the passive part" is related in the Greek not to "passive" in the English sense of "inactive," or "lacking motion." The Greek means rather "suffering," or "feeling pain." There seem only two possible explanations for Plutarch's word choice: either the act of receiving anal penetration was thought of as always notably painful, though surely any Greek knew better, or some sort of sexual act other than simple anal penetration is being referred to. "The union of male with male" is a none-too-common term in Greek to describe homosexual acts (we have met it before in Plato's *Laws*). I would suggest that the text glances at the sadomasochistic forms of homosexuality that we have seen becoming popular after the time of Alexander the Great. "Males with males" is used as a contrast to the *eromenons-eromenon*, man-boy love, that had flourished at the height of Greek civilization. The notion of one male hurting the other in the act of love goes against the ideal of friendship for our philosopher. It appears that Plutarch neither understood nor approved such relations where pain substituted for pleasure and looked with the deepest contempt on those who willingly seemed to surrender their freedom to enjoy. In context of the dialogue's question of the young groom and the older, wealthy bride, the unspoken fear is one of prostitution on the man's part, if not worse.

The quotation above is followed by a number of examples of young men who were abused or raped, and killed the older men who did it. In contrast to this, we get another collection of historical examples of male-male lovers who have behaved with all the virtues Plutarch admires — loyalty, courage, hatred of tyranny and mutual devotion (760B–762B). This is the fullest and clearest defense of pederasty surviving from antiquity. It ends with a messenger coming out of the machinery of the dialogue to announce that the wedding of the rich widow and her boy-toy has occurred. Happy wedding hymns are to be sung, and the dialogue concludes on a note reminiscent of Shakespeare's golden comedies.

Though homophobic statements are made in the course of the "Dialogue on Love," it seems untrue to call the work homophobic. It probably echoes the attitude of some in Greece at the time of its writing, admirers of Musonius and others who were trying to rid their culture of an activity which seemed entirely exploitative. Homosexuality in the dialogue is defended in terms of events in the remote past and criticized in the same terms. There are no contemporary examples here. Plutarch is at his best as an antiquarian, perhaps because he found the contemporary world of Greece too discouraging to contemplate.

Plutarch's dialogue on love is the earliest example we have of a debate on the advantages of homosexual versus heterosexual love; this sort of dispute became something of a minor genre in late antiquity, flourishing well into the Middle Ages.[98]

We get a more pessimistic assessment of the position of same-sex love in the later antiquarian Athenaeus of Naukritos, in Egypt. A political conformist, he was a friend of Ulpian, the famous Roman jurist.[99] He was writing about 230 CE, and his one surviving work is a huge dialogue, *The Wise Men at Dinner*, set at Rome.[100]

Much of the book is a discussion of food and ancient Greek symposia. Since homosexual courtship was part of symposia, the topic is discussed in Athenaeus' usual manner — long strings of citations from earlier writers. A speaker in the midst of this long discussion of boy-love sighs nostalgically, "It is a fact that even in ancient times they loved boys."[101] Later the speaker refers to the homoerotic poetry of Stesichoros, then about 800 years old, "so active was the pursuit of erotic affairs, since no one regarded erotic passion as vulgar."[102] Glancing back at Plato's *Symposium*, Athenaeus finds the discussion of love there "very indecent too [*mala aprepeis*]."[103]

Then later in the dialogue: "So beware you philosophers who indulge in passion contrary to nature, who sin against the goddess of love ... for boys are handsome even as the courtesan Glycera [Sugar] ... was wont to say, so long as they look like a woman."[104] This is followed by a string of anecdotes about impossible love—passions for statues, a peacock, a dolphin, etc.

All in all, Athenaeus represents a stage beyond Plutarch. A scholar deeply read in the Greek tradition, he looks back on pederasty with a nostalgia he struggles to conceal. He has fully accepted, though not completely internalized, the new Roman attitude of complete suppression. Unlike the speaking genius of Plutarch, there is no creativity left in our collector of facts, only an inert nostalgia. Perhaps the saddest note with regard to the end of Greek homosexuality comes from the anonymous Byzantine copyist of Manuscript A, produced in the tenth century CE. At 602D, Athenaeus is discussing the opposition of tyrants in the sixth century BCE to male lovers, and the copyist explains with a note on the margin that this was because "they fear their unified spirit."[105] After 1,600 years the facts were not forgotten.

Neo-Pythagoreanism did not end with the publication of the documents discussed in the last chapter. Philosophers in the second century CE began to publish under their own names, and we hear of Nichomachos of Gerasa, Numenius of Apamea and Moderatus of Gades, to mention some whose works have survived. Moderatus in the first century CE developed the Pythagorean notion that things are numbers to the point of defining the human soul as a number—the number four.[106] Nichomachos extended the theory in his *Numerical Theology* (which claims that the various gods of the classical pantheon are numbers), positing a god-number that is "male-female, thus in some way matter."[107] Matter then is both bisexual and evil. For these philosophers the world that can be sensed—felt, touched, and seen—was evil. They held, as Reale has said, that the "end of man involves distancing from the sensible and himself with the divine."[108] Losing the rational to the soteriological, they came to look on the increasingly mythologized Pythagoras as a prophet and wandering sage; again Reale: "Pythagoras became for the Pythagoreans what Christ was for the Christians, the son of god in human form, and his philosophy became a divine revelation."[109] Numenius, like the anonymous authors of the Pythagorean texts before him, claimed that Socrates and Plato were Pythagorean or taught doctrines that originated with Pythagoras, as did the wise men of the Jews, the Egyptians and the Persians; "Plato was just a Moses talking Greek," he wrote.[110] However, those works are extremely abstract and there is little evidence to tell us what, if any, opinion these later Pythagoreans held on homosexuality—probably the same that we have seen in the earlier documents. The final importance for Pythagorean thought in the history of homophobia is rather in a sort of underground Pythagoreanism that produced a hybrid philosophy and influence Western thought down to the present.

Plotinus, the great exponent of Neo-Platonism, was born in Egypt about 205 CE. He seems to have been culturally completely Greek.[111] He studied under Ammonius Saccus (about 175–250 CE), a porter by trade in Alexandria, along with Origin the (future) Christian. Porphyry tells us that Ammonius was raised a Christian, but left the Church when he came into contact with philosophy[112]; if Plotinus got his homophobia from Ammonius, we may suspect it was Christian, though Plotinus later urged pupils to study the wisdom of the Persians and Hindus. This idea may have come from Ammonius; and both cultures at the time had a distinctly developed homophobic element[113]; nevertheless it seems that we need look no farther than the Pythagorean tradition to find homophobia in the Alexandrian schools. At 39, Plotinus followed the Emperor Gordian, who was invading Persia. Plotinus hoped to meet magi who would tell him the secrets of the East; but, when Gordian met victory and assassination, the philosopher fled to Rome, where he taught until his death in 270 CE. Porphyry's life of his teacher begins with this unforgettable sentence: "Plotinus ... seemed ashamed of being in the body." We learn farther that when he was suffering from a bowel disorder for which his physician recommend an enema, he refused it as "unsuitable." Plotinus also "avoided the bath,"[114] meaning the public baths of Roman where nude males often saw each other. His work, collected and edited by Porphyry, has come down to us complete in one large book, the *Enneads*. Baine Harris, a Plotinus scholar, has said of Plotinus' style: "The *Enneads* probably deserves to be called the world's worst written book," though, he says, it is also one of the world's most influential books, popular in its time,[115] for Neo-Platonism in the Western tradition is "one of the basic intellectual forces, sometimes open, sometimes hidden, in the evolution of philosophy and theology ... a force that usually operated with some other interest."[116] Plotinus recognizes a triple division in the universe: objects of sense (inherently evil), objects of intellectual perception (Plato's Ideas or Forms) and the One. Salvation begins by living a moral, responsible life. Next one turns away from the objects of sense toward the Forms. Finally one in a leap of insight grasps the One and identifies one's soul with it.[117] The rejection of matter springs ultimately from the effort in the *Timaeus* and the *Laws* to explain evil by positing the soul as the source of all motion in the universe and asserting that an irregular motion exists in "the nurse or receptacle," what Aristotle was later to call *hyle* or matter.[118] The One is a Pythagorean concept, identified by Plotinus with God in Plato, though in Plotinus it becomes the "base unity of all metaphysicals. It is nothing because it is everything."[119] The One has no love for what proceeds from it,[120] yet intellectual love of the One is the only transcendence possible and a participation of the mortal soul in eternity.

Loving the unloving number from which the universe emanates seems very far indeed from the *Symposium*'s notion that love of another individual (specifically of a boy by a man) is the first step on the ladder to God. Yet Plotinus claimed to be only an interpreter in a scholastic sense of the wisdom of Plato — though clearly he is biased.[121] Again, dualism is a source for homophobia. Much radical dualism almost certainly came to Plotinus from the long-lived Platonic school of Apamea in Syria, which was deeply influenced by Zoroastrian ideas.[122] By the time of Plotinus, if not earlier, the *Vendidad*, part of the Zoroastrian scriptures, ranked male homosexuals among those criminals who may be killed on the spot.[123]

Certainly Plotinus was homophobic. In Porphyry's life of his teacher, we read that when one Diophanes "maintained the pupil for the sake of advancement, should submit to the teacher without reserve, even to the extent of criminal commerce, Plotinus started up several times to leave the room but forced himself to remain."[124] One could argue of course that what Plotinus objected to was not homosexual acts, but a kind of pedagogic prostitution. However, the *Enneads* make it clear that he objected to any form of homosexual acts:

> Those forms of Love that do not serve the purposes of nature are merely accidents attending on perversion ... they are merely accompaniments of a spiritual flow which the soul exhibits in the total of disposition and conduct. In a word; all that is truly good in Soul is according to the purposes of nature and within it appointed order, all this is Real Being.[125]

Plato's *Symposium* views all sexual acts as generative, especially homosexual ones; Plotinus' system is forced to ignore this and gets around it none too gracefully.[126] He disapproves of homosexual acts because nature "looks toward beauty and the definite [*aoriston*], which is in the column of the good."[127] Unable to perceive the generation of the *polis*, the city or community that is inherently founded by each pair of same-sex lovers in Plato's understanding, Plotinus sees homosexual love as indefinite, not part of the arithmetically perfect universe, and therefore in the Pythagorean column of evil.[128] This is perhaps understandable if we consider how far Plotinus of Lycopolis, in the Roman Empire, was from the city-states defended by armies of lovers in Plato's time.

This is as full an explanation as we have in classical sources of the argument that homosexuality is "against nature," and it depends on the Pythagorean concept of things as numbers and numbers as things. Sex, seen as an act solely in the realm of "nature" and therefore a "natural" or "unnatural" act, ignores completely the fact that sex involves two people — a political act. Having perceived order in the universe, by a kind of huge overgeneralization, the Pythagoreans assumed that, if the purpose of something was not clear or apparent, it was both purposeless and bad. One is reminded of Dr. Pangloss in Voltaire's *Candide*, who argues that the existence of noses proves humans were intended to wear glasses.

Like much of the philosophical tradition, the medical tradition, which had early and deep contacts with Pythagoreanism, carried a deeply embedded homophobic tradition into the Late Roman Empire. Famous physicians whose works remained authorities in the medical field for over a millennium had notions that were either directly homophobic or implied a homophobia. Galen of Pergamum (born 129 CE), court physician to Aurelius; Orisbasius; Rufus of Ephesus; and Soranos all taught that the emission of semen is weakening, while men who conserve that bodily fluid grow bigger and stronger.[129] Reasonably then, a wise man would only have just enough sex to reproduce and would not endanger his life with homosexual acts. Artemidorus of Ephesus regarded both lesbian desire and the desire in men to be penetrated as a form of sickness.[130] Soranos diagnosed in his *Guniacia* the desire of a woman to have sex with another woman as specifically caused by an unnaturally large clitoris and prescribed surgical removal of that organ as a cure.[131] The opinion that same-sex desire was a form of illness lingered in the medical community somewhat longer than the habit of bleeding and the administration of powered mummies as a medicine, being renounced by the American Psychiatric Association only in 1971.

The work called *Problemata* and once attributed to Aristotle was probably written in the period of late antiquity, which we are discussing; the unknown author of the *Problemata* treats male homosexuality in a medical context. The sperm ducts in some men, we are told, lead to the anus rather than the penis, so that the anus craves friction rather than the penis. Men who desire such passive sex are more likely to be either lustful (*largos*) or soft (*malakos*). Such men are "naturally womanish" (*hoi phusei thaludriai*); here the term seems to be purely based on a physical analogy: the anus that craves friction is equated to the vagina. Other men have sperm ducts that allow semen to gather either in the anus or the genitals and may have sex either by penetrating or being penetrated. Though the *Problemata* sees male homosexuality in purely physical terms (however erroneous), it also speaks of "habit" that can become like nature.[132]

A more distinctly pseudoscientific book, the *Oneirokritica* (*Judgment of Dreams*) by Artemidorus the Dalian of Ephesus (flourished in the second century CE) is an important witness to the popular understanding of sexual ethics in lower classes of the Roman Empire. His theories of dream interpretation are largely derived from Posidonius the Neo-Stoic (mentioned earlier as a disciple of Panaetius), though Artemidorus collected data for his specific dream interpretations in marketplaces and at festivals.[133] The great value of the *Judgment of Dreams* is that Artemidorus classifies dreams according to whether the thing dreamed of is according to nature, law (*nomos*) or custom (*ethos*). From a careful study by Bernadette Brooten of the *Judgment of Dreams*, the following principles emerge: Male-to-male sex is natural, legal and customary, whereas masturbation, sex between women (both the active and the passive) and autofellatio are unnatural acts. It was legal and customary for a man to penetrate a male servant and to be penetrated by an older or richer man. To be penetrated by a slave was legal but unlucky.[134]

Astrology in the Hellenistic age was not quite the fortune-telling popular entertainment it has become in our age. The stars were thought to control earthly fate; and, by a study of their inexorable courses, astrologers like Ptolemy and Vettius Valens achieved something like the philosophical mood — an indifference to fate.[135] Astrologers, too, could be quite homophobic in the Imperial age. Julius Firmicus Maternus, who wrote a textbook, *Matheseos*, on that art about 334 CE, lumped together *cinaedi*, eunuchs and viragos as persons guilty of *impuritas* — impurity[136]; and another writer on astrology, Hephastion of Egyptian Thebes, likewise considers *cinaedi*, tribades and eunuchs, as a group, all guilty of "unnatural acts."[137] Such stargazers did not create the opinions they voiced. Contempt for these classes of person was deeply imbedded in the intellectual culture. The eunuchs so condemned were probably slaves used for sexual pleasure by their masters.[138] The rather doubtful zoology expressed in the *Physiologus* likewise helped carry homophobia into the Middle Ages. The work is a bestiary, an often fanciful description of animals, dwelling long on the uncleanness of weasels and hyenas and their homosexual activity. The book went though an amazing number of translations and versions and rivaled the Bible for its popularity throughout late antiquity and into the Renaissance.[139]

Novels too reflect the temper of the times in which they were written; the Greek novel is one of the more pleasant developments of Hellenistic culture, and we find at best mixed signals about homosexuality in the surviving Greek works in this genre. Generally the central couple in a Greek novel are male and female, and the plot turns on the rather new idea of sexual love leading to marriage. Eros, which had been largely thought of as a homosexual god, now becomes a god of marriage and reciprocal loyalty and what we might recognize as "love."[140] Homosexual lovers occur as secondary characters generally, and their attraction is always asymmetrical — man-boy love, with the man chasing and the boy often fleeing or being caught between two aggressive men. The point of the novel is to exhibit the sentimental, conjugal loyalty of the heterosexual couples in contrast to the homosexual ones.[141] Achilles Tatius, writing about 380 CE in his *Leucippe and Clitophon*, has his characters going from Berytus (Beirut) to Alexandria; on the way the men fall into a conversation over which is better: boy-love or heterosexual activity; it is noted that boys get only pain from sexual union with men, while another speaker in the novel maintains that homosexual love between males is civilized and cultured.[142] In Xenophon of Ephesus' *An Ephesian Tale* (before c. 200 CE) the robber Hippothous has a remarkable sex life. His first love, a boy, was drowned; now he is in love with a boy, Habrocomes, and a girl, Antheia; he treats Habrocomes better than Antheia, but eventually leaves him for another boy. Written in the world of postdemocratic Greece, such novels view male-male sex as hardly more than comic relief; pederasty belongs to the world of dominance and submission the central lovers are trying to escape.

No history of homophobia in the later Roman Empire could be complete without a discussion of Apollonius of Tyana. Though he was reportedly born in the year 4 CE, most of our information on him comes from the *Life of Apollonius*, written by Philostratus at the command of the Empress Julia Domna, wife of Septimus Severus (who reigned 193–211 CE). The work is relentlessly homophobic. We know that Julia Domna was estranged from her emperor-husband, though details are lacking — perhaps Septimus Severus chose to practice pederasty in the old Roman fashion, and his wife resented it. Julia Domna was a Syrian by birth, and in her literary circle were Greek speakers. Philostratus in the *Life* relentlessly glorifies the Greeks,[143] so that another agenda working beneath the book's surface may be to both gratify the philhellene empress and exculpate charges of homosexuality leveled at the Greeks by homophobic Romans. It must be noted that little if anything that Philostratus says about his subject is reliable as history; though the book represents itself as a genuine biography, the *Life of Apollonius* is best regarded, as G.W. Bowerstock has pointed out, as a novel.[144] Nevertheless it is a novel commissioned by an empress and written by one of the leading pagan authors of its time, and therefore it carries considerable weight as a witness to the ethics admired by upper-class Greeks and Romans in the early third century CE.[145] We hear of a legal opinion by the jurist Paulus (exiled by Elagabalus and recalled by Severus) that a man who willingly allowed himself to be penetrated by another man would forfeit half his estate to the government.[146]

The work introduces itself as an apology. Philostratus says that he is writing to correct misunderstandings about its subject; the problem was that Apollonius was regarded in some circles, it seems, as an "intruder into philosophy," and people were unaware of his "genuine wisdom" and did not think he was an "honorable man" when in fact he was a follower of Pythagoras.[147] We have some traces of an anti–Apollonius tradition. Someone named Moeragenes wrote a substantial work that seems to have been critical of the Sage of Tyana[148]; and Lucian of Samosata, writing a century or so earlier than Philostratus in his satirical *True History*, portrayed Apollonius as a babbling religious fraud, fond of seducing boys. Hypocrisy in this latter regard is one of Lucian's stock jokes, so we may take it with a grain of Attic salt. Whatever the truth — saint or Rasputin — Julia Domna wanted Apollonius' reputation cleared up, and she got it in the *Life*.

Apollonius was, according to legend, the son of Zeus and a mortal mother, his birth attended by a lightning bolt that hung in the sky and did not fall[149]; the story is clearly an Orphic fable — the lightning bolt of Zeus had burned up the Titans, but Apollonius was declared free of Titanic *hubris* by the retreating bolt. At 15, Apollonius resolved to live the Pythagorean life.[150] We are explicitly told that Pythagoras in his office of lawgiver had declared that a man should not have sex with anyone except his wife, but Apollonius went Pythagoras one better and declared that he would neither marry nor have sex with anyone.[151] Perhaps we should see this in Orphic terms: Apollonius could dare to remain childless because he was so pure; fearing no retribution for unpurged hereditary sin, he need not have an heir. Soon Archelaus of Aegae, the king of Cicilia, made a pass at the young Apollonius in what most Greeks of the time would have thought of as the most proper manner. Of course Apollonius refused him, calling him insane and filthy. Angry, the king threatened to have Apollonius beheaded. The prophetic young sage merely laughed and predicted that on a certain day Archelaus would be beheaded — which, we are told, happened.[152] It is worth noting that Archelaus, a client king to Rome, was in the bad graces of the Emperor Augustus at the time; and Augustus did have him beheaded (17 CE), alleging insanity in his political enemy.[153] Philostratus seems to have been somewhat worried that his apotheosizing of the celibate Apollonius might be taken as a condemnation of marriage. So while in Rome, the sage encounters the body of a girl who had died on the eve of her wedding, being carried to her funeral. He touches her, and she comes back to life, presumably to be married.[154]

Apollonius, in his wanderings in Egypt, met an admirable young man named Timasion. Timasion was himself a wanderer, for he was fleeing from his stepmother, who was in love with him. When the handsome young man in his late teens refused her, she put out the scandalous report that he preferred men to women, so he bought a boat and left home. Seeing Apollonius was a philosopher by the way he dressed and read books, Timasion joined him and, hearing his story, complimented his self-control. Timasion then introduced Apollonius to the Gymnosophists, an acetic community living near the first cataract.[155] The event probably has no basis in reality beyond the fact that incestuous marriage was common in Egypt in this era. The conjunction of homosexual erotic love and incest is a major anxiety for Apollonius.[156] In the context of the court of Julia Domna, for whom Philostratus is writing, it is worth noting that there were persistent rumors that Julia Domna and her son (mistakenly called her stepson) Caracalla were lovers and in fact married.[157] Philostratus explicitly claims to have found the story of Timasion in his source, but he almost certainly invented it to turn away (probably unfounded) suspicion regarding his patroness.

Apollonius (or rather his legend) represents the most complete development we know of pure Pythagorean shamanism. The commissioning of the *Life* by Julia Domna shows beyond doubt what sort of ethics she wished to embrace at the imperial court, which in turn set the tone for the whole ruling class of the empire. It was a mixture of religion and politics that was carefully designed to appeal to Roman superstition and fondness for authority. The wise man should teach as a lawgiver, he said[158]; like the legendary Pythagoras, he underwent incubation in the Cave of Trophonius, and came out with a book of oracles.[159] According to one story, he in fact never died but walked into a temple on the Isle of Lidos and was taken up to the gods, only to appear later to convince a skeptic.[160] Romulus, the first king of Rome, is said to have undergone a similar apotheosis, having been taken up in a cloud from the Campus Marius in 710 BCE,[161] which demonstrates once again that much of early Roman "history" is in fact made of Pythagorean fables. The Severan dynasty leaned on such legends to prop its authority and establish its moral credentials; and in turn that dynasty gave prestige to the same legends, causing homophobia, which had for centuries been a feature of Pythagoreanism, to strike ever deeper roots in the ethical code of Rome and finally of the Western world. As for Elagabalus, it seems fairly clear that his assassination was largely due to his open (screaming, indeed) passive homosexuality. We are told that he was "in heat" and could not command the respect of the army because he "was the recipient of lust in every orifice of his body," appointing men to positions of great power and authority on the basis of their penis size.[162] He sometimes dressed as and chose to be referred to as a woman and regarded himself as married to a famous male athlete, Hierocles. He was very much what we might call a gender-bender: to the utter horror of Rome, he brought his grandmother Varia into the senate and allowed her the rights of a senator there, the first and only woman to be allowed that right.[163] He was assassinated after a bit more than three years as emperor, on March 12, 222. In the usual bloodbath that followed the assassination, some of his especially hated followers were killed by being pierced up the anus.[164] This form of punishment for passive homosexuality was recalled in the time of Justinian. What in 222 CE was an act of individual mutilation by enraged homophobic soldiers, became under Justinian a matter of legal punishment, officially sanctioned. The act is rich in symbolic implications; the perpetrator was reversing the quality of an act that had been originally performed for pleasure into one of pure pain. The spear or sword in substituting for the penis becomes a violent thrust of defense against the "feminine" desire for penetration. Varia in the senate, taking the role of a man at the very heart of traditional, patriarchal Rome, had exacerbated the fear of the Roman males till the murder of Elagabalus' friends had to be done by a sort of cold steel rape. The Latin word *pugna*, which normally means to fight, had since the time of Scipio the Younger been occasionally used to mean "to have sex."

When Julia Domna's great-nephew Alexander Severus became emperor (222 CE), we are told that he worshiped every morning in a private chapel (*lararium*), containing images of, among others, Orpheus, Pythagoras, Apollonius of Tyana and Abraham[165] — all representing traditions that carried homophobic elements. With Alexander Severus, we may leave off the narrative of the Caesars and turn to the religious traditions of Palestine for a final element that completes the homophobia of the end of the classical world. Undoubtedly the irresponsibility of Elagabalus had left homosexual acts, especially the passive role, in even greater contempt; and, for a century, popular philosophers with imperial patronage had preached homophobia all over the Roman world. We will not trace the accession of the terrible Diocletian, who converted the Roman state from a principate to a dominate — an even more absolute and highly centralized government. As security without declined and the barbarian howled at the door, freedom within declined, and it seemed ever more increasingly a question of survival that all things be orderly and all authority obeyed.

JUDAISM

The Jewish tradition enters history with homophobic legislation already in place. There are exactly two explicit references to homosexuality in the Hebrew scripture, both strongly disapproving. To these we turn first.

The science, or perhaps more correctly the art, of higher criticism furnishes us with all we may call history in regard to the origins of these passages. This movement of scholarship begins with Baruch Spinoza, who published (1670) his *Theological-Political Tractate* in Holland at a time when that book could have gotten its author burned at the stake anywhere else in Europe. In that work the "God Drunken Man" proposed a far later date for many of the books of the Bible than the orthodox maintained. The question of dates and sources was taken up into the vise-like grip of Prussian scholarship in the latter nineteenth century. Klostermann dubbed the texts we are primarily concerned with *Das Heiligkeitsgesetz*,[166] usually translated as the Holiness Code, of the Book of Leviticus and elsewhere. Discussion, criticism, modification and refinement of higher criticism has gone on for more than a century now: we can begin to speak with some certainty.

The traditional view is that the Torah, also known as the Pentateuch or the first five books of Moses, were written as a continual work by the prophet Moses (died 1451 BCE).[167] The Torah begins with an account of creation and proceeds though the deliverance of the children of Israel from Egypt and their receiving a body of law from God in the desert. This body of law has remained central to Jewish ethical thought and is (at least selectively) highly regarded by many Christians.

Using techniques for the close examination of literary texts (some of them developed to elucidate the text of Homer), scholars have shown that the Torah is in fact composed of a number of distinct documents, varying greatly in their age and origin, which were assembled into a steadily growing work by scribes over a period of centuries. The Yahwist narrative is probably the oldest in written form, dating perhaps to the reign of King David (about 1000 BCE). The Elohist tradition was written down two centuries or so later and fused with the Yahwist in the time of King Josiah (about 622 BCE), and so on.[168] The work we are principally concerned with, the Holiness Code, was the last major document added to the text of the Torah, and the Holiness editors are responsible for the final smoothing out of the text before it assumed its final form.[169] The fact that it was the last major document incorporated in the Torah does not mean that the Holiness Code is the youngest. Indeed, Artur Weiser has detected elements in the Holiness Code that go back to the very earliest times in Israel's history, before the tribal union that established the nation.[170] The main body of the Holiness Code in Leviticus runs from chapters 17 through 26. It appears to be an entire separate law code from that of its chronologically earlier predecessor, the Priestly Code, differing from that other material both in language as well as emphasis. Perhaps the most significant element that distinguishes the two codes is that the Priestly Code views only the Sanctuary area as a place that must be kept from all ritual defilement, while the Holiness Code sees the entire land of Israel as sacred and therefore to be kept undefiled.[171] The main thrust of the Holiness Code, as one would expect, is that Israel must be holy, both morally and ritually. Of course holiness is demanded of Israel in other threads of the tradition (e.g. Exodus 22.31 and

Deuteronomy 14:2, 21), but here it becomes "the leading motive of the entire section,"[172] with an almost obsessive force. The Book of the Covenant (Exodus 19:3 — 24:18), another work incorporated in the Torah, saw Israel's entitlement to the land of Israel as a sort of overlord-vassal relationship between God and the people (thought by A. Alt to be modeled on Hittite treaties). In a parallel, the Holiness Code is deeply concerned with the threat of expulsion from the land for unholiness.[173] If the Israelites pollute the land, it will "vomit them out," (Leviticus 18:25) as it had the earlier pagan peoples.

The Holiness Code forbids acts as varied as bestiality (Leviticus 18:23), slander (Leviticus 19:16) and a priest trimming the corners of his beard (Leviticus 21:5); but it also contains perhaps the most famous and seldom-obeyed injunction in the Bible or any other scripture: "You shall love your neighbor as yourself" (Leviticus 19:18).[174] We are concerned, however, with only two verses in the Holiness Code:

> Leviticus 18:22: And with a male you shall not lie the lying down of a woman; it is a *to'eba* [abomination].
> Leviticus 20:13: And as for the man who lies with a male the lying down of a woman, they — the two of them — have committed *to'eba*; they shall certainly be put to death; their blood is upon them.[175]

The Hebrew here is difficult to interpret; the best interpretation is that of Saul Olyan, whose work is based on strictly objective, scientific analysis of words and idioms in the Hebrew. Olyan concludes that what is being forbidden in 18:22 is the act of a male inserting his penis in the anus of another male. This prohibition is repeated in 20:13 with the change — awkwardly worded, at best — that now both the inserting and the receiving partner are condemned.[176] The word *to'eba*, usually translated as "abomination," is not specifically clear in the context of the Holiness Code, but generally it is used throughout the Hebrew scriptures (e.g. Deuteronomy 12:31) to indicate anything that God despises, from injustice to ritual uncleanliness.[177] The punishment of exclusion and death indicates the gravity with which the acts were regarded. The change from condemning the single partner to condemning both is notable in Leviticus' legislation on adultery as well, and seems to represent a later editing of the text.[178] What the text does not say is worth looking at as well. It condemns only one very specific form of homoerotic behavior. It does not deal with cult prostitution or any form of homosexuality that may have been practiced in Canaanite religion.[179] Furthermore, there is no convincing evidence that the passages are interested in gender boundaries as such, since originally only the inserting partner was condemned and the receiving one is more likely to have been accepting an improper role.[180] Nor are these laws concerned with insuring the fertility of the people, since other acts that might waste semen are not prohibited.[181] Female-to-female homosexual activity is not referred to at all.

Why then this? Again, the useful work of Saul Olyan suggests an explanation. Semen was considered a defiling agent in the Holiness Code; and, though not explicitly stated in the Holiness Code, it may be inferred from Ezekiel 4:9–15 that excrement was as well (Ezekiel "belonged to the Holiness school").[182] The command against male-to-male anal penetration seems to arise from the fear of mixing two defiling substances, excrement and semen.[183] By the same token, a man and woman who had intercourse when the woman is menstruating were to be cut off from the community[184] because semen and menstrual blood were both defiling elements. Hence there was no law forbidding female homosexual activity, since it does not generate any defiling substance,[185] nor are other forms of male-to-male homoerotic activity prohibited, since they do not threaten the creation of the doubly defiling mixture. In fact it would appear that all forms of homoerotic activity other than male-to-male penetration were left undisturbed by the legislation in Leviticus.[186] Hence the much discussed love of David and Jonathan, ("more wondrous your love to me than the love of women,"[187] said David of Jonathan), may have been quite erotic; but erotic desire would not have mattered to the ethical understanding of that time and place as long as no sodomy occurred.

There remains a word to be said about the initial formation of such rules of cleanliness and uncleanliness. We have no further specific information about the origins of the Holiness Code[188]; but, when we put that code in the context of the study of comparative religion and anthropology, some considerable understanding is gained. The inevitably linked concept of the pure and the impure exists with varying degrees of importance in virtually every culture known. Purity and impurity are not a duality; rather, they imply a trinity of forces. The impure person is thought to be out of harmony both with god or the cosmos, and the human community.[189] The work of Mary Douglas and other anthropological structuralists have shown that knowing what is clean and unclean in a given society can tell us with some considerable accuracy how that society orders its human relations. "Reflection on dirt involves reflection on the relation of order to disorder, being to non-being, form to formlessness, life to death."[190] Excrement and semen, like menstrual blood, are among the substances most commonly considered unclean; and, since such things are inevitable, the force of purity laws is not to eliminate them, but to carefully mark their boundaries, hence the boundaries of the society itself.[191] Again, to quote Mary Douglas: "The human body is never seen as a body without at the same time being treated as an image of society." Gasses, liquids or substances that go in or out of the body are considered dangerous because they bring into question the borders of the body.[192] It was precisely the borders of the Jewish state and of Jewishness itself that were deeply in contention in Palestine between the fifth century BCE and the first century CE. The legislation in Leviticus and elsewhere against menstruating women serves, as it does in other societies, to keep women in a subservient role and guarantees the dominance of men.[193] This aspect of male dominance is not directly tied to the prohibitions on homosexuality, though as we shall see when we turn to post–Biblical Judaism, male dominance becomes a major issue in regard to homophobia in the Rabbinic tradition.

Two further matters need to be mentioned in regard to homophobia in the Hebrew scriptures. First is the matter of the *kedesh* (also transliterated *qdesh*). The word occurs in Deuteronomy 23:18–19: "There shall be no *qdeshah* of the daughters of Israel; neither shall there be a *qdesh* of the sons of Israel. You shall not bring the hire of a harlot or the wages of a dog into the house of the LORD your God in payment for any vow; for both of these are an abomination to the LORD your God." The word also occurs in 1 Kings 14:24: "And there were also *kedesh* in the land. They did according to the abominations of the nations ..." (see also 1 Kings 12:15; 2 Kings 23:5–7). The difficulty here is that the meaning of the word is by no means clear and early interpretations differ.[194] The word *kedesh* originally meant simply "a holy one," hence a priest of some cult. The interpretation as "male cult prostitute" among the non–Jewish religions of Palestine, especially prostitutes who catered to male clients, cannot be confirmed: the evidence for male cult prostitutes who specialized in impregnating barren women is somewhat more substantial.[195] There is the very late testimony of Lucian of Samosata (died about 190 CE) who writes that there were male temple prostitutes who catered to males at Hieropolis in Syria; what they did was "a very sacred custom."[196] However, we don't know how old the practice was, or how widespread. Unless or until more evidence comes to light, we may suspect that some form of sacred androgyne is intended, but it seems best to suspend judgment.

Then of course there is the matter of Sodom and Gomorrah. Lot, the nephew of the patriarch Abraham, had settled with his family in the city of Sodom, according to Genesis

19. Two angels were sent to visit the city to find out if the rumor of its wickedness is fully true (Genesis 18:20–21. Lot welcomed them into his house, but

> before they lay down the men of Sodom, both young and old, all the people to the last man surrounded the house; and they called to Lot, "Where are the men who came to you tonight? Bring them out to us that we may know [*yada*] them." Lot went out to the men, shut the door after him and said, "I beg you my brothers do not act so wickedly. Behold I have two daughters who have not known man. Let me bring them out to you and do to them as you please; only do nothing to these men, for they have come under the shelter of my roof [Genesis 19:4–8].

The men of Sodom do not accept the offer but try to break Lot's door down. The angels send blindness upon the men of Sodom, and Lot escapes with his family in the morning.

> Then the LORD rained on Sodom and on Gomorrah brimstone and fire from the LORD out of heaven, and he overthrew those cities and all the valley, and all the inhabitants of the cities and what grew on the ground [Genesis 19:24–25].

It is not absolutely clear that the men of Sodom were trying to rape the male angels. The word *yada*, translated "to know," can mean "to meet socially, to become acquainted with," though it also carries the sense of sexual intercourse[197] (for example Genesis 4:1: "Adam knew Eve his wife, and she conceived ...") Since Lot seems quite horrified at what the men of Sodom want and offers his daughters in the tradition of protecting a houseguest at all cost, it seems safe to assume that what the men of Sodom had in mind was not a get-acquainted mixer with tea and cookies. Yet neither Genesis nor the numerous references to the Sin of Sodom elsewhere both in the Hebrew and Christian scriptures refer to homosexuality.[198] Even Ezekiel, the staunch proponent of the Holiness Code, sees the Sin of Sodom in a quite nonsexual context:

> Behold this was the guilt of your sister Sodom; she and her daughters had pride, surfeit of food, and prosperous ease, but did not aid the poor and needy. They were haughty and did abominable things before me; therefore I removed them [Ezekiel 16:49–50].

A parallel, indeed perhaps a double, of this text is the story in Judges 19. An unnamed Levite was traveling home with his concubine. They stopped in the town of Gibeah in the country of Benjamin. An old man offered them hospitality for the night, when

> behold the men of the city, base fellows beset the house round about, beating on the door; and they said to the old man, the master of the house, "Bring out the man who came into your house that we may know him." And the man, the master of the house went out to them and said to them, "No my brethren, do not act so wickedly [*neualah*]"[199] [Judges 19:22–23].

This time the concubine is put out for the men of Gibeah. "And they knew her and abused her all night" (Judges 19:25).

The Levite reports the rape of his concubine to the rest of Israel in a most dramatic manner, and Israel responds by almost exterminating the entire tribe of Benjamin — 25,000 are killed (Judges 20:40). Again, as with the Sodom story, it is impossible to disentangle the threat of homosexual rape from homosexuality itself. Nothing allows us to say that the anger of God or of Israel was not simply against treating guests with such violence, whether homosexual or heterosexual.

In conclusion, then, the Hebrew scriptures, which were codified in more or less their present form about 400 BCE, explicitly condemn one and only one form of homosexual activity: male-to-male anal penetration, and that solely in the context of the creation of an unacceptably high level of uncleanliness. When we turn next to the development of Hebrew thought, however, we find a homophobia vastly expanded on the basis of the far broader Greek understanding of homosexuality, and a condemnation based not on the horror of pollution, but on the fear of dominance.

JEWISH HISTORY: SEXUALITY AND POWER

The history of Israel offers plenty of contrasts, ups and downs of dominance and submission, from the time of Solomon onward. The son of David, King Solomon (died about 992 BCE), had been a king of kings; for wealth, wisdom and power he was unsurpassed in the Palestine of his time; he "reigned over all the kings from the Euphrates to the land of the Philistines and to the border of Egypt. And the King made silver as common in Jerusalem as stone" (2 Chronicles 9:26–27). But Solomon's empire was short-lived. In his son's reign the kingdom was divided (about 922 BCE) into a northern kingdom, whose throne was never stable, and a southern, which continued to be ruled by the house of David. In 722 the northern kingdom fell to the Assyrians, and its inhabitants were deported. By the mid–seventh century BCE, the remaining southern kingdom found itself caught between a rock and a hard place. Egypt and Babylon were each trying to control Palestine. Babylon won, and in 597 Nebuchadnezzar took king Jehoiachin and a great host of the skilled workers of Jerusalem captive to Babylon (2 Kings 24). A second revolt followed ten years later, and this time the city and its temple were destroyed. Those inhabitants who were not killed were taken in exile to Babylon (2 Kings 26). Tradition has Nebuchadnezzar forcing his captives into anal intercourse.[200] Eventually the Persian king Cyrus allowed the Temple to be rebuilt (515 BCE) and restored Jerusalem as an autonomous province of the Persian empire.

When Alexander the Great passed though, Jerusalem and its greatly diminished Jewish environs passed into Greek hands. A colony of Jews remained and prospered in Babylon, and another one grew up in Alexandria. Nevertheless, the central worship in the Jerusalem Temple continued to give unity to Judaism. Jerusalem remained, quietly, first as part of the kingdom of the Ptolomies, then part of the Seleucid Greek empire. Antigonos the One-Eyed, when he held the region after 311 BCE, seems to have settled Greek and Macedonian colonies throughout the region, as a protection against Ptomomaic aggression.[201] The Jewish settlements in Egypt became rapidly Hellenized, since the Ptolomies refused to trust native Egyptians with high administrative power and employed Jews instead; as result an upper class of bureaucrats grew up, Jewish by faith but educated in Greek and attracted to Hellenistic culture.[202] As Martin Hengel wrote, "From the beginning of the third century BC all Judaism must be designated Hellenistic Judaism.[203] The Book of Ecclesiastes offers advice to young men on how to behave in a royal court (e.g. 8:2–6), almost certainly the court of the Ptolomies.[204] During all this period, Greek ideas must have been slowly filtering into the lives and thoughts of Jews all over Alexander's shattered empire.

In the long period from 322 to 177 BCE, there seems to have been little resistance to Greek culture. Perhaps most importantly, even in rabbinic circles, the Greek habit of solving problems by back and forth logical discussion (which had produced the dialogues of Plato) became the norm for settling difficult questions of interpretation of the Law of Moses[205]; the ultimate product was the Talmud. Greek wisdom under the name of Solomon found its way into the Hebrew scriptures: the hypostasis of Lady Wisdom in the Book of Proverbs (8:1–36) has a distant Platonic ring to it.[206] Ecclesiastes, also attributed to Solomon, written in the third century BCE, breathes a "skeptical, pessimistic rationalism"[207] that Epicurus might have found solemnly pleasing. Somewhat later (200–180 BCE is a good guess), Joshua Ben Sira wrote, in his own name, a book of exhortations that is still in the Apocrypha, warning the pious against the corruptions of the foreigners. It was too late, for there is a Stoic flavor to even Ben Sira's thought.[208] In short, the revolt under the Maccabeans for nationalism and the purity of the faith had something of the quality of a barn door being closed after the thief has left. Greek thought, Greek rationalism, had already fused itself profoundly, inextricably, into the Jewish mind.

The revolt when it came was caused as much by concern for gold as for God. The Seleucid Greek kings, who ruled Palestine as part of a heterogeneous and always unstable empire, began to look at the treasures of the Jerusalem temple when they found themselves in need of money. There was no lack of greed on the Jewish side either, for friendship with the Greeks could be worth money. In a Greek empire knowing Greek, living as a Greek, eating forbidden foods at table with Greeks were the golden keys to jobs in the government and profits in trade from the headwaters of the Tigris to the cataracts of the Nile. Merchants and bureaucrats grew rich on gold and fat on pork, while poor farmers kept the Law and the land—and little else. The split began, as such things often do, within a family.

Onias III was the high priest of God in Jerusalem; the position had developed into a secular office of authority as well as a sacerdotal rank in Persian times, so that the high priest more or less ruled the nation as a sort of governor under the Seleucid king. Onias was a strict observer of the Law, but his brother, Joshua (better know by the Greek name he took, Jason), was a fervent worshiper of mammon. When Antiochos IV came to the throne in 175 BCE, Jason made the new king a tempting offer. If he (Jason) were installed as high priest in place of his pious brother, he would work to bring the Jews into the orbit of Greek culture. Antiochos, perhaps because he was educated as a follower of Epicuros[209] and disliked any sort of religious zeal, took Jason up on the offer. A Greek enclave was built in or near Jerusalem, and Greek education was offered to the citizens. One thread of Greek thought was the superiority of the Greeks; the young Jewish men who flocked to embrace the culture of the conquerors were taught to hate themselves and to change themselves into Greeks[210]—layer upon layer of queerness. This was all the more true because the Greek enclave included a gymnasium in sight of the Temple Mount.[211]

The gymnasium was recognized throughout Greek culture, as we have seen, not only as a place for physical culture, but also as the standard meeting place of male same-sex lovers— the gay bar of antiquity. There seems to be no doubt that it functioned in this regard in Jerusalem. Young Jewish men, anxious to get ahead in the world, flocked to the gymnasium of Jerusalem and soon were exercising naked[212] in the Greek manner. We are told further that such young men underwent painful surgery to have their circumcisions reversed[213]; probably the effort was not so much to hide their Jewishness as to become more erotically attractive to the Greek males who were educating them. The Greek ideal of boyish beauty involved the glans hidden by the foreskin; the revealing of the glans when an erection occurred was almost a sacred mystery.[214] There was a biennial festival of Dionysus celebrated at Jerusalem, with processions of men ivy-crowned.[215] We have seen that such Dionysian festivals usually involved homosexual activity. Generally it may be said that in second century BCE Jerusalem the ruling political elite, the Macedonian Greeks and their Jewish followers made participation in homosexual activity first economically advantageous, then legally all but mandatory.

Mandatory, for a brief civil war broke out when the Greek-installed high priest turned the Temple funds over to the king. As a result Antiochos attempted the complete extirpation of Judaism. Circumcision and keeping the Sabbath were outlawed, all copies of the Torah were ordered burned, and in December of 167 BCE the Temple was rededicated to Olympian Zeus, and pigs were offered on the altar.[216] Generally this seems to have been well-accepted in Jerusalem[217]; but, as the policy of forced Grecization began to be carried out in the small, outlying towns, it provoked a sudden and violent rebellion. An old priest, Matthias, in the village of Modein, killed the royal officer who was sent to set up Greek worship there. Soon Matthias and his five sons, the Maccabees, were heading a band of rebels that acted with the same intolerance that the Greeks had — those who had gone Greek were killed and the pagan altars destroyed. After a long war, Matthias' son, Judas Maccabee, took Jerusalem, cleansed the Temple, restored the Torah as the law of the land (164 BCE), and became high priest, replacing the line of priests of the house of Zadok (appointed by Solomon); by June 142 BCE after further wars, Judea was for all intents and purposes a nation independent of the fast-fading Seleucid empire. The flirtation with Greek culture and the violent reaction against it put the Palestinian Jews through what Martin Hengel has called a severe "collective cultural trauma."[218]

Judea was not, however, either a religiously unified nation or a nonaggressive one. A group that came to be known as the Essenes broke away from the Temple service because they saw the Maccabees as an illegitimate line of priests, upstart from the ancient Zadokites[219]; retiring to the desert, they set up communities that were modeled on the Pythagorean brotherhood. Likewise the description of the paradise believed in by the Essenes strongly resembled the Orphic-Pythagorean concept of the life after death.[220] They insisted on a solar calendar (rather than the ancient lunar one used in the Temple) and regularly tested the orthodoxy of their members in a way that strongly suggests that Greek and specifically Pythagorean ideas had been absorbed by the Teacher of Righteousness long before he and his followers became ascetics in the desert — Josephus compares the Essenes with Pythagoreans.[221] Even the strictest Jews lived by and believed in what they probably no longer realized were Greek concepts. Under the second generation of the Maccabees, John Hyrcanus (ruled 134–104 BCE) witnessed a second split. Unlike his father and uncles, Hyrcanus pursued a moderate sort of Hellenization; a religious party that came to be called the Sadducees grew up around him, insisting on a very narrowly literal interpretation of the Torah, which allowed Hyrcanus considerable room to make his own peace with the Greeks' world. Opposed to Hyrcanus and the Sadducees, the Pharisees remained loyal to the antiforeign zeal of the early Maccabean revolt, and to a growing body of orally transmitted commentary on the Torah, which steadily raised "the walls of the Law" ever higher — insisting on stricter and more elaborate interpretation of the Law as opposed to the approach of the minimalist Sadducees.[222]

Politics proceeded apace. Hyrcanus added to the expansions of the earlier Maccabees, using a mercenary army. He took and destroyed the Temple to Zeus on Mount Gerizim, where the half–Jewish remnant of the northern kingdom worshiped. Idumea, the ancient Edom, fell to his armies, and in 107 BCE he captured and destroyed the Hellenized city of Sameria. Internal conflict became more pronounced under Hyrcanus' son, Alexander Jannaeus (107–76 BCE); the Pharisees revolted; tradition says that he had 800 of them crucified around Jerusalem.[223] Further civil war broke out between rival sons of Jannaeus; both sides appealed for help from a new power in the region: Rome had made the Seleucid empire a province of its own growing empire, and now Pompey took Jerusalem and made the former governor of Idumea a puppet king. He was Antipas, and his son was more famous as Herod the Great.[224] From now until the utter extirpation of the Jewish state after the revolt of Bar Kochba in 135 CE, Rome was the ultimate ruler of Palestine, ruling first though the House of Herod as convenient puppets, and ruling with an ever heavier iron fist as abortive revolt succeeded abortive revolt.

If we turn to look at attitudes toward homosexuality among the Palestinian Jews, we find, perhaps not surprisingly, that all concern with uncleanness is absent from the discussion, and a strong concern to condemn particularly the penetrated party springs up. In short, purity is no longer an issue, and power is. Michael L. Satlow has studied in detail the Talmudic tradition that grew up in the first century CE among Jews in both Palestine and Babylon. This represents the originally oral interpretation of the Torah developed early by the Pharisees, but not written down until the third century CE.[225] Rabbinic sources strongly emphasize questions of dominance and submission. The pharaoh of the Exodus was said to have desired to penetrate the male Hebrews as a result of his haughtiness and desire for dominance.[226] Of course there is plenty in the Biblical account to convict the pharaoh of the Exodus of arrogant pride; however, one suspects this tradition owes something ultimately to the Hellenistic and Roman romance tradition of the arrogant tyrant, who molested boys and effeminized them. Artapanos, an Alexandrian Jew, who wrote sometime between 250 and 100 BCE[227] an epic in Greek on the life of Moses, portrays the pharaoh of the Exodus (whom he calls Chenepheres) as the quintessential Hellenistic tyrant, bringing the wrath of God on his innocent people.[228] Only fragments of Artapanos' epic survive, and we do not have a specific reference to homosexuality in Chenepheres, but Artaphanos compares Moses to Mouseaus, the teacher of Orpheus,[229] so that a contact with the same Orphic-Pythagorean sources that furnished the legend of Aristodemos, the boy-raping tyrant, to Roman legendary history seems not unlikely. Likewise in the Talmud, the man who willingly received anal penetration from another man was considered doubly guilty of a crime deserving death.[230] Female homoeroticism was not condemned, since Torah had not expressly condemned it, though marriages between women were prohibited because it was recognized as an Egyptian custom.[231] Ultimately the line of reasoning that condemned male-to-male penetration comes from an identification of the penetrated male with a woman. God, the rabbis of Palestine believed, had specifically created a woman to be penetrated and hence owned by her husband. Penetration equaled domination and ownership. Males are not made to be dominated by other males; hence the act of penetrating another male is one of willful arrogance.[232] Though Satlow explicitly denies a political agenda behind Talmudic thought on homosexuality,[233] it is clear that one existed. Centuries of being alternatively dominant and dominated politically and ideologically had left the rabbinic exegetes of Palestine with the clear notion that the sex act was inherently aggressive. This, coupled with the more ancient Jewish insistence on human worth and equality, made homosexuality appear to be an inevitable result of human selfishness and the ungodly wish to control others. Most interestingly, the Palestinian Talmud alone concerns itself with issues of homosexuality, while the Talmud produced in Babylon (and outside Roman influence) does not mention the issue,[234] though the Babylonian Talmud is about three times as long as that produced in Palestine. Nothing is said about homosexuality as producing impurity, and the Greek concept of homosexuality as "against nature" is entirely lacking in the Talmudic discussions.[235] A passage in *Sukkah* (29a) says that eclipses of the moon can be caused by homosexual acts, but other things can cause a similar upset in nature, including the death of the vice-president of the Sanhedrin.[236] Only the theme of dominance as inherent in the sex act suggest a possible Roman influence. The Talmud remains to this day a religious guide for Orthodox Jews throughout the world, though its influence outside Judaism has been far less than that of the Torah itself.

HELLENISTIC JUDAISM

More influential then the Talmud in the intellectual history of the West were the Jews of the diaspora who wrote in Greek. By the time that the Roman Empire was well underway, a considerable number of persons drifted into the category that the Book of Acts calls "God-Fearers [*ton theos sebastoi*]." Often gentile in origin, they kept some but not all of the laws outlined in Torah, omitting usually circumcision and the dietary regulations. Living both in Palestine and many of the major cities though the Roman world, such God-Fearers form a wide middle-ground between monotheistic pagans and strictly observant Jews.[237] Like the Jews of Palestine and Babylon, the Jews in the ancient diaspora were placed by their religion in a difficult bind. Since Alexander's time and to an increasing degree under Rome, the world-view of Hellenism strained toward a unity, often an imperial unity. It seemed quite reasonable that, if the world were to be governed as a single empire, all the citizens of that empire ought, reasonably, to conform to the same — essentially Greek — customs, mores and worship. Generally this proved easy enough among polytheistic peoples — Baal Shem of the Syrians or Amun Ra of the Egyptians were assimilated easily to Zeus or Jupiter, and other gods were fitted into the universal pantheon easily enough. Likewise, interracial marriages facilitate the development of a universal state (such as in Alexander's marrying a Persian princess). Philosophers too maintained the universal validity of reason. For Stoics, as an example, reason was an indestructible aspect of God.

In all this empire-building Hellenic universalism, the Jews refused to fit. For the Jews there was only one God, a God with a specific (if unspeakable) name who was jealous and refused to be identified with any other god. Worse yet to the Greeks, the Jews were antisocial. They would not eat with or marry into pagan families. They believed (which seemed sheer hubris to the Greeks) that God was the only god and that he had a special love and care for the Jews, which did not quite extend so fully to non–Jews. All of this easily brought down the contempt of many a Greek and Roman on both Jewish ideas and on the Jews as a people far too superstitious — for example, the anti–Jewish fulminations of Posidonius (135–51 BCE), who studied under Panaetius and taught, among others, Julius Caesar.[238]

The response of many Jews was a sort of one-upmanship, taking the appeal to universalism quite seriously, but claiming for their tradition the true validity as universal. As early as 150 BCE, Jewish thinkers educated in the Greek traditions began to embrace strands within that Greek tradition that seemed to support their own ancient tradition. The most important of these ideas for our purpose is the concept of natural law.[239] Most happily for the Jewish apologists, first Plato, then the Neo-Pythagoreans and the Roman Stoics after Panaetius, all agreed in condemning what the Torah had condemned — homosexuality. The defining fingerprint that allows for a distinction between Hellenistic and Palestinian Judaism is on the issue is lesbian activity; Hellenistic Jewish texts follow the Pythagorean tradition in denouncing both male-to-male and female-to-female homoerotic activity, while Palestinian Judaism remained closer to the Torah in condemning only male-to-male activity involving penetration. The apologists of Judaism who wrote in Greek were particularly ready to point out that Moses had forbidden what some Greeks had forbidden but had done so a millennium earlier. The increased emphasis on sexual conduct in the Greek-Jewish writers[240] probably derived from their position in society. Universal or would-be universal states generally legislate in matters having to do with money and taxation — merchants must deal fairly and pay the pence to Caesar. With this the Jewish writers had no problem, but there was relatively little legislation from the state in matters of sexual conduct, so Jewish writers, struggling to maintain their identity in a world where homosexuality was a norm, stoutly maintained sexual integrity against the indifference of most Greeks and Romans.

Between the Jews and the pagans there was an indefinite middle ground occupied by the *sebastoi*; called sometimes the God-Fearers, or the Pious Ones, these were persons who were not fully observant Jews, but yet maintained an identification with the monotheism and the legal traditions of Judaism. We hear of them in the New Testament as a major source for Christian converts (Acts 10.2), and Juvenal describes as common Romans who were circumcised and who kept the Sabbath. Unfortunately, our documents do not give us any clear indication of what percentage of the population were in this category.[241]

If we turn to writers who attempted to defend Judaism in Greek, we find our earliest examples in the almost honorable tradition of Hellenistic forgeries. A number of Jewish writers, generally in Alexandria, produced work under the names of famous Greek writers of an earlier age. Since they were alienated from and despised by at least some of their Greek neighbors, such literary borrowing of the identities of Sibyl or Phoclydes allowed the Hellenistic Jews to adduce witnesses to the value of the Jewish tradition from, as it were, from the hostile camp. The terrible temptation to the Jew in the Hellenistic world surely was to admit the Greeks were right — hadn't they the arts, the social organization, the raw power to control the world? By a bit of slight of hand that put a Greek name on a Jewish idea, the Hellenistic Jew might have it both ways. Of course it was trimming. The rabbis of Palestine had it right; the Torah was valid not because it was the law of universal nature, but because it was spoken by God, though few took matters with such rigor in Alexandria.

Finally, there is the odd power of the argument from nature: it makes an imagined "nature" the mirror of the constructed sexuality of dominance and gives an imagined eternal authority to the latter. Pure, spontaneous homosexual desire is, as Harmodios and Aristogeiton had known, not a desire to dominate, rape, hurt or do anything but share bodies in love and playfulness. But in patriarchal societies and those that are either aggressively dominant over others or heavily dominated by others (and the Jews had been both in a few centuries), homosexuality is often artificially linked to dominance because heterosexuality is likewise linked; homosexual desire is perceived instantly when directed at another person of the same gender as the urge to enslave, or if perceived coming from another person, as aggressive domination. What is really against nature is enslavement to the will of another or the desire to enslave. The Romans, caring nothing for the freedom of their slaves, had no compunction and thought it not unnatural to rape them, male or female. The Jews, with a nobler ethic, would neither rape nor be raped. What was lost, all but entirely in the Hellenistic world, was freedom: only the truly free can truly love.

From the surviving body of Greek Hellenistic writing we have the *Sibylline Oracles*, a collection of prophesies attributed to a pagan sibyl, written probably in Egypt, probably by a Jew in the circle of Onias IV, the high priest, who had fled Palestine and built a temple at Leontopolis (the Ptomolies found him useful as a foil to the high priest in Jerusalem, who was owned by Antiochos). The date of 163–145 BCE[242] seems a reasonable one for these oracles, although they pretend to be a thousand years older.[243] Probably they represent a pagan Greek work that was written after Philip of Macedon conquered Greece and that used the persona of the sibyl to denounce the conquerors; it was then presumably taken over by a Jewish writer for a similar purpose.[244] The pagan classical world had a tradition of a sibyl or sibyls going back to the fifth century BCE, when both Plato and Aristophanes speak with great respect of the sibyl; by the third or second century BCE, Lycophron in Alexandria was influenced by sibylline writings, and the prestige of the sibylline oracles in Rome cannot be understated. Human sacrifice had been offered at the command of certain sibylline oracles, kept in darkest secret. In 83 BCE the Roman sibyllines were lost in a fire; the Emperor Augustus labored first to replace them from various prophetesses around the Mediterranean. Augustus selected a carefully sorted collection and deposited it in the Temple of Apollo in the Forum. Nervous that oracles could be used against the Roman authority, Augustus had 2,000 volumes of disagreeable prophesies burned publicly.[245]

What has come down to us under the name of the sibyl is a book of mostly Jewish-Christian prophetic works. The Jewish sibyl is represented as a daughter-in-law of Noah named Sambethe,[246] presumably the author of our text. Our present text of the *Sibylline Oracles*, though dating from the mid–second century BCE, was regarded as extremely ancient in Roman times and had considerable prestige and authority among pagans, Jews and Christians. Clement of Alexandria thought the book was earlier than the legendary Orpheus, while Augustine put the date of the work as contemporary with the Trojan War.[247] The unknown author of the sibyllines takes a cosmological and moralistic view of history. To quote John J. Collins, the sibylline sees a "recurring pattern": sin, usually the sin of idolatry, leads to disaster, and that in turn leads to the coming of a king who will restore righteousness.[248] We will return to this insight when we deal with Paul in the Christian scriptures. All nations including the Jews are condemned by the sibyl for not keeping the "holy laws of the great God" (lines 283–84). These laws are not the Torah, but laws that everyone knows by nature — essentially "natural law." For the sibyl, "The basic sin is idolatry."[249] The ancient kings of the Greeks "began the first evils for mortals setting up many idols of dead gods" (lines 554).[250] Homosexuality is one of the sins condemned by the *Sibylline Oracles*; the Phoenicians are condemned for oral sex: Woe to them for "opening their mouths for uncleanness" (line 387).[251] When the Messiah comes and the rule of God is set up on the earth, "No longer are wretched mortals beset with deeds of shame, with adulteries and unnatural passions for boys, with murder and tumult.[252]

This new race of god-fearing men avoided "unholy intercourse with boys," unlike the Phoenicians, Egyptians, Latins and Greeks.[253] The sibyl likewise commands that men aught to "shun adultery and confused intercourse with boys" (3.764). Further on the sibyl denounces the Romans "who formerly impiously catered for pederasty and set up boys in houses as prostitutes" (5.386).[254]

Though ultimately derived from the Torah's denunciation of male-to-male anal penetration, Roman homosexual prostitution is denounced in practice as violating natural law.[255] Interestingly, the Messiah foreseen by the Jewish sibyllines is not a Jew but a king of Egypt (surely one of the Ptolomies). The Messiah is referred to by a remarkably Egyptian epithet, "the king from the sun," a title applied to the pharaoh in the Egyptian prophetic tradition,[256] which in turn suggests the traditions of the cult of Amun as sun god. We have seen in a purely Greek context the conjunction of Greek worship of Amun as Ammon with Pythagorianism and homophobia. It is worth noticing that the later, less popular, sibylline oracles, of which we have only fragments, have a distinctly Orphic quality to them.[257] Quite possibly the author of the Jewish sibyllines in Alexandria at its zenith had contact with Pythagorean thought. The sibyl's idea that idolatry is the origin of all evil is likewise important to our discussion: the idea is repeated in the Talmudic tradition (*Sifre Numbers* 3.F, pages 31b–32a) and is used by Paul in condemning homosexuality in Paul's Epistle to the Romans.

An even more universalistic attempt to unite Jewish thought with pagan survives in the poem attributed to Phoclydes of Miletos (flourished about 500 BCE). The real Phoclydes was a gnomic poet, rather the Poor Richard of ancient Greece. Only scattered fragments of his versified good advice survive, but the poem forged under his name has come down to us complete. Again, the work was produced by an Alexandrian Jew; it can be very tentatively dated between 30 BCE and 40 C. Like the earlier pseudo-sibyl, Pseudo-Phoclydes claims validity as natural law for insights that ultimately go back to the Torah.[258] The work is far more universal than the that of the "sibyl"; and, like that work, it concerns itself much with sexual conduct. Adultery, abortion, rape of a virgin and sexual relations with one's wife when she is pregnant are forbidden, along with homosexuality, both for men and women.[259] Books of wise sayings, like that of the real Phoclydes and Publius Syrus, were widely used as school-boy texts (the boy Shakespeare, for example, was probably set to copying the Latin maxims of Syrus), so Pseudo-Phoclydes may have been created to provide Jewish boys with a morally safe text for their Greek exercises.

No document in this context is more problematic than the Testaments of the Twelve Patriarchs. It is now generally agreed that it was originally written in Greek, some say by an Alexandrian Jew; though there is far less agreement about dates. What we have is an originally Hellenistic Jewish work representing perhaps a revision of a text, perhaps as old as 200 BCE, which has been reworked into a Christian text.[260] Certain elements suggest a contact with the Essenes.[261] We concern ourselves here only with the clearly pre–Christian elements in the Testaments. Perhaps the most remarkable passage for our purpose comes from the Testament of Naphtali[262]:

> Sun and moon and stars change not their order; so do you change not the law of God. The gentiles went astray and forsook the Lord, and changed their order, and obeyed stocks and stones, spirits of deceit. But ye shall not be so my children, recognizing in the firmament, and in the earth, and in the sea, and in all created things the Lord who made all things, that ye become not as Sodom, which changed the order of nature. In like manner the Watchers also changed the order of their nature, whom the Lord cursed at the flood.

This fairly clearly represents a restatement of the argument of a sort of astronomical morality in the Platonic *Laws*. Failure to recognize the order in nature (particularly the order of the sun, moon and stars) leads to immoral acts and ruin. This may be the earliest document we have that alludes to the sin of Sodom not as inhospitality, but as a sexual sin, probably homosexuality. "Changing the order of nature" in the case of the Watchers meant a sexual offence, since we learn from another work of pseudepigrapha, the Book of Enoch[263] from about the same time, that these Watchers were the "Sons of God" mentioned in Genesis 6:4–5: "the sons of God came in to the daughters of men, and they bore children to them. These were the mighty men that were of old, the men of renown. And the Lord saw that the wickedness of man was great in the earth." Elsewhere in the Testaments, the Testament of Levi warns that if sin continues, "with harlots and adulteresses ye shall be joined, and the daughters of the Gentiles shall ye take to wife ... and your union shall be like unto Sodom and Gomorrah" (Levi 14:6). The only sexual act threatened by the men of Sodom in Genesis is homosexual, and that fact in conjunction with the clear linking of moral law and the law of nature (especially in the order of the heavens) suggest that, late in the second century BCE in the more pious circles in Palestine, Jewish writers were using the *Laws* of Plato to support their own concept of Torah as universal law.

We turn for the culmination of the Greco-Judaic tradition to Philo of Alexandria, otherwise called Philo Judaeus, the philosopher and apologist of Hellenized Judaism. Philo was born in Alexandria, probably about 20 BCE; his family was very wealthy, with connections to the Roman government and their Herodian puppets in Jerusalem,[264] but we know nothing of Philo's education except the result. Philo was well acquainted with the full range of Greek philosophy — he quotes from 54 Greek authors[265] — and used it in his defense of Judaism as he understood Judaism. Philo takes it for granted that Jews would be gymnasium-educated,[266] yet how he acquired his philosophical knowledge we do not know. A rescript of the Emperor Claudius has survived, renewing the prohibition that no Jew could be educated in the gymnasia of Alexandria, but we do not know when the use of the gymnasia was first forbidden to the Jews; probably the Jews of Alexandria had their own schools, law courts, etc.[267] It is tempting to suspect that Philo's parents had him privately educated by carefully chosen Greek tutors. Since, as we have seen, the Neo-Pythagoreans were strongly opposed to homosexuality in any form, and most of them were by the first century BCE vegetarians,[268] it seems quite likely that such Neo-Pythagoreans would have been the teachers of choice for Jewish parents worried about the purity, dietary and otherwise, of their sons.

Whether he was educated by a Pythagorean or not, certainly Philo shows a strong interest in sacred numbers and mystical numerology, suggesting particularly Pythagorean knowledge.[269] He even quotes Philolaus to the effect that the number seven is a symbol of God.[270] He is likewise interested in Orphism, and knows a good deal about the mystery cults.[271] The Judaism that Philo defends with Greek philosophy is not the ceremonial Judaism of the Temple with its sacrifices and rituals, but the "quasi–Pythagorean" Judaism of the Essenes in Palestine and the monastic Therapeutae in Egypt.[272]

Philo's work is an effort to syncretize, to put together in one system, both the visible and the invisible worlds to produce a unity of Greek rationalism and Jewish piety, of nature and divinely revealed law. The surviving works of Philo constitute a commentary on the Hebrew Bible, beginning at the opening of Genesis and going though Exodus with special attention to the Jewish patriarchs Abraham, Isaac and Jacob in Genesis. The concentration on the patriarchs who lived before the Law of Moses is essential for Philo's argument that the law of nature and Torah are essentially related. The patriarchs, having no divine revelation thundered to them from a burning mountain, nevertheless lived good lives because, Philo maintains, they lived by natural law. In Philo the "unwritten law of nature" is a sort of Platonic archetype, knowable to all humans by right reason, and the written law, Torah, is its most perfect possible embodiment; this is a synthesis of Greek philosophy and Hebrew revelation, an Hellenization of Judaism or a Judaization of Hellenism.[273] There can be no conflict, Philo maintains, between Torah and right reason because both originate in God. This synthetic idea was taken up readily by the Church Fathers and transmitted though them to Augustine, Islam, Aquinas and the whole scholastic tradition in the West down to Descartes.[274]

Philo must be discussed at length and in detail because his works are probably the most extended and virulent source for homophobia we have in Greek and also because he was a pivotal figure in the transmission of those ideas to the future. As an apologist, he tried to find all the possible reasons for condemning homosexuality that he possibly could, probably because he recognized the potential hostility of much of his audience. Homosexuality is spoken of not as an act but in terms of a class of persons worthy, says Philo, of being executed. Both the "active" and the "passive" partners are condemned. The "passive" partner generally gets the more severe castigation and can be recognized, Philo says, by his appearance. We hear nothing of lesbians.

Philo is clear in his homophobia: Commenting on Leviticus 18:22, he says homosexuality is even worse than having sex with a menstruating woman:

> Much graver than the above is another evil, which has rammed its way into the cities, namely pederasty [*paiderastein*]. In former days the very mention of it was a great disgrace, but now it is a matter of boasting not only to the active [*drosi*] but to the passive [*paskhusin*] who habituate themselves to endure the disease of effemination [*thaleian*] ... and leave no member of their male sex-nature to smolder. Mark how conspicuously they braid and adorn the hair of their heads, and how they scrub and paint their faces with cosmetics and pigments and the like, and smother themselves with fragrant unguents.... In fact the art of the transformation of the male nature to the female is practiced by them as an art and does not raise a blush. These persons are rightly judged worthy of death by those who obey the law, which ordains that the man-woman [*androgunon*] who debases the sterling coin of nature should perish unavenged, suffered not to live for a day or even an hour as a disgrace to him-

self, his house, his native land and the whole human race. And the lover of such [*paiderastes*] may be assured that he is subject to the same penalty. He pursues an unnatural pleasure [*ten para phusin hedonan*] and does his best to render cities desolate and uninhabited by destroying the means of procreation. Furthermore he sees no harm in becoming a tutor and instructor in the grievous vices of unmanliness and effeminacy [*andrias kai malakias*] ... which rightly should be trained to strength and robustness.... Certainly you may see these hybrids of man and woman continually strutting about through the market, heading the processions at the feasts, appointed to serve as unholy ministers of holy things, heading the mysteries and rites of initiation and celebrating the rites of Demeter.[275] Those of them who ... mutilate their genital organs are clad in purple like signal benefactors of their native land ["The Special Laws," 3.7.37–42].[276]

This sounds remarkably modern; Philo's homophobia seems to have been bred into him by his culture, and he experiences the same sort of knee-jerk reaction to transgender behavior that many modern persons do. Probably this was the general attitude of both the pagans, whom Philo knew well, and the Jewish community in Alexandria in his time. He is no different in his contempt for the passive male homosexual than Martial or Juvenal. His attitude toward the active male has a more legalistic quality and probably comes from his more distinctly Jewish cultural milieu. His overall emphasis on homosexuality, however, is largely theological and apologetic; it was a welcome point of agreement with his pagan philosophical tradition: he was a Middle Platonist, tending to the same homophobic traditions we have seen in Plotinus, ultimately going back to the *Laws* of Plato and the Pythagorean tradition.

Philo's passing remark about the "sterling coin of nature" is as close as he brings us to the specific denunciation of homosexuality as "against nature," though his rather quaint notion elsewhere that homosexuality causes sterility is apparently part of the same complex of ideas. *Phusis*, Nature, was for him rather like the image we have of Mother Nature, a source of vitality, a creative power inherent in the universe.[277] Probably the most that can be said for the notion of homosexuality causing sterility is that it resembles the sometimes hasty, folkloric "science" that circulated in antiquity (e.g. Pliny's *Natural History*, where we learn that the north wind in Portugal makes mares pregnant). The astrologer Vettius Valens of Antioch, writing about 175 CE, said that the passive partners in male-to-male sex acts lose the ability to produce offspring.[278] Sex was a rather more serious business to people in antiquity than to many moderns; life expectancy was short, and the notion that whole cities or the human race might easily die out for lack of reproduction was very real.[279] In the sex act men thought of themselves as becoming, in Peter Brown's phrase, "human Espresso machines," boiling their blood until it fused with their spirit and produced semen that contained both the substances of the body and the soul.[280]

Philo uses "against nature" to denounce only three sins: heterosexual relations with a menstruating woman; sexual relations between different species of animals, and male-to-male homosexuality. Men who marry barren women and do not divorce them are likewise "enemies of nature."[281] All in all, the image of God that Philo draws is just sufficiently anthropomorphic and pantheistic enough to let us suspect that, to Philo, nature in a vital aspect is God's genitals, as nature in an organized aspect is God's mind. Any activity that denies order in social custom (e.g. androgyny) or the sex act (sodomy) is an insult to God's being, as it were.

Philo's Platonism is heavily influenced by the Pythagorean Platonism of Eudoros of Alexandria.[282] Harry Wolfson maintained that Philo was consciously correcting Plato,[283] and certainly this does seem to be the case, or at least he has no small ambiguity with regard to Plato's use of homosexuality. He is shocked and appalled by the homosexuality in the *Symposium*:

Plato's banquet is almost entirely concerned with love, not merely with men in love with women, or women with men, lusts subject to the laws of nature, but of men with males differing from them only in respect of age.... The greater part is taken up with common and vulgar love.... For the mind of the boy-lover is necessarily aimed at his darling, and is keen sighted for him only, blind to all other interests, private and public; his body wastes away through lust, especially if he fail in his suit, while his property is diminished ... by his neglecting it.... Ignorant of the science of husbandry, sowing not in the deep soil of the plain but in briny fields and stony hard places.... but the disciples of Moses, in their vast superiority, trained as they are from early youth to love the truth hold them in contempt and continue undeceived.[284]

Yet Philo cannot resist using the Plato that suits his purpose. He can never get very far from the Pythagorean and Platonic notion that the essence of the good life is to transcend the world of sensation and achieve a mystic union with God. Though he explicitly condemns the homosexuality of the *Symposium*, he consistently uses the *eros* language of that work to describe the relation of the human soul to God.[285] In his "Special Legislation," which is a discussion of specific laws in the Torah, such as circumcision, Philo uses the complex image from Plato's *Laws* of the Procession of the Gods, related to the sun and to a charioteer with two horses — all very Platonic. Philo adds that the regularity of the visible world demonstrates the existence of God: "just as sense is the servitor of mind, so too the beings perceived by sense are the ministers of Him who is perceived by the mind."[286] Since homosexuality causes blindness in Philo's none too scientific understanding[287] (one is reminded of the notion in folklore that masturbation causes blindness, or hairy palms), then by implication homosexuality is related to unbelief, since those who cannot see the sun, moon and stars cannot see the proof of God's existence.

Though the passage in Leviticus 18:22 serves as his starting point, the principal source for Philo's denunciation of homosexuality is not the ritual prohibition in Leviticus, but the story of Sodom and Gomorrah in Genesis. In his "Questions and Answers on Genesis," he declares that "Sodom" and "Gomorrah" are Hebrew for "blindness" and "barrenness"[288]— blindness because the men of Sodom were smitten with blindness by the angels, and sterility because homosexuality causes sterility. We are further informed in his treatise "On Abraham" that

men mounted [*epibainontes*] males without respect for the sex nature which the active partner shares with the passive. And so when they tried to beget children they were discovered to be incapable of any but sterile seed. Yet this discovery availed them not, so much stronger was the force of their lust which mastered them. Then little by little they accustomed those who were by nature men to submit to play the part of women, they saddled them with the formidable curse of a female disease. For not only did they emasculate their bodies by luxury and voluptuousness.... Certainly had the Greeks and Barbarians joined together in effecting such unions city after city would have become a desert as though depopulated by a pestilential sickness.... God abominated and extinguished to the greatest possible degree this unnatural and forbidden intercourse.[289]

Apparently Philo got the curious idea that sodomy is a sort of disease from the contemporary Greek medical tradition; Cacaelius Aurelianus quotes the Greek physician Soranus (about 100–150 CE) to the effect that the desire by a male to be penetrated is a disease.[290] This may be the first mention we have of a notion that was to crop up again and again in expressions of homophobia well into the twentieth century.

In "On the Eternity of the World" (146–50), Philo sees the destruction of Sodom as only one instance of the cyclical rise and fall of cities and empires governed by the Natural Law (*nomos tes phuseos*) or the Reason (*logos*) of God. "For the divine Logos moves in a cyclic dance which the majority of men call Fortune [*tukhe*]."[291] Here Philo is using the Cyclical Theory mentioned in Plato in his major homophobic work, the *Laws* (3.676–77 and also *Timaeus* 22.A–F) and developed in detail by the Stoics. The importance here is that in Philo for the first time clearly and unequivocally the destruction of Sodom and Gomorrah is said to be a direct result of homosexuality in those cities. We may view this as the birth of the Sodomite by name, and an important source for the statement that Justinian wrote into law that homosexuality causes earthquakes.

When he died about 60 CE, we may see Philo of Alexandria as taken away from evil to come. In 70 CE the Jews of Palestine and in 135 the Jews of Alexandria and Palestine as well rose against the oppression of Rome. Predictably, the Romans crushed them with a cold fury. Philo's own nephew, Tiberius Alexander, was a general under the command of Rome, cooperating in the destruction of his own people.[292] After 135 CE the middle ground of the Hellenized Jews disappeared. The cosmopolite universalists like Philo found themselves between two fires. Some, following Akiba and the Council of Jamnia, embraced a Judaism as purified as it could be of all taint of Greek influence — what had been the Judaism of the Pharisees — and became the Judaism of the Middle Ages in Europe. Others embraced paganism, or, as often as not, one suspects, Christianity.

8

Christianity: The Triumph of Homophobia

The Christians did not make the world ascetic. Rather the world in which Christianity found itself at work made Christianity ascetic.
— M.S. Enslin, *The Ethics of Paul*

Let me tell you: men are a hopeless lot. They know how to do nothing that comes from within themselves, not even the least thing occurs to them on their own account. They only imitate the gods, and whatever picture they make of them, that they copy. Purify the godhead and you purify men.

— Thomas Mann, *Joseph in Egypt*

An evangelist is someone with *good news* to impart. *Good* indicates the news is seen from somebody's point of view, from the Christian Jewish rather than the Roman imperial interpretation. *News* indicates that a regular update is involved. It indicates that Jesus is constantly being actualized for new times and new places, situations and problems, authors and communities.

— Dominic Crossan,
The Birth of Christianity

Very probably the crucifixion of a certain Galilean peasant-teacher went largely unnoticed in Jerusalem about 30 CE. The political situation had become steadily more unstable. Religion, nationalism and the desire to not pay ruinous taxes gave many the incentive to rebel against Roman dominance. Death by torture on a cross was Rome's last, best answer to any who objected to its rule; and, for decades to come, it was effective. Crucifixion was a horrible death: the weight of the body hanging from nails driven at the wrists caused paralysis of the muscles in the chest that made breathing possible; a cross was a marvelously simple, effective torture machine, and a few Roman troops could kill scores times their number with an efficiency that made it their method of choice.

The teacher was Jesus, and his followers were to dominate the religious and moral outlook of Western civilization for a long age. He was crucified as an outsider, an outcast from the society, a deviant who was causing too much trouble, or might cause too much. Just how deviant he was from Roman culture and from the culture and religion of Judea is difficult to assess: the very brilliance of the sun hides its shape from any observer. Within two decades of his crucifixion, Jesus was being proclaimed as God made flesh, and all the ideal concepts humans have of God were marshaled to describe him. To any modern human, it is perhaps easier to conceive of God than to conceive of a truly human human. Theologians of the new religion who hammered out and nailed down with the terminology of Greek philosophy a creedal definition of Jesus Christ as "very God of very God and very man of very man" made the assumption that to be truly human was to be purely heterosexual. Modern science has made that assumption no more tenable than the six days of creation. The analogy is not far-fetched, for any consideration of creation is a consideration of nature, and that in turn must involve placing the human race in the context of nature. Once it is admitted that the word "nature" often means nothing more sublime or eternal than a habitual way of thinking, then homophobia becomes far less than deeply grounded; nothing is by nature "pure" — distilled water is hydrogen adulterated with oxygen. Considering Christianity, if one adds to that the consciousness of a human being who sees through and has little respect for conventions, especially those conventions that shun and declare impure and subhuman various persons, you then have a high likelihood for — not a Christianity without homophobia — but a Jesus without it. It is unworthy of him. Indeed, in a curious way the basic world view of Christianity resembles or is analogous to the scientific view that we have already mentioned of homosexuality. Christians often view the world as a circled camp of the "saved," the church, or those relatively few individuals whom God looks upon with some sort of special favor. Outside the church is another group, the great mass of humans who are outcast from the favor of God. Jesus and his followers, motivated by love, move from the inner circle outward to rescue and lead into the inner circle those poor sinners who are outside. If we compare this to Frank Muscarella's description of older chimps who led in and socialized in the dominant group younger, outcast chimps in a homosexual context, the analogy is startling. This chapter is an examination of how Christianity became homophobic and works with what a feminist theologian has termed an "hermeneutic of suspicion," that Christianity absorbed its homophobia from the ambient culture, not from its shunned, demonized and crucified founder.

No part of the origins of homophobia is more difficult to write about than Christianity. This is because, quite obviously, of all the matters discussed in this history, Judaism and Christianity are the ones still most alive and are the most active participants on a battlefield of ideological contention. The very meaning of the word "Christianity" is in some sense up for grabs. By that term do we mean exclusively the teachings of Jesus as far as they can be known from extant sources, or do we include the interpretations included in the writings of Paul and other authors in the New Testament? Shall we add the interpretation of the Church Fathers down to the Nicene Creed? What of the post–Nicene writers, the popes of the Middle Ages, and the Reformers?

It seems clear that in any serious consideration of the early history of what became the Church we must speak not of Christianity, but of Christianities — a broad, polyform movement begun by and centering on Jesus but perceiving Jesus in very diverse ways. This should not surprise us; schools of ancient philosophy as diverse as the Cynics, Stoics and Platonists all claimed the historic Socrates as their founder, in each case perceiving the barefoot philosopher of Athens differently. It was not until more than a century after Jesus' death that some of his followers began to declare others of his followers "heretics" and state that those followers has so incorrect an understanding of the founder that they were unworthy of the title "Christian." It is not the historian's job to sort out such rival claims in terms of the theologically valid or invalid. Rather we shall here attempt to state as far as it can be discerned what events happened that led to the Church's becoming (though it has never really been a unitary entity) the major carrier of homophobia in the Western tradition from the end of antiquity.

This work cannot hope to find for its readers that philosopher's stone of theologians, the historic Jesus. The attitude of Jesus himself toward homosexuality is nowhere clearly recorded. If we turn to the generation or so after Jesus, extant documents begin to shed light on the matter, and an area of inference exists at an earlier period. Clearly there was from very early in the history of Christianity a homosexuality-friendly element among at least some followers of Jesus. Followers of Jesus, however, were not entirely new creatures, though often the apostles said and hoped that it were so. Old prejudices, old ideas of what it meant to be a good person were often retained by those pious persons — pagan or Jew or God-Fearer — who converted to the new faith. The homosexuality-friendly element soon found itself isolated, while a strongly homophobic element came to dominate the followers of Jesus to the exclusion or near exclusion of any tolerance of homosexuality. In this way Christianity duplicates the fate of Western culture as a whole, shares it, adds to it. The homophobia that appears very early in Christianity is double-barreled — that is, it is opposed to both gay and lesbian activity; also it is concerned primary with gender-bending rather than impurity. These facts distinguish Christian homophobia from Jewish and suggest that the former had Pythagorean rather than Jewish roots.

The notion, so profoundly shocking to so many modern Christians, that Jesus of Nazareth may have condoned homosexual acts, may even have had a boyfriend himself, is not new. A few voices have cried in the wilderness to that effect for a long time. Until quite recently they have lacked much hard evidence, and the culture has so smothered and silenced them that the idea can hardly be said to have been current.

Archeological discovery such as the finding of the Gnostic library in Egypt, the Essene scrolls in Palestine, and the fragment of the Letters of Clement, as well as the growing freedom felt by many scholars to discuss homosexuality even in texts that have long been known, have made it possible to trace the history of the homophobization of Christian thought as it became institutionalized as the Church. Following John Dominic Crossan, we may discriminate two diverse attitudes with coined Greek names: "sarcophilic" (that is, flesh-loving) Christianity and "sarcophobic" Christianity (that is, flesh-fearing), where "flesh" is shorthand for the complex of bodily needs and desires our flesh is heir to. Sarcophobic Christianity embraced the dualism of Plato and the Pythagoreans, seeing the mind or soul or inner self as entirely separate from the material body. For sarcophobic Christianity the body and all its desires are a prison (*soma sema*, "the body is a tomb"), a place where the soul has to dwell temporarily but one that constantly hinders it on its journey back to God. Sarcophilic Christianity, on the other hand, retained the ancient Jewish sense of humans as one thing, not two — flesh and spirit are not, in this view, opposed, but unitary.

In a way orthodoxy as it took shape endeavored to have it both ways. The creed framed at Nicea declares Jesus to be both truly human and "very God of very God." The caveat imposed on this is to deny that homosexuality is in any way "natural," that is, belonging to the world of material beings which experience sexual desire along with thirst and hunger. Jesus is shown in the gospels, which were canonized as the standard accounts of his life, as not even tempted by sexual desire, let along manifesting it in any way, homosexual or heterosexual; however, there was a very old, minority view of the matter that stated things otherwise.

The standard answer to the question that every adult Christian implicitly asks, "What must I do about sexual desire?" was given curtly by Paul — get (heterosexually) married and satisfy your desires with your spouse. "It is better to marry than to burn [with lust, presumably]" (I Corinthians 7:9).[1] Women, Paul thought, were "weaker vessels," and therefore male domination of them in marriage was the natural thing. The notion that sexual desire was particularly something to be repressed seems to have come from the very deeply ingrained mixture of sex and power in the ancient world. To have sex was not a simple pleasure like drinking water or eating figs. It required a partner and that partnership was all but universally thought of as inherently unequal. In heterosexual marriages the male was thought of as somehow owning the female. There seem occasionally to have been equal sexual partnerships in a homosexual context, at least among the Greeks, at least in the sixth and fifth centuries BCE; but, by the time Christianity entered the world, such relationships were hardly more than an antiquarian's dream. Asking ordinary people to imagine, then enact such equal relationships when all they had known in the home or in public life was power-based relationships seems to have been more than the new faith could seriously do.

The earliest documents we have that concern Jesus of Nazareth are not narratives but collection of sayings attributed to Jesus, such as the Q document and the Gospel of Thomas; these date from about 30 CE to about 60[2]—all written within the lifetimes of persons who could have known Jesus. This sayings tradition clearly presents Jesus as a Cynic teacher; "The Jesus movement began as a homegrown variety of Cynicism in ... Galilee," said Burton Mack.[3] Christian art, even more than texts, portrays Jesus often in the garb and pose typical of a Cynic teacher.[4] In all of Judea at the time, Galilee was the single area where there was no hostility between the Greco-Roman culture and the Jewish.[5] Sepphoris was the capitol of the Galilee region, a city built by Herod with a Greek democratic constitution on the manner of a *polis*.[6] Cynicism, of all the schools of philosophy that grew up in Greece, stood outside of and was critical of those power relationships that were so deeply a part of culture—in Rome, Athens or Jerusalem.

Cynics, like Platonists, Stoics, and Epicureans, looked to Socrates as their ultimate source; but the Cynics chose the Barefoot Socrates as their source rather than the logic-chopping Socrates of Plato. Cynicism as a philosophy in classical times had a few basic attitudes: that the pursuit of wealth, power, glory was the pursuit of illusions; that one should be sensitive to all the ills of life, in oneself and others; and above all, that one should seek freedom and self-reliance.[7] The Cynics often made fun of popular superstitions about the gods, though we do hear of one Cynic, Oenomaus of Gadera, in Palestine, in the early second century CE, who claimed to have direct revelation from Herakles.[8] "Consider the ragged cloak to be a lion's skin," wrote an anonymous Cynic of the fist century BCE, "the staff a club, and the wallet land a sea from which you are fed."[9] Cynicism gets its impetus from what Thoedore Gomperz called "the contrast between a well-founded self-esteem and a mean situation."[10] The individual Cynic protested his (or her—female Cynics existed) own worth independent of the comforts and trappings of culture. There is what a modern sensibility might call a "queer" quality to many of the ancient remarks attributed to the Greek Cynics, resulting from a self-chosen separation from the ordinary goals of most people. The Cynic lifestyle, which often involved begging and living in destitution, was a kind of willing protest against the foolishness of unexamined assumptions. When Diogenes the Cynic met a boy who showed him the finely made knife a man had given him as a love-gift, Diogenes smelled the prostitution and called the knife "a pretty blade with an ugly handle."[11] Oscar Wilde would hardly have said more. This game of "gotcha," as Burton Mack has pointed out, had great humor and serious assumptions under it[12]—the Greek word was *spuadalogeloios*. One might compare, with the added frankness characteristic of Cynics, Jesus' criticism of the Pharisees as swallowing camels and straining out gnats (Matthew 23:24).

However, the Cynics had two real founders and to the end of the movement a sort of bicameral double nature, following either Antisthenes or Diogenes. Antisthenes of Athens (about 446–366 BCE) was a disciple of Socrates. Like Socrates he maintained the unity of the human will, the unlimited right of free speech and public criticism and a rational deduction of the rules of life.[13] His ideal was humans in the "state of nature," looking to the animals, rather than to any ideal; human softness, love of luxury, is the cause of suffering, he maintained,[14] though he is pictured in Xenophon's *Symposium* as having a house in Athens and not disdaining the invitation to a good supper.[15] He was looked to as the founder of the ascetic, pleasure-hating wing of Cynicism: "I'd rather be mad than feel pleasure," he often said, perhaps reflecting the fact that he was also initiated into Orphism.[16] However, it is not clear that he was opposed in principle to pederasty; the wise man, Antisthenes is reported to have said, "will not disdain to love [*erasthesesthai*], for only the wise man knows who is worthy to be loved [*eran*],"[17] and "a good man deserves to be loved [*axierastos*]," using in all three examples the Greek verb that usually refers to homosexual love.

Diogenes of Sinope (404–326 BCE), the second founder of Cynicism, "practiced what Antisthenes preached."[18] His father ran a mint, and it said that Diogenes fled to Athens to avoid a charge of adulterating the coinage of Sinope.[19] Living in a discarded storage jar for a while, Diogenes avoided the entrapments of civilization, as well as its comforts. He had no disdain for pleasure per se, but was all too aware that it often cost freedom itself, a price he was unwilling to pay. He got his pleasures as best he could. He is said to have masturbated in public; "I only wish I could relieve hunger as easily by rubbing my belly."[20] In a first century BCE forgery attributed to Diogenes,[21] the philosopher tells how he visited the young men's gymnasium. The young men are exercising naked in the Greek manner and Diogenes joins them. A handsome, beardless young man extends his hand, inviting Diogenes to wrestle. Diogenes wrestles with the young man and gets an erection, so he "stood there and rubbed [*etriboman*]" himself. The custodian upbraids Diogenes for doing this, and Diogenes replies that if something caused the wrestles to sneeze, no one would complain against them. So, he reasons:

> now are you upset that someone quite spontaneously experiences an erection while rolling around with a handsome lad? Or do you suppose that while the nostrils are completely responsive to nature, this other part of us is in the power of our deliberate choice?.... Do you think that your regulation will be able to place bonds and restraints upon excitable nature when boys happen to roll around with adults?[22]

The story illustrates a number of points in Cynic thought; the boy invites Diogenes to wrestle, implying that the relationship was his free choice. Radically for that age, Diogenes recognized marriage only if it happened with the woman's consent.[23] And Diogenes' defense indicates that he believes homosexual response was a simple natural reaction, as masturbation was. For the Cynics, nature was the savior of humankind: "Nature is mighty and, since it has been banished from life by appearance [*doxas*], it is what we restore for the salvation of mankind."[24] Elsewhere, Pseudo-Diogenes recommends masturbation in a heterosexual context.[25] Indeed masturbation in a homosexual context seems to have been his preferred sexual outlet. Generally the tradition has it that Diogenes accepted homosexuality as natural, though he rejected all forms of "gender-bending"— any hint of males trying to look or act like females was offensive to him,[26] perhaps because females had so little freedom in that society. Diogenes is said to have taken Monimos as a pupil and boy-love. Said to have been the servant of a Corinthian banker, Monimos threw the money off his master's table to get himself dismissed and followed Diogenes out.[27] The world was illusory, Monimos maintained, and truth was to be found only in instincts and impulses; law, like the *nomos* that protected the banker's table, had no validity.[28] This rather remarkable act of throwing the money off a banker's table was later repeated, we are told, by a Jewish peasant who got himself crucified for doing it.

The difference in the attitude toward pleasure between the followers of Antisthenes and

Diogenes seems to have been essentially practical rather than theoretical. Antisthenes was far more willing to participate in society than Diogenes; and his followers saw this as an effort to help the deluded non–Cynics who needed to see a Cynic up close; the disadvantage of this is that any participation in society limits one's freedom and can also lead to a reliance on the comforts that a settled, organized society offers to some of those who cooperate. Diogenes, on the other hand, was uncompromising; he practiced *askesis*, rigorous self-discipline, to wean himself from any love of pleasure as an end in itself, an end that may destroy freedom. In the context of a society that forbids some forms of pleasure (such as homosexuality) the Antisthenic Cynic may abstain from that pleasure in order to continue a relation to society, while the more severe Diogenetic may engage in that activity as a form of social criticism, exhibiting the naturalness of pleasure and the absurdity of rules against it.

We hear little of the Cynics in the second and first centuries BCE; however, in the first through the third centuries CE, a body of Cynic letters appears, anonymous in fact but attributed in good Hellenistic style to famous Cynics of the past. These letters reveal a deep split in Cynic thought in the period. One group of Cynics, called the austere Cynics, harked back to Diogenes; the other, called humane Cynics, followed principles they believed they found in Antisthenes and Aristippos. The austere Cynics stoutly maintained the *anaideia*, the shamelessness and contempt of commonly held conventions that Diogenes had so proudly displayed; they held that the crowd "know neither reason nor truth,"[29] though from sympathy and a sense of duty the Cynic sages tried to save humans from their illusions. One of the letters attributed to Diogenes (though written in the second century BCE) has him saying: "Nature [*phusis*] is mighty and since it is banished from society by appearance [*doxa*] it is what we restore for the salvation of mankind."[30] Acts of shamelessness including the fart were a standard form of Cynic social criticism.[31] On the other hand, the humane Cynics lived more conventional lives, often as settled workers, rather than wandering beggars.[32] The austere Cynics maintained Diogenes' attitude toward homosexuality. One of them, writing in the name of Heraclitos, protests against the Roman habit of raping slaves: "Your slaves who have to put up with wrong though fear are to be pitied. You yourselves are accused of ordering them to do worse and worse."[33] When we turn in more detail to the history of early Christianity, we shall see this split in Cynic thought curiously reflected in Christian thought.

We do not know how Cynicism came first to Palestine. The Hellenistic cities built there by Alexander's successors probably had their Cynic teachers from an early date; among Cynic philosophers in the region, we hear of Meleager of Gadera, who was educated at Tyre about 100 BCE; Philodemos, perhaps 50 years later; and Oenomaus, also of Gadera, about the year 200 in the Christian era. Little definite can be said about any particularly Palestinian form of Cynicism, but what we know about Herakles, the favorite deity of the Cynics in this area, is suggestive.

We have seen earlier that Herakles filled a niche in Greek mythology that answered to Gilgamesh in the oldest Sumerian paradigm. As Gilgamesh had his Enkidu, Herakles had a number of boy-loves, including Iolaos and Hylas. At Tyre and the other coastal Phoenician cities, Herakles was worshiped as a dying, rising-again god under the Semitic name of Melqart. Every year, in the later winter or early spring, an image of Herakles-Melqart "died," was burned, and then, in a way we do not understand, the god was believed to return to life again.[34] A Greek version of the myth says that Iolaos returned Herakles to life after he had been killed by the monster Typhon.[35] In this regard Iolaos corresponds to Asclepias, the official Greek god of healing, whose symbols included a dog.[36] We can then assemble a sort of Greek-Semitic myth system that includes Cynics, if only by virtue of a pun (*kunos*, the same word as Cynic, means "dog" in Greek: the Cynics were dog philosophers). The fullest explanation we have for why the Cynics had their doggy name has nothing to do either with sex "in the doggy position" or mythology.[37] The most direct link of Cynic, dogs and healing is through the healing office of Semitic gods worshiped in Tyre, Ashkelon and the other cities of the coast; Sed-raphe' and Eshmun for example, and the goddess Gula, "she who by the touch of her pure hand revives the dead." Gula also had the dog for her symbol.[38] Archeological evidence has been found for a short-lived cult of dogs in the coastal city of Ashkelon about 400 BCE. Scholars believe the sacred dogs of Ashkelon were associated with a healing cult, as dogs are generally in legend, since dogs lick their own wounds to heal them.[39] Perhaps then we may understand the enigmatic prohibition in Deuteronomy 18:23: "You shall not bring ... the wages of a dog into the house of the Lord.[40]" Not only were dogs impure because they were associated with a foreign religion; they were impure because they consumed the filth of wounds and sores. Were the priests of Eshmun-Iolaos likewise consumers of impure substances, in either healing rituals or homosexual acts — or both? Of course the healing properties of licking a wound are real. Not only does such a process remove bacteria; saliva also contains mild antibiotics which aid in healing. We read that Jesus healed using his own saliva. In Mark 7:31–37 he heals a man who is deaf and has a speech impediment by spitting and touching the man's tongue. In Mark 8:22–26 Jesus restores sight to a blind man by spitting on his eyes. Anyone familiar with the religion of the Cities of the Coast in the first century would be very likely to think that Jesus was acting like a dog. But did he also sometimes act like a Cynic?

There is remarkable unanimity of scholarly opinion that Jesus of Nazareth lived and taught in the manner of a Cynic — an austere, wandering Cynic at that,[41] which was the Cynic school most accustomed to ignore popular conventions, including any prohibition on homosexuality. The mild Cynics, on the other hand, were more respectful of popular morality. The evidence is so overwhelming on this point that it does not require repeating here; Gerald Downing's *Christ and the Cynics* is recommended for those interested in the general point. However, it remains to be asked whether there is evidence that Jesus tolerated or even practiced homosexuality as his Cynic contemporaries did. From the Q document, written about 50 CE, perhaps in Tiberias in Galilee,[42] we read:

> To what then shall I compare the men of this generation, and what are they like? They are like children sitting in the marketplace and calling to one another,
> "we piped to you and you did not dance;
> we wailed and you did not weep."
> For John the Baptist has come eating no bread and drinking no wine; and you say, "He has a demon." The Son of man has come eating and drinking; and you say, "Behold a glutton and a drunkard, a friend of tax collectors and sinners!" Yet wisdom is justified by all her children [Luke 7:31–35 = QS 18 (Mack, 86–87)].

Ron Cameron has pointed out that in this passage John the Baptist is described in terms that would indicate the more conventional, mild Cynic, who lived an ascetic life (Antisthenes), while Jesus is described in terms suggestive of the austere Cynics (Diogenes), who took their pleasure when they could get it.[43] By the mid–second century CE the Palestinian Cynic Oenomaus of Gadera had declared that there were really not Cynics of Diogenes or of Antisthenes, but only Cynics of Herakles.[44] It will be good to begin the exploration of such a question by looking at Jesus' attitude to the principal homophobic institution of his time and place: the ceremonial law. In Canonical Mark (which comes from the earliest stratum of the tradition)[45] we read:

> And a leper came to him [Jesus] beseeching him and kneeling said to him, "If you will, you can make me clean." Moved with pity, he stretched out his hand, and touched him and said

to him, "I will, be clean." And immediately the leprosy left him and he was made clean. And he sternly charged him and sent him away at once, and said to him "See that you say nothing to anybody. Go, show yourself to the priest and offer for your cleansing what Moses commanded, for a proof to the people" [Mark 1, 40–44].

Leprosy (by which the ancient texts mean a number of diseases, modern Hanson's disease among them) made anyone suffering from it unclean according to Torah (Leviticus chapters 13–14). I have chosen for the sake of clearness to use the term "Torah" to distinguish the body of law in the first five books of the Bible in order to prevent confusion with other systems of law. To even approach another Jew as the leper does was forbidden. To touch a leper, as Jesus does, was to make oneself unclean, to share the uncleanness of the leper. The author of Mark is showing us two things about Jesus that it will be of utmost importance to discuss here: (1) Jesus is a miracle worker, and (2) Jesus is not an observant Jew.[46]

"Miracle worker" is not an epithet for Jesus that many modern, scientifically minded persons are likely to find immediately palatable. However, it is important here because it places Jesus in direct opposition to the religious orthodoxy of his time and place. Jesus was a magician.[47] Judaism at this time and religions in general see themselves as founded on miracles: the Red Sea parts for the Children of Israel; the bush is burned before Moses but not consumed. These were miracles already in the remote past in Jesus' time, and they were cited by the Temple authorities as granting validity to the official religion; the religion of the Temple and the communal orthodoxy rested on those stupendous, long-ago miracles. Now here was this fellow from Galilee (just about nowhere) exhibiting a personal and individual power to perform miracles.[48] Miracles are, as Claude Levi-Strauss has said, "additions to the objective order of the universe ... naturalization[s] of human actions, a treatment of human actions as though they were an integral part of physical determination"[49] by making inner wishes and objective order one. Perhaps they appealed to the profound sense of self that Cynics had. Later Christians were to use the Argument from Nature against homosexuality without quite realizing, it seems, that any notion of a universe where a miracle is possible cannot well support that theory.

If performing a miracle were not enough, Jesus did it by touching the unclean. Jesus the Magician was radically counter to the culture of his own time and place. Our modern sensibility may begin to appreciate this in terms of Magical Realism. Colonialized third-world people and those dispossessed within Western society often have recourse to magic as a kind of protest against the overwhelming power of orthodoxy — whether the power of an institutionalized Church or the orthodoxies of modern, Western science, which, like a church, claims finality for its vision of the world. When Jesus' hand touched the stinking sores of the leper, he defied the rules of the Temple; when those sores healed miraculously, Jesus defied the power of the Temple.

Jesus seems not to have much respect for the Sabbath. In Mark 2:23, he approves his disciples gleaning on the Sabbath and cites the example of David, who ate consecrated bread out of desperate need. The Sabbath laws were closely tied to the Holiness Code. When Jesus repeats the Ten Commandments at Mark 10:19, there are only seven commandments — idolatry, honoring father and mother, and the Sabbath are not mentioned[50] (compare Exodus 20:3–17). Sabbath observance was an essential element of Jewish self-identity; it singled them out as a people to whom God had given special laws. The commandments that Mark and the other gospels show Jesus as respecting are more or less the ethical norms that most pious gentiles lived by as well. But what of the ethical norm of homophobia?

Unlike his near contemporary, Philo, Jesus does not understand the sin of Sodom as sexual; in Mark 6:11, he says that any town that is inhospitable and does not receive his disciples will be judged more harshly than Sodom; the sin of Sodom was, therefore, inhospitality by implication. If one takes all of Jesus' sayings recorded in the canonical gospels quite literally, it is difficult to see him approving of what the religious right has lately termed "family values," especially with regards to children obeying their parents; consider Matthew 8:21–22, 10:35–37, 12:46–50; Luke 9:59–60, 14:26–27. Jesus' teaching on marriage in Mark 10:1–12 has often been cited to the contrary. This passage offers little respect for the text of Torah, however; divorce, Jesus says, is an invention of Moses, not God, and then only a concession to human hardheartedness. Marriage is based on Creation (v. 6); its visible sign is that male and female become "one flesh [*hoi duo eis sarkas mian*]" (v. 8). Marriage is based on God joining together the couple, rather than any human institution (v. 9). Marriage is an act of God, for Jesus, tantamount, it seems, to a miracle. "Joining together" may mean physically, socially, emotionally — the matter is far from clear. That "marriage" is exclusively limited to male-female couples is a common modern reading, not quite explicit in the texts. Again, one sees no more room in this understanding for the Greek concept of nature applied to gender, than for more conventional customs of marriage per se. The whole ground of thought on gender and marriage shifts almost imperceptibly, nevertheless radically, in a manner familiar from Cynic sayings, but not from Jewish tradition.[51] Likewise, Mark 10:11 undercuts the prevailing male-centered idea of honor and shame on which much (especially Roman) homophobia was based. Shame is attached to the penetrated male in male-to-male homosexual acts because he acts like a woman — a person without honor in the definitions of the society; Jesus sees women as having quite as much honor as men.[52] When later in this study we see Paul denouncing homosexual acts between men as "dishonorable," we must wonder how much he knew, or understood, Jesus' sayings. Jesus' understanding of the proper relationship of his followers is that they should be as brothers and sisters under the fatherhood of God, without patriarchal or hierarchal relationships among themselves (Matthew 23:8–9). "Jesus will tear the hierarchal or patriarchal family in two along the axis of domination and subordination," as Dominic Crossan has said.[53] John Boswell has shown that in common first century Greek "brother" and "sister" were frequently used by both same- and opposite-sex couples who were erotically linked, but not genetically related.[54]

One passage, which comes from the fairly late Gospel of Matthew (dated by Burton Mack around 85–90 CE),[55] has Jesus saying:

> I say to you everyone who is angry with his brother shall be liable to judgment; whoever insults [*hos d' an epei to adelpho autou Raka*, literally "whoever says to his own brother Raka"] shall be liable to the council, and whoever says "you fool [*mora*]" shall be liable to the hell of fire [Matthew 5:22].

The word *raka* is obscure and not Greek. Warren Johannson has suggested that *raka* comes from the Hebrew word *rakha* ("soft," translating the Greek *malakos)* and is related to an Akkadian prefix used to indicate a woman's name; hence, *raka* means a passive male homosexual, and by extension the Greek (and English) *moron* (literally a fool or dull-witted person) means an aggressive male homosexual.[56] I can find no text from antiquity that indicates that *moron* can mean "aggressive male homosexual"[57]; however, if we accept Johannson's reading, then Jesus seems to be offering sympathy to those to whom homophobic insults are offered, regardless of their sexual identity.

All of this suggests that Jesus did not greatly value the codes of his time that were incidentally homophobic. One finds none of the sexual pessimism that would later pervade Christianity, insisting that virginity was an essential part of the highest spiritual state possible.[58] Jesus, in other words, is not deeply grounded in the Platonic dualism of flesh opposed to spirit — he is not sarcophobic. Rather he appears much more clearly in the Jewish tradition of sarcophila — flesh and spirit are not antithetical but really one thing. If we look for explicit statements about homosexuality in the earliest documents we have, we must turn to the vexed question of the "Bethany Youth."

The discovery by Morton Smith of two remarkable fragments of an early version of the Gospel of Mark in the library of the ancient monastery of Mar Saba has turned the attention of scholars to the possibility of a homosexual relationship between Jesus and a young man from Bethany. The dust of expert opinion has not completely settled on this matter; Morton Smith is a scholar whose opinions cannot be summarily dismissed, except on doctrinal, ultimately dogmatic grounds; and New Testament scholars as reputable as Dominic Crossan have accepted that the Secret Gospel is all Smith claims it to be. The text of the Secret Gospel allows for a unification of fragments of a story scattered throughout Mark and the other gospels. The following is based on a careful overview of the subject by Miles Fowler.[59] A rich young man,[60] unnamed in the Secret Gospel but called elsewhere Lazarus,[61] came to Jesus asking how he could inherit eternal life. Lazarus was acquainted with the circle of the high priest in Jerusalem, about a mile and a half from Bethany.[62] "And Jesus looking upon him loved him" (Mark 10:21).[63]

The verb in that verse, *agape*, is used by Homer for the love that Odysseus feels for his only son, Telemakhos. Mark's Greek is distinctly influenced by the Septuagint, the Greek translation of the Hebrew scriptures circulating in the Hellenistic world perhaps as early as 200 BCE[64]; in the Septuagint (the LXX), the word *agape* can mean any form of love from the love of God for God's people (Deuteronomy 7:8, "Because the Lord loved [*agapan*] you and is keeping the oath which he swore to your fathers..."[65]) to more fleshly love. In Genesis 29:20 we are told that Jacob loved (*agapan*) Rachel, whom he married; farther on we read that Amnon, son of King David, loved (*agapasin*) a woman named Tamar (Themar in the Greek); he seems to have gone through a depression, "love sickness," for her and eventually raped her (2 Samuel 13:4–14, termed 4 Kings in the LXX translation). The Song of Solomon in the Septuagint regularly uses *agape* for the emotion felt for the beautiful Sulemite maiden, whose breasts and navel are described in wonderfully erotic poetry. Likewise in later Greek, to the time of Jesus and afterward, *agape* can mean the range of human emotion covered by the English word "love" — both erotic and nonerotic, as could two other Greek words, *philia* and *philein*.[66] In the Greek, however, the most interesting word in Mark 10:21a for our purpose is the one translated "looked on," for who does not know, as Yeats says, that "love comes in at the eye?"[67]

Jesus then tells Lazarus to sell all that he has, give the money to the poor, and follow him — very much in the manner of Cynic dispossession. Lazarus can't bring himself to do it and turns away. Later Jesus and the disciples are on their way to Jerusalem, when Mary Magdalene,[68] the sister of Lazarus, meets them, distraught that her brother has died: "Jesus wept. And the Jews said, behold how he loved him [*ide pos ephilie*] John" (11.35–36).[69]

At Bethany Jesus has the tomb opened (though according to the Gospel of John, Lazarus has been dead long enough to be stinking), goes in and touches the body.[70] Lazarus rises from the dead and becomes known as the Beloved Disciple. The Secret Gospel of Mark continues the story:

The youth loved him [Jesus] at first sight and began to plead with him to stay. And coming out of the tomb, they go to the young man's house, for he was rich. And six days later Jesus called him. And when evening came the young man went to him wearing a shroud [*sindona*] over his nude body. And he stayed all night, and Jesus taught him the secret of the kingdom of God [Secret Gospel 1.8–14].[71]

One of the most remarkable and interesting visual depictions of the Raising of Lazarus from ancient times is from double-registered sarcophagus now in the Museo Pio Cristano (part of the Vatican Museums).[72] The artist of this Christian sculpture put Jesus and the raising of Lazarus in a pagan mythic context that is both erotic and homosexual. Apparently something like the Secret Gospel of Mark was known to at least some Christians in Rome. The raising of Lazarus is shown in the upper-left-hand register; of this much must be said. The remainder of this remarkable sculpture is taken up with water-imagery — Jonah and the whale, and Moses striking a rock with his fingers and waiting for water to gush from it. Jonah is shown in the pose of Endymion. Jonah is associated with the death and resurrection of Jesus (Matthew 12:40), which in turn is part of the motif of creation out of water, as well as the raising of Lazarus. The myth of Endymion has a moon goddess, Selene, falling in love with a beautiful young shepherd, Endymion; at her request, Zeus grants Endymion immortality; but he spends most of it sleeping in a cave, only to be wakened by Selene in order to love her. Keats describes Endymion's waking:

> Opening his eyelids with a healthier brain,
> He said: "I feel this thine endearing love
> All through my bosom: thou art as a dove
> Trembling its closed eyelids and sleeked wings
> Aabout me...[73]

On the Pio Cristano sarcophagus' upper-left corner, Jesus is shown, youthful and unbearded, standing before the tomb of Lazarus in tunic and pallium; he stands with his weight on his left leg, his hips curving to the left and his left hand on his left hip; with his right hand (now broken off) he gestures for Lazarus to come forth from the tomb. The pose of Jesus in this sculpture is, according to the canons of Roman masculinity, distinctly effeminate — not only the beardlessness, but the hips swished to the left and the hand on the left hip are not just suggestive; they are explicit. Whoever carved this scene wished to show Jesus unmistakably as a *cinaedus*.[74]

The Gospel of Mark continues the story: about to leave Bethany for Jerusalem, Jesus

> sent two of his disciples, and said to them "Go into the city and a man carrying a jar of water will meet you; follow him and wherever he enters say to the householder, 'The Teacher says, Where is my guest room, where I am to eat the Passover with my disciples'" [Mark 14:13–14].

"A man carrying a jar of water" was anomalous in that culture; carrying water was woman's work, so this man was in his way bending gender, acting womanlike in public. Furthermore Jesus knew in advance that this man would provide the room for what was to be the last supper of Jesus and his disciples.

After the Last Supper, the Gospel of John describes Jesus as doing what in that culture was thought of as a womanly thing; he washes the disciples' feet and dries them with the towel he is wearing (John 13:5). Then, still wearing a towel, one assumes, Jesus reclines on a couch (the Greek manner of eating) with the others to eat the Passover meal. The Disciple whom Jesus Loved (Lazarus)[75] reclined with his head on Jesus' bosom — this "lying spoons" was, as we have mentioned, the usual way that men and their boy-loves ate at *symposia* in the Greek tradition. Jesus then

> took bread and when he had given thanks, he broke it, and said, "This is my body which is for you. Do this in remembrance of me." In the same way, also the cup, after supper, saying, "This cup is the new covenant in my blood" [I Corinthians 11:24–25].[76]

Jesus then went into the Garden of Gethsemene to pray. Judas came followed by a band of soldiers. Judas kissed Jesus (apparently the usual greeting), and the soldiers took him away to be crucified.

> And a young man [neaniskos] followed him, with nothing but a linen cloth about his body; and they seized him, but he left the linen cloth and ran away naked [Mark 14:51].

Miles Fowler identifies this youth as, again, Lazarus, still wearing the single piece of cloth that he had been buried in as a sign of his resurrection.[77]

Finally, the two sisters, Mary and Salome, went to the tomb where Jesus had been buried, three days following the crucifixion. There they saw someone, probably their brother, Lazarus, dressed in a gleaming white robe such as Jesus had worn. Persons who read this narrative in first century Palestine would have been likely to remember the image of Iolaos, who in Tyre was said to have effected the resurrection of Herakles, the son of Zeus. Jesus had raised Lazarus from the dead; now he announces Jesus' resurrection: "He is risen, he is not here," Mark has the youth saying; "But go tell his disciples and Peter that he is going before you to Galilee; there you will see him" (Mark 16:6–7). Christianity had begun.

Of course the Secret Gospel of Mark proves nothing. Jesus and the youth look at each other lovingly, Jesus stays at his house six days; the youth, nearly naked, is baptized by Jesus in a secret ritual at night. All of this is suggestive, what gay men a few generations ago would call "minty," but there is no explicit statement that the young man and Jesus were sexually intimate. Nevertheless, the intimations remain. Quite early in the history of Christianity, some Christians were doing things on the authority of the Secret Gospel of Mark that others, like Clement of Alexandria, found shameful and shocking. Clement uses wine imagery; the followers of a teacher named Carpocrates had mixed the "spotless and holy words" with "shameless lies" in their interpretation of the secret baptism.[78] Very likely those "lies" were stories that Jesus and Lazarus had an homoerotic encounter. The Carpocratians probably maintained that some sorts of erotic activity were an integral part of Christianity. We turn next to a more careful interpretation of the story, then to what happened to homosexuality in the doctrines of the new and swiftly developing Church.

We have briefly noted that homosexuality was an issue in the Cynic Letters, many of which were written around the same time as the Gospels. Two issues of wealth and social organization, and sexuality and free love were at the heart of the questions that first century Cynics debated in a pagan context. The followers of Diogenes maintained that one must dispossess oneself entirely of worldly goods to live the free and purely natural life; that life might include sexual acts with either men or women as the occasion presented itself, without regard to social customs or prejudice. The followers of the other, less austere Cynics (Antisthenes, for example) maintained that one may live within human society, owning a modest few possessions and provisionally living by accepted social norms, while at the same time criticizing those norms that were most clearly unnatural, harmful and smothering to integrity. It is instructive to keep in mind this conflict within the Cynic movement as we look at a parallel conflict within Christianity. The argument of Voltaire and Rousseau was old when those philosophers were born into it.

It is possible to discern from a very early period in the Church an antinomian, liberal faction and a more legalistic, conservative faction. By the end of the second century CE the conservative faction was winning and set about repressing the documents of their defeated opponents. What survived and was eventually adopted as the state religion of the crumbling Roman Empire was rather far from what the Galilean peasant had preached in the dusty fields to hardscrabble farmers and out-of-luck fishermen. If we look for the antinomians in early

Christianity, we may start in the New Testament itself and with the primary Christian initiation rite — baptism.

Baptism became the central, essential Christian rite of initiation; to be baptized, Paul says, is to participate in the resurrection of Jesus (1 Corinthians 15:28–29), replacing the Jewish rite of circumcision, which in the Rabbinic tradition had been taken as a rebirth ritual. Separation from the foreskin is like separation from the tomb according to the Talmud (Pessharim, 8, 8, and 'Euyot, 5, 2).[79] "The Baptism of John" was a kind of historical re-enactment, an attempt to symbolically recreate Israel as a righteous people. The world had been created by God, who commanded it to rise from the watery chaos; Israel had been created by God's parting of the Red Sea for the Israelites to pass though. Now John was seeking a renewal of the people by symbolically passing them though the River Jordan, from which they emerged cleansed of their sins, like Israel from the Red Sea. Such an interpretation of baptism was certainly known to Paul (I Corinthians 10:2) and was viewed by both Origin of Antioch and Hippolytus as parallel to the Resurrection.[80] Moreover, John's baptism was a challenge to the services of the Temple, since John claimed repentance and baptism could gain forgiveness that the Temple offered only through expensive sacrifices.[81] In the Christian context, baptism has always been seen as the central initiation rite, performed once only, and securing the baptized the right to the common meal that was the central celebration of the early Church.[82] As John's baptism broke down the distinction between rich and poor, Christian baptism was believed to break down even more barriers; Paul wrote:

> For as many of you as were baptized into Christ have put on Christ. There is neither Jew nor Greek, there is neither slave nor free, there is neither male nor female [*ouk eni arsen kai thelu*], for you are all one in Jesus Christ [Galatians 3:27–28].

John's baptism was public, however, a mass undertaking in broad daylight; anyone who was repentant might be baptized immediately. The baptism of Lazarus by Jesus was quite another matter. Jesus' baptism was a secret ritual, performed only on those who has been prepared by long instruction from Jesus; it seems not to have been for the crowds. It was so secret in fact that only the Gospel of John among the four canonical gospels even mentions that Jesus baptized at all. In the Secret Gospel, the baptism is at night, and the one baptized is naked. It appears that what is being symbolically re-enacted here is the fall from the Garden of Eden, and it is being reversed: the one baptized is going back to God, back into Eden, back into the state of naked innocence.[83] Clement of Alexandria, who preserved the fragments we have of the secret Gospel of Mark, says the soul must approach God *gumno*, naked; and in the early Christian tradition both the person baptized and the one baptizing were naked.[84] If we take the story of Eden very far back, we find in one tradition not male and female, not Adam and Eve, but only Adam, a single androgynous creature from whom Eve was later "taken out." Here we come to the central question of Jesus' attitude toward sexuality. Was the androgyne to be thought of as an asexual being, childlike, therefore ascetic as Crossan thinks[85] (forgetting Freud's insight that children are quite sexual), or is there a possibility of some form of sexuality? If Jesus' kingdom was a "radically egalitarian one," as Crossan thinks, then in the most radical reading there is no distinction between male and female, and therefore two same-sex persons making love are no different from a male-female couple making love. Paul, as we will see, was to maintain that males and females are distinct and inherently both different and unequal. The notion of sexual dimorphism implying inequality is all but universal in this age; the only place it is questioned may be in the more radical followers of Diogenes of Sinope. In a perhaps less radical sense, if the polarity of power disappears, then there is no longer a possibility of one partner being the aggressor, the other the victim of penetration. The Roman Empire falls either way.

Morton Smith, who discovered the Secret Gospel of Mark in 1958, has written perhaps the most thorough analysis of the ritual of Lazarus' baptism in that document. Jesus' baptism was an act that conferred "spirit" (*pneuma*) on those baptized.[86] In John 20:22, Jesus confers the Spirit on his disciples by breathing on them. To any Greek reader, *pneuma* has this double meaning; and, to the ancients, it had further overtones. "To breathe into to" was to inspire (the English word is from the Latin, meaning the same thing) and inspiration is what the beloved, the boy, received from the lover, the man in Greek pederastic relationships. Just how spiritual or how physical this was in the case of Jesus and Lazarus we are not privileged to know.[87] Morton Smith concludes that those whom Jesus baptized were "united with" Jesus and that his baptism was an ecstatic experience, a transcendence of Torah and a freeing from it; probably Jesus used his hands in some way during the rite.[88] Perhaps we are talking about mutual masturbation by two men, not penetration.

This, in turn, may lead us back to the Cynic tradition. We have seen that Diogenes of Sinope practiced homosexual masturbation; the tradition of Diogenes' masturbation is referred to in the first century CE Cynic Letters, and Galen (about 129–200 CE) was aware of the practice by Diogenes and commented that it might have been nothing more than the way a poor and homely philosopher relieved himself.[89] Dio Chrysostom, writing about 100 CE, says that masturbation was invented by the god Pan, and that Diogenes the Cynic recommended masturbation, then gave a public demonstration of it, adding, "If all men were like myself, the Trojan War would never have happened."[90] His point was that masturbation eased sexual tension without transferring it to the social sphere, and thus would have prevented the abduction of Helen, which started the war. It seems not unlikely to conclude that masturbation was the sexual practice of choice among Cynics of the austere school; against the background of the general Roman dislike of the practice, public masturbation on the part of Cynics takes on the aura of social protest.

To experience intense sexual pleasure by touching another person, being penetrated by him or her or penetrating him or her, or even to desire such, is to risk that obsessive relationship known as "falling in love." Such an obsession can very easily become possessive; it can reduce the person desired to the level of an object, something to be grasped at and owned. The Austere Cynic practice of masturbation may have been a radical effort to deal with the problem of sexual desire and sexual objectification. Not everyone wants to be touched, penetrated or owned, particularly by this or that individual. The conflict between those who desire and those who do not takes on the quality of a war, Trojan or not. "Universal love goes with masturbation," a great modern Cynic has said, because "it saves a person from judging others by the confused standards of male, female, old, young, beautiful, hideous."[91] Relieved manually of the sharp edge of sexual desire, one can relate universally to the human. Clearly a Cynic ethic of masturbation (largely homosexual) existed in the first century CE. Jesus was near to Cynicism of his day; and if we are to look for historical evidence of his practicing it, it is in the water at Bethany that we must look.

If Jesus and Lazarus practiced masturbation, then the challenge to the Torah was considerably less severe. As we have seen, male-to-male anal penetration was punished by the death of both parties concerned; however, Torah regarded "emission of semen" (apparently through masturbation or nocturnal emission) as a relatively mild defilement (Leviticus 15:16–18). The theme of masturbation into water opens a wide mythological prospect to us. In some Egyptian mythological accounts, the world came into being when Amun, the Creator, masturbated and deposited his semen in the Waters of Chaos.[92] Josephus mentions a false Messiah who came from Egypt and was crucified in Palestine about 20 CE. Did he leave Egyptian elements behind in the tradition of Palestinian messianism?

At this point it may be not inappropriate to quote at length what has come to be known as Egerton Gospel Two. This is a badly mutilated fragment from a papyrus manuscript; the actual manuscript can be dated between 150 and 200 CE, though the text dates from a time well before the split between the synoptic and Johanine traditions; the manuscript has many places where words are lacking entirely. This is the tentative restoration of F.F. Bruce[93]:

> ... enclosed in its place, ... placed below invisibly, ... its weight immeasurable, ... And they were perplexed at his strange question, Jesus as he walked stood on the bank of Jordan and stretching out his right hand, filled it [with seed] and sowed it on the river. Then ... [? he blessed] the water which had been sown [with seed] ... in their presence and it produced much fruit ... to their joy (?).... [94]

Are we to understand that what Jesus sewed on the Jordan was "seed" as Bruce reconstructs the text? Or as others read the obliterated word, "water?" The noun is lost in the decayed papyrus; but, whatever the substance, the verb is clearly "sowed," the noun regularly associated with distributing grain for germination. The Jordan (where Jesus had been baptized) seems to bear fruit, which would suggest "seed" or "semen." Sowing water on water is even odder than sowing seed. As a metaphor for spiritual development, planting seed was a commonplace in Greek and Persian thought.[95] At any rate, the substance seems to have been near at hand; but the fragmentary nature of this passage leaves it more suggestive than instructive.

An ecstatic tradition in Christianity has been largely marginalized, though never quite eliminated. There is evidence for an ecstatic prophetic tradition in northern Israel going back to the seventh century BCE that stood outside of, if not in opposition to, the legalistic tradition that later found its center in Jerusalem. We hear of prophets like Elijah, who was called "mad" (2 Kings 9:11); and Celsus, writing about 175 CE, was acquainted with ecstatic *goetes* in Samaria, who practiced glossolalia and claimed absolute divine authority.[96] In the Book of Genesis as we have it, there are two narratives of the creation of humanity; a fairly late editor combined the traditions of the Northern Kingdom (later the area of Samaria and Galilee) with those originating in Judea.[97] The Northern narrative can be distinguished by its use of "Elohim" as the term for God. In distinction from the Priestly Code, which emphasized his work as a lawgiver, the Elohist saw Moses primarily as a prophet.[98] This was combined very early with the Yahwist to form a single "prophetic" narrative of the history of the world and early Israel.[99] The textually first story of Creation in Genesis shows God creating humanity at the very beginning as two distinct individuals: "male and female he created them" (Genesis 1:27)[100]; the creation of the Sabbath, among other things, shows this as the work of the Priestly editor.[101] The textually second narrative (beginning in the middle of Genesis 2:4) gives a rather different version: a single being, "man," was created; then this Adam was divided into two beings, Adam and Eve (Genesis 2:18–23). The northern, Samaritan, Galilean tradition in ancient Israel had what we may call a sort of anthropology, which saw humans as originating from a single androgynous being, "man," while the southern, Priestly tradition had a more distinctly dualistic anthropology, where "male" and "female" are seen as distinct categories. It was, it seems, with this particularly ecstatic and self-possessed aspect of marginal Judaism that the fusion with the equally self-possessed, if more rational, Cynicism took place.

According to Clement of Alexandria (our sole source for the Secret Gospel), the two versions of Mark's Gospel — Canonical Mark and Secret Mark — were both written by Mark, the evangelist, based on the preaching of Peter, whom Mark had known at Rome.[102] Clement says that Canonical Mark was written "for those who were being instructed." The Secret Gospel, on the other hand, was written by the same evangelist for those who "made progress" in the teachings of Christianity.[103] Clement sees Christians as separated into a less enlightened group and "those who made progress" (a Stoic phrase), who were somehow more sophisticated. For Clement there is a Christian mystery analogous to the pagan mysteries like that at Eleusis. Peter in particular, and the other disciples of Jesus in the Gospel of Mark, are shown as not knowing what the secret was and being rather thick-headed about it; apparently Mark knew the secret, though it was being revealed to Peter at or after Jesus' resurrection.[104] Whoever edited Secret Mark into the text we have as the Gospel of Mark in our canon seems to have deliberately and drastically cut out most of the resurrection story. Since Jesus' activity with Lazarus prefigured Jesus' own resurrection, probably Mark originally made Lazarus a major figure in the story of Jesus' resurrection.[105] It seems quite likely that either explicit homosexuality or something that offered an almost unavoidably homoerotic interpretation was part of the secret that was imparted to Peter and the others after the Resurrection, and part of the text of Secret Mark. We know that Christianity found many of its earliest adherents in the "God-Fearers" scattered throughout the ancient world. Those "God-Fearers," to judge by the texts we have looked at, were, without exception, homophobic. Perhaps a homosexual or bisexual Jesus was a fact that the early evangelists realized was too much to be accepted by those God-Fearers. Only after a period of instruction and enlightenment could such a secret be imparted to those whose moral frame of reference was, after all, like all humans, a part of a finite, very limited world.

If we turn to the other great Christian rite, the Eucharist, we may likewise pick up hints, though no solid proof, of a Greek-related homosexual context. Certainly the act that Jesus performed in giving his disciples bread and wine and telling them that they were his blood and body has no parallels in any Jewish tradition known to us. Morton Smith quotes two magical texts from classical antiquity in which a cup of wine becomes the blood of the god to be drunk as a mean of union with the divine.[106] Most interestingly, this idea appears in a Cynic context from first century BCE Palestine.

Meleager (Greek Meleagros) the Cynic was born in the Palestinian Greek colony of Gadara about 135 BCE[107]; he wrote of being educated in the Palestinian seacoast city of Tyre, but he also seems to have spoken both Syrian and Phoenician,[108] suggesting there may have been a native-speaking school of Cynicism in first century BCE Palestine. He knew Jews, at least secondhand, for he speaks with jealousy of his beloved Demo, who consorts naked "with some sabbath keeper."[109] He wrote biting satires in verse like those of Menippos, though very little of his satirical work has survived; nor do we have his *Symposium*, though the very title suggests Meleager may have dealt at length with homoeroticism. Meleager is principally remembered for his love poetry—135 short love poems in which he mentions 14 persons of both sexes as his love objects.[110] He seems to have enjoyed his student years in Tyre:

> By love I swear it!
> Tender are the boys whom Tyros nurtures,
> Yet Mysikos is the sun,
> and when he illuminates the world
> bright stars fade under his light.[111]

Almost certainly this epigram plays off the famous epigram attributed to Plato, where the soul of the dead Aster is compared to a star that rises again. Sometimes such sidereal rising was thought of as out of the great ocean that was thought to circle the world. A contemporary of Meleager, the philosopher Philodemos, also of Gadera (about 110–30 BCE), accused the Cynics of practicing homosexuality.[112] Meleager seems to have preferred mutual sex:

> My heart is not boy-crazy. What pleasure is there, O Love,
> In man-mounting [*androbatein*] one who holds-back unwilling.

Since hand washes hand — beautiful is it to stick with a wife
Rather than wander after a male who's no more than a pair of tongs stained with depilatory.[113]

The joke is on men who try to play the boy, using chemicals to remove their pubic hair. The serious point is, regardless of gender, a favorable opinion of mutually satisfying sex, which is a rare idea in antiquity.[114] However, it is to the heteroerotic Heliodora and Zenophilia poems of Meleager that we turn for the most remarkable parallels to the Christian rite of consecrating the Cup. Meleager writes:

> The wine cup is happy. It rubbed against
> Warm Zenophilia's erotic mouth. O bliss!
> I wish she would press her lips under my lips
> and in one breathless gulp drain down my soul.[115]

The implication is that in some way, by rubbing the mouth of the beautiful Zenophilia, Meleager's soul enters the wine cup, and now Zenophilia can take him into her by drinking. The theme of drinking the beloved in a cup of wine becomes more clear in a number of poems by Meleager written about the beautiful Heliodora.

Agkhe, kai palin eipe, palin, palin, "Heliodoras."
     Fill the cup and say again, again, again, "Heliodora's." Speak the sweet name. Temper the wine with but that alone. And give me, though it be yesterday's, the garland dripping with scent to wear in memory of her. Look how the rose that favors Love is weeping, because it sees her elsewhere and not in my bosom.[116]

He wept for Heliodora's death:

> Tears, the last gift of my love, even down through the earth I send to thee in hades, Heliodora.[117]

The themes that link Meleager's poetry and the Gospel are as follows:

1. A beloved person dies, and a Cynic weeps for him/her.
2. In the context of a symposium, a Cynic consecrates wine in a cup by placing a soul in it.
3. There is an implication that the beloved will rise again (Myiskos, Lazarus, Jesus).

Our knowledge of Tyre and its connections with early Christianity are limited. Mark tells us that Jesus "arose and went away to the region of Tyre and Sidon. And he entered a house and would not have anyone know it" (Mark 7:24).[118]
     There follows in Mark (vv. 25–30) the encounter between Jesus and the Syro-Phoenician woman, usually considered the most convincing evidence we have of Jesus' Cynic connections.[119] Luke 10:14 has Jesus contrast Tyre and Sidon favorably to the Palestinian Jewish towns of Capernaum, Bethsaida, and Chorasin. If we look at the Last Supper in a Greek context, we may add a fourth element to those above, for, as all early Christian sources agree, "the Lord Jesus on the night when he was betrayed took bread, and when he had given thanks, he broke it, and said ... in the same way also the cup..." (1 Corinthians 11:23–25).
     Dominic Crossan has pointed out that Jesus is acting in a countercultural role; he was serving food to his friends. The apostles, who were sitting at that Last Supper, would have associated Jesus' activities with what slaves would normally do, female slaves at that.[120]
     The gift of bread and wine is symbolic of an open commensality — equality in the

circle of Jesus' followers; however, in the earliest Christian tradition available to us, emphasis is placed on the cup rather than the wine in it.[121] This seems to be more than mere metonymy. Any Greek reader of the autograph copy of Paul's epistle to the Corinthians in the first century CE would have known that a cup was commonly a gift to a boy on his coming of age and entering into a pederastic relationship.[122] The fact that the wine used in communion is always mixed with water also points to a Greek influence on the rite, since the ancient Greeks were proud of the fact that they (unlike the barbarians) always drank their wine mixed with water.

The latest of the canonical gospels, the Gospel of John, has long been recognized by some as embodying a homoerotic sensibility.[123] The marvelous prologue to the Gospel is essentially a creation story, which calls Jesus the divine *Logos* (John 1:1). It has been suggested that this extremely difficult word (which can mean "word" and many other things in Greek) should be interpreted in light of Philo of Alexandria's notion of a *logos*, which was an intermediary between God and the material world.[124] The pagan Hermetic treatise *Poimandres* (Greek for "Shepherd of Men"), perhaps a century later than the Gospel of John, begins with a creation story that seems to embody a similar idea:

> Out of the Light a holy Word [*logos*] descended upon the watery substance, and I thought this word was the voice of Light.... The fire was quick and violent and the air, being light followed the Breath [*pneuma*] as it rose.[125]

Both Philo and *Poimandres* have a common origin in Plato's *Timaeus* and the Demiurgos there, who makes the material world from a divine plan. The presence of Logos theology and the descent of a divine emanation onto water leads us back to creation/baptism imagery in the Secret Gospel as well.

According to Oscar Cullmann, the Gospel of John embodies the theology of the Hellenistic Christians, represented by Stephen,[126] which, as we have seen, was strongly antinomian. The background in which Jesus moves in the Gospel of John is one of heterodox, Samaritan Judaism, opposed to the orthodoxy of the Temple.[127] Morton Smith notes that the Gospels of both John and Secret Mark draw independently on an earlier source — probably an Aramaic one.[128] Such a source must surely have been among the very earliest Christian writings. W.K.C. Guthrie saw in Jesus saying "I am the true vine.... I am the vine" (John 15:1–5) a reference to Dusares, the Dionysus of the western Semitic peoples. Dusares was very ancient, the equivalent of the "wild Dionysus" that the Orphics and Pythagoreans so hated.[129] The narrator of the Gospel of John is referred to, in the text as we have it, only as the "beloved disciple" — "the disciple whom he loved [*matheten ... egapa*]" (John 19:26); "the other disciple, the one whom Jesus loved [*matheten hon ephilei ho Iesous*]" (John 20:2); "that disciple whom Jesus loved [*mathetes ... hon egapa ho Iseous*]" (John 21:7 and 20) — or as "the other disciple."[130] The beloved disciple and Peter often confront each other in the Gospel of John, and clearly that Gospel prefers the beloved disciple. The oldest form of the Secret Gospel of Mark had Jesus and Lazarus in the water, "naked man with naked man." In the Gospel of John, chapter 21, the beloved disciple and Peter are out fishing after the resurrection; Peter is naked. When the risen Jesus appears to them, Peter hurries to put his clothes on (verse 7), modest before Jesus but not the other disciple. Rudolph Bultmann saw the beloved disciple as representative of Hellenistic Christianity in contrast to the Judaic Christianity represented by Peter and Mary; and A. Kragerud saw the same disciple as representative of prophetic Christianity as against institutionalized Christianity.[131] The author of the Gospel of John is much concerned with Torah but only as a prophetic work that predicted Jesus' ministry, not as a body of prescriptions and proscriptions.[132] Finally, Oscar Cullmann posits tentatively that there were two groups of disciples, both going back to Jesus — the larger, headed by Peter, and a smaller group resting "on a more inward relationship" to Jesus, headed by the beloved disciple.[133] We would add to Cullmann's notion the possibility that those two groups of Jesus' disciples may have held very different opinions of homosexuality.[134]

To summarize then: there is no evidence of homophobia in anything we have that can be reasonably attributed to the historical Jesus. On the other hand, while there is also no absolutely clear evidence of either homosexual activity on the part of the historical Jesus or of his approving of homosexuality, nevertheless, there is fairly clear evidence of what might be called a homophilic ambience around the historical Jesus. Jesus lived in an area of Jewish-Hellenistic Palestine, where the already fading traditions of Greek pederasty still survived; and many of his earliest followers were recruited in that context. If there is homophobia in the Christianity that was inherited as a vital element in the formation of the modern Western tradition, that homophobia entered Christianity after Jesus and not through him.

AFTER JESUS: HOMOPHOBIA IN THE FORMATION OF CHRISTIANITY

Whatever happened between Lazarus and Jesus in the water at Bethany, it is clear that, within a generation of Jesus' death, some but not all of his followers were preaching and practicing an antinomian gospel. There was fairly clearly a split in the very early church over the question of Torah: how much of the commandments of Torah were Christians obliged to follow? The split was between legalists and antinomians. Antinomianism meant freedom from the law — specifically Torah. Morton Smith maintains that Jesus claimed that he had transcended Torah and that his followers, endued with the spirit, had too.[135] Others, led in the early years by Jesus' brother James adhered more closely to Torah and the common practices of the time and place.

The opposition between love and law is very old and has never been fully worked out in Christianity. The Catholic tradition has tended to follow a theory of natural law, while Protestantism has sought its validity in a strict understanding of Scripture. As Philo saw Torah as a Platonic shadow of ultimate reality, law can be at best only what Reinhold Neibuhr has called "an approximation of love."[136] As we have seen, the moral certainties that natural law present are in fact quite uncertain, and Scripture looks all too time-bound, approving of tyranny, slavery, the oppression of women and other practices that we find ethically repugnant.[137] No one can argue that any and all acts based solely on homosexual desire are ethical; at the same time it seems obvious that some homosexual acts can arise from love and be truly moral. It is a serious and ongoing failure of Christianity as a whole that it does not recognize this.

The split may have its roots well before the execution of Jesus; we have seen that there are hints that Jesus and his birth family — his mother and brothers — may not have gotten along very well. Soon after his death there was a drastic split in the young church, a split between the "Hellenists," antinomian Christians who were largely Greek-speaking, and the "Hebrews," conservative, Torah-observant Christians who spoke Aramaic.[138] James, called James the Just, had been converted to Christianity by a vision of the risen Jesus,[139] and soon he was leading the conservative faction. On the liberal or antinomian side a man named Stephen made a ringing speech denouncing the Torah and those who practiced it — and got himself stoned to death for his trouble.[140] Morton Smith analyses the split in terms of the attitude toward baptism. The Baptism of Jesus seems to have been a profoundly emotional rite, performed secretly, one on one, and after several days of preparation. Soon after Jesus' death, his movement began to have a mass appeal. The fact that Jerusalem was a center visited by Jews from all over the Roman empire helped spread the new faith very quickly to Rome, and to Alexandria — we hear very early of an Alexandrian Jew named Apollos who became a Christian.[141] Ecstatic converts were baptized by Peter with, it seems, little attention to any preparation beforehand, and apparently in public.[142] Almost certainly they did not immediately receive the "Secret of the Kingdom of God" in the way that Lazarus had — whatever it was. The response to Christianity was so great that church leaders were forced to emphasize numbers over careful instruction. The Church very early in its life began to suffer from its own success.

Interestingly, Heggisppus (about 90–180 CE), writing in the generation after the Apostles, says of James the Just, leader of the legalists: "He did not anoint himself with oil nor did he go to the baths.... He did not wear wool but linen."[143]

James was also a vegetarian.[144] The refusal to use the baths (public baths, where homosexual activity was frequent) strongly reminds us of Plotinus two centuries later, a Platonist deeply influenced by the Pythagoreanism of Amminius Saccus. Likewise the refusal to wear wool was part of a very old Pythagorean tradition.[145] Vegetarianism was also a common mark of the Pythagoreans. It is therefore possible to surmise that in James the Just we have Pythagoreanism entering Christianity at a very early date, probably after having made a considerable excursion through the Essenes and there losing its foreign, non–Jewish, identity. The Epistle of James (written perhaps 90 CE), which has entered the canon of the New Testament, is almost certainly not actually the work of James the Just. It mentions Jesus Christ only twice and has a strong emphasis on Torah.[146] On the other hand, it is clearly influenced by Cynic ideas.[147] Robert Grant has seen in the phrase "wheel of becoming" (James 3:6) an Orphic idea that the author of the epistle does not fully understand.[148] Once again it appears that much of the Orphic-Pythagorean and other quasiphilosophical influences on early Christianity occurred through Hellenic Judaism.

James the Just was soon recognized as a "pillar of the Church," as a leading authority able to define and enforce what was and was not permissible to Christians. The antinomians saw Torah as no more than "a cultural artifact," while others saw it as the unalterable will of God. Though some political arrangement we do not fully understand, the non–Christian leaders in Jerusalem persecuted the antinomians, killing Stephen and driving many out of the city, while James the Just and his followers were left alone.[149] Antinomianism was not likely to appeal to any government, Jewish or Roman, based on law.

There was, then, a wide divide in the earliest days of Christianity over law. Inextricably linked to the Torah was some form of homophobia. If antinomian Christians in the early years of the church saw love as the only law, they may have practiced love in a most canonically unapproved fashion. Jewish-Christians, on the other hand, probably maintained at least the minimal command against male-to-male sexual penetration and probably saw homosexuality in a wider sense, like Philo, forbidding all forms of homosexuality both between males and between females.

9

The Birth of Modern Homophobia

> I am afraid that nature itself is but primarily custom, and that custom is but second nature.
>
> — Blaise Pascal, quoted by
> Andre Gide in *Corydon*

Homosexuality was in a tentative situation in the second and third century classical world. Wandering Stoic preachers like Dio preached against it in the great cities, and Roman emperors had begun to trim at it, fear it, distrust it. The final crystallization of the Greco-Roman world was to produce European civilization in many respects as it endures to this day. We have seen that there is little evidence in the early days of Christianity of any homophobia. Soon Christianity was to undergo the same sort of transformation that had affected the larger culture, and join with the pagan philosophers and the Roman Emperors in denouncing a certain sort of love. We begin where Christian homophobia seems to have begun.

PAUL

The only explicitly homophobic statements in the New Testament are in the writings of Paul; and it is to Paul, who called himself the "Apostle of the Gentiles," that we turn next. Paul was born in Tarsus, a Greek colony city on the Mediterranean coast of Cicilia, about the same time as Jesus[1]; from the very beginning he was a man with one foot in the Hellenistic world and the other in the Jewish — Tarsus was famous for its schools of philosophy as well as the haughty Greek pride of its inhabitants.[2] The ancient deities of the Hittites continued to be worshiped at Tarsus as well. We hear of Ba'al of Tarsus who was identified with Herakles, the Greek hero-god. Sometimes called Sundan, the myth had him the son of Zeus who was sacrificed in the fire annually.[3] Paul's family were Jews; he was, he tells us a "Hebrew of Hebrews," apparently from a family that continued to speak Hebrew, which even in Palestine was old-fashioned, if not archaic, for that time.[4] Educated in the Greek schools in Tarsus,[5] Paul seems to have finished his education in the conservative religious schools of Jerusalem,[6] becoming a Pharisee. Generally we may conclude that he was a fairly representative example of a Hellenistic Jew.

Converted in midlife to the growing Jesus movement, Paul became a wandering missionary, founding churches in Greece and Asia Minor and writing letters to them, letters that rank second only to the Gospels in importance as Christian Scripture. There are two references to homosexuality in the surviving body of Paul's letters.[7] The longer of these, that in Romans chapter 1, will furnish not only a full overview of Paul and homophobia but a context for the whole topic within early Christianity. Always in dealing with the writing of Paul, we should bear in mind what the author of the Second Epistle of Peter said of Paul's Epistles, "there are some things in them hard to understand" (3:16). This is perhaps an understatement.

We know a good deal about the situation that provoked the Epistle of Paul to the Romans. Christian missionaries had reached the city quite early and converted a considerable number of the Jews living in Rome; this had led to violent conflicts in the synagogues, which spilled onto the streets. The Emperor Claudius had banished a large number of Jewish-Christians and their opponents as well from the city. When Nero came to power in 54 CE, he lifted the ban, and the squabbling elements returned.[8] As Jerome Carcopino has shown, many of the early Christians in Rome were recruited from the ranks of the Neo-Pythagoreans and attempted for generations to retain an identity both Pythagorean and Christian[9]; we have seen in some detail that the pre–Christian Neo-Pythagoreans were strongly homophobic and that they used the argument from nature to denounce homosexuality. It appears that Paul, who had never been to Rome, was writing to help calm these troubled waters and perhaps prevent another expulsion, or worse.

Perhaps there was a wider argument in Rome at this time of which we know very little. Edward Gibbon says succinctly, "Of the first fifteen emperors Claudius was the only one whose taste in love was entirely correct."[10] The contrast with his successor, the flamboyantly polysexual Nero, must have been jarring. Claudius, very heterosexual in his tastes, had a long, quiet and prosperous reign; perhaps heterosexuality had come to be taken as a norm by his enormous household of slaves. Perhaps the stormy situation that provoked the Epistle of Paul to the Romans involved a conflict of the more heterosexist household slaves of Claudius against slaves of Nero, who may have maintained a freer attitude. Clear and certain information on the topic is, however, lacking.

The situation in Rome was radically different, it seems, from that in the churches that had grown up in Greece or the sphere of Greek cultural influence. Churches such as that at Antioch met in private homes of wealthier members; there were Jewish homes, where ritually clean meat was served, and non–Jewish homes which probably accommodated those who ate only *kosher* food.[11] The Greek tradition that male slaves should be free from homosexual coercion survived. However, the available information suggests that in the early Roman church, many of the members belonged to the household of the Emperor Claudius and may have been forced to meet at one, very large house,[12] though they were ethnically diverse — Jews, Greeks, Latins (who if they were free, were accustomed — at least before conversion — to sexually use their slaves, regardless of gender), former God-Fearers, Orphic-Pythagoreans, and others. It was essentially an imperial situation, and aspects of personal preference could not easily be respected.

As a kind of prologue, Paul discusses the origin of human sin; he speaks of the whole race, Jews and non–Jews together, as collectively guilty of sin, particularly the sin of homosexuality. Here is the passage itself:

> For the wrath of God [*orga Theou*] is revealed from heaven against all ungodliness and wickedness [*adikian*, injustice] of men who by their wickedness suppress the truth. For what can be known about God is plain to them because God has shown it to them. Ever since the creation of the world, his invisible nature, namely his eternal power and deity has been

clearly perceived in the things that have been made. So they are without excuse; for, although they knew God, they did not honor him as God or give thanks to him; but they became futile in their thinking [*dialogogismois*]; and their senseless minds were darkened. Claiming to be wise [*sophoi*, wise ones], they became fools and exchanged the glory of the immortal God for images resembling mortal man or birds or animals or reptiles.

Therefore God gave them up in the lusts of their hearts [*en tais epitumias*] to impurity [*akatharsian*], to the dishonoring [*mazesthai*] of their bodies among themselves [*ta somata auton en heautois*] because they exchanged the truth about God for a lie and worshiped and served the creature rather than the creator, who is blessed forever! Amen.

For this reason God gave them up to dishonorable passions [*eis pathe atimias*]. Their women exchanged natural relations [*phusikan khresin*, uses or needs of nature] for unnatural [*eis ten para phusin*, that against nature], and men likewise gave up natural relations with women [*ten phusiken khresin ten theleias*] and were consumed [*exekauthesan*] with passions [*orexei*] for one another, men committing shameless [*askhemosunen*] acts with men and receiving in their own persons the due penalty for their error.

And since they did not see fit to acknowledge God, God gave them up to a base mind and improper conduct [*ta me kathekonta*, literally "that which is against duty"]. They were filled with all manner of wickedness, evil, covetousness, malice. Full of envy, murder, strife, deceit ... disobedient to parents ... [Romans 1.18–30].

In order to deal with this complex passage, it will be convenient to summarize its points, then consider each item individually. In summary this runs:

1. God's wrath is provoked by those who willfully suppress the truth.
2. The truth of God can be known by looking at the created world.
3. Humans willfully and foolishly ignored the truth of God and worshiped beastlike idols instead of God.
4. Because of their idol-worship, God gave humans over to lusts and impurities.
5. Those lusts and impurities consisted of same-sex sexual relations, both of women with women and men with men.
6. Many other sins are included in the evils to which God gave up humans.

Items 1 and 2: Paul restates briefly the argument from nature. By looking at natural objects — in effect by science — humans can know God. This essentially is the Pythagorean religion of seeing, which is opposed to the old Dionysian religion of eating. We have noted at great length in this work that this idea is not by any means original with Paul. It was first stated by Plato in the *Laws* and elaborated upon and developed by virtually every Greek philosopher after Plato. The axiom: "Live according to nature" was almost universal in Greek philosophical thought, though what this implied with regards to homosexuality was subject to wide disagreement. Early Stoics believed that homosexual acts were a part of a fully natural life, while Platonists looked on such acts as unnatural.

Item 3: Paul does not explicitly say that homosexual desire and acts are a direct result of willfully ignoring the appearance of God in creation, though he later refers to such acts as "against nature." Rather, the result of ignoring God in nature was idolatry, specifically worshiping animal-shaped idols (probably we should see this as a direct reference to the animal-shaped idols of Egypt, though the Jews' worship of the Golden Calf in the wilderness may also be hinted at). As Bernadette J. Brooten has noted, this echoes ideas put forth in the Wisdom of Solomon, which denounces idolatry.[13]

Items 4 and 5: As a response to humanity's sinful worship of idols, God gives them up to shameful same-sex lusts, and acts. Homosexual acts do not provoke "the wrath of God"[14]; instead they are a result of it. Thus, Paul implies, there is a pattern of action and, response. Humans give up God and turn to idols: God gives up humanity to homosexuality. Homosexuality is not itself a result of turning from nature to the unnatural but a sign or result of divine abandonment.[15] Paul sees homosexual acts both for males and females as *atimazo*, "to degrade, to dishonor." He seems quite close to seeing homosexuality less as a crime than as a punishment for the crime of idolatry. Homosexual acts are described with words that imply a universally accepted societal norm, the ancient Mediterranean ethic of shame, rather than the particularly Jewish ethic of Torah.

Item 6: Having concentrated on homosexuality as a result of the typical human sin, idolatry, Paul gives a longer list of various other sins, which, Hans Lietzmann finds, contains distinct echoes of Stoicism.[16] It seems worth noting that the vice-list includes disobedience to parents, though we have seen that the historical Jesus seems not to have been overly worried about that sin. Romans were, however, worried; essential to Roman culture was the dominance of the *paterfamilias*, the male head of the family who controlled everyone in the family with an iron grip. The Greek institution of pederasty offered boys training outside the family to become free and independent. A phrase in a vice-list is not usually considered grounds for an elaborate doctrine, but it seems clear that Paul was considerably more ready to give in to the cultural norms of the dominant society than Jesus was.

"Sin" (*hamartia*) is used by Paul in a curious manner, mythologically, almost personified as an independent being; sin for Paul is a power greater than any individual human; humans are less sinners individually than victims collectively of Sin.[17] Sin thus personified is less a matter of defectiveness, or what we might call bad choices, and more a powerful spirit, active in the world. Paul uses the concept of demons that was developed (or at least given intellectual standing) by Speusippos and Xenocrates, though ultimately the notion goes back to the most ancient and apparently universal forms of animism.[18] As references in other letters of Paul show, Hellenistic Judaism was very much interested in such "elemental spirits."[19] Humans, Paul believes, are slaves of Sin (Romans 6:16, 17, 20;), sold into sin as slaves were sold (7:14); and Sin rules them like a monarch (5:21). All this tends to exculpate the individual sinner, since a slave must obey his or her master, as Paul's audience knew only too well. Rather, Paul sees Sin as a part of the human condition; all are sinners because they are descended from the original sinners, Adam and Eve (5:12). In contemporary Jewish thought, Torah was graciously given to Israel by God as a solution to this problem. Salvation was extended to all Israel, but obeying the Torah was the condition of remaining within the covenant community.[20] However human weakness, the innate inability to obey the Torah, made Torah ineffective, according to Paul — the law was "weakened by the flesh" (8:3). Paul, seeking to bridge the gap between pagans and Jews, offers a universal vision of all humanity bound under Sin, enslaved as the Israelites were in Egypt, and freed by the gracious act of God. As sin is a universal condition, so Paul seems to see the deliverance from sin as universal: "For God has consigned all men in disobedience, that he may have mercy upon all" (Romans 11:32).

Paul saw Christ as "the end of the law" (Romans 10:4). Elsewhere he sees Christians as the offspring of Sarah, a free woman, as opposed to those who are under Torah, who are offsprings of a slave woman; as Jerome Murphy-O'Connor (a Paulist priest) has said, "Believers could see themselves as partners in a new covenant without in any way being bound by the Law."[21] The corresponding myth to being a slave to sin under the law is life in faith through Christ.[22] In a remarkably subtle way Paul has it both ways — enough respect for the Torah to satisfy James the Just and enough freedom to make conversion possible for the pagans. It was clear to Paul[23] and others that Jesus had not understood careful obedience to the Torah as essential to salvation. To those Christians in Rome the question of what Torah meant and how it related to daily life was an essential issue. Should males be circumcised as well as baptized, as an initiation rite in the new covenant? Should one eat pork, or meat at all (the latter forbidden by Orphics)?[24] Should one engage in same-sex lovemaking? The Roman Christians had been so vexed by such questions that their commotion threatened the peace of the city. In one way the Epistle to the Romans is Paul's attempt to address the issue of the relation between the Jewish idea of what is a moral life and the Christian understanding of that issue. Law, or the conventional understanding of law, is not the answer for Paul. In his epistle to a group of Christians whom he knew better, the Galatians, he deals more directly with the issue. "For all who rely on the works of the law [*ex ergon nomou*] are under a curse" (Galatians 3:10). Joseph B. Tyson has interpreted the difficult term "works of the law" as those activities that distinguished the Jews from the Gentiles — primarily the food laws and circumcision. Paul is not opposed to "good works" but is striving to free Christianity from the narrowing bounds of Jewish nationalism and ethnocentrism, and to establish it as a universal religion, "for the Jew and also the Greek."[25] At this point it is important to remember that in Romans (and not in Galatians) Paul addresses those Christians who had been God-Fearers — persons who by their participation in the Roman Empire had a more or less universal outlook, yet by their participation in the Pythagoreanized moral outlook of so many Romans were homophobic. Certainly for this audience of Paul and perhaps for Paul himself (as a man from Tarsus and hence a Hellenistic Jew), the universe itself was essentially homophobic. Homosexuality was "against nature."

Jesus is the Messiah, for Paul; but he is above the law, the Torah; Jerome Murphy-O'Connor has written: "Paul saw the Law as subsumed in Christ. The perfection of love ... was all the Law could possibly demand.... It was up to each believer to decide how in any given set of circumstances the creative self-sacrificing demonstrated by Christ should be given reality."[26] The Epistle to the Galatians is the only epistle of Paul that does not seem to be addressed to a church (or rather churches in this case) that was not founded from the membership of a Hellenistic synagogue.[27] Paul's vice-list in Galatians 5:19–21 is remarkably similar to that in 1 Corinthians 6 but lacks reference to homosexuality. It is tempting to speculate that Paul, whose homophobic statements were addressed to churches of God-Fearers and Hellenistic Jews, was actively attuning his message to the moral expectations of the persons he was addressing. In short, Paul continues the antinomian tradition that Jesus expressed. There seems little room in this for a new law, a law of nature, but there it is.

The question of Christian antinomianism (that is, of whether law, Torah, is valid) has been debated for centuries.[28] However, it seems that Paul may be using a sort of two-leveled approach to the issue. In 1 Corinthians 3:1–9, he speaks of the members of the Corinthian church as babies (*nepios*) and complains that he must address them as babies, rather than as "spiritual persons" (*neumatikois*). Later in that same epistle Paul restates his essential antinomianism:

> "All things are lawful for me," but not all things are helpful. "All things are lawful for me," but I will not be enslaved by any [1 Corinthians 6:12].

In Galatians 4:1–7, Paul combines the imagery of children, slavery and the law:

> I mean that the heir, as long as he is a child, is no better than a slave, although he is the owner of all the state; but is under guardians and trustees until the date set by the father. So with us; when we were children, we were slaves to the elemental powers of the universe [*stoikheia tou kosmou*]. But when the time had fully come, God sent his Son, born of a

woman, born under the law, to redeem those who were under the law, so that we might receive adoption as sons.... So through God you are no longer a slave, but a son, and if a son, then an heir.

Likewise in 1 Corinthians 8, Paul discusses the ethics of eating food that had been offered to idols (it was a common pagan practice to offer food to various deities before eating it). He says that, to those with knowledge (*gnosis*, v. 1), such gods are nothing. In and of itself, eating such food is harmless. However, some weak Christians may find the fact of others eating food offered to idols a stumbling block; they might eat such food against their consciences. Therefore, one ought to not eat such food in order not to offend. Carrying the point further, Paul asks rhetorically, "Am I not free?" (9.1) and defends his right as a free apostle among other things to "lead about a sister-wife [*adelphen gunaika*]" (9:4) as other apostles do. The nature of Paul's relationship to the sister-wife was probably as ambiguous to many in his time as it to everyone today; the suggestion is that it at least looked as though they had an improper sexual relationship. Similarly in Romans Paul recommends not eating meat at all, not because eating meat is evil, but because some Christians (probably former Pythagoreans) think it is, so out of love one should abstain (Romans 14:1–4). Hence there are two manners of possible conduct, dictated by one rule. One may eat whatever is available if it does not offend others, but out of love for others, one should not eat meat if it offends. Love is the only rule.

All of this suggests an analogy to Stoic practice, especially the Romanized Stoicism of Panataeus. Less out of love and more out of a desire to appear proper, many Roman Stoics like Cicero saw not the high and pure rationality of Zeno and Chrysippos as the proper guide to living, but convention, custom and civil practice; they particularly avoided anything that smacked of Cynic practice.[29] We have seen Cicero denouncing as unseemly homosexual practices in public, yet maintaining a deep relationship, both erotic and loving, to his slave Tiro. The use of the word *kathekonta* in Romans 1 clearly indicates that Paul was thinking in Stoic terms. The Geneva Bible of 1560, which was annotated by Calvinists, who knew something about Stoicism (John Calvin did his dissertation on the Stoics), says in a marginal note on the above quoted passage, "All things are lawful to me" (I Corinthians 6:12), and "Here he [Paul] speaketh of things indifferent of their nature and first as touching carnal liberties." The annotator must have been thinking of *adiaphoria*, the common Stoic term for things that were morally indifferent. The word *kathekonta* was not quite invented by the Stoics; but it was such a buzz word among them that, especially in any statement about natural ethics, a Stoic association is inevitable. The author of Acts has Paul allude to Stoic concepts in his speech before the Athenians (Acts 17:28), and the presence of Stoicism in Paul's thought is generally agreed to be pervasive.[30] The Stoic connection may at the very least deepen the suspicion that Paul was thinking of appearances rather than abstract ethics in Romans 1.

As we have seen, Clement of Alexandria, writing more than a century later, says that the Church in Alexandria had two Gospels of Mark, one for those who were being instructed in the faith, and another for those who were mature. This second version had homoerotic overtones. Anyone who has attempted to raise a child knows that some things safe and permissible for an adult to handle (a carving knife, for example, or a piece of expensive glass art) may not the sort of things that should be given to a child. Rules like "don't play with matches" may seem merely arbitrary to a child who sees adults lighting candles and grills with them every day. If we want to see Paul as fully consistent (though there is no guarantee that he was), we may maintain that there was a sort of esoteric secret gospel, revealed to those who were ready to handle it, and an exoteric, public gospel proclaimed from the rooftops. Still Paul, in the passage from Corinthians quoted above, returns to what appears to be a form for the argument form nature: "the body [*soma*] is not meant for immorality [*porneia*]" (1 Corinthians 6:13). This is preceded by one of Paul's vice-lists (vv. 9–10), which includes homosexuality, and followed by explicit warnings against sex with prostitutes. (*Porneia* originally comes from the Greek verb meaning "to sell," and had the specific meaning of selling sex; however, by Paul's time the word had come to be applied to a wider range of activities. The word is almost always used to distinguish a sexual activity, not necessarily homosexual).[31] One wishes that one could say that Paul was sympathetic to the slaves who were forced into the brothels of antiquity, but rather he seems to regard those persons only as sources of defilement — scarcely human. The implication of 1 Corinthians 6:13 is essentially that the nature of the body as *soma* is not for certain activities, though here the essential gendered idea of the body widely held in Paul's time is not at question (Paul's example is a man having sex with a female prostitute). If there was a secret gospel concerning freedom with regard to homosexuality, Paul kept the secret very well.

Paul had a much-hyphenated identity — a Roman-Hellenized-Jewish-Christian. As a Roman he would have seen male-to-male homosexual activity as an expression of dominance, one man demonstrating his superiority over another. The verb Paul uses to describe male-to-male sex acts in Romans 1:27 — *katergazomenoi* from *katergazomai* — generally has destructive and aggressive meanings: "to overpower, to work down, bruise, destroy."[32] Likewise, the term for female-to-female homosexual activity, *exekauthesan*, has to do with "inflammation, busting into flame, fever," suggesting the Hellenistic notion that lesbian women were somehow sick or afflicted with an unnatural condition. Bernadette Brooten has explored at length the Hellenistic medical tradition of seeing women who sought out same-sex partners as diseased, often as afflicted with an oversized clitoris, a disease that the males who controlled such women attempted to cure by surgical removal of the clitoris.[33] The Roman and Hellenistic understanding of homosexuality was generally highly negative, and the evidence suggests that Paul shared that understanding. The argument from nature was restated in several Hellenistic Jewish works, as we have seen. The Wisdom of Solomon, Pseudo-Phoclydes, and particularly the Sibylline Oracles, all echoed the notion that homosexuality was "against nature" and thus put that essentially Pythagorean Greek idea into a Jewish context. We have evidence of a direct influence from one of these sources: Clement of Alexandria, who had the opportunity to read the entire Sibylline Oracles, says that Paul appealed to them for support.[34] The texts as we have them of Paul and the sibyl have only the general resemblance of denouncing idolatry and homosexuality as linked. Possibly Clement is referring to some portion of the Sibylline Oracles now lost.

Modern efforts to understand why Paul introduces homophobia and the argument from nature into his writing have to a considerable degree split down denominational lines. The Jewish tradition sees God essentially as active in history,[35] rather than nature. God created the world; but God's primary revelation, in the Jewish tradition, is not in nature but in miraculous acts affecting whole peoples — the parting of the Red Sea, the giving of the Torah, etc. "The heavens are telling the glory of God; and the firmament proclaims his handiwork" (Psalms 19:1). But law, Torah, is a special revelation of God's will, not inscribed in nature. Torah is particular, given to one people, once in history. In so far as Paul was deducing law from nature, he was thinking in the Greek tradition, not the Jewish. Roman Catholics have generally taken the argument from nature as valid. Protestants have generally seen it as unreasonable and intrusive to Paul's case. Thomas Aquinas discusses law and natural law at great length in the *Summa* (Questions 90–93, among others),[36] which was placed on the altar at the Council of Trent beside the Bible as equal in authority.[37] The First Vatican Council (1869–70) taught natural theology as the official doctrine of the Church.[38] After Vatican II,

Paul IV in *Humananae Vitae* (1968) affirmed the authority of the Church to define and interpret natural law and "all the moral law."[39]

Protestants, on the other hand, have generally held grave doubts about the appeal to natural theology. Immanuel Kant maintained that we cannot know God by reason, and David Hume disposed of the possibility of a natural ethic, saying that one cannot derive an "ought" from an "is." In the twentieth century, Karl Barth argued that a Christian's knowledge of God must come from Jesus Christ and the Scriptures, not from an application of reason to nature; for Barth, the argument for the existence of God from nature is "intellectual work-righteousness," evidence of human arrogance, since it assumes that humans can save themselves.[40] The problem remains then: If we take the argument in Romans 1 in a literal manner, then we must believe that humans can know God though the observation of nature; hence, both Christ and Scripture are unnecessary. Perhaps the nearest we can come in a theological solution is to follow Wiard Popkes in regarding Paul's argument here as a sort of framework, intended to lead up to the point Paul is really interested in — the salvation of those both with and without Torah.[41] In summary, then, the Protestant position is that the argument from nature in Romans 1 is essentially intrusive to Paul's argument; and, though many Protestants retain the homophobia Paul expresses there, they nevertheless tend to marginalize the text.

We turn next to Paul's other pronouncement on homosexuality: the vice-list in 1 Corinthians 6:

> To have lawsuits at all with one another is defeat for you. Why not rather suffer wrong? Why not rather be defrauded? But you yourselves wrong and defraud and even that your own brethren. Do you not know that the unrighteous will not inherit the kingdom of God? Do not be deceived; neither the immoral, nor idolaters, nor adulterers, nor sexual perverts [*oute malakoi, oute arsenokoitai*], nor thieves, nor the greedy, nor drunkards, nor revelers, nor robbers will inherit the kingdom of God. And such were some of you. But you were washed, you were sanctified, you were justified in the name of the Lord Jesus Christ and in the Spirit of our God [1 Corinthians 6:9–11].

Since this is another of Paul's vice-lists and the only unambiguous reference to homosexuality in I Corinthians, it is not clear that the circumstances of the Corinthian church that Paul was writing to have much to do with the denunciation of what the Revised Standard Version hastily translates as "sexual perverts" (more on this soon). Corinth was essentially a Roman colony in Paul's time, with Latin as its official language.[42] The church there, which, unlike the church at Rome, Paul had known personally, was involved in an ethical dispute. Certain persons, whom we have already referred to as *pneumatikoi*, were acting in a way that violated accepted social standards of the time: some males were wearing long hair: "Does not nature itself teach you that a for man to wear long hair is degrading to him [*atimia auto*]?" (1 Corinthians 11:14).

At this time women in the Corinthian church were wearing their hair down, in what would have struck contemporaries as a loose and improper fashion.[43] Men with long hair certainly disturbed Paul violently; long hair in a man was often looked upon as a sign of homosexuality in Paul's world, as short hair in a woman could mark a lesbian[44]; we have seen Philo's denunciation of it above. For Paul to say that proper differentiation between men and women, according to nature, depended on the length of hair tends to undercut any logical understanding of an argument from nature in Paul's thought. Hair grows quite as fast on the heads of males as it does on those of females — that is "nature." We cannot be sure that this hair-splitting matter was about homosexuality, however; all that is clear is that Paul was concerned that members of the Corinthian church maintain sociably determined gender appearance (a position any Cynic would have agreed with), especially in consideration of *tous aggelous* (v. 10), which may be read as either messengers from other churches or as supernatural beings. Murphy-O'Connor believes that Paul was being followed around the Mediterranean by suspicious agents of the morally strict Church of Jerusalem, then controlled by James the Just.[45]

The *pneumatikoi*, who troubled Paul at Corinth, represent the opening crack of a schism that a century later was to trouble the Church profoundly—the Gnostic movement. Such "Spirit People" understood Jesus and the apostles (in Corinth, probably Apollos) who preached Jesus' gospel as conveying a kind of mystery wisdom. The true realization of the Kingdom of God was in the present for them, not something only fully realized after death or at the end of the world.[46] Apparently they had experienced secret baptism and took the tradition of antinomianism quite seriously. Paul, on the other hand, saw Christianity as essentially apocalyptic[47]—the Kingdom of God is not here, but there, beyond death, "pie in the sky, by and by, when you die," or more likely after the eschaton, the end of the world order as we know it. One suspects that Paul may have held both ideas—he may have held that the apocalyptic Gospel laden with moral warnings was suitable for those Christians who were immature and felt themselves in need of rules, while the spiritual Gospel with implied antinomianism was suitable for those who were mature.

As for the form the prohibition of homosexuality comes in, the vice-list is an ancient rhetorical device, both pagan and Jewish. There was an ancient game popular in Rome that involved tiles with the name of a different vice written on each, and dramatists like Plautus in the *Pseudolus* use the device of a chain of vices.[48] Paul may have picked up his string of vices in 1 Corinthians 6 almost anywhere.

However, the exact meaning of the words "*oute malakoi, oute arsenokoitai*" ("sexual perverts" in RSV) is one of the thornier problems in New Testament scholarship. The two plural nouns designate classes of persons, but exactly what the distinguishing feature of those classes is remains far from clear. The structure of the Greek may be represented thus:

Neither (class A of persons) nor (class B of persons) will enter the kingdom of God.

Class A are called *malakoi* in Greek and class B *arsenokoitai*; the problem is determining what exactly those words mean. Bernadette Brooten's reading of the two words as "'weak/soft persons' or 'men who assume a passive sexual role with another man' (*malakoi*), and 'those who have sex with men' (*arsenokoitai*)'" is probably not far wrong.[49] Such an interpretation, however, leaves the list repetitive; a more precise reading would probably be that Paul is condemning both "bottoms" (*malakoi*) and "tops"—the insertive partner—(*arsenokoitai*). The first noun, *malakoi*, is problematic because it has such a wide number of meanings throughout the range of Greek, while the second word, *arsenokoitai*, is obscure because to the best of our knowledge this is the first and certainly one of the few times it was ever used. A small stream of ink has been spilled trying to make out the meaning of both words.

Malakoi is related to the Greek word *malakiao*, "to be soft or tender," hence *malakizo*, "to make soft, to enervate ... to be softened or effeminate." *Malakoi* in the Attic singular, *mallakos*, can mean persons who are "modest of life, soft, mild, gentle"; or in a bad sense, "womanish, faint-hearted, cowardly ... unable to bear pain ... easy, careless or remiss."[50] Not even a well-educated pagan Greek like Dionysus of Halicarnassus could always be sure just whether someone in a text who is referred to by the adjective *malakos* was being praised for sweetness of behavior or condemned as "womanish [*theludria*]."[51] By late antiquity the term was used to mean "masturbation," and a long tradition of Christian prohibition of that "secret sin" rests on this reading.[52] Clearly, however, as a term of abuse, the word is part of an elaborate misogynistic world-view that saw the genders as very distinct, and women as soft, weak and lacking courage; to denigrate a man (or call him sinful) as *malakos* was simply to include him in the despised class of women when he could and should "be a man." *Malakos* is a sort of general insult; the homosexual act of a man being willingly penetrated by another man is not the real focus of the evil associated with being classified with that word. Rather, the weakness of submitting to an act that relegated one to the class of sex object, slave, or moral and physical coward in the understanding of the person who used the word is what gave *malakos* its sting.

Arsenokoitai is obscure, not from its wealth of meanings, but from its lack. It was later assumed to have something to do with male homosexual acts because of its apparent derivation and because it seems to be associated with *malakoi* in 1 Corinthians 6:9; however, neither of these is an absolute guarantee of even a general meaning. Like a great many Greek words, *arsenokoitai* is compounded from root words, in this case *arsen*, which means "male," and *koite*, "a bed or place to sleep." Like the English euphemism, "to sleep with," *koite* takes on an erotic connotation, so it is difficult not to suspect that *arsenokoitai* means something like "males who have sex with males." However, the formation of Greek words from such roots is not by any means clear or consistent, and it is possible that other implications attached to the word, beyond merely "males who have sex with males."[53] The word occurs in the Sibylline Oracles (2.73), but it is not clear if this particular portion of the text is older than Paul or later. The Vulgate (fourth century BCE or earlier) translates this passage as "*neque molles neque masculorum concubitores.*"[54] This was translated into English by Gregory Martin and others in the 1590s as "Nor the effeminate nor liers with mankind" (Douay-Rheims Version). The Latin world *molles* is analogous to the Greek *malakio* in that it primarily means "soft" and also has the wide and confusing range of meanings that the Greek word has, "male who accepts penetration" among them: it can mean "effeminate," or "weak." *Masculorum concubitores*, "men who lie together," involves a word related to *concubitus*, "a lying together ... copulation, coition."[55] However, the word *concubitores* is related to the English word "concubine" and implies a sexual relationship, marriage-like but with less legal dignity than full marriage, usually a state entered into by a master and a slave.[56] Both Paul and those he wrote to are unlikely to have had much knowledge of sexual relations, either heterosexual or homosexual, that did not involve a dominant and a submissive person, so since *arsenokoitai* surely means something different from *malakoi*, the phrase "aggressive top," if slangy, seems likely to convey as near as we can get to a meaning.

The difficulty in knowing just what the words mean is a useful reminder of the imprecision of language and our tendency to read into ancient texts concepts that the original writers might have found not just strange but outright unthinkable. Nor are words always perfectly clear to those who use them. The slangy English word "sissy" is obviously from the world "sister." To call a man a sissy is generally to call him a coward — not an effeminate male homosexual per se (though it can mean that). However, one can easily imagine scholars 2,000 years from now, who did not have the advantage of a great many modern slang texts, doing so. One could easily produce a learned monograph on the two or three instances in which "sissy" appears in rare twentieth century texts and proving that it meant only and exclusively "passive homosexual male."

In conclusion, Paul condemns homosexual acts, in general, both between men and between women. His condemnation seems to come to him less from the Hebrew scriptures or from the understanding of rabbinical Judaism (both of which left lesbian activity out of their condemnation) and more from the Hellenistic-Jewish tradition, represented by Philo and various pseudepigraphal works. Paul's homophobia would have been taken for granted as a moral norm by a large part of his audience, whether they were philosophically inclined pagans or God-Fearers. Many modern liberal Christian theologians would say that we should not take Paul literally on this point — the homophobia in Romans is bound to the understanding of its time and place, and two ambiguous words in 1 Corinthians create a weak text on which to build the condemnation of as many as ten percent of the human race. Nevertheless, the condemnation of homosexuality in Leviticus and that of Paul have had immense influence in the world, largely, one suspects, because they resonated so well with Late Hellenistic culture.

Homophobia and very authoritarian or tyrannical government are frequently found together, as far back as Hipparchos in sixth century BCE Athens. Sadly, the same seems to be true with Paul. His approval of the state in Romans 13:1–8 gives little comfort to those who thought of Roman imperialism as evil: "Let every person be subject to the governing authorities. For there is no authority except from God, and those that exist have been instituted by God. Therefore he who resists authorities resists what God has appointed" (Romans 13:1–2). Caesar is "almost divinized," an attitude that goes well with Roman Stoicism, though it is hard to reconcile with the position of Hebrew prophets who opposed wicked kings and queens in the name of God; nor was Jesus very taken with the rulers of his time.[57] Perhaps the only point that Paul really wished to make was that one had better pay taxes to stay out of trouble with the authorities.[58] Likewise the writer of Ephesians (Paul or one of his disciples) commands, "Slaves, be obedient to those who are your earthly masters in fear and trembling and singleness of heart, as to Christ" (Ephesians 6:5). Small wonder that American abolitionists in the nineteenth century found it difficult to argue from the Bible for the end of slavery in the South. Many early Christians (like many nineteenth century Christians) were slaveholders with no apparent pinch to their consciences for it.[59] Cynics who found homosexuality natural were among the very rare voices in antiquity who were bold enough to denounce slavery as "unnatural."[60]

Nor is Paul always ready to regard women as truly equal. Bernadette Brooten has admirably summed up Paul's position on women as both "culture bound and forward looking." Paul's theory of nature in ethics maintains a natural source for "men to be superordinate and women to be subordinate."[61] Paul's condemnation of homosexuality in both men and women springs from that same none-too-well-thought-out theory of natural ethics; male or female homosexuality violates the proper subordination. That Paul and all his addressees lived in an Imperial Roman world, where the whole structure of society was built on subordination, should not surprise us. As John J. Winkler concluded, "for 'Nature' read 'culture.'"[62]

There is, in all of this, what Sherlock Holmes would call the "dog that did not bark."[63] Early Christian ethical statements against homosexuality are plentiful, but denunciation of slave-rape is strangely lacking. We know that Romans routinely raped their slaves in both a heterosexual and a homosexual context. No doubt it was understood that Christians who owned slaves would not use them sexually, but no advice, commands or injunctions seem to explicitly cover the subject — and certainly there is no advice to slaves to resist. The silence is suspicious. One finds a few Cynic voices raised against slave-rape, and slavery in general,[64] but they were marginalized. Already persecuted and already enjoying wide support in the upper classes, Christianity seems to have made a frightfully conscious decision to support the status quo of antiquity in regard to the power one human might hold over another.

Paul and his homophobia represent the strand of early Christianity that was (to quote Morton Smith) "safe, sane and successful."[65] For all his writing about Christian liberty, his basic message appealed to the more conservative elements in the growing Christian movement; in the second century CE, when the canon was determined of what writings were to be considered authoritative for "orthodox" Christians, the letters of Paul held a prominent place, while other, more radical works were left out and perished, either of neglect or outright destruction by zealots of a newly organized Christianity. The gospels enshrine the words of Jesus because, by the time the gospels were written, then canonized, those words were thought of as too sacred to be left out; but a canonized Jesus, locked in print and exalted to the highest heaven, is much easier to bow to and ignore than a living one, angry sometimes and sometimes loving with all the ambiguity of that word.

EARLY CHRISTIANITY: CHRISTIAN PSEUDOPIGRAPHA

If we look at early Christian material that did not make it into the canon of the New Testament, we find homophobia like that of Paul and worse. The number of examples is so great that a representative sampling must suffice. We begin with apocalyptic literature, representing a tradition deeply embedded in Christian thought (e.g. Matthew 24); typically apocalyptic literature is produced by minority, alienated communities — the Essenes, for example.[66] One of the major elements of the typical apocalypse is a visionary journey to the other world, and a description of the rewards of the saved punishments of the damned.[67] Such tours of the other world are generally thought to have Orphic-Pythagorean sources, deriving ultimately from a lost Greek account of Orpheus in the Underworld,[68] combined with Jewish prophetic sources and others as well. The Book of Revelation, the major canonized Christian apocalypse, attributed to John the beloved disciple, does not mention homosexuality.[69] The Apocalypse of Peter was written in Greek, probably in Egypt, probably between 200 and 250 CE; Clement of Alexandria and the Muratorian Canon both consider it authoritative; and Sozomen, the church historian writing about 440 CE, says it was read as scripture in the churches of his native Palestine.[70] Willis Barnstone comments that the work reflects with profound sadism the horrors of war[71]— the eternal war of good and evil. Instructed by Jesus, Saint Peter sees a vision of hell after the Last Judgment where men and women

> chew their tongues and they are tormented with red-hot irons and have their eyes burned. These are the slanderers and those who doubt my righteousness.... Other men and women who cast themselves down from a high slope came to the bottom and were driven by their torturers to go up the precipice and were thrown down again, and had no rest from their torture. These were those who defiles their bodies, behaving like women. And the women with them, these are those who behaved with one another as men with women.[72]

Pythagorean tours of hell generally do not describe such specific torments for specific sins[73]; one suspects these tidy lists may derive from Egyptian sources ultimately going back to the Book of the Dead (which, as we have seen, is homophobic) where a specific and gruesome deity is appointed to punish each specific sin. On the other hand, the concept of homosexuality as gender-bending has a Greek quality to it. Probably the image of homosexuals being thrown off a cliff repeatedly may derive ultimately from the famous Lovers' Leap on the island of Lesbos, where legend said Sappho threw herself to her death because of her unrequited love for a fisherman. All in all, the Apocalypse of Peter is a wonderfully syncretistic work, looking back to the Jewish prophetic tradition, the Egyptian understanding of the afterlife, the Orphic Greek tours of hell, perhaps Persian influence and predominantly Christian influence.[74] In the isolated, alienated and persecuted Christian communities of Egypt, where it originated, it must have offered great comfort to its earliest readers to find that those who shunned them, persecuted them, killed them would one day get their pay back in awful and endless pain, though such licking of one's lips over vengeance is not a firmly rooted Christian norm. A harem of pleasure-boys was a privilege of a Roman governor; something to entertain himself with when he was not doing the hard work of persecuting Christians. The fact that the Apocalypse of Peter picked up homosexuals as a group to put in hell only indicates that the author was too hurt and angry to think straight.

The Apocalypse of Paul is derived from that of Peter; the original manuscript (Greek) of this work was sealed in a marble box along with the sandals of Paul the Apostle and buried under what was believed to be Paul's original house in Tarsus. This is a trick all too familiar to those who remember the coffin of Numa filled with Pythagorean manuscripts. The apocalyptic manuscript and both lost soles were discovered under miraculous circumstances in 388 CE.[75] The work survives in Latin and other translations. Paul, accompanied by an angelic interpreter, tours hell and asks why this or that group of persons is being punished:

> And I looked and saw others hanging over a channel of water and their tongues were very dry and much fruit was placed within their sight and they were not allowed to take of it; I asked: "Who are these, sir?" And he said to me: "These are they who broke their fast before the appointed hour: therefore they pay these penalties unceasingly.... And I saw other men and women covered in dust and their faces were like blood, and they were in a pit of tar and brimstone, and they were running in a river of fire. And I asked: "Who are these, sir?" And he said to me: "These are those who have committed the iniquity of Sodom and Gomorrah, men with men. Therefore they pay the penalty unceasingly."[76]

THE CHURCH FATHERS

When we turn from the early Christian pseudepigrapha to the Church Fathers, we begin to breathe a very different air — one less touched at least with brimstone. Paul had begun the process of fusing Christianity with classical philosophy and culture in general in his famous speech on the Areopagos in Athens.[77] For many centuries to come, Christian thinkers were busy trying to answer the question that Tertullian asked: "What has Athens to do with Jerusalem?"[78] If we take Tertullian's symbolic "Athens" to mean the Athens of Harmodios and Aristogeiton, the answer is a resounding "nothing whatsoever!" The dominant culture in the Greco-Roman world, both among the elite and, as far as we can discern it, the lower classes, was strongly homophobic by the time the Church Fathers began to write. The synthesis that intellectuals such as Clement of Alexandria and Justin Martyr strove to make was, in ethical terms, that of Christianity with Stoicism (the Stoicism of Panaetius)[79] and, in metaphysical terms, that of Christianity with Platonism (the heavily Pythagoreanized Platonism of Plotinus). Both systems of thought were homophobic before the Church Fathers came to them.

Clement of Alexandria (about 150–210 CE) wrote a number of books that mediate between the pagan tradition and the Christian. Born in Athens of pagan parents, he converted to Christianity, he came to Alexandria and became a teacher in the catechetical school there until driven out by the persecution of the Emperor Severus. His *Paidagogos* (*the Tutor*) and *protreiptikos pros Hellenas* (*Exhortation to the Greeks*) (written perhaps around 200 CE) are the major sources for our knowledge of early Egyptian Christian manners and morals, especially the upper class. As with so many early Christians, Stoicism was a major influence on Clement — often the specific influence of Musonius Rufus can be traced in his work.[80] His *Hypotyposes* is lost in the original Greek, but Photios, who read it in the original, said that it taught metempsychosis — a Pythagorean-Platonic idea.[81] Besides his Christianity, Clement's writing, especially the *Tutor*, is based heavily on Musonius Rufus, in particular Musonius' lost work, *peri paideis*[82]; we have already seen the homophobia of that pagan philosopher. Philo of Alexandria is likewise a major influence on Clement. He repeats the now commonplace notion that Pythagoras and then Plato were familiar with the writings of Moses, and stole their ideas from him.[83] Interestingly, he mentions a rumor that Pythagoreans do not marry, and maintains that they do[84]; possibly the rumor that Clement heard had reference to the monastic Theraputae Philo knew about and thought of as Jewish. Clement is himself sufficiently influenced by Pythagorean writing to devote much ink to numerology.[85]

For Clement, as for Philo before him, the universe was created essentially sexually. The definition of "male" and "female" and the interaction of those principles is a metaphor for the creation of the world.[86] Bernadette Brooten finds in Clement's use of the word *allelobasias*, "same-sex sexual contact," the origins of a Christian concept of homoeroticism,[87] which, predictably, Clement condemns along with all pleasure. Specifically he condemns four forms of homoerotic activity: passive males, passive females, active females[88] and active males.[89] Clement's major condemnation of homosexuality is in the *Tutor*. An example shows a cosmology of classical homophobia: "The male seed contains within itself nature's thoughts. To shame nature's thoughts by irrationally bringing them on unnatural paths is totally godless."[90]

Matter containing thought in it is a Stoic concept. The image of sowing seed on barren ground is from the gospel (Luke 8:5–8), while the application of this to the homosexual act of one male ejaculating on another's body is from Plato's *Laws*. In a fragment of one of Clement's lost works, he defines "nature" as follows: It means (1) the truth of matters, their essence, (2) the genesis of things which come into existence, and (3) the providence of God. The first definition is grammatical. The last two definitions are taken from Aristotle.[91]

Likewise, Clement sees luxury — wearing cosmetics, jewelry, fine clothes and shaving — as a major cause of homosexuality in men. Luxury confounds "nature; men suffer the things of women; and women behave like men in that women, contrary to nature, are given in marriage and marry [other women]."[92] Men should show their stronger, Christlike nature by wearing beards — proof of their right to rule. When Adam's rib was removed, all softness left men.[93] For Clement sex is permissible only to preserve and continue the creation of the universe — by sexual contacts within marriage that produce children; non-generative sex — homosexuality, and male sex with barren, pregnant or menopausal women — should be avoided. Indeed pleasure itself should be avoided: Pleasure sought for its own sake, even within the bounds of marriage, is a sin and contrary both to law and reason.[94] "The clear conclusion that we must derive is that we must condemn sodomy, all fruitless sowing of seed, any unnatural methods of holding intercourse, and the reversal of the sex role in intercourse."[95] "You shall not corrupt boys [*paidophthoria*].... Sow not where you do not intend to reap, nor touch anyone at all besides your own wife."[96] Again, this is the Alexandrine rule.[97] Clearly the sexual mores of Clement imply the subjugation of women; sex for him is a microcosm of the macrocosm, and the order of the universe involves not only exclusive heterosexuality but also the subordination of women — concepts that are inherently linked in Clement's thought.

Justin, who earned the title of Martyr in the time of Marcus Aurelius, was born of pagan Greek parents in Neopolis, near Samaria, in Palestine, about 100 CE.[98] Well-educated and much-traveled, he studied philosophy first under a Stoic, then a Pythagorean, next a Platonist, finally becoming a Christian about 132 CE.[99] His writings are apologetic — intended to recommend Christianity to a non–Christian audience — and they mention homosexuality only in passing but always with contempt, sneering at Zeus and Ganymede for "man-mounting" (*androbatein*)[100] and at Apollo for "effeminacy" (*kinaidia*).[101] He makes no argument for homosexuality as evil, because he knows he doesn't need to. His pagan audience already considers it evil, and Justin merely uses the homosexuality of the fading old gods as a stick to beat them with. He was appalled by the cult of Hadrian's lover, the deified Antinous and the sexual orgies that accompanied it, the "sacred nights of Antinous," which indeed became a straw dog of choice to Christian apologists.[102] In his *First Apology* he protests against those pagans who raised abandoned boys to sell them into prostitution and "godless, open and intemperate sex [*ta atheo kai asekei kai akratei mizei*]" with men.[103] Nevertheless, like Philo, Justin cannot dispense with Plato. He saw Plato as having read the Torah, and Justin manages to extract from the *Timaeus* a prophecy of Christ's crucifixion.[104] Justin's disciple, Tatian the Assyrian, became something of a Gnostic; we posses only one of his works, *Against the Greeks*; but he too, like Justin, denounces homosexuality, specifically Crescens the contemporary Cynic[105] philosopher who "made his nest" in Rome and loved money and boys (*paiderastia*).[106]

If we look for the "libertine" Christians, those who may have regarded homosexuality with no horror or contempt, we must search in the dusty byways, where what has been anathematized for nearly two millennia may lurk in fragments of crumbling parchment and stray words that leaked all but unnoticed out of the pens of writers who had other things in mind. The nearest we are likely to come is those obscure heretics, the Carpocratians.

In a simplified polemic, Hegesippus traced the origins of all Christian heresies to the death of James the Just; after James's death there seems to have been a conflict between Symeon and Thebuthis as to who should lead the Church. Symeon won, and Thebuthis started his own movement, from which, says Hegesippus, many heresies developed, including those of the Carpocratians.[107] It seems fairly certain that James had insisted on a strict legalism in the Church; Thebuthis is hardly more than a name to us, but his rebellion against the picked successor of James may have had meaning in the moral sphere as well. The Carpocratians are the group of Christians that the fragmentary letter of Clement of Alexandria associates with the Secret Gospel of Mark, secret baptism and the whole conglomerate of ideas associated with homosexually friendly antinomianism in early Christianity. Clement of Alexandria speaks of the Carpocratians' "unspeakable [*arretous*] acts," using a term usually associated with the mysteries of Dionysus,[108] which were generally concerned with gender-bending. Probably they saw the secret baptism in Mark as a homosexual act.[109] Like most Gnostics, Carpocrates saw the world as inherently evil and created by a power far less than God, "angles much inferior to the unbegotten father."[110] Strongly influenced by classical philosophy, especially Orphism, he considered the body a prison.[111] However, on Christian antinomian grounds, Carpocrates reversed the polarity of Pythagorean puritanism and declared that in order to be fully free of the bodily prison, one must sin gloriously:

> The souls which in a single life on earth manage to participate in all sins ... will be freed so that they no longer come to be in a body.... Through faith and love we are saved; all else is indifferent, after the opinions of men, and is sometimes considered good, sometimes bad. Nothing is evil by nature.

Epiphanes, the son of Carpcrates, continues:

> The justice of God is a kind of sharing along with equality.... All beings beget and give birth alike, having by justice an innate equality. The Creator and Father of all with his own justice appointed this.... For God made all things to be common property.... With a view to the permanence of the race he has implanted in males a strong and ardent desire which neither law nor custom nor any other restraint is able to destroy.... Consequently one must understand the saying "you shall not desire" as if the lawgiver was making a jest.[112]

The emphasis on common property suggest the statement in Acts 2:44 where the believers held all their property in common. Apparently the Carpocratians held at least one very old tradition of the Church. As for considering the commandment against desiring a joke on the part of God, one is reminded of the Cynic concept of "serious jesting." Leaving aside metaphysics that are likely to strike the modern reader as odd, the call for justice and equality is perhaps the most appealing aspect of Carpocratian thought and the one that is most likely to go back to the historical Jesus. Calls for equality and justice become all too rare in the Church of the second and third centuries, and it seems rather little wonder that the Carpocratians were so soon disowned. The Carpocratians did not long survive; a Roman persecution of the church in Alexandria about 202 CE probably destroyed the sect, along with any text they may have had of the Secret Gospel of Mark. Origin of Antioch, who was in Alexandria a generation later, looked for but could not find a Carpocratian, and he seems not to have known about any Secret Gospel.[113]

In short the Secret Gospel vanished; the Carpocratians and other sects of early Christianity that may have practiced an antinomian gospel were marginalized within the Christian community; and Christianity as a whole became very conservative about sexuality in general and homosexuality in particular. The "Two Ways" section of the Didache forbids "corruption of boys [*paidophthoria*]" (2. 2)[114] though no clear date for that text can be fixed. It seems to derive from Jewish sources,[115] as one would expect, given the reference to uncleanness. The charge that homosexuality was "against nature" is frequently repeated, both by Greek and Latin Church Fathers[116]: by Tertullian (about 200 CE), for example (*On the Crown*, 6), and Lactantius (*Divine Institutes*, 6, 23; written about 308 CE and influenced by the Sibyllines). Isadore of Seville (died 636 CE) defined "natural law" (Latin *ius natural*) as "that which is contained in the gospel by which each is commanded to do to the other what he would have done to himself."[117] The Council of Ancyra (314 CE in what is now Turkey), condemned homosexuality (Canon 17). Numerous other examples of ecclesiastical disapproval could be cited.[118] Generally, homosexuality was taken up in the sweeping ascetic movement of the Church. Sex in general was looked on with deep suspicion; it might be tolerated only in the strictest of circumstances: between married couples for the purpose of creating children.

The roots of asceticism in the ancient world are in Pythagoreanism and Plato's dualism: matter and the physical world were seen as evil and opposed to spirit and the divine order; sexual activity was only a contaminant on the soul.[119] Hippolytus in his *Refutation of Heresies* quotes Empedocles to the effect that sex, even sex in marriage, helps the disruptive work of Strife.[120] Paul almost offhandedly recommended that females who were virgins would be better off remaining such (1 Corinthians 7:29). In context the passage is referring to Paul's expectation of the Second Coming and the end of the world in his own lifetime. However, this passage and the general temper of the times led to an overwhelming tradition of ascetic thought and practice. Lifelong virginity for both men and women became the Christian ideal.[121] Monasticism flourished. It seems that denunciations of sex in its totality does not belong to the history of homophobia; only when homosexual activity is partitioned off from heterosexuality and condemned uniquely does true homophobia occur. Of course the monastic tradition forbade both male homosexuality and lesbian activity.[122] Basil the Great of Caesarea (330–379 CE) in his *On the Renunciation of the World* said to "fly from intimate association with comrades of your own age and run away from them as from fire." If one must talk with another young monk, one should do it with "head bowed lest perchance by gazing fixedly into his face, the seed of desire be implanted in you by the wicked sower."[123] Heterosexual marriage itself was looked at darkly.[124] Towns were being depopulated by citizens fleeing to nunneries and monasteries. Philo had warned about 20 CE that homosexuality would cause the desolation of cities; now asceticism was accomplishing that goal.

THE CHRISTIAN AUTOCRACY: IRONY ON THE THRONE

That the followers of a man who had been crucified by the State Supreme eventually came to dominate that state is perhaps too much irony to be laughed at — at least by those who suffered and died for their theologically defined "crimes." By 313 CE when Constantine became Roman emperor, the Empire was dying a slow, painful death. Plagues followed the reign of Marcus Aurelius, followed by civil wars and barbarian invasions. Gradually the emperor, who had been essentially a civil leader, became, though a series of generals who ascended the throne by right of conquest, a military leader. Diocletian (245–313) had imposed a severe order and persecuted the Christians for what proved to be the last time. Dying childless, he bequeathed the throne not to an heir but to chaos, as the custom was. Converted to Christianity by what he said was a miraculous vision, Constantine moved the capital of the failing Empire to Byzantium, renaming it Constantinople, granted tolerance to Christians and attempted to assure them of doctrinal consistency by convening the Council of Nicea in 325.

The Roman emperors had long been thought of as more or less divine. The tradition went back to the Etruscan kings, who were thought of as gods on earth. Theoretically an emperor was not a god until he was voted such by the senate after his death, though emperors like Domitian had had themselves worshiped during their lives. As a Christian, Constantine could not, of course, parade himself as a god, though he came as near as he reasonably could — his statue as Apollo was set up in the New Rome while priests solemnly sang the Kyrie, and when Constantine died he was buried in his great Church of the Holy Apostles as virtually a thirteenth apostle.[125] Divine kingship, which the immediate heirs of Augustus had inherited from Etruscan sources and bolstered with Macedonian statecraft, was artfully combined by Constantine with Christianity.[126] The legislation of this "thirteenth apostle" could be remarkably harsh, especially in the realm of sexual morality: "It was offenses against chastity that roused his most inexorable and most terrible wrath.... His edicts against adultery and rape breathe the hatred of an avenger rather the prudence of the head of an empire." Parents who were accessory to the seduction of their daughter had molten lead poured down their throats.[127] Jews who threw stones at a "convert to the worship of God" were to be burned at the stake; likewise punished by burning at the stake were tax collectors who abused their office, and forgers.[128] Burning at the stake (which had been an Etruscan form of the death penalty)[129] replaced crucifixion as the Imperial death penalty of choice against the poor and slaves. The laws of Constantine and his sons are occasionally worded very oddly for laws; instead of great legal experts like Paulus and Ulpian, who had composed legal texts for Hadrian or Antoninus Pius, Constantine employed rhetoricians who wrote laws as flowery and passionate as popular fiction.[130] A Christian rhetorician, Lactantius (about 250–325 CE), was appointed by Constantine to tutor his eldest son.[131] In his book *On the Deaths of the Persecutors*, Lactantius takes a sadistic pleasure in the details of his subject. It was, as Ramsey McMullen has noted, "a brutal age, and men attributed brutality to God"; although the violence and harshness of Constantine was far more Roman than Christian.[132] Bishops became, under the legislation of Constantine and his immediate successors, the moral monitors of the people; and the books of moral discipline that had grown up in the churches, the penitentials, came to have, under the authority of local bishops, a force equivalent to civil law.[133] Heavily influenced by Neo-Platonic thought, the Church grew increasingly antiegalitarian and antidemocratic.[134] Any respect or influence individual homosexuals may once have had in their local churches was soon drowned in the rising tide of the Church Universal and Homophobic. Closet doors slammed. The image of Christ, once a beardless youth with more than a hint of the homoerotic, increasingly became stylistically identical to the iconography of the emperor, bearded, stern and patriarchal; and individual churches, which had once been independent, self-governing little democracies, came under the control of a theoretically universal hierarchy.[135] Church and state became one.

No antihomosexual legislation of the Emperor Constantine has survived; however, his son Constans I was co-emperor for a few years after his father's death and is said to have enacted laws against homosexuality in Italy, north Africa and Ilyricum. The moral force of these laws was undermined by the sexual affairs Constans had with some young German soldiers who were his prisoners of war; at any rate the effect of his laws seems to have ended when Constans was murdered by a rebellious general at the age of 27 on January 18, 350 CE, at Augustodanum.[136]

Constans' brother, Constantius II, survived long enough (he reigned as sole emperor 350–61) for the text of his law to survive. His decree of December 4, 342, is highly significant for the history of antihomosexuality legislation: men who "marry" or "have sex with" (the Greek *gamos* can mean either) another man are to be burned alive.[137] Essentially this legislation was repeated in the Constitution of Valentinian (364–75); the decree of August 6, 390, by Theodosius the Great; and finally the laws of Theodosius' son, Arcadius (395–408). All these laws affected only the willing passive partner in male homosexual acts; it was not until the legislation of Justinian that both male partners came to be punished.[138] The same codes increased the protection of slaves against their masters' sexual advances, implying that homosexual rape had come to be considered a crime so horrible that even slaves should be protected from it.[139] The shadow of late Roman legislation against homosexual acts is long indeed. We find about 603 CE the laws of the Visigoths in Spain punishing homosexuality with castration[140] in obvious imitation of Justinian's practice with the unfortunate bishops. The Holy Roman Emperor Otto I enacted legislation in 966 demanding strangulation and burning at the stake for some homosexual acts.[141] According to Byrn Fone, more than 100 civil and ecclesiastic prohibitions against homosexuality were enacted in the new states of Europe before the year 1000 CE.[142]

It is not the intent of this work to extend beyond the classical era: the age of Justinian is the very latest to which any historian will consider classical antiquity to extend. John Boswell, Byrne Fone and others have written full and readable histories of homosexuality and its opponents in Europe through the Middle Ages and into modern times. Obviously, homosexuality did not cease to exist because emperors and bishops said it should. The medieval fondness for male pairs of military saints like Sergios and Bacchos seems to have filled the gap that Harmodios and Aristogeiton left in the Greek heart.[143] In Syrian-speaking regions Saint George seems to have taken up much of the reverence that was once placed on Eshmun as a sort of personification of life itself.[144] When Ralph H. Brewster visited the great Greek Orthodox island monasteries of Mount Athos in the early 1930s, he found institutions that remarkably resembled ancient pederasty there; when a young man decided to become a monk at Athos, he often took a boy from his native village with him; the boy would grow up on Athos as a servant to the older monk and might stay to become a monk himself.[145] Naturally there were rules against homosexuality, but Brewster is clear that it happened anyway. Perhaps the greatest contribution to scholarship of John Boswell was his discovery of a same-sex bonding ritual in the liturgy of the Church in the middle ages. Boswell could not date evidence for the ritual earlier than the eighth century.[146] It is not quite clear that this "brother-making" ceremony was ever thought of in erotic terms; nor can it be seen as in any way a secret tradition that goes back to the baptism of Lazarus.

Homophobia struck in waves generally; here and there, now and then there were quiet times when lesbian and gay persons could go about their lives in relative peace and security.

But such security was never very secure; laws remained on the books and circumstances might arise at any moment to see that they were enforced. Homosexuals were forever looking over their shoulders. The stake, the gallows always loomed in the distance, and it is a tribute to the integrity of the human heart that so many dared to do and be for so long under such threats. The number of persons known to have been gay or lesbian in the last 1,500 years is impressive, and the contribution of those persons to the whole of Western culture is incalculable. The Renaissance, the rebirth of so many classical ideas, was, in regards to homosexuality, all too frequently a rebirth of the homophobia of late antiquity rather than of the ideas of early antiquity, which had valued homosexuality. All and all, that this may be attributable to religious factors. One sociologist has called religion "culture crystallized." Religion is essentially conservative; and Christianity, along with the rest of classical culture, crystallized as homophobic between about 200 and 550 CE. Only in the memory of persons now living has democracy become really independent of religion and begun a return to tolerance, if not acceptance, of homosexuality. Yet the ancient tradition persists: on June 30, 1986, Chief Justice Warren Burger of the United States Supreme Court cited ancient Roman law in a decision supporting the rights of states to outlaw sodomy in private between consenting adults.

No account of homophobia in the late Roman empire would be complete without mention of the "Sedition of Thessalonika" (390 CE), as Gibbon called it; Gibbon's Imperial prose tells the tale incomparably: Thessalonika

> had been protected from the dangers of the Gothic war by strong fortifications and a numerous garrison. Botheric, the general of those troops, and, as it should seem from his name, a barbarian, had among his servants a beautiful boy, who excited the impure desires of one of the charioteers of the circus. The insolent and brutal lover was thrown into prison by the order of Botheric, and he strongly rejected the importunate clamors of the multitude, who, on the day of the public games, lamented the absence of their favorite and considered the skill of a charioteer as an object of more importance than his virtue. The resentment of the people was embittered by some previous disputes; and as the strength of the garrison had been drawn away for the service of the Italian war, the feeble remnant, whose numbers were reduced by desertion, could not save the unhappy general from their licentious fury. Botheric and several of his principal officers were murdered.... The fiery and choleric Theodosius was impatient of the dilatory forms of a judicial inquiry.... The punishment of a Roman city was blindly committed to the undistinguishing sword of the barbarians.... The promiscuous carnage continued without discrimination of strangers or natives, of age or sex, of innocence or guilt; the most moderate accounts state the number of the slain at seven thousand.

Apparently Botheric was only enforcing a Roman law against homosexuality when he imprisoned the charioteer.[147] Ambrose, the bishop of Milan and teacher of Augustine, was so distressed by the massacre of the citizens of Thessalonika that he excommunicated the emperor Theodosius until the Emperor publicly did penance.[148] Thessalonika, at the head of the Thermaic Gulf in ancient Macedonia, had been evangelized by Paul and was the object of his earliest extant epistle. Dionysus and Isis had been worshiped there in Roman times. A Christian, Demeterius, was martyred there in 303 CE, and Bishop Damasius I of Rome (366–84) made one Acholius his vicar apostolic in Thessalonika. It was in Thessalonika ten years before the massacre that Theodosius issued his famous edict of February 28, 380, making the form of Christianity represented by the bishops of Alexandria and Rome the only legal religion of the Empire[149]; it is fair to say the city was as Christian as any in the Roman Empire of the later fourth century. Nevertheless, the citizens of Thessalonika were willing to murder the Roman garrison for the sake of a chariot driver in the amphitheater who was in love with a boy. This suggests that, no matter how violent were the laws issued by emperors or the sermons preached by bishops, homophobia had not taken hold on the hearts of Roman citizens nearly so deeply as chariot racing had.

It is to a preaching monk that we turn for the final examples of homophobia in the classical world. "Saint John Chrysostom," says John Boswell, "probably wrote more about the subject of same-sex sexuality than any other pre–Freudian writer."[150] John, who came to be called *Chrysostom*, "Goldenmouth," for the eloquence of his preaching, was born in Antioch in Syria about 347 CE, son of a civil administrator. Well educated (he was a pupil in rhetoric of the famous Labanios), he was baptized in 368 and spent some time thereafter as a monk in the country. He lived winter and summer for two years in an unheated cave on Mount Silpios, fasting often and eating, when he ate at all, barely enough to stay alive. He literally could not stomach the life of a hermit; his gastric system gave out, and he had to leave for the city or die.[151] Returning to Antioch, he was ordained and began the famous series of sermons including the Sermons on Romans in 381 CE. John Chrysostom's Greek prose style is generally considered the best of any of the Church Fathers; it can stand beside the likes of Lysias and the other orators of Athens.[152] His learning and eloquence spans and sums up a long age of ever-growing moral outrage, fear and loathing of homosexuality. John's native Antioch was one of the last great cities of antiquity — alive with performances in the theaters, races in the Hippodrome, swarming with merchants sharpening for a dime and beggars whining for a crust. Men and women, young and old, of every shade of sexuality strove and compromised for a contingent and brief life. As we have seen often in this work, pederasty was often looked upon as an essential formative force in the free, democratic *polis*; the legend of Harmodios and Aristogeiton as self-giving martyrs was the ideal of independent Athens. John Chrysostom understood this profoundly, and as a result he strove mightily to destroy the city as a basic unit of human organization.[153] Coming as he did out of a Christian tradition in which the Church had been isolated and persecuted by the larger society for centuries, he looked upon everything outside the Church and the individual household as evil. He wanted, in fact, to substitute for the city a loose conglomeration of independent, patriarch-headed households.[154] The poor, who swarmed in Antioch as they do in every great city, were an especial object of Chrysostom's care and affection. "The greatest of things," he wrote, "is charity.... without virginity indeed it is possible to see the Kingdom [of God], but without almsgiving this cannot be."[155] In this light his famous sermon on homosexuality appears as just one more attack by Chrysostom on what he perceived as the irredeemably corrupt city. Working his way at a leisurely pace though Paul's Epistle to the Romans, he takes his text for his fourth homily on Romans from Romans 1:26. Those who have sex with persons of the same gender, Chrysostom says, cannot protest that they did it for pleasure, because

> that which is contrary to nature hath in it an irksomeness and displeasantness, so that they could not fairly allege even pleasure. For genuine pleasure is that which is according to nature. But when God hath left one, then all things are turned upside down ... whence they are quite out of the pale of pardon, and have done an insult to nature itself.[156]

In order to prove that homosexual acts are not really pleasant, Chrysostom must allege that homosexuals are in fact insane and only think they are having pleasure when in fact they are harming themselves:

> ... the punishment was in this pleasure itself. But if they perceive it not, but are still pleased be not amazed for even they that are mad ... while doing themselves much injury ... smile and revel over what has happened.[157]

Nevertheless, hell is the "threatened" punishment for homosexuality, Chrysostom says. "How many hells shall be enough for such?" he asks rhetorically, then invokes the image of fire raining down on Sodom.[158] Homosexuality is, Chrysostom, says the worst sin of all:

> these I say, are even worse than murderers ... for the murderer dissevers the soul from the body, but this man ruins the soul and the body. And name what sin you will, none will you mention equal to this lawlessness.[159]

Women, Chrysostom agrees, can be guilty of homosexuality as well as men:

> Which is an evident proof of the last degree of corruptness, when both sexes are abandoned and both he that was ordained to be the instructor of the woman and she who was become a helpmate to the man, work the deeds of enemies against one another ... for they both [men and women] dishonored nature and trampled on the laws.... Since this war was not twofold or threefold but even fourfold.... For even women again abused women, and not men only. And men stood against one another, and against the female sex as happens in a battle by night.[160]

The perfect ideal for Chrysostom is for men and women to become one in the sex act, but homosexuality produces sex as aggressiveness. Moreover, female-to-female sex destroys for Chrysostom the hierarchical nature of what he sees as the proper relation of men and women — the man instructs the woman, and the latter serves as a helper to the man. He uses the extended metaphor of slaves who are sent to the market to buy certain things; the slaves are diverted and waste their time watching "juggler's feats." When the slaves return late, they are beaten. Hence homosexuality is only a diversion, and God as our master will punish us severely for not doing what we were sent to do.[161] Predictably, the passive male partner in homosexual acts comes in for a particular denunciation:

> For I should not only say that thou hast become a woman, but that thou has lost thy manhood, and hast neither changed into that nature nor kept that which thou haddest, but thou hast been a traitor to both of them at once, and deserving both of men and women to be driven out and stoned as having wronged either sex.[162]

Chrysostom's fourth homily on Romans represents the climax and consummation of homophobia in the late classical world; it inherits and echoes the whole range of homophobic thought from Plato through the Pseudepigrapha on Sodom. It seems after this sermon unlikely that there would be any softening in Chrysostom's stand on the "greatest possible sin." Yet in his treatise "On Suspect Cohabitations" an odd, uncharacteristic note is sounded. Unmarried male and female Christians who live together, says Chrysostom, must have separate bedrooms, yet two male Christians who live in the same house may share "a single room, a single cushion, one bed and the same blanket." In the same treatise he denounces what seems to be male prostitutes who do business "in the center of town practicing their base acts upon other males as if they were in the middle of the desert."[163] The duality in Chrysostom always involves the Great City as a sinkhole of iniquity. He had spent his early adulthood in the desert living as a hermit with an older hermit. Perhaps the mention of the desert here is merely an ordinary sort of rhetorical device, springing from the convention that homosexuals should be run out of town. Still the ash falls from Freud's cigar at the mention.

In comparing his one sermon on homosexuality and homosexuals with his series of eight sermons on the Jews, a final, clearer understanding appears. The sermons are as violently anti–Semitic as the fourth sermon on Romans is homophobic. Much of the language of European anti–Semitism, from the fourth century through the twentieth, can be found in Chrysostom's work. Perhaps it should be remembered that Chrysostom was a saint, not a prophet; his rhetorical stance is of one on the defensive, one who felt his church threatened by the popularity of the synagogue. He did not foresee an age when the Christians would feel themselves the vast majority.[164] Though there is a clear thread (one of millions) that runs from his Sermons on the Jews to Auschwitz and Treblinka, he probably thought of his own group, the Christians, as survivors rather than instigators of a holocaust.

The moral must be applied. The fundamental error that unites homophobia and anti–Semitism is thinking of ourselves as the good people in a besieged city. We inside are the saints, the Christians, the liberals, the gay liberationists, the good citizens of besieged Rome; and those outside, battering our walls, are the demonic ones — the faggots or the Jews or the Fundamentalists or the Communists or the Capitalists. The essence of hatred between any groups comes from failing to recognize ourselves as polymorphously human and containing at least some germ of what threatens us from without.

For John Chrysostom the city won at least a temporary victory. He was elected patriarch of Constantinople in 397 CE and was soon over his head in politics civil and ecclesiastical. His Cynic freedom of speech soon got him in trouble with the Empress Eudoxia, and he died in exile (more or less murdered) in 407.[165] The image of John Chrysostom, prematurely old and chronically ill, run out of Constantinople by a vengeful monarch, returns us to two bishops mentioned earlier. We do not know what became of Isaiah and Alexander, the bishops accused, tortured and mutilated by Justinian for pederasty. Shamed, torn, and bleeding, they left the city and history as well — or rather, they departed for the middle ages. The basic pattern of homophobia that was set by the early fifth century in the fading Roman Empire endured well into living memory. Countless thousands died as a result of laws enacted on the model of the much admired Roman Law. Thousands, indeed millions more had their lives warped, confined and stunted by homophobia external or internal. A recent sighting of the exiled bishops was in a cornfield in the western United States; one witness said he looked like a scarecrow. Alas, he was human, and his name was Matthew Shepard.

Chapter Notes

INTRODUCTION

1. Hannah Arendt. *Eichmann in Jerusalem: A Report on the Banality of Evil* (New York: Penguin, 1963).

CHAPTER 1

1. Sture Brunnsaker, *The Tyrant Slayers of Kritios and Nesiotes* (Stockholm: Svenska Institute, 1971), 14.
2. Mable Lang has made the best of a bad case defending Aristotle in "The Murder of Hipparchus," *Historia* 3 (1954–55), pp. 395–407. Her arguments are answered by Thomas R. Fitzgerald in "The Murder of Hipparchus: A Reply," *Historia* 6 (1957), 275–86.
3. Plutarch, "Life of Solon," 1.
4. Aristotle, *Constitution of Athens*, 13, 5.
5. Aristotle, *Constitution of Athens*, 18, 1.
6. Herodotus, *Histories*, 5, 61.
7. Thucydides, *History of the Peloponnesian War*, 6, 54.
8. Aristotle says (*Constitution*, 18, 2) it was the tyrant's illegitimate half brother, Thessalos; however, this is quite unlikely, and Charles W. Fornara in "The 'Tradition' about the Murder of Hipparchus" (*Historia* 17 [1968], 400–424) argues that the mention of Thessalos is an interpolation on Aristotle's text. J.B. Bury in his judicious *History of Greece*, 3rd ed., affords Thessalos only a footnote (205).
9. Thucydides, *History*, 6, 56.
10. Aristotle, *Constitution*, 18, 2.
11. Aristotle, *Constitution*, 19, 5.
12. Aristotle, *Constitution*, 91, 2.
13. Thucydides, *History*, 6, 59.
14. William Scott Ferguson, *Hellenistic Athens*, 276–77.
15. Herodotus, *Histories*, 7.8a.
16. Thucydides, *History*, 6, 59.
17. Brunnsaker, *Tyrant Slayers*, 120, n1.
18. Diodorus Siculus, *History*, 20, 46, 2.
19. Pausanius, *Travels in Greece*, 1, 29, 15.
20. A law to this effect, issued apparently by Pericles, was found in a fragmentary marble inscription (*Inscriptiones Graeci*, I, 2, no. 97), and the matter is widely testified in the literary sources: See Dinarchos, *Orations*, 1, 101; Iseos, *Orations*, 5, 47; Demosthenes 4:1, 20, 18, 29 127 ff., 159 f. 21, 170 and 23, 143.
21. Heraclitus of Pontius, in his *Peri Erotikon* (*On Love Affairs*) tells the story of two male lovers, Chariton and Melanipos of Agrigentum, who withstood the tyrant Phalaris (570–54 BCE) and were tortured to death (Athenaeus, *Deipnosophists*, 602 b–c). However, Phalaris is largely a legendary character, and it is doubtful that Heracleides had accurate information. The story may have been made up by someone in Agrigentum to steal the glory of Athens' Tyrant Slayers. See Muller, Historia Graecae 11, 210.
22. Athenaeus, *Deipnosophists*, 13, 602d. Erixias in his *History of Colophon* said that the people of Samos dedicated a gymnasium to Eros and called it the *Eleutheria* (Place of Freedom), but we do not know when this occurred. See Athenaeus, 561f–562a.
23. See Aelian, *Varia Historia*, 9.4, and Alciphron, letter 8.
24. See Walter Kirkpatrick, *The Family in Classical Greece*, 157.
25. Athenaeus, *Deipnosophists*, 512a. He goes on to cite the Apple Bearers, a special corps of eunuchs tending on the king of Persia.
26. Other than this passage, the earliest reference I know of to a male virgin in Greek is in the late *Palatine Anthology* and all the writings of the Church Fathers. Evidentially Greek men were not passionately devoted to maintaining their virginity.
27. Aeschines ("Timarchos," 1, 13, 14) says the law went back to the legendary Drako, famed for his draconian severity.
28. Aeschines, 1, 19–20.
29. K.J. Dover, *Greek Homosexuality: Updated with a New Post Script*, 92–93.
30. Aristotle, *Politics*, 6, 2 (1317 a 40).
31. See P. Cartledge, "The Politics of Spartan Pederasty," 201.
32. Greenberg, *Construction of Homosexuality*, 26–29. I know of only one explicit statement of such a magical transmission in the Greek, but it seems quite likely that what exists in other cultures in a similar context existed in Greece. For semen as a means of magically transferring personal attributes, see Theodore Gaster, *Thespis: Ritual Myth and Drama in the Ancient Near East*, 257–59. The only example Gaster cites from the Greek context is Odysseus in the tenth book of the *Odyssey*, where that hero resists the sexual advances of Kirke in order to preserve his own virility.
33. Richard D. Mohr, *Gay Ideas: Outing and Other Controversies*, 140. Italics Mohr's.
34. Mohr, 198.
35. Mohr, 199.
36. Mohr, 199.
37. Mohr, 200. This fact is attested by Masters and Johnson.
38. Pausanius, *Description of Greece*, I, 31, 1.
39. Alciphron, letter 7 in *Alciphron, Aelian and Philostratus*.

40. When a young man allowed the older to have sex with him the word for this act was *kharitas*, a word that has come over into English as "charity," implying some favor freely given.

41. The word in Greek carries the same original meaning as the English word — to "blow into" or "breathe into."

42. John Boswell, *Same Sex Unions in Pre-Modern Europe*, 28–107.

43. Oswyn Murray, "Life and Society in Classical Greece," 216.

44. See for example the ridicule of such young men in the comedies of Critinos, in Comedia Attica Fragmenta, I, 29.

45. Pausanius, *Tour of Greece*, I, 8, 4–5. A note in the Loeb edition gives Critios *flourit* as 445 BCE.

46. The two best and most nearly complete copies of the two statues are in the Museo Nazionale in Naples; they are said on no certain authority (Brunnsaker, 47) to have been found in the ruin of Hadrian's villa. This origin seems not unlikely since that emperor cultivated a more or less pederastic relationship with the unfortunate Antinous and had that young man sculpted in the austere style of the Early Classical, like the Harmodios and Aristogeiton statues.

47. Brunnsaker thinks that Harmodios is about 20 (65) and Aristogeiton a well-preserved 30 (52).

48. A stamnos painted about 470–60 BCE shows the killing of Hipparchos painted by the "Copenhagen painter." This represents an artistic tradition largely independent of the statues; the Tyrannicides are likewise shown as the same size and nearly the same age. See Brunnsaker, 108–09.

49. John Boardman, *Greek Sculpture: The Archaic Period*, 18–23.

50. See for example the *Lysis* of Plato.

51. Hans Georg Wunerlich, *The Secrets of Crete*, 330.

52. Claude Chalme in *Les choers des jeunes filles en Grece araaique* demonstrates the existence of schools in which women taught younger women to sing in the religious choruses.

53. Bernadette J. Brooten, *Love Between Women: Early Christian Responses to Female Homoeroticism*, 24.

54. Brooten, 22.

55. Brooten, 17.

56. Claude Calame, *Les choer des jeunes filles in Grece arcaaique*. See also Arthur Evans, *The God of Ecstasy*, 73.

57. Plutarch, "Life of Lycurgos," 18–19. "Their exercises and dancing were incitements to marriage, operating on the young men with the rigor and certainly, as Plato says, of love, if not of mathematics." Dryden's translation.

58. Whitney Jennings Oates and Charles Theophilus Murphy, eds., *Greek Literature in Translation*, 960–61.

59. Dover, *Greek Homosexuality*, 180–81.

60. Dover, 174–75.

61. Christine Downing, "Athena," 490–91.

62. Pierre Grimal, *Dictionary of Classical Mythology*, 295.

63. Frank Muscarella, "The Evolution of Homoerotic Behavior in Humans."

64. Muscarella, 53.

65. Muscarella, 60.

66. Muscarella, 62.

67. Muscarella, 64.

68. Muscarella, 62.

69. Benjamin R. Foster, translator and editor, *The Epic of Gilgamesh*, xii–xiii. The earliest known Sumerian manuscripts are from about 2100 BCE. The work was translated and adapted into various languages in Mesopotamia and Syria. The text is divided into 12 tablets in most modern editions. All quotations are from this edition.

70. Berit Thorbjornsrud, "What Can the Gilgamesh Myth Tell Us About Religion and the View of Humanity in Mesopotamia."

71. Tablet II, line 115.

72. Tablet VI.

73. Tablet VII.

74. Arthur A. Brown, "Storytelling: the Meaning of Life and the Meaning of *The Epic of Gilgamesh*.

75. N.K. Sandars, *The Epic of Gilgamesh: An English Version with an Introduction*, 21. Sandars notes a parallel with the legendary Minos, king of Crete.

76. Sandars, 12.

77. Thorbjornsrud makes an especial point of the parallel of Achilles choosing death and fame over life and immortality by sexual reproduction as a parallel to Gilgamesh's rejection of Ishtar. Sandars comments on a possible Mycenaean epic tradition which may have transmitted many of the ideas in the Gilgamesh epic to Homer.

78. Both names have a variety of spellings. "Melquart" is sometimes "Melkart" or the older "Melcarth," while "Eshmun" is often "Esmun" or "Eshmoun." I have regularized the spelling to what seems most common in modern sources.

79. William Foxwell Albright, *Archaeology and the Religion of Israel*, 80–81.

80. Stephen Herbert Langdon, *The Mythology of All Races*, Vol. V: *Semitic*, 336–51.

81. Michael C. Astour, *Hellenosemitica: An Ethnic and Cultural Study in West Semitic Impact of Mycenaean Greece*, 259.

82. Edward Tripp, *Crowell's Handbook of Classical Mythology*, s.v. Apollo, 65.

83. Trip, s.v. Apollo.

84. Friedrich Hrozny, "Hittites," *Encyclopædia Britannica*, 1945. Hrozny suggests that the name of Odysseus (in Latin Ulysses) may be an Etruscan version of the name derived from the Hittite *Ullush*, going back to the Babylonian word *ullu*, which means "carried away, distant."

85. Greenberg, 124–25.

86. Walter Berkert, *Structure and Story in Greek Mythology*, 120. Berkert explains the mutilation and public humiliation as ritually placing them both beyond and inferior to ordinary men. There is specific reference both to the worship of Dea Syria and to the Galloi priests of Pessinus and Hieropolis.

87. Quoted in Frazer, *Adonis Attis Osiris*, 169. From Iambilikhos, *Of the Mysteries*, 3–4. Probably the priests of Ba'al on Mount Carmel who "cut themselves after their manner with knives and lancets" (I Kings 18; 28) were following the same ritual, though neither castration nor homosexuality is mentioned. The name "Iambilikhos" is usually transliterated as "Iambilichus" in English.

88. Tripp, s.v. Apollo.

89. Grimal, *Dictionary of Classical Mythology*, s.v. Themis.

90. "*Corpora veste levant et suco pinguis olive,*" says Ovid. "They stripped themselves and 'nointed them with oil of olive fat," in Golding's translation (*Metamorphosis*, 10.185).

91. Ovid, *Metamorphosis*, 10.171–75. Equivalent to 10.165–66 in Ovid's original (Golding is not as succinct as Ovid).

92. Grimal, s.v. Apollo.

93. Lucian of Samosata, *Dialogue of the Gods*, 14.

94. Langdon, *Mythology of All Races*, 52.

95. Langdon, 74–75.

96. Eudoxos of Cnidos says that Iolaos revived Herakles with the smell of a burned quail (Athenaeus 9.392, D–E). See Astour, *Hellenosemitica*, 236–38. In the fourth century CE St. Jerome speaks of "Adonis who was Tammuz" and says that his death was wept over in a cave at Bethlehem (Langdon, 76). Greek myth likewise preserves

the relationship of Ishtar and the serpent; Typhon is said in one version of the myth to be the offspring of Hera, born without a father (Grimal, s.v. Typhon).

97. Grimal, *Dictionary of Classical Mythology*, s.v. Iolaos.

98. *Pindar: Olympian Odes: Pythian Odes*, edited and translated by William H. Race, 44–45.

99. Pindar, "Olympian I," lines 32–42.

100. Pindar, "First Olympian," lines 75–78.

101. J.B. Bury, *History of Greece*, 178–79. The source for this is, of course, Herodotos.

102. J.B. Bury, *History of Greece*, 210, 214.

103. Gaster, *Thespis*, 32. Yet another name for the lament for the crop deity was Ioulo, a feminine name that suggest Iolaos, the boy, was likewise a vegetation deity. Ultimately the myth is the hot sun of late spring and summer killing the tender vegetation of the spring. As the sun returns from winter, so the vegetation returns.

104. The Greek *isonmein* means "equal law."

105. Michael W. Taylor, *The Tyrant Slayers: The Heroic Image in the Fifth Century BC Athenian Art and Politics*, 85–86, following F. Jacoby in his *Atthis*.

106. Pausanius, 1, 15, 4.

107. Taylor, *Tyrant Slayers*, 90 and following.

108. Aristotle, *Politics*, 1271b.

109. Sextus Empiricus, *Pyrrhonian Sketches*, 3.199–200. The Lexicon of Hesychus in the fifth century CE defines *Kreta trooron* to mean pederasty. We might add the testimony of Timaeus of Taormina and that of the third Dythrimb of Bacchalydes.

110. In Athenaeus of Naucritus, *Deipnosophists*, 12, 602, a.

111. The story is told fully in the seventh book of Herodotus.

112. The Greek word is *philia*— a love feast.

113. M. Detienne, *Dionysus Slain*, 70.

CHAPTER 2

1. W.K.C. Guthrie, *The Early Pre-Socratics and the Pythagoreans*, 155.

2. Alexis, *The Samian Chronicle*, book 2, cited in Athenaeos, Deipnosophists, 540c–d. See also 514f–15a.

3. Gillian Clark (*Iamblichus: On the Pythagorean Life*, 5), cites Apollodorus that Pythagoras was flourishing (meaning that he was about 40) in 532 BCE. This was within the reign of Polykrates.

4. Iamblichus, *Life*, para. 11.

5. J.B. Bury, *History of Greece*, 233.

6. Iamblichus, *Life*, para. 35 in Clark, who cites various authorities for the date.

7. See the epitome by Justin Justinianus of Pompeius Trogus 20.4, cited in Clark, note on 13.

8. Justin, in Trogus, 20.4.

9. Probably this punishment was an arcane effort to cleanse his soul of his guilt and cause it to lose the memory of secrets; the Gulf of Tarentum, according to *The Krater*, was an upper-world entrance to a purifying bath for souls and one that induced forgetfulness. See Peter Kingsley, *Ancient Philosophy*, 135–40. Hippasos was something of a Pythagorean loose cannon; Iamblichus (*Life*, ch. 35) has him on the democratic, anti–Pythagoras party in Crotona. James A. Phillip in *Pythagoras and Early Pythagoreanism*, 31, calls Hippasos "a legendary figure of whom we know next to nothing," which is true enough, but the fact that such legends arose tells us what we need to know. Guthrie (*History of Greek Philosophy*, vol. I, *The Earlier Pre-Socratics and Pythagoreans*, 149, 320) regards him as historical and gives full information.

10. See Walter Berkert, *Lore and Science in Ancient Pythagoreanism*, 116–19, for the sources that call Pythagoras a tyrant. The evidence is scanty and widely scattered in ancient literature, possibly because Pythagoras was a hero to many in late antiquity, and there was something of a whitewash of his reputation.

11. Berkert, *Lore*, 116.

12. W.K.C. Guthrie, *Early Pre-Socratics*, 179. Guthrie dates the cataclysmic second uprising about 454 BCE; Berkert in *Lore*, 117, gives c. 450 BCE. The major source of information for this event is Polybios, 2.39.

13. Berkert, *Lore and Science*, 192, from Timaeus the Historian. See also Iambilichus, *Life of Pythagoras*; and chapters 17 and 18 in Kenneth Sylvan Guthrie, *Pythagorean Source Book and Library*. The word *sundon* means a large piece of cloth and could also mean a loose garment, or a shroud.

14. Walter Berkert says that the "sayings of Pythagoras" are "like a pile of gravel — there is no pebble which we can say it must be primitive rock, but any single one may be." *Lore and Science*, 188.

15. Adapted from a list in Kenneth Sylvan Guthrie, *Pythagorean Source Book and Library*, 159 and following.

16. Pausanius, 8.37.5.

17. Berkert in *Lore and Science*, 114, thinks Kerkropes is a figment of ancient philology.

18. Aristotle, quoted in Cicero's *On the Nature of the Gods*, 1.107. Aristotle added that Orpheus never existed — which may be one of the reason he fell from favor with the Macedonian government after his patron Alexander died.

19. Kingsley, *Ancient Philosophy*, 115 and 133.

20. Ion of Khios (flourished 452–421 BCE) in *The Presocratics*, trans. Kathleen Freeman, 36b.2.

21. C. Kerenyi, *Dionysus: Archetypal Image of Indestructible Life*, 241.

22. W.K.C. Guthrie, *Orpheus and Greek Religion: A Study in the Orphic Movement*, 46–47.

23. Phanokles (date unknown) in Stobaeus *Flor*, 64.14. These are fragments of a lost work called *Love Stories* or *Beautiful Boys*. He says that Orpheus was torn apart by women because he had lured their husbands away.

24. Erwin Rohde, *Psyche*, 285.

25. *Iliad*, 6.132. "Mainomenoio Dionusoio"— but the epithet has connotations of a divine madness, such as prophets have.

26. Eva Cantrella, *Bisexuality in the Ancient World*, 6.

27. Clement of Alexandria, *Protrepicus*, 2.30.

28. C. Kerenyi, *Dionysus*, cites the authority of J.J. Bachofen and Rudolph Otto.

29. Larry J. Alderlink points to dualism in the oldest known Orphic text, the Deverni papyrus found in Macedonia, in *Orphism and Bacchic Mysteries: New Evidence and Old Problems of Interpretation*, 10–12.

30. W.K.C. Guthrie, *Orpheus and Greek Religion*, 79. Guthrie is analyzing Orphic fragment 28 in Kern's *Orphic Fragments*. Generally I follow Guthrie.

31. Orphic Fragment 80 in W.K.C. Guthrie, *Orpheus*, 102. Guthrie compares him to the bisexual creatures described by Aristophanes in the *Symposium* of Plato.

32. W.K.C. Guthrie, *Orpheus and Greek Religion*, 101.

33. Guthrie, *Orpheus and Greek Religion*, 80, thinks Phanes produced a new Earth and Heaven by Nix, his daughter.

34. Guthrie, *Orpheus*, 108, on the authority of Plutarch, Diodorus Siculus and Firmicus Maternus.

35. Guthrie, *Orpheus*, 209, suggests that the Orphic initiates reenacted this by bathing in milk.

36. Guthrie, *Orpheus*, 120.

37. Erwin Rohde, *Psyche*, 340. Kerenyi suggests that instead of heart we should understand penis.

38. Orphic Hymn 37.2 calls the Titans "the original source of care worn mortals."

39. Rohde, *Psyche*, 285.

40. George Thompson, *Studies in Ancient Greek Society*, vol. 2, 258–62, believes ancient Greek dualistic thinking came from the division between master and slave. Greenburg, *Construction of Homosexuality*, 203, extends this to the dichotomy between male and female.

41. Aristophon in Athenaeus, 563 b. Gulik's translation.

42. Alexis in Atheanaeus, 562a–b. Gulik's translation.

43. Herman S. Schibli, *Pherekydes of Syros*, 33.

44. Aristotle, *Physics*, 2.13b.4. Translation by W.D. Ross.

45. Iamblichus, *On the Pythagorean Life*, 2.

46. James Henry Breasted, *A History of Egypt*, 523.

47. Berkert, *Lore and Science*, 161. This is from Heraclitos, frag. 81, in Berkert's translation. Kathleen Freeman in *Ancilia to the Pre-Socratics*, 30, gives the milder "Original chief of wranglers." The pejorative word means something that tradespeople do in the street, so trickery, wrangling and cheating are all possible translations. I note in passing that Heraclitos was a bitter enemy of Pythagoras. See Guthrie, *Orpheus*, 225.

48. Timaeus the Historian, frag. 131, in Berkert, *Lore and Science*, 143.

49. Berkert, *Lore and Science*, 159.

50. *Life of Pythagoras*, 143, in Berkert, 143. The story seems likely to be based on some Greek's research in the legal records of Crotona, perhaps in the Hellenistic age.

51. Herodotus, 2, 81. This is coincidentally confirmed by the excavations of the Italian Francesco Saverio Cavallari, who found a linen cloth in what seems to have been the grave of an Orphic. See Fritz Graff, "Dionysian and Orphic Eschatology," 252.

52. See for example R.B. Parkinson, "Homosexual Desire in Middle Kingdom Literature," 81.

53. It seems too much to argue that the famous Gold Plates that were buried with the Orphic dead and provide instructions on how to get around in the underworld were derived in some way from the Book of the Dead, but the parallel is striking.

54. Henry Breasted, *Development of Religious Thought in Ancient Egypt*, 302.

55. Book of the Dead, A 20, B 27, trans. Walter Beyerling; *Near Eastern Texts Relating to the Old Testament*, trans. John Bowden, in Greenberg, 132.

56. Greenberg, *Construction of Homosexuality*, 127–35. Greenburg cites Walter Beyerling, *Near Eastern Texts Relating to the Old Testament*, trans. Bowden, 64.

57. For a list and discussion of Pythagoras' miracles, see Berkert, *Lore and Science*, 141–43.

58. W.K.C. Guthrie, *Early Pre-Socratics*, citing Aristotle frag. 191 and 192 in Rose.

59. Geoffrey Graham, correspondence with author, Dec. 2, 1996.

60. Erik Hornung, *Conceptions of God in Ancient Egypt: The One and the Many*, 240.

61. Hornung, 172–85.

62. Giovanni Reale, *History of Ancient Philosophy*, vol. 1: *From the Origins to Socrates*, 297–300, points out that reincarnation is found in Pindar, but Pindar does not seem to attribute the idea to Pythagoras. Probably it was Orphic.

63. Evans, *The God of Ecstasy*, 159. Compare Guthrie, *Orpheus*, 49–52, who uses the example of Olympias to prove that women took part in the Orphic rites. Olympias was a queen, and a person remarkable for willfulness; one has the impression that she took part in anything she wanted to.

64. *Pythagoras and Early Pythagoreanism*. Phoenix. *Journal of the Classical Association of Canada, Supplementary*, vol. VII (Toronto: University of Toronto Press, 1966), 10.

65. Diodorus Siculus, 6.10.11.2.

66. Athanaeus, 12.602a. Plutarch, in his "Pelopidas" 18, attributes the founding to the legendary Gorgides. Probably Epameinondas renewed a custom that had fallen into disuse.

67. Cornelius Nepos, "Epameinondas," 10.1.

68. Asopichos, the lover of Epameinondas, is mentioned by Athanaeus, 605a.

69. Leonard Taran, *Parmenides: A Text with Translations and Critical Essays*, 263. Fragment 18 (in another work by Aurelianus) seems to have something to do with homosexuality, but all efforts to make clear sense of it have failed. See p. 264 in Taran for bibliography and a summary of the scholarship.

70. Berkert, *Lore and Science*, 284.

CHAPTER 3

1. J.B. Bury, *History of Greece*, 328.

2. Bury, 340.

3. Thucydides, *History of the Peloponnesian War*, 5, 84–105.

4. Xenophon, *Hellenica*, 2.2.3., trans. Carlton W. Brownson, in the Loeb ed.

5. Thomas Gould, *Platonic Love*, 120.

6. Eric Robertson Dodds, *The Greeks and the Irrational*, 209. Socrates' mental withdrawal (*Sym.* 174D–75C and 220D–D) links him to the abstracted states of shamans.

7. For a general account of the goings on at symposia see Paul Brandt, *Sexual Life in Ancient Greece*, 167–76. Generally they seem to have been second only to the gymnasia as places where the older men met the younger for erotic purposes.

8. Daniel E. Anderson, *The Masks of Dionysus*. Anderson makes a case (163 n2) that Diotima may be a substitute for the historic Aspasia, the famous mistress of Pericles, and possibly "the main stream of Western philosophy was born of a woman."

9. Plato, *Symposium*, 202E.

10. *Symposium*, 206C. Translator W.R.M. Lamb's note in the Loeb ed., 1967 (p. 191), points out that "begetting" here must apply "indifferently to both sexes."

11. *Symposium*, 206D. See Gould, *Platonic Love*, 48.

12. *Symposium*, 209C.

13. Gould, *Platonic Love*, 126.

14. Anderson, *Masks of Dionysus*, 97.

15. Gould, 24, with notes to Euripides.

16. Plutarch, *Alkibiades*, 4.

17. So Martha Nussbaum reads it, in *The Fragility of Goodness*, 195 and following.

18. So Anderson, *Masks of Dionysus*, 123–24.

19. *Hamlet*, 3.4, 89–90.

20. For a convenient summary of the scholarship on Plato's attitude toward Pericles, see J.C. Rowe, *Plato: Phaedrus, Translation with Commentary*, 204–05. Plato was about three when Pericles died, though the philosopher's stepfather was near the circle of Pericles. Jeno Platthy in *Plato: A Critical Biography* points to evidence that Plato preferred his mother's side of the family and that of his stepfather to that of his biological father. There seems to have been some sort of scandal attached to the latter, but the details are not reliable.

21. John Herman Randall, Jr., *Plato: Dramatist of the Life of Reason*, 166.

22. Victoria Tejera, *Plato's Dialogues One by One: A Structural Interpretation*.

23. Diskin Clay, "Reading the *Republic*," 21. Italics Clay's.

24. Randall, *Plato*.

25. There was a shift in Greek shortly after Plato's time, and the form of the subjunctive changed particularly. It is likely that many Greeks a century after Plato's death would not have fully grasped the subjunctive here.

26. *The Republic*, 468B, trans. Paul Shorey, Loeb ed., 1969.

27. In his *What Plato Said*, Shorey refers to homosexual acts as "unnatural practices" (see 361).

28. *The Republic*, trans. Paul Shorey, vol. I, 489.

29. W.K.C. Guthrie, *Early Pre-Socratics*, 317 and n1.

30. Aristotle, *Politics*, 1268A 32 (book 2, chapter 4).

31. R. Hackforth, *Plato's Phaedrus*, 3–8.

32. Tejera, *Plato's Dialogues*, 50. Phaedrus is old enough to have his own boy lover, but Socrates is much older than Phaedrus.

33. Plato, *Phaedrus*, 245C.

34. Plato, *Phaedrus*, 246B–D.

35. Adrastia, here a goddess. The Orphics spoke much of her—perhaps we should compare Kali-Durga in the Hindu tradition.

36. Plato, *Phaedrus*, 248D–E.

37. Vlastos, *Platonic Studies*, 25 n. 76 and 224–25.

38. Dover, *Greek Homosexuality*, 163.7.

39. William S. Cobb, "The Symposium and The Phaedrus," 147–48.

40. Giovanni R.F. Ferrari, in *Listening to the Cicadas: A Study in Plato's Phaedrus*, suggests that orgasm was forbidden "because it is too strong, too self-dissolving" (268) and then compares this to the Oneida Community, founded in upstate New York in the nineteenth century by John Humphrey Noyes, who recommended his fellow communards refrain from all but orgasm (268–69) in a heterosexual context.

41. Plato, *Theaetetus*, 150, C7–8.

42. Plutarch, "Platonic Questions," *Moralia* 999F–1000A.

43. Plutarch, 999E.

44. Robin Waterfield, *Xenophon: Conversations of Socrates*, 220.

45. Paul Cartledge, "The Politics of Spartan Pederasty," 19, 87–88.

46. Xenophon, *Lacedemonians*, 2, 12–13; Plutarch, "Pelopidas," 19; Strabo, *Geography*, 10, 4, 19–21, and Vern Bullough, *Sexual Variance in Society and History*, 101.

47. In Guthrie, *The Greeks and Their Gods*, 312.

48. Quoted in James K. Feibleman, *Religious Platonism: The Influence of Religion on Plato and the Influence of Plato on Religion*, 57.

49. W.K.C. Guthrie, *Orpheus and Greek Religion*, 209. Of course that play is a farcical comedy, and Socrates is the butt of the joke. Orphism seems to have been very unpopular at Athens at the time, but it is quite unlikely that Aristophanes would have introduced this element if there were not a factual base for it.

50. Dodds, *The Greeks and the Irrational*, 208.

51. Dodds, *The Greeks and the Irrational*, 211.

52. Dodds, *The Greeks and the Irrational*, 209.

53. Platthy, *Plato: A Critical Biography*, 95–96.

54. Athanaeus, *Deipnosophists*, 11, 508C–D.

55. Alice Swift Rigionos, *Platonica: The Anecdotes Concerning the Life and Writings of Plato*, 170–73.

56. Diogenes Laertius, *Lives of the Philosophers*, (8, 85, 7) says that Philolaus was the first to put Pythagorean teaching in writing.

57. Aristotle, *Metaphysics*, I, 6 (987B.22).

58. For reasons that will be explained in due course, the *Laws* will be considered in another place.

59. Plato, *Timaeus*, 34–36

60. For a full account and discussion of this matter, see W.K.C. Guthrie, *A History of Greek Philosophy*, vol. V: *The Later Plato and the Academy*, 424–35. Pages 431–35 discuss the Pythagorean nature of what we know of the speech.

61. Dodds, *The Greeks and the Irrational*, 210.

62. L. Campbell, *The Statesman*, xxv–xxvi. Also Platthy, *Plato*, 95–96. In K.S. Guthrie, The Pythagorean Source Book and Library.

63. Tejera, *Plato's Dialogues*, 234–35. The fragments attributed by Stobaeus to Archytas are not reliable, but we do know that he held power in Tarentum longer than he constitutionally could.

64. Rigionos, *Platonica*, 162–63. The epigrams attributed to Plato in the *Greek Anthology* and elsewhere were circulated by Pseudo Aristippos. The evidence that they are by Plato is weak, but the facts of personal history that are implied in them are more likely to be reliable. Shelley translates the epitaph to Aster thus:

> Thou wert the morning star among the living,
> Ere thy fair light had fled;—
> Now having died thou art as Hesperus giving
> New splendor to the dead.

65. Theopompos in Athenaeus, *Deipnosophists*, 11, 508C–D.

66. Platthy, *Plato*, 71. The figure of eight percent that Platthy gives may be deceptive. The figure of 60 known disciples is probably too small. The four that became tyrants were probably much better known than many of Plato's disciples whose names have not come down to us.

67. Platthy, 182, cites numerous sources; however, Dodds (*Greeks and the Irrational*, 213 and n. 30, 227–28) calls the evidence late and weak. The best evidence seems to be the citation from Diogenes Laertius that follows.

68. Diogenes Laertius, *Lives of the Philosophers*, 8.5.83, like other late sources, calls Alkmaeon a disciple of Pythagoras, and says that he held that "the soul is immortal and that it is continuously in motion like the sun [*sunekhes hos ton helion*]." Guthrie (*History of Greek Philosophy*, 341–51) points out that Aristotle denies that Alkmaeon was a Pythagorean. Perhaps this idea of the astronomical soul is a distant echo of the worship of Ra as the sun god in Egypt, though sun-worship was hardly unique to the Egyptians.

CHAPTER 4

1. The military facts here generally follow Bury's *History of Greece*, 728–29.

2. S.A. Cook, F.E. Adcock, and M.P. Charlesworth, eds., *The Cambridge Ancient History*, 197–98.

3. N.G.L. Hammond, *Philip of Macedon*, 1.

4. Hammond, 3.

5. Aristotle, *Politics*, 5, 10, 1311a.

6. Theopompos, frag. 225. Theopompos' information should perhaps be taken with a grain of salt; though he admired Philip he was both anti–Macedonian and anti–Pythagorean.

7. Theopompos in Polybios, 8, 9, 6–13.

8. Quoted in all innocence in Peter Green, *Alexander of Macedon, 356–323 B.C.: A Historical Biography*, 39.

9. Hammond, *Philip of Macedon*,16–17.

10. Alfred S. Bradford, ed., *Philip II of Macedon: A Life from the Ancient Sources*, 9.

11. Hammond, *Philip of Macedon*, 8.

12. Hammond, 183.

13. Robin Lane Fox, *Alexander the Great*, 52.

14. Hammond, *Philip of Macedon*, 17.

15. Plutarch, *Moralia*, 14B–C.

16. Athenaeus, *Deipnosophists*, 11, 508C–E. See also Demosthenes, 9, 12, 57–62 (the "Third Philippic") and

Aeschines III, *Against Ctesiphon*, 89–90. Euphreios was arrested in connection with an uprising in his home town and executed by Parmenion on orders, no doubt, from Philip II. Theopompos calls Euphreios a murderer.

17. Green, *Alexander of Macedon*, 26–30. The quotation is from Chaucer's "Prologue to the Canterbury Tales," referring to the Wyf of Bathe.

18. Athenaeus, *Deipnosophists*, 13. 557C–E. We may mention Audata, Phila, Eurydice and Philinna among his minor wives—the last is described as a dancing girl and whore. See Green, *Alexander*, 525 n55.

19. Hammond, *Philip*, 51, 121.

20. Plutarch, "Life of Pelopidas," 18.5.

21. Plutarch, *Moralia*, "The Sayings of Kings," 178, A.12, trans. Frank Cole Babbitt (Cambridge: Harvard University Press, 1968), 45.

22. Green, *Alexander of Macedon*, 41.

23. Plutarch, "Life of Alexander," 2, 7.

24. Plutarch, "Life of Alexander," 3.3–4. This is indirectly confirmed by the court historian Callisthenes—see John Maxwell O'Brian, *Alexander the Great: the Invisible Enemy*, 18.

25. For a full discussion of the serpent in Orphism, see Hans Leisegang, "The Mystery of the Serpent," 194–260. Writing about 177 CE, Athenagoras in his *Libellus pro Christianis*, 20, says that Zeus transformed himself into a serpent to rape Rhea and thus begot Persephone.

26. Green, *Alexander of Macedon*, 272–73.

27. Leisegang, "Mystery of the Serpent," 257–58.

28. Green, *Alexander of Macedon*, 54.

29. Margaret Bieber, *Alexander the Great in Greek and Roman Art*, 25.

30. Theophrastos, quoted in Athenaeus, *Deipnosophists*, 10.435.A. Theophrastos was at the court of Philip just about this time. Coincidentally the story is also told of St. Thomas Aquinas that he resisted the blandishments of a prostitute hired for that purpose by his parents.

31. Plutarch, "Life of Alexander," 72, 2, calls Hephastion a *neon* (young man) at the time of his death; Alexander was 30 at the time. The not overly reliable Quintus Curtius Rufus says that (3, 12, 6) that Hephastion was the same age as King Alexander: "Et sicut ae tate par erat regi."

32. Pseudo-Diogenes, "Letter 24," *Cynic Epistles*. Malherbe dates this letter about 200 CE (page 15). See also Fox, *Alexander the Great*, 56. Fox accepts the letter as giving an accurate understanding of Alexander.

33. Diogenes Laertius, *Lives of the Philosophers*, 4, 14.

34. Hammond, *Philip*, 157.

35. Ernest Baker, "Greek Political Thought and Theory in the Fourth Century," in *Macedon*, 442–43.

36. Pseudo-Plutarch, *Moralia*, "Life of Lycurgos," 843, F. This is a second century CE work by an unknown author which has found its way into the *Moralia*.

37. Pseudo-Plutarch, 842, B–C.

38. Hammond, *Philip*, 157.

39. Baker, "Greek Political Thought," in *Macedon*, 440–41.

40. Pseudo-Plutarch, *Moralia,* "Life of Lycurgos," 841E.

41. Pseudo-Plutarch, 842C–D.

42. Ernest Baker, "Greek Political Thought," in *Macedon*, 442.

43. Greenberg, *Construction of Homosexuality*, 160–62.

44. Bullough, *Sexual Variance in Society and History*, 299–300.

45. Vivian Ng, "Homosexuality in Late Imperial China," 76–78.

46. Ng, 78.

47. Greenberg, *Construction of Homosexuality*, 162.

48. Ng, 88.

49. Ng, 87.

50. Jonathan D. Spence, *Emperor of China: Self-Portrait of Cawing Hi*, 125–29.

51. These events surrounding Philip's death follow the account in Diodorus of Sicily, 16, 93. Exceptions are noted.

52. Diodorus uses *philos* for Philip's feeling toward Pausanios of Orestis. The word can mean either friendship or sexual love. The relationship of Pausanios to Atollos is called *philos* in the same context, while Philip's feeling for the Other Pausanios is termed *agapomenon*, which can also mean sexual love but is more often used for a love that is intense, but nonsexual. *Agape* in Homer is what Odysseus feels for his son, and the Kloine form of the word *agape* is used in the New Testament for God's love for the human race. A bit later in the passage Pausanios the Historian uses *erotas*, a word that has unmistakable sexual meaning, so we will do well to translate both *philos* and *agape* as "like" or "love" in a nonsexual sense. Justin in his *Epitome of Trogus* makes Philip sexually attracted to both pages (9, 6, 5), but that work is both late and generally unreliable.

53. Justin, 9, 6. This is the only source for the joke. William Woodthorp Tarn calls Justin's history "a heap of rubbish."

54. Green, *Alexander*, 107–10. Olympias is known to have a hand in at least five other political murders, one of them the roasting of a child to death. Apparently she did a lot of reading.

55. Possibly this is one source for the superstition of 13 being an unlucky number.

56. Demosthenes, "Second Olynthian," 15–20.

57. Andrew Stewart, *Faces of Power: Alexander's Image and Hellenistic Politics*, 73.

58. Stewart, *Faces*, 72–74.

59. Theophrastos in Athenaeus, *Deipnosophists*, 10, 435A. One wonders where the historian got this bit of information.

60. Stewart, *Faces*, 72–74. For Alexander's *anastole*—crook neck, in contemporaneous documents as a sign of the *kinedos*, the effeminate male, see a quotation from Alexis, the writer of New Comedy in Athenaeus, 13, 585.A.

61. Plutarch, "Life of Alexander," 4, 1–2.

62. J.D. Beazley, "Greek Art and Architecture," in *Macedon*, 541–42.

63. Ephippos in Athanaeus, 573, c–538.A. Ephippos was Alexander's chamberlain, so an eye-witness to this. William Tarn calls him "a scurrilous gossip monger" (*Alexander*, 73), but Tarn was trying to make Alexander into a Victorian gentleman.

64. Plutarch, *Moralia*, 245.E; 304.E; "Life of Lycurgos," 15, 5.

65. Detienne, *Dionysus Slain*, 25.

66. Richard Isay, *Being Homosexual: Homosexual Men and Their Development*, 82.

67. Barry M. Dank, "The Homosexual," 174–210. I have chosen to use this essay because it is a thoroughly scientific work that has the great advantage for this present study of being a generally pre-Stonewall work; thus it captures well the deeply homophobic attitudes of the time.

68. Green, *Alexander of Macedon*, 40; O'Brian, *Alexander*, 21, and others.

69. Plutarch, "Life of Alexander," 26, 1–2.

70. O'Brian, *Alexander*, 57.

71. So Dikaiarkhos, the pupil of Aristotle, wrote in his *On the Sacrifice at Ilium*, Athenaeus, 603, A–B.

72. Quoted in Mary Renault, *The Nature of Alexander*, 47.

73. Arrian, 2, 12.

74. Green, *Alexander of Macedon*, 60.

75. Plutarch, "Alexander," 8, 4.

76. Pausanius, 1, 22, 6.

77. Green, *Alexander of Macedon*, 364.
78. Katherine Callen King, *Achilles: Paradigms of the War Hero from Homer to the Middle Ages*, 179.
79. W.M. Clarke, "Achilles and Patroculus in Love," 95–110.
80. "Their [Achilles and Patroclos'] love and the name of their friendship he [Homer] conceals, assuming that what goes beyond the limits of goodwill is obvious to the educated among his readers" (Aeschines, "Timarchos," 142).
81. Thorbjornsrud, "What Can the Gilgamesh Myth Tell Us," 112–37.
82. Tarn, *Alexander*, 145.
83. W.K.C. Guthrie, *Orpheus and Greek Religion*, 148–49.
84. Plutarch, "Alexander," 67, 2–6. Ptolemy omitted this incident, probably to spare Alexander's reputation. Diogenes Laertius, *Lives of the Philosophers*, 6, 63, says that Alexander was granted the title of Dionysus in Athens during his lifetime, which supports both the incident at Camarina and the opinion that he was worshiped as a god before he died. Camarina is identified by Alexander Polyhistor as Ur— apparently the ancient city near Erech (Uruk) in Sumer, where the myth of Gilgamesh originated. Mythically Alexander was right at home.
85. The "reason is nowhere given," Tarn, *Alexander*, 117.
86. Tarn, *Alexander the Great*, 123. Tarn attributes this to "a will of iron." The evidence suggests rather that Alexander had very few heterosexual urges to resist.
87. Green, *Alexander of Macedon*, 152–53. "His interest in women was (to put it mildly) tepid."
88. Plutarch, "Life of Alexander," 21, 11.
89. I follow Green (*Alexander of Macedon*, 245), who follows Tarn in regarding Barsine (allegedly the first wife of Alexander) as a fictitious person. However, she was the sort of woman that Alexander *might* have married— ten years his senior, well educated and twice a widow with several children. For a bibliography of the debate on her existence, see Green, *Alexander*, 539, note 5. Mary Renault believes that the whole matter was invented by a young man named Heracles, who wished to pass himself off as a son of Alexander following the latter's death —*Nature of Alexander*, 100–101.
90. Tarn, *Alexander*, 76.
91. Stewart, *Faces of Power*, 184–85. The picture was exhibited in Greece and sold for an enormous sum; apparently Alexander never saw it.
92. Hephastion died in October of 324 BCE; Alexander died June 10, 323, and his posthumous son, Alexander IV, was born in August of that year. Mary Renault (*Nature of Alexander*, 158–59) speculates that Bagoas the eunuch may have "disinhibited" Alexander so that he could inseminate Roxane. It seems more likely that the loss of Hephastion may have caused Alexander to turn to his wife.
93. O'Brian, *Alexander*, 57. Green, *Alexander of Macedon*, 245.
94. Green, *Alexander of Macedon*, 418–21.
95. Dank, *Homosexual*, 183.
96. "...quae vocata est Cinaedopolis probrosis ibi relictus a rege Alexandro." Pliny the Elder, *Natural History*, 5, 31, 134. Pliny is giving a detailed description of the cities around the Anatolian coast.
97. Green, *Alexander of Macedon*, 202–04. Green calls Alexander of Mollosia "the Lyncastrian," an alternate designation for the same person.
98. Green, 333.
99. Green, 441–42. Renault (*Nature of Alexander*, 137) speculates that Bagoas had lived with one of his masters for a time in Macedon and so learned Greek.

100. Plutarch, "On the Fortune of Alexander," *Moralia*, 333, A. See also 1099, and "Life of Alexander," 676, F. Green (*Alexander*, 440) thinks Alexander was angry because the governor was trying to make his sexual choices for him.
101. Quintus Curtius, *Life of Alexander*, 10.1.26. This act is said to have been held contemptible by the Persians.
102. Green, *Alexander of Macedon*, 442.
103. Aelian, *Varia Historia*, 3.23. This was in the last year of Alexander's life, and we know that Bagoas the eunuch was accused before Alexander of robbing tombs and that Alexander had him crucified. However the chronology is not clear enough to show whether this was just before or just after Hephastion's death. Pliny the Elder says that the House of Bagoas in Babylon was not the property of Bagoas the eunuch (*Natural History*, 13.41), but this is uncertain. See Fox, 531. Mary Renault believes Bagoas the eunuch survived Alexander.
104. George Hart, *A Dictionary of Egyptians Gods and Goddesses*, 15.
105. Elizabeth Riefstahl, *Thebes in the Time of Amunhopte III*, 136.
106. P.H. Newby, *Warrior Pharaoh: The Rise and Fall of the Egyptian Empire*, 15.
107. Newby, 180–81.
108. Greenberg, *Construction of Homosexuality*, 132.
109. Greenberg, 128–29 and notes 20 and 21.
110. Breasted, *Development of Religious Thought*, 247.
111. Schibli, *Pherekydes of Syros*, 38.
112. Arrian, *Anabasis of Alexander*, 3, 3, 1.
113. Green, *Alexander of Macedon*, 527 note 27.
114. Fox, *Alexander*, 206.
115. Fox, 211–12, speculates that the priest may have intended to greet Alexander with "*o paidion*" ("my boy"), but in imperfect Greek said "*o padios*" instead, which was misheard as *pai Dios*, "son of Zeus," instead.
116. Newby, *Warrior Pharoah*, 8–10.
117. Green, *Alexander of Macedon*, 274–75.
118. Strabo, 17, 1, 43 (814C in the Loeb edition). Strabo's source is Kallisthenes, Aristotle's nephew, who was waiting outside the oracle at the time.
119. Greenberg, *Construction of Homosexuality*, 128–29.
120. Hart, *Dictionary of Egyptian Gods and Goddesses*, 78.
121. Fox, *Alexander*, 207. Nineteenth century explorers found that the upper-class men at Siwa would ×freely loan their sons to their male friends for sexual uses.
122. Hart, *Dictionary*, 12. The inscription beside the sculpture reads: "King of the south and north, Setep-en-Amon-meri-re, son of the sun, lord of risings, Arksandres" (Green, 276). We note in passing that the title "son of the sun" parallels the epithet that Pindar applied to athletes — "sons of the sun"— and that that poet was one of the first Greeks to write about Ammon (Amon).
123. Plutarch, "Life of Alexander," 35, 1–7; Strabo, 16, 1, 5.
124. Valerius Maximus, 3, 3, sec. 1.
125. Fox, *Alexander*, 227.
126. Robert J. Kus, "Alcoholism and Non-Acceptance of the Gay Self: The Clinical Link," 25–42.
127. O'Brian, *Alexander*, 210–16. O'Brian's whole book is a moving documentation of the alcoholism of both Alexander and his friend and the mental and physical degeneration that alcoholism brought on.
128. Plutarch, "Life of Alexander," 72, 4.
129. Implied in *Iliad*, 23, 241–48. Expressly stated in *Odyssey* 24, 76–75.
130. Diodorus Siculus, *History*, 17, 115, 3.
131. O'Brian, *Alexander*, 226–8.

132. Quintus Curtius, *History of Alexander*, 10, 4, 4; "ut corpus suum ad Hammonem ferri iuberent."

133. Arrian, *Anabasis of Alexander*, 7.11.

CHAPTER 5

1. Diogenes Laertius, *Lives of the Philosophers*, 3, 2.

2. So says the Anonymous Prolegomena to Plato, though this is late and may be influenced by Christianity (Rigionos, *Platonica*, 198).

3. Minor M. Markle III, "Support of Athenian Intellectuals for Philip," 92.

4. Green, *Alexander of Macedon*, 79–80.

5. Rigionos, 14. Indeed this is a huge riddle — did the Old Academy headed by Speusippos invent what is later known as Pythagorean dogma, or did it predate both Plato and the Old Academy? On the evidence of Aristotle, it seems likely that most of the ideas we now call Pythagorean are pre–Plato.

6. Czarists of Pergamum, *Historical Notes*, in Athenaeus, *Deipnosophists*, 9, 506, E, 275 Loeb ed.

7. Tejera, *Plato's Dialogues*, 102–03.

8. Tejera, 102.

9. Athenaeus, *Deipnosophists*, quoting Dionysus of Sicily, 546, D.

10. Diogenes Laertius, *Lives of the Philosophers*, 3, 51–55.

11. Tejera, *Plato's Dialogues*, 101.

12. Tejera, 133.

13. Aristotle, *Metaphysics*, 1072, B, 30; *Nicomachean Ethics*, 1096, B, 6.

14. Robert S. Brumbaugh, *Plato's Mathematical Imagination*, 5.

15. Speusippos, quoted in F.W. Russell, *The School of Plato*, 145.

16. Dikaiarkhos, *Life of Plato*. This was read from one of the charred scrolls found at Herculanaeum by Konrad Gaiser (Platthy, 145).

17. Diogenes Laertius, *Lives of the Philosophers*, 4, 1, 1.

18. Emile Brehier, *History of Philosophy: The Hellenistic and Roman Age*, 31.

19. Peter Green, *Alexander to Actium*. The main sources are Aristotle's *Nicomachean Ethics*, 1152 B, 7 ff, 1153 B, 5 ff, 1172, B 36–73, A 12.

20. John Dillon, *The Middle Platonists*, 19.

21. See W.K.C. Guthrie, *Later Plato and the Academy*, 228 and following, for an analysis of pleasure in this late and "weary" dialogue.

22. Athenaeus, *Deipnosophists*, 546 D.

23. Timotheus, *On Lives*, in Diogenes Laertius, *Lives of the Philosophers*, 4, 4.

24. Giovanni Reale, *A History of Ancient Philosophy, vol. III: The Systems of the Hellenistic Age*, 70. Quoting Speusippos in Clement of Alexandria, *Strom*, 2, 22, 131.

25. John Burnett, *Early Greek Philosophy*, 10–11. Burnett refutes at length and with abundant examples W.A. Heidel's theory that *phusis* originally meant "growth." It is Heidel's interpretation that John Boswell uses in *Christianity, Social Tolerance and Homosexuality*, 13–14, n22.

26. *The Cambridge History of Later Greek and Early Medieval Philosophy*, 33.

27. Werner Jaeger, *Paideia: The Ideals of Greek Culture*, 159–61. Jaeger bases this on Fragment 9 of Anaximander and thinks that this idea of Anaximander's influenced Pythagoras (162).

28. Jacqueline de Romilly, *The Great Sophists in Periclean Athens*, 45–46.

29. Arthur W.H. Adkins, *From the One to the Many*, 113–15.

30. Fragment 920 in Adkins, 119.

31. Adkins, 123.

32. Dover, *Greek Homosexuality*, 60–61.

33. de Romilly, *Great Sophists*, 117, citing a passage of Thrasymachos (the Sophist whom Plato used as a straw man in the *Republic*).

34. Dodds, *The Greeks and the Irrational*, 188.

35. Plato, *Lysis*, 214 B. See also *Meno*, 81C; *Phaedo*, 96A; and *Philebus*, 59A.

36. W.K.C. Guthrie, *Later Plato*, 280.

37. Joseph P. Maguire, "Plato's Theory of Natural Law," 158–59. For detailed evidence, see notes 33, 160.

38. Maguire, 158–59.

39. Maguire, 162–63.

40. John Wild, *Plato's Modern Enemies and the Theory of Natural Law*, 150–51.

41. Russell, *School of Plato*, 115.

42. Stobaeus, 2, 30.

43. Clement of Alexandria, *Strom*, 2, 19, 3.

44. Russell, *School of Plato*, 119.

45. Wild, *Plato's Modern Enemies*, 132–33.

46. Plato, *Symposium*, trans. Walter Hamilton, 63.

47. Dillon, *The Middle Platonists*, 34.

48. Dillon, 34.

49. Dillon, 35.

50. Plutarch, "De esu charn," i, 996, C.

51. Platthy, *Plato*, 83.

52. Platthy, 119.

53. Cicero, *The Nature of the Gods*, 1, 34.

54. W.K.C. Guthrie, *The Later Plato*, 484–85.

55. W.K.C. Guthrie, 484. We will see when we come to the reign of Justinian that earthquakes as a sign of divine displeasure have occasionally touched off waves of persecution against homosexuals, as well as other minorities.

56. W.K.C. Guthrie, *Aristotle: An Encounter*, 22–23.

57. W.K.C. Guthrie, *Aristotle: An Encounter*, 74–75.

58. Burnet, *Early Greek Philosophy*, 83, n2.

59. W.K.C. Guthrie, *Orpheus and Greek Religion*, 245–46.

60. Diogenes Laertius, *Lives of the Philosophers*, 5, 31. The fact that falling in love is opposed here to marriage proves Aristotle had male-male love in mind. Marriage was a much less emotionally significant matter for Greek of this period.

61. John Boswell's translation of this word as "bad habit" in *Christianity, Social Tolerance and Homosexuality*, 49, note 18, does not stand the test of Liddle Scott's dictionary; the word is related to words for small wild animals, and maggots in a sore; Dioscuourides uses it to describe malignant cancers. Perhaps the old-fashioned English term for an emotional compulsion, "maggots in the brain," would be an apt translation of Aristotle.

62. Dover, *Greek Homosexuality*, 168–69.

63. Aristotle, *Physics*, 2, 1, 192B–193B.

64. Robert M. Grant, *Miracle and Natural Law in Greco-Roman and Early Christian Thought*, 6–7.

65. Diogenes Laertius, *Lives of the Philosophers*, 5, 11–16.

66. Athenaeus, *Deipnosophists*, 566, D–E; Stephanos of Byzantium under "Phaselis"; Valerius Maximus, 8, 14, 3.

67. Diogenes Laertius, *Lives of the Philosophers*, 5, 69–70.

68. Diogenes Laertius, *Lives of the Philosophers*, 4, 5.

69. These two points are raised by Tejera (*Plato's Dialogues*, 139–40).

70. W.K.C. Guthrie, *The Later Plato*, 321n3.

71. For example, Paul Freindlander, *The Dialogues*, 389. W.K.C. Guthrie in *The Later Plato* (321–23) sums up the evidence pro and con admirably.

72. Athenaeus, *Deipnosophists*, 11, 509.

73. Ferguson, *Hellenistic Athens*, 104–06.

74. Cicero, *Tusculum Disputations*, 4, 34 (72). Cicero mentions Dikaiarkhos (Dicaearchos, in Latin) several times favorably in his letters to Atticus (4, 2, 3, 13, 31, 2) as an exponent of the practical life.

75. L.A. Seneca, *Epistles*, 94, 38.

76. Cicero, who had studied under him (*De Finibus*, 1, 1, 2), calls him the greatest of all the Stoics, and Pompey went out of his way to hear him lecture on Rhodes.

77. Cicero, *Of Law*, 2, 6. For a part of these laws, see Diodorus Siculus, 12, 11–21.

78. Tejera, *Plato's Dialogues*, 140.

79. Tejera, 142.

80. Tejera, 143.

81. W.K.C. Guthrie, *The Later Plato*, 322, n1.

82. Howard Tarrant, *Thrasyllian Platonism*, 6.

83. Howard Tarrant, 7.

84. Tarrant, 179.

85. Tarrant, 193.

86. Tarrant, 6, n6.

87. Tarrant, 208.

88. Friedlander, *The Dialogues*, 387.

89. Tarrant, 148.

90. Tarrant, 210.

91. Aristotle, *Politics*, 2, 4, 1262 A 32, apparently referring to the passages we have discussed earlier in the *Republic*. However, the *Politics* is one of the texts of Aristotle edited in Rome by Andronicus in the first century BCE, so we may not preclude tampering with the *Politics* either.

92. Dillon, *The Middle Platonists*, 115, 125.

93. A Magils is mentioned in an Arabic source as a Pythagorean philosopher; others identify him with Megillos of Akragas, who is said to have taught Plato music. See Holgar Thesleff, *The Pythagorean Texts*, 115, for Klenias, 107.

94. Berkert, *Lore and Science*, 150–51.

95. Diogenes Laertius, *Lives of the Philosophers*, 1, 10, 109, 112.

96. Berkert, *Lore and Science*, 155.

97. R.G. Bury, *Laws*, 313, n1. This discussion generally follows Bury's translation.

98. W.K.C. Guthrie, *The Later Plato*, 362.

99. Gould, *Platonic Love*, 131.

100. W.K.C. Guthrie, *The Later Plato*, 365, n3.

101. Schibli, *Pherekydes of Syros*, 109–13. The evidence for this in Pherekydes is very late, and Schibli suspects it is a Christian reading of the text of Pherekydes. Nevertheless Pherekydes was almost certainly influenced by Zoroastrian sources (see 69 n50, 71). The concept of individuals having two souls occurs in Egyptian religion as well — the *ba* and the *ka* were thought of as separable aspects of the total person, which might survive the individual's death.

102. Gould, *Platonic Love*, 138.

103. It is perhaps not entirely coincidental that such a fine on bachelorhood was enacted in Geneva under John Calvin.

104. Schibli, *Pherekydes of Syros*, 2.

105. His sundial is referred to by Diogenes Laertius, *Lives of the Philosophers*, (1, 119). Of course astronomy and astrology were not distinct until the modern era.

106. Schibli, 16. For reasons not clear, Pherekydes spelled their names "Zas" and "Khthonie" rather than "Zeus" and "Kthonia," the usual spellings.

107. Schibli, 37.

108. Schibli (11, n4) gives numerous citations to the effect that Pherekydes was Pythagoras' teacher.

109. Schibli, 120 for the River of Rebirth and 38 for Egyptian connections. John Burnett (*Early Greek Philosophy*, 83) thinks that the *Phaedo* is inspired by Pythagorean sources. It is notable that in that dialogue Socrates arrives

at an assurance of life after death, yet in the (probably much earlier) *Apology*, he is quite uncertain on the issue.

110. R.G. Bury, *Laws*, 293, n2. For a clear repetition of the Pythagorean pairs of opposites, see *Laws*, 717A.

111. Sextus Empiricus, *Pyrrhonian Sketches*, 3, 199–200; Aristotle, *Politics*, 1271B. Henri Jeanmaire saw a pederastic ritual related to the Bull Cult on the Chieftain's Cup, from pre–Hellenic Crete. See William Armstrong Percy III, *Pederasty and Pedagogy in Ancient Greece*, 23–24. Percy's thesis that pederasty was invented by a seventh century BCE Cretan king seems exaggerated.

112. Laius was the father of Oedipos the king, and he is reported to have kidnapped and seduced a lad named Chrysippos; following Plato later Greek scholars sometimes speak of Laius as the "inventor" of homosexuality.

113. This refers to a favorite manner of homosexual intercourse among the Greeks: the penis of the man is rubbed on or between the thighs of the boy. No actual penetration occurs.

114. For a text of the *Laws*, I have used the translation by R.G. Bury in the Loeb edition. However, I have occasionally made the references to homosexuality more explicit using the Greek text there.

115. The word more often is used to refer to persons coming together in a non-sexual context. Plato is one of the few sources that use it to indicate sexual activity; see *Symposium* 91c and 206c.

116. Adultery with a woman is generally implied by the word.

117. Dillon, 40.

118. Diogenes Laertius, *Lives of the Philosophers*, 4, 16–17.

119. Diogenes Laertius, *Lives of the Philosophers*, 4, 18.

120. Dillon, *Middle Platonists*, 41.

121. Diogenes Laertius, *Lives of the Philosophers*, 4.21, translated by R.D. Hicks, in the Loeb series.

122. Diogenes Laertius, *Lives of the Philosophers*, 4, 19. The authority here is the Roman Favronius. This seems doubtful, since he is the only authority and the story has Polemon meeting Xenocrates when the former was a "lad" (4.16, *meirakion*) and Xenocrates probably was in his late sixties.

123. W.K.C. Guthrie, *The Later Plato*, 392.

124. Platthy, *Plato*, 137.

125. Quoted in Plutarch, "Life of Romullus," 30, 6.

126. Diogenes Laertius, *Lives of the Philosophers*, 4, 22.

127. Numenius in Eusebius of Pamphilia, *Preparation of the Gospel*, 14, 731A. He blames Archisilaus' homosexuality on his association when young with Theophrastos.

128. Diogenes Laertius, *Lives of the Philosophers*, 7, 1–3.

129. David Sedley, "The Protagonists," 4–6.

130. Daniel Babut, "Les Stociens et l'Amour," 1.

131. Giovanni Reale, *The Systems of the Hellenistic Age*, 217.

132. Reale, 217.

133. Diogenes Laertius, *Lives of the Philosophers*, 7, 158.

134. Diogenes Laertius, *Lives of the Philosophers*, 7, 148.

135. Reale, *Systems of the Hellenistic Age*, 244.

136. Plutarch, "De Stoic Repug," 1035A.

137. Plutarch, "De Alex. Magni Fortuna," 329 A–B.

138. Gerald Watson, "The Natural Law and Stoicism," 224.

139. Watson, 222–23.

140. Reale, *Systems of the Hellenistic Age*, 213.

141. Gisela Striker, *Essays in Hellenistic Epistemology and Ethics*, 218–19.

142. S.G. Pembroke, "Oikeiosis," 115–22. The illustration is from Aristotle; Pembroke notes (124) the analogy with the Freudian concept of id, ego and super-ego.

143. Pembroke, 130.

144. Josiah B. Gould, *The Philosophy of Chrysippus*, especially 186, n2.

145. Stobaeus, *Anthology*, 2, 5, A.

146. Stobaeus, *Anthology*, 2, 11, S.

147. Stobaeus, *Anthology*, 2, 5 B.

148. Stobaeus, 2.88, 8–90, 6.

149. Diogenes Laertius, *Lives of the Philosophers*, 7, 130.

150. Athenaeus, *Deipnosopists*, 561C.

151. Antigonos of Karustos, *Biography*, in Athenaeus, 563E.

152. J.M. Rist, *Stoic Philosophy*, 53.

153. Plutarch, "Against the Stoics on Common Conceptions," 28, *Moralia*, 1072F–1073D. Representing a moderate Platonism, Plutarch protests that this is impossible for most persons. As examples of what sex is really like, however, he cites tag lines from Homer that refer to heterosexual activity.

154. William Scott Ferguson, *Hellenistic Athens*, 145.

155. Epicurus, "The Vatican Sayings," 42–43.

156. Donald Dudley, *A History of Cynicism from Diogenes to the Sixth Century AD*, 127.

157. For a summary of opinion on this point, see *The Cambridge History of Later Greek and Early Medieval Philosophy*, 105, n1.

158. Berkert, *Lore and Science*, 200.

159. Plutarch, "Convivial Questions," 8, 7, 727B.

160. Justin Martyr, *Dialogue with Trypho, a Jew*, 250–51.

161. Antigonos in Athenaeus, *Deipnosophists*, 565D–F. *Kinaidos*, plural *kinaidoi*, Latin *cinnaedus* (hence the English "cinnaedus") is usually translated as "effeminate" or some such. The word's derivation is obscure, but it seems to have meant men who cross-dress or act like women (sexually or otherwise). See Byrne Fone, *Homosexuality: A History*, 41 and notes, for discussion.

162. Green, *Alexander to Actium*, 113.

163. Ferguson, *Hellenistic Athens*, 20.

164. Ferguson, 64.

165. Green, *Alexander to Actium*, 199–200. For a more detailed discussion of Macedonian law in Egypt, see Pierre Gadget, *Alexander the Great and the Hellenistic World*, 113.

166. Ferguson, *Hellenistic Athens*, 28–29.

167. Ferguson, 22.

168. Ferguson, 66, 69.

169. Ferguson, 42–45.

170. *The Hellenistic Monarchies and the Rise of Rome*, vol. 7 of *The Cambridge Ancient History*, 224. The quotation is from *De elequentis* and reflects Demetrius of Phalerium's unique prose style.

171. Athenaeus, *Deipnosophists*, 542B–543A.

172. Green, *Alexander to Actium*, 48. Apparently this was the gilded bronze statue, the remains of which were found by archaeologists, that had been thrown down a well about 200 BCE at the end of the Macedonian domination.

173. Antiphanes, Fragments 4, 85; Taylor, *Tyrant Slayers*, 187. Antipanes was a writer of the New Comedy.

174. Ferguson, *Hellenistic Athens*, 73–74.

175. Ferguson, 75, n4; Plutarch, "Table Talk," 7, 8, 712C. The New Comedy of Menander is apt for banquets "for in all these plays there is no homosexual love of boys" (*oute gar paidos eros arrenos*).

176. Jaeger, *Paideia*, 364.

177. *Hellenistic Monarchies*, 227.

178. Diodorus Sicilus, 19, 105, 1–5; Pausanius, 9, 7, 2; Justin Martyr, *Dialogue with Trypho*, 15, 2.5. The date of this event cannot be set with certainty. Some modern historians say 310 BCE. Kassander had already killed Olympias, Alexander's mother. Alexander's sister Cleopatra survived about another year after this; she was the last descendant of Philip II.

179. Ferguson, *Hellenistic Athens*, 107.

180. Athenaeus, *Deipnosophists*, 603E. Antigonos of Karustos says the king invited the philosopher to a drinking party at the house of Antigonas' male lover, the flute player Aristocles.

181. Ferguson, *Hellenistic Athens*, 234.

182. Gadget, *Alexander*, 137.

183. Dio Chrysostom, "Oration 21," written early in the second century CE, seems to be the first explicit notice we have of this and is based on Dio's study of the older sculpture at Olympia in contrast to later works nearer his own time.

184. Green, *Alexander to Actium*, 389. The oppressive laws of Demetrius in Athens were a brief exception.

185. Margaret Walters, *The Nude Male: A New Perspective*, 53.

186. Summarized in Le Vay, *Queer Science: The Use and Abuse of Research into Homosexuality*, 82–44, 280.

187. Gary P. Leapp, *Male Colors: The Construction of Homosexuality in Tokugawa, Japan*, 1–2, 47–54.

188. Jean-Pierre Lehmann, *Roots of Modern Japan*, 89.

189. Lehmann, 226.

190. Leapp, *Male Colors*, 52.

191. See *Thesmorphoria*, line 134 and following.

192. Sonya Lida Taran, "EISI TRIXES: An Erotic Motif," 90–107.

193. *The Greek Anthology*. All references are to the original division into books and number of poem.

194. Apollonius of Rhodes, *The Voyage of Argo*, 1, 1197–1200 (68).

195. Apollonius, 1, 1234–35.

196. Arthur Darby Nock, *Early Gentile Christianity and Its Hellenistic Background*, 17. Quoted from *Sylloge inscriptionum graecarum*.

197. Nock, 18.

198. Nock, 21.

199. Marjorie Leach, *Guide to the Gods*, 11.

200. Cited in Nock, 22, n2.

CHAPTER 6

1. Plutarch, "Life of Amellius Paulus," 1. Of course this is a myth; the point is they believed it.

2. A.E. Astin, *Scipio Aemelianus*, 17.

3. Astin, 13.

4. Plutarch, "Life of Aemilius Paulus," 326.

5. Astin, *Scipio*, 14–15.

6. Alexander W. Mair, *Encyclopædia Britannica*, 1945, s.v. "Polybius." The approximate date for his birth is given as 201 BCE.

7. F.W. Wilbank, introduction to *Polybius: The Rise of the Roman Empire*, 12.

8. Polybius' description of the festivals for boys and men in Arcadia (*History*, 4, 20) does not specifically allude to pederasty, but it indicates the customs of the age of pederasty had survived unchanged in Arcadia down to the historian's own time.

9. Wilbank, introduction to *Polybius*, 13.

10. Astin, *Scipio*, 20. Donald Earl (The Moral and Political Tradition of Rome, 27) has pointed out the prominence of references to ancestors in the inscriptions found on the tombs of the Scipio family, especially the last Scipio. However, we cannot fully trust that these inscriptions are contemporary with the persons buried there; for more on this see *Remains of Old Latin*, 2–8, n1, 2.

11. Polybius, *History*, 31, 23.

12. Suetonius," Terrence," 3, 1.

13. Polybius, 31, 24.

14. Wilbank, introduction to *Polybius*, 14.

15. Franz Altheim, *A History of Roman Religion*, 303–05. Cicero's *Dream of Scipio* has the general (whom Cicero greatly admired) meeting his ancestors in the underworld — all very Pythagorean. About three centuries after Scipio's time, Juvenal's "Second Satire" depicts the utter horror of the souls of Roman heroes in the underworld when a man guilty of voluntarily being sexually penetrated joins them. In a sort of ectoplasmic homosexual panic, the heroic souls "wish to be ritually purified" (lines 153–58). Amy Richlin thinks Juvenal's notions on this point go back at least to the time of Scipio the Younger ("Not before Homosexuality," 553).

16. Plutarch, "Roman Questions," 101. Of course it came to the same thing.

17. Appian, *Punica*, 132. He was writing in Greek. Diodorus Siculus says (31, 26, 5) that Polybius taught Scipio philosophy — though this seems unlikely (see Astin, 339). Probably Diodorus was thinking of Scipio and Polybius' relationship in terms of Stoic pederasty.

18. Valerius Maximus, 6, 1, 10–11. Valerius not a very good source, since his intention is to be a moral instructor rather than a historian; and his examples are taken from writers like Fabius Pictor, who are likewise more tendentious than scientific.

19. Suetonius, "Life of Terence," 1. Likewise Gaius Laelius, one of Scipio's most intimate friends, was some years older than he (Plutarch, "Sayings of the Romans," 200C, where Laelius refers to Scipio as *neoteroi*). The effort is, of course, to maintain Scipio's reputation as a Roman hero; if he was thought to have been the sexual aggressor on a younger, foreign-born Terence, it would be acceptable to Romans of the early Empire.

20. Wilbank, introduction to *Polybius*, 27–32. At the last, disastrous battle against Philip II, Demosthenes carried a shield with "Tukhe" painted on it — and left it behind in the field.

21. Polybius, 31, 28–29. It seems fair to say that Scipio was assuming the public colors of a *rubus neckus*.

22. Plutarch, "Sayings of Romans," *Moralia*, 200, A, 3. Cato carried on a long feud with the Scipio family, destroying the career of Scipio's adoptive grandfather, Scipio the Elder. The fact makes his praise of Scipio the Younger even more remarkable.

23. Earl, *Moral and Political Tradition of Rome*, 37. See Aulius Gellius, *Attic Nights*, 4, 20, 1.

24. Aulius Gellius, *Noctes Atticae*, 6, 12. Following Charles Forburg's translation in the 1844 *Manual of Classical Erotology*, "inner side of the couch" means the side facing the center of a circle or square of couches at a banquet. In the Greek tradition this is where the younger man reclined, on his side, facing the center, with the older man behind him.

25. Macrobius, *Saturnalia*, 3, 14, 7.

26. Amy Richlin, *The Garden of Priapus: Sexuality and Aggression in Roman Humor*, 165.

27. Richlin, *Garden*, 29.

28. Astin, *Scipio*, 235.

29. Edward Vernon Arnold, *Roman Stoicism*, 101. I have chosen to give his name in the Latin form rather than transliterate the Greek (Panaitios) because he was above all a Roman philosopher, and his work is known almost entirely though the Latin of Cicero and Seneca.

30. Cicero, *De Officiis*, 1, 127–29.

31. Diogenes Laertius, *Lives of the Philosophers*, 7, 34. Since the Library of Pergamos was pillaged by Antony, we may date this in Republican times.

32. For a full treatment of the early Stoics' somewhat ambivalent attitude toward slavery, see David Brion Davis, *The Problem of Slavery in Western Culture*, 72–79.

33. Cicero, *Republic*, 3, 25, 37. Attributed to Panaetius in Arnold, *Roman Stoicism*, 279.

34. M. Rostovtzeff, "Rhodes Delos and Hellenistic Commerce," in *Rome and the Mediterranean 218–133 BC*, 631.

35. Cicero, *De Officiis*, 3, 3, 13. It is generally conceded that this work of Cicero is a free translation of a lost book, *pari kathakontos*, by Panaetius. See Arnold, *Roman Stoicism*, 101.

36. Cyril Baily, "Roman Religion and the Advent of Philosophy," in *Rome and the Mediterranean*, 463.

37. R.T. Wallis, *Neoplatonism*, 118.

38. Earl, *Moral and Political Tradition*, 41.

39. Stobaeus, 2, 63, 25–64 (Panaetius, fragment 109), 396 in Sedley.

40. Striker, *Essays*, 253.

41. Cicero, *De Officiis*, 1, 148. See Striker, *Essays*, 256.

42. Pembroke, "Oikeisos," 231–32.

43. Arnold, *Roman Stoicism*, 242–44.

44. F.H. Sandbach, *The Stoics*, 128.

45. Seneca, *Epistles*, 116, 5, trans. Inwood and Hackett.

46. Arnold, *Roman Stoicism*, 104. It was Posidonius, the disciple of Panaetius, who has preserved for us the clearest evidence we have that the *Laws* as it now exists may be partly a forgery. Both Panaetius and Posidonius probably read their Plato in the library of Pergamon; it is possible that copies of both the original and the amended *Laws* existed there. When the Roman army burned the library of Alexandria, Antony replaced it with the Pergamon library. Nevertheless a tradition of Platonic scholarship continued in Pergamon; many of the best manuscripts of Plato's dialogues come from the library of the bishop of Pergamon in Byzantine times.

47. Rist, *Stoic Philosophy*, 195.

48. Cicero, *De Officiis*, 1, 36 (129).

49. Cicero, *De Officiis*, 1, 36 (page 130). The rather quaint footnote of Walter Miller at this point calls these "foppish manners," 133a.

50. Cicero, *De Officiis*, 125 (128).

51. Martin Hengel, *Judaism and Hellenism*, 87.

52. *Cambridge History of Later Greek and Early Medieval Philosophy*, 57.

53. Astin, *Scipio*, 240.

54. Ramsay McMullen, "Roman Attitudes to Greek Love," 340–358, 344. See also J.N. Adams, *The Latin Sexual Vocabulary*, 228–29.

55. Greenberg, *Construction*, 153. The sole evidence is a single relief showing Mars as a wolf-god with naked youths. The notion that pederasty was a rite universal among the Indo-Europeans cannot be proven.

56. Michael Grant, *History of Rome*, 11–13. For an earlier view, skeptical of an Etruscan invasion, see *Hellenistic Monarchies*, 379–80. Grant's opinion has benefited by 50 years of archeology.

57. Otto Wilhelm von Vacano, *The Etruscans in the Ancient World*, 127. At each quarter of the moon the *lucomon* would show himself to his people, wearing a purple robe sewn with silver stars, his face painted with vermillion and riding a chariot pulled by white horses; the effort was to impersonate the supreme god, Tin.

58. Jacques Heurgon, *The Rise of Rome to 264 BC*, 48.

59. Ervin Staub, *The Roots of Evil: The Origins of Genocide and Other Group Violence*, 61.

60. Athenaeus, *Deipnosophists*, 522E–F.

61. Gordon W. Allport, *The Nature of Prejudice*, 37.

62. Quoted in Athenaeus, 517D–518A. Possibly Theopompos' interest in the subject was provoked because homosexuality was first being seriously questioned in his day. Greenberg (*Construction of Homosexuality*, 152 and note 147) points out that this Etruscan fondness for

boys is confirmed both in Aristotle and in Etruscan tomb paintings.

63. Heurgon, *Rise of Rome*, 44. He cites the example of Tarquinia, who exercised a power behind the throne comparable to that of Eleanor of Aquitaine or Marie de Medici.

64. For example, Paegnium in *Persa*. His name is from the Greek *paignion*, a toy or plaything. See Saara Lilja, *Homosexuality in Republican and Imperial Rome*, 302–03.

65. Raymond Bloch, *The Etruscans*, 69–70.

66. von Vacano, *Etruscans*, 36.

67. Grant, *History of Rome*, 19.

68. Albert Grenier, *The Roman Spirit in Religion, Thought and Art*, 38.

69. Grant, *History of Rome*, 15. Perhaps the irony should not go unnoticed that Rome, whose puritanical attitude toward homosexuality was vastly influential, had as its first monument a sewer.

70. Heurgon, *Rise of Rome*, 118.

71. Huergon, 117–18.

72. Huergon, 140–55.

73. Grant, *History of Rome*, 36.

74. Hugh Last, "The Kings of Rome," *Hellenistic Monarchies*, 396.

75. Jerome Carcopino, *La bisilque puthagoricienne de la Porte-Majeure*, 161; Heurgon, *Rise of Rome*, 98; Franz Cumont ("Frontier Provinces in the East," *Imperial Peace*) in Thesleff, says the same thing. See Thesleff, *Pythagorean Texts*, 53.

76. Heurgon, *Rise of Rome*, 97.

77. Otto Kiefer, *Sexual Life in Ancient Rome*, 134.

78. George Dumezil, *Archaic Roman Religion*, 34–35.

79. Dumezil, 675.

80. Dumezil, 472.

81. Michael Grant, *History of Rome*, 52.

82. Grant, 54.

83. Staub, *Roots of Evil*, 21–22, table 1.

84. Staub, 29.

85. Staub, 61–62.

86. Staub, 56.

87. Milton Kleg, *Hate, Prejudice and Racism*, 128–29. Summarized from *The Authoritarian Personality*.

88. Michael Grant, *History of Rome*, 115.

89. Dumezil, *Archaic Roman Religion*, 512.

90. *Livy: With an English Translation in Fourteen Volumes*, 25.1. All quotations from Livy are from this series but given in the standard divisions of Livy's text.

91. Livy, 25, 12.

92. Dumezil, *Archaic Roman Religion*, 525.

93. Livy, 16, 19. Livy notes the parallel with Alexander.

94. Seneca, *Epistles*, 108, 17–21. It appears that many Jews outside of Palestine simply gave up eating meat altogether rather than attempt to obtain ritually pure flesh food.

95. Michael Grant, *History of Rome*, 119.

96. Heurgon, *Rise of Rome*, 97–98.

97. Livy, 2, 33.

98. Diodorus Siculus, 24, 93; Strabo, 4, 179–80.

99. *Encyclopædia Britannica*, 1945, s.v. Fabius Pictor.

100. Andreas Alfoldi, *Early Rome and the Latins (Jerome Lectures 7th Series)*, 173.100.

101. Alfoldi, 173. One recognizes here another element in the fascist personality — the belief in destiny.

102. Michael Grant, *The Ancient Historians*, 169.

103. Erick S. Gruen, *Culture and National Identity in Republican Rome*, 13.

104. Gruen, 27–28.

105. Huergon, *Rise of Rome*, 129.

106. von Vacano, *Etruscans*, 80.

107. Gruen, *Culture and National Identity*, 31.

108. Alfoldi, *Early Rome and the Latins*, 158–59.

109. Alfoldi, 151.

110. J. Wright Duff, "The Beginnings of Latin Literature," *Rome and the Mediterranean*, 402–05.

111. Alfoldi, *Early Rome and the Latins*, 159.

112. Alfoldi, 158–59.

113. Serge Lancell, *Carthage: A History*, 23–24.

114. Carlin A. Burton, *The Sorrows of the Ancient Romans: The Gladiator and the Monster*, 40. Burton traces *devotio* to Hittite, Hebrew, Greek and Roman sources (44). Ennius quotes Dacius as saying: "Hear O gods, quickly, for steadfastly and with full forethought I lay down my life for the people of Rome."

115. Burton, 44.

116. Alfoldi, *Early Rome and the Latins*, 23, from Timaeus, and Servius. Modern scholars do not know what "Elissa" or "Eli-shat" originally meant, in fact.

117. Alfoldi, 152. Part of this may be explained by Pictor's hatred of the Sabines in general — his family and the Sabine Claudian gens (clan or family) had a long-running feud.

118. Stuart James ("Sources for the Tradition of Early Roman History," in *Hellenistic Monarchies*, 367) says that the story of the Rape of the Sabines was "precedent for the force put upon the bride before she entered her husband's house.

119. Last, "Kings of Rome," in *Hellenistic Monarchies*, 395–96.

120. Alfoldi, *Early Rome and the Latins*, 59.

121. Certainly a Roman touch: among the Greeks for a boy to wear his hair long was a sign that he was prepubescent and out of bounds for sexual activity; Roman males wore their hair short all their lives, and women wore theirs long.

122. Alfoldi, 58.

123. Earl, *Moral and Philosophical Tradition of Rome*, 66–67.

124. For example see Plutarch's "Life of Numa" throughout.

125. Cicero (*Republic*, 2, 28) notes the discrepancy.

126. Last ("Kings of Rome," in *Hellenistic Monarchies*, 374–77) argues that the complex order of the priestly colleges at Rome must have had a single organizer; hence there must have been a single mastermind who fits the character of Numa.

127. Grenier, *Roman Spirit*, 53 n2.

128. Jerome, Eusebius, *Chronicle*, Year of Abraham, 1777 and 1848 (240 and 168 BCE).

129. W.Y. Sellar, *The Roman Poets of the Republic*, 65–66.

130. Nels W. Forde, *Cato the Censor*, 81.

131. Ennius, fragments 1–13 in *Remains of Old Latin*, 2–7.

132. Grenier, *Roman Spirit*, 127. For more on Epicharmus as a Pythagorean, see Diogenes Laertius, *Lives of the Philosophers*, 8, 78. Some notebooks (*hupomnmata*) attributed to Epicharmus were among the Neo-Pythagorean pseudepigrapha.

133. Dumezil, *Archaic Roman Religion*, 490.

134. Dumezil, 493.

135. Forde, *Cato*, 45.

136. Forde, 46. Forde disagrees with those skeptics who doubt the story of the meeting of Cato and Nearchus. For the skeptics, see Forde, 265 n1.

137. Plutarch, "Life of Cato the Elder," 2, 3–4. In his *De senectutae* (12.39–40) Cicero attributes the same sentiments to Archytas and has him add that the body is the cause of "treason against the state ... rape, adultery and every similar offence." Almost certainly both Plutarch and

Cicero are quoting from the same work made popular by Cato the Elder.

138. Forde, *Cato*, 46.

139. Cato, *De re rustica*, 154–55. Citations from *Marcus Porcius Cato on Agriculture: Marcus Terentius Varro on Agriculture*, trans. William Davis Hooper.

140. Dumezil, *Archaic Roman Religion*, 418.

141. Gruen, *Culture and National Identity*, 52–56.

142. Gruen, 56.

143. Forde, *Cato*, 104; Gruen, 65.

144. Livy, 34, 2–3.

145. Cato, *De re rustica*, 43. We must note that the text we possess of this, Cato's only surviving book, shows signs of having been considerably revised in late classical times. Nevertheless, such are almost certainly Cato's sentiments, if not his exact words.

146. Plutarch, "Life of Cato the Elder," 22, 4.

147. Plutarch, "Life of Cato the Elder," 22, 5.

148. A.A. Long, *Hellenistic Philosophy: Stoics, Epicureans, Skeptics*, 104–05. The main source is Lactanius' *Institutes* and Cicero.

149. Diogenes Laertius, *Lives of the Philosophers*, 8.

150. Aulius Gellius, *Attic Nights*, 9, 12, 7.

151. Richlin," Not Before Homosexuality, 523–73, 561–62.

152. Gruen, *Culture and National Identity*, 71, citing Festus on the word.

153. Plutarch, "Life of Cato," 23, 3–4; Pliny, *Natural History*, 29, 14. Gruen (78) dismisses this remark of Cato's as "obvious hyperbole."

154. Plutarch, "Life of Cato," 20, 6. Plutarch remarks (with a certain Greek amazement) that among the Romans "even fathers-in-law avoided bathing with their sons-in-law, being ashamed of their nakedness." The custom seems not to have survived to the fourth century, for Augustine in his *Confessions* says that his own father noticed in the bath he (Augustine) was undergoing puberty.

155. Aulius Gellius, *Attic Nights*, 10, 15, citing Fabius Pictor as an authority.

156. "Seeing others naked is the cause of homosexuality." So said Lucillius (died 102 BCE), a poet in the circle of Scipio the Younger. Cicero repeats the idea in his *Tusculum Disputations*, 4, 33. Since Lucillius must have know Panaetius personally and Cicero was a great admirer of Panaetius' work, the notion that nudity causes homosexuality probably comes ultimately from that philosopher.

157. G.S. Pembroke, "Oikeiosis," 130.

158. Cicero, *De Officiis*, 1, 35 (126–27).

159. Kiefer, *Sexual Life in Ancient Rome*, 148.

160. Burton, 93–96. Burton's main source here is Plutarch in the second century CE. Is this notion involved in Jesus' prohibition on looking upon a woman to lust after her, at Matthew 5:2?

161. Livy, *Aburbe Condita*, 34, 1–4; Plutarch, "Life of Marcellus," 21, 5. Gruen (*Culture and National Identity*, 70) points out that Livy is unreliable in detail at this point. One is reminded of an incident in American history: When the famous nineteenth century Italian sculptor Antonio Canova presented the United States with a glorious statue of George Washington, showing the first president naked to the waist, Congress was so appalled by "Washington looking like he just came out of the bathtub" that it consigned the statue to an obscure corner in the basement of the Capitol Building, where it rests today. "Plus ça change, plus c'est la même chose," as Alphones Karr remarked—"the more things change, the more they remain the same."

162. Margaret Walters, *Nude Male*, 49.

163. "The Greek custom is to conceal nothing; the Roman custom and that of the warrior is to furnish each statue with a coat of armor," Pliny the Elder, *Natural History*, 34, 5, 10

164. Grenier, *The Roman Spirit*, 57 (figure 7).

165. Burton, 12–13. This hatred of mimes explains why the Catholic Church refused actors burial in consecrated ground as late as the eighteenth century CE.

166. When Pedanius Secundus was murdered by one of his slaves in 61 CE, the senate had all 400 of his slaves executed (Shelton, 175).

167. Cantrella, *Bisexuality*, 101.

168. Whether force was involved or seduction cannot accurately be determined and does not matter for our purposes. The Romans considered that aspect quite irrelevant in matters of male homosexuality. See Jonathan Walters, "Soldiers and Wholes in a Pseudo-Quintilian Declamation," 109–114, 109.

169. Cicero, "Pro Milo," 49; Valerius Maximus, 6, 1, 12; Quintilian, *Oratory*, 3, 11, 4; Quintilian, *Minor Declamations*, 3, 3, 6; Dionysus of Halicarnassus, *Roman Antiquities*, 16, 4, 8.

170. Gruen, *Culture and National Identity*, 62.

171. Thesleff, *Pythagorean Texts*, 51.

172. Evans, *God of Ecstacy*, 118.

173. Luther A. Martin, *Hellenistic Religions: An Introduction*, 93.

174. Diodorus Siculus, *History*, 4, 4, 2.

175. Martin, 99.

176. Martin P. Nilsson, *The Dionysitic Mysteries of the Hellenistic and Roman Age*, 15.

177. Livy. 39. 8. It is worth noting in passing that Livy uses the word "nature" here in a value-free manner—nature might incline men to homosexual acts, by implication, though Livy is obviously horrified at the goings-on he describes.

178. Livy, *History of Rome*, 39, 13.

179. John Bremmer, "An Enigmatic Indo-European Rite: Pederasty," 287. Some disagree: see Nilsson, *Dionysitic Mysteries*, 17n.

180. Livy, *History of Rome*, 39, 18.

181. Nilsson, *Dionysitic Mysteries*, 20, on the authority of Severus' commentary on Virgil.

182. Livy, 40, 29.

183. A member of "a distinct class of more or less permanent civil servants who did the clerical work in the administrative offices." Note by Sage and Schlesinger in Livy, vol. 12, 91.

184. Various other, less complete accounts of the incident differ substantially only in the number of books found; the numbers range from 3 to 12. Sage and Schlesinger discuss the matter in all the detail it deserves at note 4, 90 in Livy, vol. 12.

185. Grenier, *Roman Spirit*, 163. One also suspects that these texts forbade blood sacrifices, which, for all the Pythagorean influence, were and remained a major part of Roman public religion.

186. Forde, *Cato*, 209–10.

187. Thesleff, *Pythagorean Texts*, 47 and 47 n3.

188. Thesleff, 92.

189. Thesleff, 99–102.

190. Dillon, *Middle Platonists*, 118.

191. Iamblichus, *On the Pythagorean Life*, trans. and notes by Gillian Clark. I use the paragraph numbers from this text throughout as reference.

192. Iamblichus, 4.

193. Iamblichus, 13.

194. Clark, 6 n1.

195. Iamblichus, 18.

196. Iamblichus, 27. Clark notes the similarity to the cave of Minos; clearly we are in the world of the shaman.

197. Iamblichus, 29.

198. Martin, *Hellenistic Religions*, 134.

199. Martin, 136.

200. Iambilicos, 30.

201. Iamblichus, 34.

202. Iamblichus, 48.

203. Iamblichus, 76.

204. Iamblichus, 210.

205. Iamblichus, 77.

206. Iamblichus, 203.

207. Giovanni Reale, *The Schools of the Imperial Age*, 262.

208. Diogenes Laertius, *Lives of the Philosophers*, 8, 24, and following.

209. W.K.C. Guthrie, *Early Pre-Socratics*, 201.

210. Dillon, *Middle Platonists*, 121. Dillon reverses the older opinion of Zeller and others that Eudorus was the source of the texts Alexander Polyhistor published.

211. Gellius, *Attic Nights*, 16, 6, 7, 6, 6, 9.

212. Cicero, "Introduction to the *Timaeus*." (This is Cicero's introduction to his Latin translation of Plato's book — the translation itself is lost.) The work had to be translated into Latin again, by Erigina Scotus at the court of Charles the Bald, in medieval France.

213. Dillon, *Middle Platonists*, 117.

214. Thesleff, *Pythagorean Texts*, 41.

215. Dillon, 125.

216. Dillon, 115. Thesleff, 48. Dydimus' successor was, as we have seen, the even more Pythagorean Thrysillos at the court of Tiberius; the post then seems to have become hereditary among Thrysillos' descendants. For a century or more not a Caesar ruled in Rome without a Pythagorean philosopher to whisper in his ear.

217. Richlin, *Garden of Priapus*, 216. The *Lex Scantinia* about a century earlier is thought by some to have prohibited homosexual acts, but this is not certain. See Cantrella, *Bisexuality*, 141, 144.

218. K.S. Guthrie, *The Pythagorean Sourcebook and Library*, 91, 22C–19222D (for this work I give first the page number, then the section number and letter according to Guthrie's edition).

219. K.S. Guthrie, *Pythagorean Sourcebook*, 209.4. Taken from book 1 of Stobaeus. Original in the Koine dialect, but taken from a Doric document. Guthrie believes (203) that this portion of the document may derive from Aristoxenos, the pupil of Aristotle and author, or a work on Pythagoras. For more on Aristoxenos, see Philip, *Pythagoreans and Early Pythagoreanism*, 14.

220. K.S. Guthrie, *Pythagorean Sourcebook*, 233. Taken from book 10 of Stobaeus. The original begins in Doric but soon shifts to Attic Greek.

221. Gellius, *Attic Nights*, 4, 11, 1–13. It is not clear where this interpretation comes from. In the passage Gellius quotes Aristoxenos, the pupil of Aristotle, but the specific interpretation of "beans" as "testicles" is not attributed to Aristoxenos. Gellius is thought to have studied with M. Cornelius Fronto (*Attic Nights*, 2, 26, 1; 12, 29, 2; 19, 8, 1), the teacher of Marcus Aurelius, who may be a source for the homophobia in that emperor.

222. Dio Chrysostom, *Discourses 12–30*, 398.

223. Dio Chrysostom, 30, 11–12, and notes 3 and 4. which point out the Pythagorean sources (409 in Loeb ed.).

224. Dio Chrysostom, 30, 17.

225. Cohoon (in Dio Chrysostom, *Discourses 12–30*, 395–98) cites scholars who suspect Cynic influence, especially Antisthenes, as well as Orphic-Pythagorean in the "Oration on Charidemos." Diogenes the Cynic was famous for his defense of masturbation and public practice of it. For Diogenes it was no more than a convenient relief, analogous to eating. Possibly Antisthenes gave that act a more religious significance. Could he have gone so far as to see it as a way to rid one's body of Titanic substance?

226. Thesleff, *Pythagorean Texts*, 111.

227. Ennius, frag. 467. Quoted in Augustine's *City of God* from Cicero's *Republic*.

228. Earl, *Moral and Political Tradition of Rome*, 29.

229. Cantrella, *Bisexuality*, 110–11. This is the clearest and most complete discussion of the *Lex Scantinia* I know of. Cantrella does not know what the fine for the passive partner was but thinks it was the same. I expect it was more severe.

230. Shelton, 9–10. The point was that the aristocrat retain the integrity of his own body.

231. Sextus Empiricus, *Outlines of Skepticism*, 3, 199. Also "We say that in Persia homosexual acts are customary, while in Rome they are forbidden" (1, 122).

232. Richlin, *Garden*, 222. For a full discussion of homosexuality in Plautus, see Lilja, *Homosexuality*, 302–20.

233. Richlin, 221.

234. Richlin, 225.

235. Shelton, 173–76.

236. Davis, *Problem of Slavery*, 83. One is reminded of the curious compromise of Panaetius/Cicero maintaining that theoretically pederasty was permissible, but ought not to be practiced because it was against common (Roman) custom.

237. Plautus (254–184 BCE) takes it for granted in his comedies that the male slaves are sexual objects to their masters. See *Asinaria*, 703; *Captivi*, 867; *Mostrella*, 847; and *Pseudoli*, 785 and 1189. J. Jachmann, *Plautinshes und Attischos*, 58, demonstrates that this is the native Roman attitude, not the Greek comedy Plautus used as a frequent source.

238. Lilja, *Homosexuality*, 302.

239. Judith P. Hallett, "Female Homoeroticism and the Denial of Roman Reality in Latin Literature," 209–27, 212. The evidence is a single line in a comedy by Plautus.

240. Richlin, "Not Before *Homosexuality*," 335–36.

241. Seneca, "Controversies," 4. Preface 10 quotes an earlier orator as saying that *impudencia*, receiving passive sex, was "a crime for the freeborn, a necessity for the slave and a duty for the free man," implying that the masters were not only allowed but expected to rape their male slaves as a sort of rank demonstration.

242. Seneca the Younger, *Letter 47*.

243. Herodotus, *Histories*, 6, 32. He calls eunuchs *paidas ektetmesthai*—"boys hollowed out." Some of this may be the exaggerated propaganda of war, but there seems no doubt that it often happened.

244. Wainwright Churchill, *Homosexual Behavior among Males*, 149–50.

245. Brandt, *Sexual Life in Ancient Greece*, 510 and n1.

246. Sonya Lida Taran, "EISI TRIKHES: An Erotic Motif," 90–107, 105.

247. Brandt, 512.

248. Shelton, 200.

249. Pliny, *Letters*, 7, 4, 4–6. Unfortunately this epigram is lost.

250. Cicero, *Letters to his Friends*, 16, 10, and 13–16. Tiro recovered and was freed; he lived after the assassination of Cicero by Anthony to edit and preserve, because of his love for his dead master, Cicero's voluminous writings.

251. Statius, *Silvae*, 2, 1, 6. See also Martial, 6, 28–29, 1.

252. Royston Lambert, *Beloved and God: The Story of Hadrian and Antinous*, 83.

253. Richlin, "Not Before Homosexuality," 526.

254. Richlin, 530–31.

255. Richlin, 541–45. Examples come from the time of Cicero (first century BCE) to that of Juvenal (late first century CE).

256. Richlin, 552–53.

257. Ovid, *Metamorphosis*, 9,666–727. Latin from the Teubner edition.

258. Juvenal, 2, 117–20, 124–25, 129. For a thorough analysis of the poem and what it tells us about the position of *cinaedi*, see Richlin, "Not Before Homosexuality," 543–45.

259. Boswell, *Same Sex Unions*, 66–67. Though written in Latin by a member of the court of Nero, the novel does have a Greek quality to it. See note 72 there.

260. Lucian, *Dialogues of the Courtesans*, 5.1–3. See Boswell, *Same Sex Unions*, 83.

261. Shelton, 304.

262. Seneca, *Controversies*, 1, 2, 23.

263. Hallett, "Female Homoeroticism," 179–97, 185–87. The epigrams are 1, 90, 7, 67 and 7, 70.

264. Hallett, 213.

265. Miriam T. Griffin, *Nero: The End of a Dynasty*, 169. Sources in Dio Chrysostom of Prusa (a rhetorician and philosopher born about 50 CE).

266. Griffin, 208–15.

267. McMullen, *Roman Attitudes*, 496 and n43 there. Compare Boswell, *Christianity, Social Tolerance and Homosexuality*, 82. Boswell never mentions the castration of Sporus.

268. Griffin, 287 n6. We note in passing the fact that one of Nero's less famous catamites was a boy named Pythagoras. See Dio Chrysostom, *Discourses 12–30*, 63, 13, 2.

269. Cicero, *Philippic*, 2, 18, 45. The usually humane Cicero approves the union; Curio the Elder is furious.

270. Boswell, *Same Sex Unions*, 84–85.

271. Staub, *Roots of Evil*, 59.

272. Allport, *Nature of Prejudice*, 19–22.

273. Staub, 60.

274. Lipmann, quoted in Kleg, *Hate, Prejudice and Racism*, 139.

275. Kleg, 140–41.

276. Kleg, 143.

CHAPTER 7

1. Procopius, *The Secret History (Anecdota)*, 9, 16. For the method of "legal" proceeding in such cases, see *Secret History*, 20, 16. Averil Cameron (*Procopius and the Sixth Century*, 62) believes Procopius should not be trusted on his accounts of specific acts of Justinian after chapter 19. However, the executions described here are confirmed in greater detail in Johannes Malalas (*Chronographia*, 18, 168) as well as in the works of Theophanes, Zonaras (50.14), and Cedrenus (368 in the Paris ed.); for a full discussion of Procopius' reliability, see Averil Cameron, 49–66. Gibbon's account in 44, 3 of the *Decline and Fall of the Roman Empire* is vivid but none too balanced.

2. Procopius, *On the Buildings*, 1, 2, 5–12. See Baker, below, for details of this monument.

3. John W. Baker, *Justinian and the Later Roman Empire*, 97. Justinian also used the title *Isopostolos*, "Equal of the Apostles," and Byzantine monarchs regularly called themselves "Emperor and Priest." "Caesaropapism," the entire unity of religious and secular authority in one person, seems an understatement to describe Justinian, since he was able to install Pelagius, his papal legate, as pope in 556 CE. See Baker, 111 and passim.

4. Lord Kinross and the editors of the Newsweek Book Division, *Hagia Sophia*, 45.

5. The idea that natural disasters are evidence of divine anger is not necessarily Christian in origin; Firmillian, the bishop of Caeserea, reported a series of earth-quakes in Cappadocia and Pontus (both in what is now Turkey) in 234 CE. The people blamed the Christians for provoking the disaster, and a persecution drove many Christians out. See *Letters of St. Cyprian*, 75.10.

6. Greenberg, *Construction of Homosexuality*, 235. This is an extension of *Institutes*, 4, 18, 4. "He who exercises his shameful lust with a man is punished by the sword on the basis of the *Lex Julia*." Eva Cantrella notes (181) this means any form of male homosexuality.

7. Baker, *Justinian*, 205.

8. Procopius, *Secret History*, 11, 34–36. Procopius calls homosexuality a "sickness" (11, 40); this was a relatively progressive opinion for the period.

9. Baker, *Justinian*, 99–100.

10. Baker, 206–10.

11. Procopius, *Secret History*, 15, 11. John Calvin comes immediately to mind, and Cromwell.

12. I take it that Alexander and Isaiah were accused of being lovers. Justinian was fond of punishing the offending body part (thieves' hands were cut off, for example), so it appears that Alexander was assumed to be the penetrator and Isaiah the receiver. By this period "pederasty" meant any form of male-to-male sexual activity, regardless of the ages or social status of the persons involved.

13. Cora Lutz, "Roman Socrates," 14–15.

14. Tacitus, *Histories*, 3, 81. The historian finds this a most unreasonable display of philosophy.

15. Arnold, *Roman Stoicism*, 118. Arnold thinks of him as a Stoic.

16. Tacitus, *Annals*, 14.57. The word "tyrannicide" doesn't occur in the text, but the descriptions are not out of keeping with language used to describe Harmodios and Aristogeiton.

17. Arnold, 400–01.

18. Dudley, *History of Cynicism*, 128. Quotation from Musonius Rufus, fragments 8, 8.1.

19. Arnold, 401.

20. Domitian put many to death "under the charge of philosophizing" (Dio Cassius, 67, 12). See also Arnold, 401–02.

21. Lutz, "Roman Socrates," 3–150, 7.

22. Lutz, 29–30.

23. Musonius, 38 in Lutz trans. All references to Musonius' essays are by page number in the Lutz text. I have occasionally used the Greek to remove the fig leaf from Lutz' sexual terms.

24. Musonius, in Lutz, 84.

25. Musonius, in Lutz, 84–88.

26. Musonius, in Lutz, 89–90.

27. The scholar an-Nadim saw a copy of this in the Library of Baghdad in 988 CE (Lutz, 20), but the manuscript probably perished when Hulaku the Mongol took the city in 1258 CE.

28. Babut ("Les Stociens," 59) notes that this is a departure from the teachings of the old Stoics and believes (61) that the Stoic position was that boy-love should be friendly, not physical — a point amply refuted by the long treatise, used above, from the Old Stoics.

29. Richard Carrier, "On Musonius Rufus: A Brief Essay." Open advocacy of abolition was "virtual suicide" among the Romans; Carrier notes the swiftness with which a slave uprising in the time of Tiberius was put down. Tacitus, *Annals*, 4, 27.

30. Carrier.

31. Arnold, *Roman Stoicism*, 117. We have already noted the homophobic interpretation of Gellius on beans. Gellius was an antiquarian with wide and varied interests, but it is possible that he may have picked up some of his ideas on this point from Musonius.

32. Lutz, "Roman Socrates," 19.

33. Arnold, 118–19.
34. Mikhail Ivonovich Rostovtzeff, *The Social and Economic History of the Roman Empire*, 586–87, n17–19.
35. Rostovtzeff, 123.
36. Rostovtzeff, 121.
37. W.W. Buckland, "Classical Roman Law," in *The Imperial Peace*, 831.
38. *Dio Chrysostom, Discourses 12–30*, 7, 135. My translation. The pun is on *aphrodisiazo*, "to have sexual intercourse." However, the meaning of the word was not limited, as Dio says, to heterosexual intercourse; he adds the well-known argument from nature to limit the term.
39. Dio Chrysostom, 7, 139.
40. Dio Chrysostom," Oration 7," 52.
41. Dio Chrysostom, 66, 7.
42. Lambert, *Beloved and God*, 86. We hear of Pylades and a dancer named Apolaustus. There was a school for imperial pages in Rome, where boys were probably taught more than how to fold napkins.
43. Anthony R. Birley, *Hadrian: The Restless Emperor*, 42.
44. Birley, 139. Birley says the reasons for Sabina's dislike of Hadrian are unclear. The evidence seems obvious.
45. Birley, 41–42.
46. Birley, 58–65.
47. Lambert, *Beloved and God*, 19.
48. Lambert, 22.
49. Birley, *Hadrian*, 158.
50. Tertullian (*Apology*, 13, 9) is the authority for this — not a friendly witness in the least.
51. Birley, 158.
52. Lambert, *Beloved and God*, 142–62.
53. *Historia Augusta*, 14, 6. Lambert on the strength of a passage in Tacitus says that this does not imply effeminacy in Hadrian, but this author rather suspects that it does. Circumstances alter cases.
54. Lambert, 117.
55. Lambert, 118–19.
56. Birley, *Hadrian*, 251.
57. Hallett, "Female Homoeroticism," 193.
58. Lambert, *Beloved and God*, 144–47.
59. Origin, *Contra Celsum*, 3, 36.
60. Lambert, 166.
61. Lambert, 181. Lambert thinks that Hadrian really believed in Antinous as a god (149); however, the emperor's wonderful poem on his own death:

> Little soul, little wanderer
> body's guest and companion
> to what place will you set out for now?
> to darkling, cold and gloomy ones —
> and you won't make your usual jokes

(translation by Birley, 301) suggests that Hadrian had no expectation of help or affection in the afterlife, from Osiris-Antinous or any other god.
62. Lambert, 143.
63. Lambert, 148.
64. Lambert, 159–60.
65. Lambert, 166.
66. Birley, *Hadrian*, 289–90.
67. Lambert, 170–72. The *Historia Augusta* says he was adopted because of his beauty, a fact not apparent from the single surviving portrait on a coin.
68. Birley, 291.
69. Birley, 292.
70. Birley, 295.
71. Marcus Aurelius, *Meditations*, 1, 16, 2.
72. R.B. Rutherford, *The Meditations of Marcus Aurelius: A Study*, 118.
73. Both the *Historia Augustae* (2.1) and Aurelius Victor (*de Caesares*, 15) say that Antoninus was *calrus moribus*,

of pure morals. However, Julian the Apostate mentions that Antoninus was *saphon ou ta es Aphroditen*, "not wise in matters of love." Perhaps Julian had in mind the mistress Antoninus took after his wife's death.
74. Aurelius, *Meditations*, 1, 17, 7.
75. Aurelius, *Meditations*, 3, 16, 1.
76. *Historia Augustae*, "Aurelius," 2, 4.
77. *Historia Augustae*, "Aurelius," 2, 4.
78. Fronto, letters 23–29. See Lambert, *Beloved and God*, 84 and n34, 253.
79. *Historia Augustae*, 4, 3. "Hadrian closely supervised his rearing and called him 'Verissimus' [most truthful]."
80. Boswell, *Christianity*, 130. See reference (n 29) to *Enchridion*, 10, and *Discourses*, 4, 11, 19. The difference on this point between Epictetus and his teacher, Musonius, seems to arise from Epictetus' deep interest in logic. See *The Cynics*, 198.
81. Gibbon, 1, 4, 2.
82. Wilhelm Weber, "Hadrian," in *The Imperial Peace*, 315.
83. Wilhelm Weber, "Antoninus," in *The Imperial Peace*, 335.
84. Weber, 372.
85. Weber, "The Antonines," in *The Imperial Peace*, 378.
86. Weber, 380.
87. Weber, 381. The always gossipy *Historia Augusta* says ("Commodus," 5.8) that he allowed every part of his body, "even his mouth," to be defiled by young men. The statement is repeated almost word for word about Elagabalus, suggesting it was more of a standard insult than a veritable fact.
88. Weber, 381.
89. Weber, 388–92. His concubine, Marcia, who helped assassinate him, is said to have been something of a Christian (383).
90. Aurelius Victor, *De Caesares*, 28, 6. Victor lived in the time of Julian, 361–68 CE.
91. W.W. Buckland, "Classical Roman Law," in *The Imperial Peace*, 806–44, 829. Just how fully this was put in practice is obscure.
92. *Encyclopædia Britannica*, 1945, s.v. "Plutarch."
93. Plutarch, "Dialogue on Love," 750C–D, in *Plutarch's Moralia in Sixteen Volumes*, vol. 9, trans. Edwin L. Minor, F.H. Sandbach and W.C. Helmbold, 306–441.
94. Plutarch, "Dialogue on Love," 752B.
95. Plutarch, "Dialogue on Love," 752F.
96. Plutarch, "Dialogue on Love," 751C.
97. Plutarch, "Dialogue on Love," 768D–E.
98. Boswell, *Christianity, Social Tolerance*, 126 for examples.
99. The presence of Ulpian in Athenaeus' dialogue is sufficient proof that the work is not influenced by Christian thought; according to Lactantius, *Divine Institutes*, 5, 2, Ulpian was the major codifier of anti–Christian laws. Some sense of the man's cruelty can be gathered from fragments preserved in the *Digests* of Justinian; see 1, titles 16, 17, title 2.3. etc.
100. *The Deipnosophists of Athenaeus of Naucritos*, viii–ix. All quotations are from this text.
101. Athenaeus, 564A.
102. Athenaeus, 601B.
103. Athenaeus, 508D.
104. Athenaeus, 605D.
105. Athenaeus, 247n.
106. P. Merlau, "On the Neopythagoreans," in *Cambridge History of Later Greek and Early Medieval Philosophy*, 94.
107. Merlau, 95.

108. Reale, *Schools of the Imperial Age*, 249.

109. Reale, 262.

110. Merlau, 97–99. Moderatus made the same claim (90) — that Plato and the Early Academy had taken doctrines from Pythagoras — called *kleptodoxia* in Greek.

111. A.H. Armstrong, *Cambridge History of Later Greek and Early Medieval Philosophy*, 169.

112. Eusebius, *History of the Church*, 6, 19, 7, quoting Porphyry.

113. We cannot date the homophobia of the extant Persian texts with precision, but the tradition may have existed in Plotinus' time, likewise with the prohibition of homosexuality in the Hindu Code of Manu.

114. Porphyry, *Life of Plotinus*, 2.

115. Eunapius (*Lives of the Sophists*, 455) says that in his time copies of Plotinus were more common than copies of Plato. Eunapius was born in 347 CE.

116. R. Blaine Harris, "Brief Description of Neoplatonism," 1–20, 1–2.

117. Harris, 6–7.

118. Merlau, "On the Neopythagoreans," in *Cambridge History of Later Greek*, 25–26.

119. Harris, 4.

120. Plotinus, *Enneads*, 5, 5, 121, 41–49, in Armstrong, 261.

121. Harris, 2.

122. Franz Cumont, "The Frontier Provinces and the East," in *The Imperial Peace*, 605–48, 642.

123. Green, *Alexander to Actium*, 186. With this we may compare Philo's equally humanitarian regard — see below.

124. Porphyry, *Life of Plotinus*, 10.

125. Plotinus, *Enneads*, 3, 5, 7.

126. Plotinus, 64 and 170–171n.

127. Plotinus, 3, 5, 20.

128. Armstrong (Plotinus, note 2, 168–69) points out that Plotinus substitutes the Platonic word *aoriston*, "indefinite," for the Pythagorean term *apeiron*, "unlimited." The reference to columns is to the parallel lists of Pythagorean opposites in Aristotle's *Nichomachean Ethics*.

129. See for example Soranos of Ephesus, fragment from unidentified work, 1, 30–31; Cantrella, *Bisexuality*, 188.

130. Artemidorus, *On Acute and Chronic Diseases*, Tarrant Passim, 4, 9, 132–33.

131. Brooten, *Love Between Women*, 163. The operation (performed, like all surgery at the time, without either anesthesia or asepsis) is described in horrible detail.

132. Pseudo-Aristotle, *Problemata*, 4, 26, 879B–880A; see Brooten, 149 n17.

133. Brooten, 176–77, 176 n2.

134. Brooten, 181–83. Brooten seems to regard penetration as always implying that the penetrator is superior to the one penetrated, something not necessarily true.

135. Nock, *Early Gentile Christianity*, 90.

136. Brooten, 34–37.

137. Brooten, 137–38.

138. For a general discussion of the contempt and hostility of the Romans toward eunuchs, see Walter Stevenson, "The Rise of Eunuchs in Greco-Roman Antiquity," 495–511.

139. Boswell, *Christianity, Social Tolerance and Homosexuality*, 141–43.

140. David Kostan, *Sexual Symmetry: Love in the Ancient Novel and Related Genres*, 43, 57.

141. Kostan, 58.

142. Tatius, *Leucippe and Clitophon*, paragraphs 27, 28, and 35.

143. Moses Hadas and Morton Smith, *Spiritual Biographies in Antiquity*, 96.

144. G.W. Bowerstock, ed., in Philostratus, *Life of Apollonius*, intro., 9–22, 19.

145. Translator C.P. Jones, in Bowerstock, 14, calls it "a mirror" of the class of Julia Domna.

146. Boswell, *Christianity, Social Tolerance and Homosexuality*, 122–23. Besides the doubt of the legal standing of this opinion expressed by Boswell, we must add doubts of its genuineness — the text dates from long after Paulus' time, when antihomosexual law was fashionable.

147. Philostratus, *Life of Apollonius*, 1, 2. All quotations are from Jones's translation.

148. Philostratus, 1, 3. This work has not survived, though Origin the Christian has preserved fragments of it.

149. Philostratus, 1, 5.

150. Philostratus, 1, 8.

151. Philostratus, 1, 13. For Pythagoras as divine messenger, see 1, 1.

152. Philostratus, 1, 12

153. Bowerstock, in Philostratus, 37, n8.

154. Philostratus, 4, 45.

155. Philostratus, 6, 3.

156. David Kostan, *Sexual Symmetry*, 111.

157. Aurelius Victor, *de Caes*, 21, 2–3; *Historia Augusta*, "Severus," 21; Eutropius, 8, 20, 1; *epitome*, 21, 5; Orosius, 7, 18, 2. Caracalla was widely regarded as a tyrant, and sexual enormities were part of the Roman stereotype of the tyrant. The confusion of mother and stepmother arises because Septimus Severus was married twice. Victor, Eutropius and Orosius incorrectly believe that the mother of his sons was his first wife, rather than Julia Domna.

158. Philostratus, *Life of Apollonius*, 1, 17.

159. Philostratus, 8, 19. This bringing up of a collection of oracles from the underworld suggests a specific relation to Etruscan mythology.

160. Philostratus, 8, 30–31.

161. Philostratus, 1, 16.

162. *Historia Augusta*, "Heliogabalus," 5, 1–2. Birley's translation. The spelling of his name is confused in the Greek sources, and Birley uses the Latin form. The most correct form seems to be Dion Cassius' "Elagabalus," which I have used.

163. *Historia Augusta*, "Heliogabalus," 12. Nero, of course, had enrolled one of his horses in the senate, but the gender of the animal is obscure, and it proposed no legislation.

164. *Historia Augusta*, "Heliogabalus," 15, 6.

165. *Historia Augusta*, "Alexander Severus," 29. Christ was also among the images he worshiped. Eusebius says (*History of the Church*, 6.21–28) that Alexander Severus' mother had been a pupil of the Christian Origin in Antioch (which does not mean that she was a Christian). Nevertheless Ulpian, the jurist, flourished under Alexander and codified virulent anti–Christian legislation.

166. Klostermann, "Hat Ezechiel in Lev., 18–26," in *Zietschrift for Luth. Theologie*, 1877, 406–45. The concept was refined by Julius Wellhausen (1844–1918), often thought of as the founder of modern Biblical criticism.

167. This is the date given by Bishop Ussher. Various other chronologies based on the text of the Bible vary slightly.

168. Nahum M. Sarna. "Biblical Literature: Hebrew Scripture," 158–59.

169. Saul M. Olyan, "'And with a Male You Shall Not Lie the Lying Down of a Woman': On the Meaning and Significant of Leviticus 18:22 and 20:13," 179–206, 179 n1.

170. Artur Weiser, *The Old Testament: Its Formation and Development*, 140. Weiser thinks it was compiled from various sources about the time of Ezekiel (around 540 BCE).

171. Olyan, 203.

172. S.R. Driver, *An Introduction to the Literature of the Old Testament*, 47–48.

173. Driver, 58.

174. Unless otherwise specified, all quotations from the Bible are from the *New Oxford Annotated Bible with the Apocrypha* (New York: Oxford University Press, 1977).

175. Translation by Olyan, "And with a Male," 180.

176. Olyan, 183–86.

177. Olyan, 180, n3. Olyan notes quite correctly that John Boswell's interpretation of the word in *Christianity, Social Tolerance and Homosexuality*, 100–101, as solely applying to the ritually unclean "is simply unfounded."

178. Olyan, 187.

179. Olyan, 198–99. Olyan quietly implies this interpretation is unworthy of consideration.

180. Olyan, 199.

181. Olyan, 202.

182. Olyan, 202–203. Deuteronomy 23:12–14 presents a quaint and charming picture: soldiers are commanded to bury their excrement outside the camp for fear that the Lord would take offence by seeing it "and turn away from you."

183. So Olyan. The same point is made by Martin Samuel Cohen, "The Biblical Prohibition of Homosexual Intercourse," 2–20, 10. Cohen sees the importance of semen as arising from its being on the boundaries between life and not-life, a deeply problematical substance. However, the importance of semen may have arisen from the fact that the ability to ejaculate semen was a sign of manhood, and therefore was involved in the deep roots of male dominance.

184. Olyan, 203–04. The Priestly Code on the other hand imposed only a seven-day purification for menstrual intercourse (mixing of semen and menstrual blood) — compare Leviticus 20:18 (Holiness Code) with Leviticus 15:24 (Priestly). One may note in Hinduism that when a particularly powerful purifying agent is required, the five purifying substances obtained from a sacred cow are mixed. See Parker, below, 96.

185. Olyan, 206.

186. Cohen, "Biblical Prohibition of Homosexual Intercourse," 2–20.

187. 2 Samuel 1:23. I quote for aesthetic reasons the translation of David Alter in *The David Story*. Alter's note on this passage denies an erotic reading but refers to the affection that develops between soldiers, which seems in its way very telling.

188. Olyan, "And with a Male," 197.

189. James J. Preston, "Purification," 91.

190. Mary Douglas, *Purity and Danger*, 5. However, Douglas' argument that homosexuality was forbidden in the Holiness Code because the receptive partner does not conform to his class of being (54–72) is shown by Olyan (198 and n62) to be untenable, since the oldest form of the law was against the inserting partner only.

191. Preston, 92.

192. Mary Douglas, "Social Conditions of Enthusiasm and Heterodoxy," 71.

193. Parker, 94.

194. Michael Satlow, "'They Abused Him Like a Woman': Homoeroticism, Gender Blurring and the Rabbis in Late Antiquity," 1–25.

195. Green, *Alexander to Actium*, 94–96.

196. Lucian, *de Dea Syria*, 27. There is, however, some doubt as to the authorship of this book. William F. Albright (*Archaeology and the Religion of Israel*, 159) accepts the text. Albright says that the *qedeshim* were equivalent to *cinaedi* or *galli* (the later are the self-castrated priests of Cybel at Rome).

197. Cantrella, *Bisexuality*, 195.

198. Boswell, *Christianity, Social Tolerance and Homosexuality*, 94–95. Greenberg (136) points out that the Lord was already angry with Sodom when the angels went there,

so some possibility of abhorrent sexual acts being involved cannot be excluded.

199. The Hebrew word is probably better translated "madness." Interestingly the Septuagint translates it *aphrodusine*— meaning "to have sex," and Jerome's Vulgate translation completes the Hellenization of the text by paraphrasing it "*scelus contra naturam*," — an "evil act against nature." Thus in brief the progression of interpretation can be demonstrated that is typical of the whole culture. See Cantrella, 195.

200. Greenberg, *Construction of Homosexuality*, 122, n176.

201. Green, *Alexander to Actium*, 499.

202. Green, 503.

203. Hengel, *Judaism and Hellenism*, 104.

204. Hengel, 31.

205. Eduard Lohse, *The New Testament Environment*, 21.

206. Hengel, 162–63.

207. Green, *Alexander to Actium*, 502.

208. Green, 502.

209. Moses Hadas, *Hellenistic Culture: Fusion and Diffusion*, 17. In Hebrew, *epikoros* means "infidel." Antiochos was a pupil of Philonides of Laodicea, a famed Epicurean teacher.

210. Hadas, 31.

211. Green, *Alexander to Actium*, 508–11.

212. See *The Book of Jubilees*, 3, 31.

213. Green, 510.

214. Herodotos says (*Histories*, 2, 36, 3–37, 2) that the Egyptians practiced circumcision, choosing cleanliness over appearance. Of course Herodotos was unaware of the Jews. For a general discussion of the Greek distaste for circumcision, see Dover, *Greek Homosexuality*, 127–31.

215. 2 Maccabees 6:7; Green, 516.

216. Green, 516.

217. Lohse, *New Testament Environment*, 23.

218. Hengel, *Judaism and Hellenism*, 305.

219. Lohse, 29.

220. Hadas, *Hellenistic Culture*, 218.

221. Hengel, 237–38, 245.

222. Lohse, 30–31.

223. Lohse, 30–32.

224. Lohse, 34–35.

225. Satlow, "They Abused Him Like a Woman," 1–25, 9.

226. Satlow, 19–20.

227. John J. Collins, *Between Athens and Jerusalem: Jewish Identity in the Hellenistic Diaspora*, 33.

228. Collins, 61.

229. Collins, 33.

230. Satlow, 10.

231. Sifra on Leviticus, 18, 3; Aharei Mot, Parasha. 9. Bernadette Brooten (*Love Between Women*, 66) cites abundant evidence for female-female marriages in Hellenistic Egypt.

232. Satlow, 15–16.

233. Satlow, 23–24.

234. Satlow, 11.

235. Satlow, 24.

236. Greenberg, *Construction of Homosexuality*, 200.

237. For a full discussion of the God-Fearers in the Hellenistic era, see Joseph Klausner, *From Jesus to Paul*, 34–49.

238. Collins, *Between Athens and Jerusalem*, 4–6.

239. Collins, 143.

240. See Collins, 143, for Pseudo-Phoclydes' interest in sexual mores.

241. Collins, 164–65.

242. Collins, 71.

243. Collins, 62.

244. John Dominic Crossan, *The Historical Jesus*, 111. For an interesting history of the entire pre–Christian apocalyptic genre, see John J. Collins' *The Apocalyptic Imagination*, referred to below.

245. "Sibylline Oracles," *Encyclopedia of Religion*.

246. "Sibylline Oracles," *Encyclopedia of Religion*.

247. Willis Barnstone, *The Other Bible*, 501.

248. Collins, *Between Athens and Jerusalem*, 63.

249. Collins, 150.

250. Collins, 150.

251. *Pseudepigrapha*. In Greek the phrase "to sleep in Phoenicia" meant to have oral sex. It is said the term comes from the famous Phoenician dye, a red-purple color. Men who performed oral sex on women would get red mouths from their menstrual blood.

252. *The Sibylline Oracles*, 5, 15, 430. This is from a revision by Barnstone (*The Other Bible*, 505) of the text translated by R. H. Charles in *Pseudepigrapha*.

253. *Sibylline Oracles*, 3.573–96. Charles notes (389) that this passage is "especially Essene."

254. Collins, *Between Athens and Jerusalem*, 151.

255. Collins, 151.

256. Collins, 68–70.

257. Collins, 153. The fragments are in Theophilus and Lactantius.

258. Collins, 145.

259. Pseudo-Phoclydes, lines 209–12. We note in passing that Pseudo-Phoclydes said that men should wear their hair short, women long; evidently this attitude was picked up in some revised form by Paul in I Corinthians.

260. R.H. Charles (*Pseudepigrapha*, 282) suggests that the original text came from 109–106 BCE in the circle of those in Palestine who admired the conquering John Hyrcanus.

261. Collins, 153–56.

262. Charles' translation.

263. 1 Enoch 11:2. Charles' translation. According to Charles this is originally from a Hebrew source. The Watchers also appear in Daniel 4:17 from about the beginning of the Maccabean period.

264. David Winston, introduction to *Philo of Alexandria*, 1–2.

265. Samuel Samdmel, *Philo of Alexandria: An Introduction*, 15.

266. Hengel, *Judaism*, 68; Philo Judaeus, *Spec leg*, 2, 230; Philo Judaeus, *De Som*, 69, 129–30.

267. Sandmel, *Philo*, 9.

268. Guthrie, *Orpheus and Greek Religion*, 196.

269. Sandmel, *Philo*, 22–23. The similarity of Philo's arithmology and the mystical manipulation of numbers in Rabbinic *gematria* is coincidental in detail. However, one suspects that both share a Pythagorean origin. The best study of Philo's numerology is the German work cited by Sandmel, 174 n5.

270. Philo, "On the Creation," 100. See also his "Allegorical Interpretation," 1, 15, for seven as meaning a virgin. Likewise in "Every Man is Free," Philo uses a Pythagorean *symbola*, in sec. 2.

271. Collins, *Between Athens and Jerusalem*, 198–99.

272. H. Chadwick, "On Philo," in *The Cambridge History of Later Greek and Early Medieval Philosophy*, 147.

273. Sandmel, *Philo*, 118–22. Sandmel is relaying largely on Helmut Koestler's analysis of the concept of the law of nature in antiquity.

274. Harry Austryne Wolfson, *Philo*, 446–47.

275. Colson's note on this expression (634) says he can find no other references to homosexual or eunuch priests in connection with the goddess Demeter. In fact the phrase in Greek "to celebrate the rites of Demeter" was a euphemism for defecation, since feces were used to fertilize the fields, sacred to Demeter, the corn-goddess. Diogenes Laertius says that Diogenes the Cynic used to shock people by "celebrating the rites of Demeter" and making love in public (6, 69). Possibly Philo has some Cynics in mind at this point.

276. *Philo*, translation by F.H. Colson, vol. 7, 498–501.

277. Grant, *Miracle and Natural Law*, 15. Grant finds Philo's concept of nature most closely resembles the Stoics.

278. Vetius Valens, *Anthologia*, 2.17.68; Brooten, 129. Valens' explanation of why this happens is not clear, but it seems that evening stars make men feminine (*thalonousi*) and hence unable to contribute the essentially male substance needed for generation.

279. Peter Brown, *The Body and Society*, 6–8.

280. Brown, 17.

281. Brooten, *Love Between Women*, 247.

282. Dillon, *Middle Platonists*, 143.

283. Sandmel, *Philo*, 123.

284. "The Contemplative Life," 7.59–64, in *Philo of Alexandria: The Contemplative Life, the Giants, and Selections*.

285. H. Chadwick, "On Philo," in *Cambridge History*, 153. For a fuller discussion of Philo's notion of the divine *eros*, see Erwin R. Goodenough, *Jewish Symbols*, 8, 12–15.

286. Philo, "Special Legislation, 3, 13–18, trans. Colson, 7. The ideas here are especially close to those of Paul in Romans 1, discussed below.

287. For a complete discussion of Philo's inconsistent attitude toward science, see Grant, *Miracle and Natural Law*, 89–91.

288. Philo, "Questions and Answers on Genesis," 122. This interpretation is repeated in "On Drunkenness," 222–23. According to Gesenius' *Lexicon of the Old Testament* (1847), "Sodom" certainly means "burning," and "Gomorrah" seems to mean "culture" or "habitation." This free play with Hebrew word meanings is common in Philo; whether he actually knew Hebrew or got his often dubious meanings from some other source is still in question. See Sandmel, *Philo*, 131.

289. *Philo*, vol. 6. Philo uses the same Greek verb that Plato uses in the *Republic*, likening homosexual mating to the rutting of animals.

290. Bullough, *Social Variance*, 143–44. From Aurelianus' *On Acute Diseases and On Chronic Diseases*, 4, 9, 131–37.

291. "Immateriality of the Soul," 176; see also Dillon, *Middle Platonists*, 154.

292. Sandmel, *Philo*, 11.

CHAPTER 8

1. For the New Testament passages on marriage and their later interpretations, see Uta Ranke Heinemann, *Eunuchs for the Kingdom of God*, 37–46.

2. Crossan, *Historical Jesus*, 427–29. The letters of Paul, written in the same period, give a bit of information on the career of Jesus as well.

3. Burton L. Mack, *The Lost Gospel*, 120. The major effort to discover and document the kinship between the early Jesus documents and the Cynics was done in several books by Gerald Downing; Downing and other Christian writers have generally failed to mention the positive attitude of the Cynics toward homosexuality. The general relationship between first century Cynicism and early Christianity seems well grounded both in the documents and in the opinion of modern scholars — see Crossan, *Historical Jesus*, 72–88. For a dissenting opinion on the influence of Cynic thought on the Q document, see C.M.

Tuckett, "A Cynic Q?" 349–76. Likewise Theissen and Merz (*The Historical Jesus: A Comprehensive Guide*, 215–16) give short shrift to the Cynic influence. They conclude that the image of Jesus in the early Gospel tradition was attempting to go the austere Cynics one better.

4. John Dominic Crossan, *The Essential Jesus*, 20.

5. Crossan, *Historical Jesus*, 16–19.

6. John E. Stambaugh and David Balch, *The New Testament in Its Social Environment*, 90–91.

7. Theodore Gomperz, *Greek Thinkers: A History of Ancient Philosophy*, vol. 2, 152.

8. Dudley, *History of Cynicism*, 162–63. Herakles was the special god of the Cynics.

9. Pseudo-Diogenes, "Epistle 26," in *The Cynic Epistles*. The editor, Malherbe, dates the work on page 15. The staff, ragged cloak and wallet (a bag worn on a shoulder strap) are the standard gear of a wandering Cynic.

10. Gomperz, 148.

11. Diogenes Laertius, *Lives of the Philosophers*, 6, 62.

12. Mack, *Lost Gospel*, 116–18.

13. Gomperz, 139.

14. Gomperz, 142–45.

15. Dudley, *History of Cynicism*, 1–2, 8–9.

16. Diogenes Laertius, *Lives of the Philosophers*, 6, 3–4 (vol. 2, 4–5 in the Loeb edition).

17. Diogenes Laertius, *Lives of the Philosophers*, 6, 11–12.

18. Gomperz, 155.

19. Diogenes Laertius, *Lives of the Philosophers*, 6, 20–21. Several variants of this story are given.

20. Diogenes Laertius, *Lives of the Philosophers*, 6, 69.

21. Dating according to Abraham J. Malherbe. *The Cynic Epistles: A Study Edition*. Missoula, Montana: the Scholars Press, 1977. 15. The letter is, of course, a forgery, but it indicates the opinion of Cynics of its time.

22. Pseudo-Diogenes. "Letter 35" Sec. 2–3, trans. Benjamin Fiore, in *The Cynic Epistles*. At the end of the incident Diogenes goes to the sea to bathe, implying he had had an orgasm.

23. Pseudo-Diogenes, *The Cynic Epistles*, 15.

24. Pseudo-Diogenes, "Letter 6." Malherbe gives no date for this letter.

25. Pseudo-Diogenes, "Letter 44." Malherbe dates it second or third century CE (page 15).

26. F. Gerald Downing, *Cynics and Christian Origins*, 52 n97.

27. Diogenes Laertius, *Lives of the Philosophers*, 6, 84.

28. Dudley, *History of Cynicism*, 40–41.

29. Heraclitos, "Epistle of Heraclitos," 7, 2.

30. Pseudo-Diogenes, quoted by Devek Krueger, "The Body and Society: The Shamelessness of Diogenes in Roman Imperial Culture," 221–33, 232.

31. Krueger, 233. Cynics perfected the use of flatulation as social criticism, farting during the speeches of demagogues.

32. Malherbe, *Paul and the Popular Philosophers*, 13–21.

33. "Letter," 9, 8.

34. The evidence from Greek and Latin sources is readily available in Frazer, *Adonis, Attis and Osiris*, 1. 110–12. Frazer spells the name "Melcarth." The cult of Herakles-Melqart spread as far west as Spain among the Phoenician colonies.

35. Astour, *Hellenosemitica*, 246.

36. Astour, 306–7.

37. Dudley (*History of Cynicism*, 5) cites a scolion to Aristotle that there are four reasons why the Cynics had that name: 1) they were indifferent like dogs to comforts and luxuries; 2) they were shameless like dogs, having sex in public; 3) they guarded their philosophy, snarling at those who would assault it; 4) they knew their friends from their enemies, barking at the latter.

38. Astour, 306–07.

39. Lawrence Stager, "Why Were Hundreds of Dogs Buried at Ashkelon?" 24–43.

40. The footnote to this passage in *The New Oxford Annotated Bible* says "dog" here means "a male cultic prostitute." This seems to be a clever guess for a serious meaning, based upon certain sexual positions. The passage can be taken literally: the author of this study remembers certain pious Baptists in the rural American South who would not buy or sell puppies or dogs because of this passage.

41. Gerald F. Downing, *Christ and the Cynics: Jesus and Other Radical Preachers in the First Century Tradition*, xiii: "Jesus was a Cynic"; Crossan, *Historic Jesus*, 75–88: "the parallels [in Jesus' teachings] to Stoic-Cynic admonitions are ... quite striking," 295; Mack, *Lost Gospel*, 120.

42. Crossan, *Historical Jesus*, 429.

43. Mack, 158. See Ron Cameron, "'What Have You Come Out to See?'" 35–69. For early Christian sculpture of John the Baptist as Cynic, see Crossan, *Essential Jesus*, 176–77. Generally John is shown in the philosopher's single pallium, while Jesus is a much smaller, nude youth ankle deep in the Jordan — for example plates 11 and 74.

44. Dudley, 163. Oenomaus' tone is one of "mocking skepticism" (170), so we may suspect that he had little respect for the resurrection rituals of Herakles in Tyre. On the other hand there is slender evidence that Oenomaus may have been a friend of the famous Rabbi Meir (162).

45. Crossan, *Historical Jesus*, 461.

46. Crossan, *Historical Jesus*, 323.

47. "Magic, simply, is what any socio-religious ascendancy calls its deviant shadow" (Crossan, 309). Hence, the violent objection by many contemporary fundamentalists to any portrayal of magic in fiction. Theissen and Merz dissent on this point: "No where else do we find a charismatic miracle worker whose miraculous deeds are meant to be the end of an old world and the beginning of a new" (309).

48. Crossan, *Historical Jesus*, 137–67, and especially 157.

49. Quoted in John Middleton, "Theories of Magic," 88.

50. Ernst Lohmeyer (*Das Evangelium des Markus*) tries to argue that Jesus' short list of commandments comes from a Galilean Torah, but this passage in Mark would be the only solid evidence for the existence of such a radically different Torah.

51. For an example of Cynic marriage see Diogenes Laertius, *Lives of the Philosophers*, 6, 93, 96–97. Krates married Hipparkhia without parental consent or public avowal but only because she loved him and wanted to be with him — the sort of Romantic love that would have made an ancient Roman or an eighteenth century upper-class father quake and fume. Dudley (*History of Cynicism*, 49–50) maintains that the "dog marriage" of Hipparkhia and Krates was a historic fact and dates it about 320–10 BCE.

52. Crossan, *Historical Jesus*, 330–02.

53. Crossan, *Historical Jesus*, 300. The traditional author of the earliest gospel is John Mark, who in Acts 15:36–40 is shown as having a bitter argument with Paul. Perhaps we do not know all the issues involved.

54. Boswell, *Same Sex Unions*, 131.

55. Mack, *Lost Gospel*, 183.

56. Johansson quoted in Greenberg, *Construction of Homosexuality*, 211.

57. If we shorten the first "o" in *moron* the word means "blackberry" (related to the English "mulberry"); by a perhaps excessively imaginative stretch, a slangy reference to the painful thorns of blackberries seems possible.

58. For a well-documented overview of the Church's negative attitude toward marriage and positive attitude toward virginity in the first 400 years of its existence,

see Heinemann, *Eunuchs for the Kingdom of Heaven*, 46–52.

59. Miles Fowler, "Identification of the Bethany Youth in the Secret Gospel of Mark."

60. *Neaniskos*, a man over 18 or so and under 30, approximately.

61. K.A. Eckhardt may have been the first to suggest the identity of the "Rich Young Ruler" with Lazarus. He believed that "John" was the name taken by the young man after he had been raised from the dead. See Cullmann below, 77.

62. Fowler, 2. He notes the parallel with John 18:15.

63. *Ho de Iesus emblepsas auto agapasen auton.* The *Novem Testamentem Greaece*, ed. Alexander Souter (Oxford: Clarendon Press, 1910 [1953]), is used for the Greek text of the New Testament throughout. The textual machinery there gives no variant readings for this verse.

64. Robert M. Grant, *A Historical Introduction to the New Testament*, 120. Darby Nock: "The importance of the linguistic usage of the Septuagint; for the study of that of the New Testament in general ... can hardly be over-emphasized" (*Early Gentile Christianity*, 44).

65. *Septuagint*, ed. Lancelot C.L. Brenton. This is substantially a reprint of the Roman text published 1586–87 under Sixtus V (*Priveligium*, dated May 9, 1587) and based on Codex Vaticanus from the fourth century CE. Vaticanus is the oldest complete manuscript extant and represents the nearest we have to the common text the author of Mark would have known. The text of the Septuagint cannot be exactly dated; it may go back as far as the second century BCE and is still in use as scripture by the Greek Orthodox Church, much in the way that the Vulgate was used by the Roman Catholic Church before Vatican II.

For a detailed discussion of Hebrew words for "love"—sexual and nonsexual, in the Scriptures, see Robert Baker Gridlestone, *Synonyms of the Old Testament: Their Bearing on Christian Doctrine*, 110. Generally *agape* translates the Hebrew *ahav*; "it indicates desire, inclination, or affection, whether human or divine."

66. Boswell, *Same Sex Unions*, 6–7 nn4–6.

67. For a very full and elaborate discussion of eye-imagery and falling in love at the sight of an attractive person in classical antiquity, see Robert Burton's *The Anatomy of Melancholy*, 3, 2, 2, 2.

68. Fowler, "Identification of the Bethany Youth," 8–9. Lazarus' sisters were Mary Magdalene and Salome. In the Gospel of Thomas 61:2, Salome says Jesus has shared her couch and eaten at her house. This probably only means he has eaten her food and accepted her hospitality by eating on a couch she owned. There is also a fragmentary Gospel of Mary (Magdalene), which shows signs of editing and anxiety about the role of women in the church. See *The Complete Gospels: Annotated Scholars Version*.

69. Morton Smith, *Clement of Alexandria*, 154, suggests that we should read this as the Jews accusing Jesus of loving Lazarus in a manner they did not approve of.

70. Secret Gospel, 1:7; Fowler, 3. The apparently later tradition recorded in John 11:43 has Jesus only calling to Lazarus. Of course touching a human corpse was a defilement according to Torah (Numbers 19:11–13).

71. Fowler's translation, 3.

72. Plate 19, 112 in Crossan, *Essential Jesus*.

73. John Keats, *Endymion*, lines 465–69.

74. For a fuller description, see Crossan, *Essential Jesus*, 191–92. Curiously, and perhaps not entirely by accident, this same pose recurs in the engraving by Samuel Hollyer of Walt Whitman for the 1855 edition of *Leaves of Grass*.

75. Fowler, "Identification of the Bethany Youth," 5–6.

76. This is the oldest surviving account of the event, written by Paul, perhaps around 60 CE.

77. Fowler, 7–8. I know of no other convincing explanation of the nude youth in Canonical Mark.

78. Clement, trans. in Smith, *The Secret Gospel*, 16.

79. Morton Smith, *Clement of Alexandria*, 179–80.

80. Morton Smith, 173.

81. Crossan, *Historical Jesus*, 230–32.

82. Stambaugh and Balch, *New Testament*, 59–60.

83. John Dominic Crossan, *Four Other Gospels: Shadows on the Contours of Canon*. Crossan is working with the insights of Jonathan Z. Smith in particular on this point.

84. *Clement of Alexandria*, 65. For nude baptism, see *The Apostolic Tradition*, 21, 11.

85. Crossan, *Historical Jesus*, 298. The whole issue (without reference to homosexuality) is discussed at length in Crossan's chapter there. On the other hand, Darby Nock denies the whole point: "The baptized convert is not thought of as a child, but as one miraculously changed into a new and full-grown adult" (*Early Gentile Christianity*, 64). (He is quoting, with approval, F.C. Burkitt — see n1 there.)

86. Smith, *Secret Gospel*, 104.

87. Remarkably, I John 3.9 says that Christians are somehow secure from sin because Christ's "seed [*sperma*]" remains in them. The Greek *sperma* can mean literal seed (grains of wheat, mustard, etc.), but it also has the meaning of "semen" (for example in the Septuagint Genesis 38, 8–10 where Onan spills his seed, not wishing to make a woman pregnant; otherwise in Leviticus *koite spermatos* is the seed of the marriage bed). I John comes from the same "community of the Beloved Disciple" that produced the Gospel of John.

88. Smith, *Secret Gospel*, 112–13 and n12.

89. Galen, *Porneia*, 65.

90. Dio Chrysostom, 6, 16–18. Cohoon's translation. For the generally negative attitude the ancient Romans took towards masturbation, see John P. Elia, "History, Etymology, and Fallacy: Attitudes Toward Masturbation in the Ancient Western World," 1–19.

91. Quentin Crisp, *The Naked Civil Servant*, 112–13. Crisp adds that, because of his practice of homosexual masturbation, the variations in his relationships caused him "concern but not anguish."

92. Hart, *Egyptian Gods and Goddesses*, s.v. "Amun," 47. The high priestess of Amun at Thebes was married in a *hieros gamos* to the god and carried the remarkable title of "The Hand of Amun." Amun was regarded as the father of the pharaoh.

93. Theissen and Merz, *Historical Jesus*, 43–44.

94. F.F. Bruce, *Jesus and Christian Origins Outside the New Testament*, 163. I have quoted the entire text with the tentative restorations from Bruce's text. Bruce speculates that this may have had some baptismal significance (164). The scholars who compiled *The Complete Gospels: Annotated Scholar's Edition*, conjecture that the word that Bruce reconstructs as "seed" was perhaps "water" (412–16). This fragment is there referred to as "Egerton Four," dating as a text from 50–100 CE, perhaps in Syria and closer to the Johanine tradition than the Synoptic.

95. Nock, *Early Gentile Christianity*, 94 and n3 there.

96. Benjamin Wisner Bacon, *The Gospel of the Hellenists*, 81–90.

97. For a detailed discussion of the distinction between the Priestly narrative and that of the Yahwist/Elohist tradition in the formation of Genesis, see Driver, *Introduction to the Literature of the New Testament*, 8–10.

98. Driver, 118.

99. Driver, 117.

100. A favorite paraphrase of this by many modern persons opposed to homosexuality is "God made Adam and Eve, not Adam and Steve."

101. Driver, 10–11.

102. Grant, *Historical Introduction*, 119. That Mark based his work on Peter is confirmed by Papias, as quoted in Eusebius, *History of the Church*, 3, 39, 15, as well as by Justin Martyr and Iranaeus.

103. Morton Smith's translation of Clement's "Epistle to Theodore" (Smith, *Secret Gospel*, 14–17).

104. Grant, *Historical Introduction*, 121–22.

105. Fowler, "Identification of the Bethany Youth," 8.

106. Smith, *Secret Gospel*, 102–03. It is going very far afield indeed, but one is reminded of Eibhlin Dhubh Ni Chonaill, the Irish poet of the later eighteenth century. Learning that her husband had been shot dead in a feud, she hurried to his body in time to drink his blood, then began to chant a magnificent requiem for him.

107. Dudley, *History of Cynicism*, 121–22.

108. *Greek Anthology*, 7, 419. "Heaven born Tyre and Gadara's holy soil reared him [Meleager].... If you are a Syrian, Salam [*ei men Suros Salam*]." Translated by Patton in the Loeb edition.

109. Meleager, in *Greek Anthology*, 5, 160.

110. Dudley, *History of Cynicism*, 121–22.

111. Meleager, "Mysikos," in Barnstone, *Greek Lyric Poetry*, 201–02.

112. Downing, *Cynics and Christian Origins*, 173, citing a fragment of Philodemos found in the ruins of Heraculaneum.

113. Meleager, in *Greek Anthology*, 5, 208. John Boswell finds this poem ironic (*Christianity, Social Tolerance*, 124), though he does not explain why.

114. Ausonius, the fourth century CE Latin poet, was much influenced by Meleager (indeed, some of his Latin epigrams are translations of poems by Meleager, which have survived in the *Greek Anthology*). Ausonius' epigram, 128, concerns a Syrian named Eunus who is accustomed to performing oral sex on a woman, Phyllis. One suspects the influence of Meleager, since such behavior would have been quite foreign to a Roman.

115. Meleager, Barnstone's translation, in Barnstone, *Greek Lyric Poetry*, 203.

116. Meleager, in *Greek Anthology*, 5, 136, Paton's translation.

117. Meleager, in *Greek Anthology*, 7, 476, Paton's translation.

118. Sidon, 20 miles away, was a sister city to Tyre; many ancient manuscripts omit the words "and Sidon."

119. Downing, *Cynics and Christian Origins*, 156 n26; the only passages in late antiquity where someone accepts being called a "dog" willingly are Cynic.

120. Crossan, *Historical Jesus*, 403–04. Crossan with a Joycean fondness for puns says, "long before Jesus was host, he was hostess."

121. Matthew 26:27; Mark 14: 23; Luke 22:20. Elsewhere "cup" is used in association with martyrdom.

122. Bremmer, "An Enigmatic Indo-European Rite: Pederasty," 285. Drinking wine mixed with water was thought of as a uniquely Greek custom, and children were forbidden to drink wine.

123. Raymond de Becker, *The Other Face of LOVE*, 91–92.

124. Joseph B. Tyson, *A Study of Early Christianity*, 218 and 306.

125. *Poimandres*, in Barnstone, *The Other Bible*, 570.

126. Oscar Cullmann, *The Johanine Circle*, 43–45.

127. Cullmann, 46.

128. Smith, *Secret Gospel*, 45–62.

129. Guthrie, *Orpheus and Greek Religion*, 256–58. One is tempted by the theory (admitting that one cannot prove it) that the prohibition in Exodus 23:19, "You shall not boil a kid in its mother's milk," represents a reaction against the cult of Dusares as a drunken wine god, paralleling the Pythagorean reaction against Dionysus. Boiling goats' flesh in milk was a rite of wild Dionysus that the Orphics objected to. Maimonides, *Guide to the Perplexed*, 3, 48, says the prohibition in Torah against boiling a kid in its mother's milk is a prohibition of a pagan ritual. Theodore Gaster in *Thespis* (1961 edition) found what he believed was a reference to this ceremony of boiling in the Ras Samara texts; however, the reading was based on a single mutilated character in one clay tablet, and Gaster later withdrew the suggestion. For a detailed comparison of this to the Dionysus myth and Jesus, see Kerinyi, *Dionysus*, 256–58. Kerinyi rightly emphasizes that Jesus said he was the true vine, in contrast to the false (presumably Dusares). The most likely immediate source for Jesus' words are Jeremiah 2:21 in the LXX and Psalms 80:9.

130. Cullmann suggests (*Johanine Circle*, 73) that in the oldest form of the Gospel of John, the disciple in question was only referred to as "the other [*allos*] disciple"; "beloved" was added by a later editor.

131. Cullmann, 74.

132. Terence Callan, *Forgetting the Root: The Emergence of Christianity from Judaism*, 40–41. Callan suggests, as others do, that the Gospel of John was written by Christians who were in the painful process of being thrown out of the synagogue when Christianity and Judaism were pulling apart, about 90 CE.

133. Cullmann, 94. Compare "The more we learn about Judaism and Christianity in the first century, the more variegated each becomes" (Dominic Crossan, "Divine Immediacy and Human Immediacy: Towards a First Principle in Historic Jesus Research," 123).

134. It is perhaps worth noting that Irenaeus of Lyons (*Against the Heretics*, 5.33, 4) calls Papias of Hierapolis in Phrygia (wrote about 130 CE) the "hearer of Saint John" and the friend of Polycarp, the martyr of Smyrna. "Hearer" is a standard term in the vocabulary of classical Greek pederasty for the younger male. At the very least, this suggests that early Christians were not adverse to taking over the language of homosexuality — even if John and Papias' relationship was purely limited to the mouth and ears.

135. Smith, *Secret Gospel*, 112–13. The earliest documentation we have of this seems to be the Epistle of Paul to the Galatians.

136. Reinhold Niebuhr, "Love and Law in Protestantism and Catholicism," 142–59, 157.

137. Neibuhr, 158.

138. Tyson, *Study of Early Christianity*, 279.

139. 1 Corinthians 15:7. See Robert Eisenman, *James the Brother of Jesus*, 166, 706–10.

140. Tyson, 280–82. The speech of Stephen is partially preserved in Acts 7, though Tyson, based on the work of Schmithals (*Paul and James*), believes reasonably that the author of Acts has watered down denunciations of Torah in Stephen's speech. Eisenmann (166–67, 185–87) argues that James and Stephen are the same person on the basis of certain phrases (this is most unconvincing).

141. Stambaugh and Balch, *New Testament*, 160–67.

142. Smith, *Secret Gospel*, 119.

143. Quoted from Eusebius, both *History of the Church* and *Jerome*, by Eisenman, *James the Brother of Jesus*, 310–11.

144. Eisenman, 260–64. This was a characteristic of Rechabitism, a quasimonastic form in the Jewish tradition. The surviving fragments of the Gospels of the Ebionites, the Hebrews and the Nazareans, all coming from the Jewish Christians, portray both John the Baptist and Jesus as vegetarian. See Tyson, *Study of Early Christianity*, 229–30.

145. Herodotus, 2, 81. See W.K.C. Guthrie, *Orpheus and Greek Religion*, 198.

146. Tyson, 146–47. As late as Eusebius, the Epistle of James was not accepted into the canon. Martin Luther called it "an epistle of straw."

147. Downing, *Christ and the Cynics*, xii.

148. Grant, *Miracle and Natural Law*, 89.

149. Tyson, 282.

CHAPTER 9

1. John Murphy-O'Connor, *Paul: A Critical Life*, 4.

2. Strabo, *Geography*, 14, 5, 3, claims that Tarsus surpassed Athens in philosophy and general education.

3. James G. Frazer, *Adonis Attis Osiris*, 142–43.

4. Murphy-O'Connor, 36–37. Legend, which cannot be confirmed, has Paul's parents leaving Gischala in Palestine about the time Paul was born.

5. Murphy-O'Connor, 49–51.

6. Murphy-O'Connor, 59–62.

7. I omit reference to the homophobic statement in 1 Timothy 1:10 because the Pauline authorship of this is very doubtful, and it repeats a term in 1 Corinthians that will be discussed at length.

8. Murphy-O'Connor, 332–33. It was not until 62 CE that Nero married Popiea, who had Jewish connections.

9. Jerome Carcopino, *De Pythagore aux Apotres*, 80; Hadas, *Hellenistic Culture*, 196.

10. Edward Gibbon, *Decline and Fall of the Roman Empire*, 1.313 n40.

11. Murphy-O'Connor, 147–51.

12. Peter Lampe argues on the contrary that the Roman church may have met at many households (Brooten, *Love Between Women*, 217 n2).

13. Brooten, *Love Between Women*, 232. In Exodus 32:6, the Israelites have made themselves a golden calf idol to worship, and in their worship, "the people sat down to eat and rose up to play [Heb. *zakhak*]." The verb *zakhak* can have a sexual connotation in the Hebrew; Paul quotes this in Greek at 1 Corinthians 10:7.

14. C. Cragg in *The Interpreter's Bible* on this passage follows C.H. Dodd in saying that "the wrath of God" does not here mean that God is angry in any human way. To thus anthropomorphize God is a sentimental error. Rather this means "the inevitable of cause and effect in a moral universe."

15. The more conventional reading of this passage is that homosexual acts are the sin, not the punishment. For example William M. Ramsay in *The Westminister Guide to the Books of the Bible* writes "in homosexual practice, Paul sees a symbol of the reversal of the Creator's intention in human relationships" (page 434). Clearly, the text does not bear such an interpretation.

16. Brooten, *Love Between Women*, 259 n128.

17. Murphy-O'Connor, *Paul*, 335–36. "Sin" for Paul is not quite equivalent to Satan, however.

18. Justin Martyr at his conversion (about 150 CE) thought of himself as needing to be freed from the power of demons, which were for him the pagan gods. Elaine Pagels, *The Origin of Satan*, 117–18.

19. Callan, *Forgetting the Root*, 37. Callan's prime reference is Colossians 2:8 — a letter that some think may be later than Paul. Nevertheless, such ideas did exist among first century Jews of the diaspora. Nock (*Early Gentile Christianity*, 98–99) compares this with Galatians 4:3 and with ideas of subservience to fate, which can be observed in the Hermetic tradition.

20. Murphy-O'Connor, *Paul*, 336.

21. Murphy-O'Connor, 207. Klausner calls this sort of reasoning "Talmudic casuistry for an anti–Talmudic purpose" (607).

22. Tyson, *Study of Early Christianity*, 295.

23. Paul must have known essentially all the information about Jesus that we have as the Q document, though he takes rather little interest in the historical Jesus (Murphy-O'Connor, 91–93).

24. The Orphic way of life was initiation (frequent prayers and ceremonies) and abstention from meat (which was regarded as murder) (W.K.C. Guthrie, *Orpheus and Greek Religion*, 196–97). We cannot be certain if those Christians Paul mentioned who refrained from eating meat did so because they were converted Hellenistic Jews who had simplified the problem of keeping kosher by not eating meat at all, or converted Orphics who did not eat meat for deeper reasons. The latter case seems more likely; most Jews who keep kosher are not troubled by non–Jews who eat meat (kosher or not).

25. Tyson, 290–93.

26. Murphy-O'Connor, *Paul*, 205.

27. Galatians 4:8. The believers in the remote province of Gallatia in what is now Turkey (mostly Celts and fond of freedom) had not formerly been believers in God. See Murphy-O'Connor, *Paul*, 192–93. Abundant testimony survives for the custom of homosexuality among the Celts: Aristotle, *Politics*, 2, 9; Diodorus Siculus, 1, 50, 5 and 32; and from a late source, Bardesanes' *On Fate*, says that among the Gauls it was customary for young men to marry each other (in Eusebius, *Preparation of the Gospel*, 6, 10 [277 A]). The Celts of Galatia may have had the same custom.

28. For an extensive bibliography and summary of modern theologians on this issue, see Brooten, *Love Between Women*, 281–82 n52.

29. Miriam Griffin, "Cynicism and the Romans: Attraction and Repulsion," in *The Cynics*, 190–204, 192–94.

30. Lohse, *New Testament Environment*, 249–50. The best summary I know of on the topic of Stoicism in Paul is Nock, *Early Gentile Christianity*, 94–97.

31. Boswell, *Christianity*, 103 and n42.

32. Liddell and Scott, *Greek-English Lexicon*, 739.

33. Brooten, *Love Between Women*, 143–73. By a gruesome analogy some fundamentalists Christians in our own time have tried to treat male homosexuality by castration.

34. *Pseudepigrapha*, 370.

35. Tyson, *Study of Early Christianity*, 96–97.

36. For a detailed discussion of Aquinas on homosexuality, see Boswell, *Christianity*, chapter 11, esp. 328.

37. Also in the *Summa* Aquinas approves the medieval Church's dealing with heretics: "the Church, no longer hoping for his [the heretic's] conversion, looks to the salvation of others by excommunicating him and separating him from the Church, and furthermore delivers him to the secular tribunal to be exterminated from the world by death (2, 2, 11, 3).

38. All who do not believe this are declared anathema by that council. Brooten, *Love Between Women*, 223–24, and note 21. 224. This incidentally was the same council that declared the infallibility of the pope, approving Pius IX's *Syllabus complectens*, which rejected the liberty of faith, conscience and worship of all faiths except that of the Church, demanded that civil governments accept the power of the Church over them and finally stated that the pope "neither can be nor ought to be reconciled with progress, liberalism and modern civilization." Pius IX has recently been declared a saint by John Paul II.

39. Paul IV, *Humanae Vitae*, 1.60. See John A. Hardon, *The Catholic Catechism*, 372–77. The claim of the Church seems to be over both reason and observation of natural phenomena. For the modern Church on masturbation and homosexuality, see Hardon, 353–56.

40. Barth's position is discussed at length by Brooten, 223–25. Interestingly, she notes (224 n23) that Barth's most trenchant points were scored in a 1934 book written against those — Catholics and others — who supported Hitler.

41. Popkes in Brooten, 224 n22.

42. Jerome Murphy-O'Connor, "I Corinthians 11:2–26 Once Again," 265–74, 267.

43. Murphy-O'Connor, "I Corinthians," 269. For a very different opinion on how women should wear their hair, see I Peter 3.3: "wives ... let not yours be outward adorning with braiding of hair." Evidently the early church never developed a standard doctrine on female coiffure. Nock, 94–95, translates the difficult passage in I Corinthians 11:14 as "the physical facts indicate what is right" — though unless we take this to mean only something like "social conventions prove," it doesn't have a very clear meaning.

44. Jerome Murphy-O'Connor, "Sex and Logic in 1 Corinthians 11, 2–6," 482–500, 485–87, 490. However, Murphy-O'Connor overlooks examples of male philosophers who wore their hair long, such as Apollonius of Tyana, a homophobic Pythagorean nearly contemporary with Paul. It seems very probable, but not quite certain, that homosexuality was the issue. Apollos is thought by Murphy-O'Connor to have been a disciple of Philo of Alexandria (*Paul*, 275–76). We have seen the Pythagorean leaning of Philo; we know, further, that Apollos had preached in Corinth (Acts 19:1, 1 Cor. 3:4–6). Is it perhaps stretching the evidence beyond all probability to speculate that Apollos had introduced long hair at Corinth in a Pythagorean (and implicitly homophobic) context?

45. Murphy-O'Connor, *Paul*, 192–93.

46. Crossan, *Four Other Gospels*, 228–29. Crossan finds clear indication that Jesus in the Gospel of Thomas saw the Kingdom of God as a here and now event.

47. 1 Corinthians 7:29–31. Paul sees marriage as irrelevant at best, because "the appointed time has grown very short ... the form of this world is passing away."

48. Adolf Deissmann, *Light from the Ancient East*, 315–17. Deissmann presents (316 n6) Latin equivalents for Paul's vices in 1 Cor. 6; "*malakoi*" equals "*patice*," and "*arsenokoitai*" equals "*cinaedus*." Hermann Usener (Deismann, 317 n2) would read "*arsenokoitai*" as possibly meaning "*pernites adulescentum*."

49. Brooten (260 nn 132–33) provides a useful bibliography of the dispute.

50. All definitions in this part from the old Liddell-Scott Greek dictionary. Clearly the source of the definition of a word as meaning both "womanish" and "unable to bear pain," is a person who has never given birth to a child.

51. Dionysus of Halicarnassus, *Roman Antiquities*, 7, 2, 4. The historian had found one Aristodamantes called *malakos* in an earlier text and states that he is unsure of the meaning.

52. Boswell, *Christianity*, 107 and 363–64. For a sixth century CE example, see J.J. Ferraher, "Masturbation," *New Catholic Encyclopedia*, vol. 19, 1967, which cites 1 Cor. 6:10 as forbidding masturbation.

53. Boswell (*Christianity*, 341–48) discusses the word at great length. His statement (347 n31) that Clement of Alexandria did not use the word to describe male-to-male sex ignores the fact that the word has a clearly vulgar ring to it in Greek, and Clement strongly objected to using coarse or sexually explicit language. See *Paidagogos*, 2, 6. This habit parallels Cicero's *decorum*, which, since the Greeks had little use for Latin literature, is probably derived from Panaetius in both Cicero and Clement. Likewise John Chrysostom in his sermons omits the word, not because he did not regard homosexuality as a sin but because it was too impolite for his audience (see his Homilies 16 and 17).

54. We cannot be sure this passage was actually translated by Jerome about 404 CE. Jerome only fully translated the Gospels into Latin: the rest of the Vulgate represents his retouching of the earlier Old Latin version of the Bible.

55. Latin definitions from E.A. Andrews, *A Copious and Critical Latin-English Dictionary*.

56. Adams, *Latin Sexual Vocabulary*, 160–61.

57. For example Mark 10:42, Luke 7:25, 22:25; and worst of all he called Caesar's puppet, King Herod, a "fox" in Luke 13:32. It might be better for Paul's reputation if we think he was unaware of such teachings; he was beheaded under Nero about 65 CE.

58. J.I.H. McDonald, *Biblical Interpretation and Christian Ethics*, 194–95.

59. Davis, *Slavery in Western Culture*, 86–87.

60. Pseudo-Heraclitus, "Letter 9," 4–5, in Malherbe, *The Cynic Epistles*. General scholarly opinion dates this work from the first century CE (Malherbe, introduction, 22).

61. Brooten, *Love Between Women*, 191–92.

62. John J. Winkler, *Constraints of Desire*, 17.

63. See "Silver Blaze" by Conan Doyle.

64. Pseudo-Heraclitus ("Epistle 9" in Malherbe, *The Cynic Epistles*) argues eloquently that both slave and free are equally citizens of the cosmos, a concept that the Cynics shared with the Early Stoics. One may compare favorably Alexander the Great's statement that we all are members of a single household.

65. Smith, *The Secret Gospel*, 133.

66. John J. Collins, *The Apocalyptic Imagination*.

67. This is an element of all 15 of the Jewish apocalypses reviewed by Collins, *Apocalyptic Imagination*, 6.

68. Richard J. Bauckham, "The Apocalypse of Peter: An Account of Research," 413–50. This provides a good general overview of the extremely complicated source question. For Pythagorean influence, see especially 427–28.

69. The mention of "dogs" among those who are excluded from the heavenly city in Revelation 22:15 may be an oblique reference to homosexuals, though the matter is controversial.

70. Brooten, *Love Between Women*, 304 and n7 there.

71. Barnstone, *The Other Bible*, 533.

72. Edgar Henneke and Wilhelm Schneemelcher, eds. and trans., *New Testament Apocrypha*, vol. 2, 671–81. The portion quoted is from the Greek fragment found at Akhmin, Upper Egypt. A fuller text of the work survives in Coptic.

73. Bauckham, "Apocalypse of Peter," 4729–30. Later Jewish sources are cited resembling the specificity in the Apocalypse of Peter.

74. Bauckham, 4732. Persian influences are hardest to document, because all our sources are relatively late and difficult to date with precision.

75. Barnstone, *The Other Bible*, 537. Apparently the angel Moroni was not involved in this discovery.

76. Henneke and Schneemelcher, *New Testament Apocrypha*, vol. 2, 773–94. Thomas Silverstein, who edited the texts in 1935, speculated that this was a direct source for Dante ("Did Someone Know the Vision of St. Paul?"). In hell Dante meets the sodomite Brunetto Latini, his old teacher, on the sandy bank of the dike along the River Phlegethon (*Inferno*, 15). The dry sand suggests a direct contact with the Apocalypse of Paul, though Dante treats his source with genius. For a fuller discussion of this region of Dante's hell, see Bruce W. Holsinger, "Sodomy and Resurrection," 243–74.

77. Acts 17. Of course in a sense the effort had begun earlier with Philo's Neo-Platonism.

78. Henry Chadwick, *Early Christian Thought and the Classical Tradition*, 2–3.

79. Downing (*Cynics and Christian Origins*, 191) suggests that the Christian conformist ethics "may stem from the long lived marriage of Jewish and Stoic civic ethics."

80. Downing, *Cynics and Christian Origins*, 142–44.

81. H. Chadwick, "On Philo," in *Cambridge History of Later Greek*, 172. Metempsychosis does not occur in the Latin translation of Clement's *Hypotyposes* made by Cassidorus. The idea, however, does occur in Origin of Antioch, often thought to have been a pupil of Clement (Chadwick, 190).

82. C.P. "Musonius in Clement," *Harvard Studies*, 1901, 191–200; Lutz, *Roman Socrates*, 20.

83. Clement, *Stromeitais*, 5, 5, 29, 3. This idea seems to go back to Posidonius, who declared that "Moskhos" was the philosopher of the Asians. Jewish and early Christian writers often assumed that "Moskhos" was a form of "Moses."

84. Clement, 3, 4.

85. Clement, *Strom*, 4, 11.

86. Denise Kimber Buel, *Procreative Language in Clement of Alexandria*, Ph.D. dissertation (Harvard University, 1995), in Brooten, *Love Between Women*, 325 n86.

87. Brooten, 331. Brooten develops her argument though a long discussion of hyenas and rabbits, going back to Genesis, chapter 2.

88. Brooten, 324–25.

89. Clement, *Paidagogos*, 2, 10. Brooten counts only the first three.

90. Clement, *Paidagogos*, 2, 10, 83, 3, in Brooten, 325.

91. Grant, *Miracle and Natural Law*, 16.

92. Clement, *Paidagogos*, 2, 3, 21, 3; Brooten, *Love Between Women*, 322 n76.

93. Clement, 2, 2, 19–20; Brooten, 323.

94. Clement, 3, 10, 92.

95. Clement, 3, 10, 86.

96. Clement, *Paidagogos*, 2, 10, in Boswell, *Christianity*, 359. For a remarkably close parallel, see Musonius Rufus in Lutz, *Roman Socrates*, 84.

97. Brooten, 326. Compare Boswell, 147.

98. Irwin Edman, *Marcus Aurelius and His Times*, 244.

99. Justin Martyr, *Dialogue with Trypho*, 2; Edman, 245.

100. Justin, *Second Apology*, 12, 5.

101. Justin, *First Apology*, 25. In this passage he also heaps contempt on Zeus for surrendering to his lust for a woman, Antiope.

102. Justin, *First Apology*, 24, 29, 4. Clement of Alexandria was likewise aghast — *Protreiptikos*, 4, 49. Tertullian of Carthage (writing about 200 CE) compared Antinous to a public whore and regarded Antinous' deification as ludicrous (*Apology*, 13, 1). The position is repeated by Jerome, *Commentary on Isaiah*, 2; *Of Illustrious Men*, 22; and *Against Jovinian*, 2, 7; among others. Some pagans like Celsus were equally appalled — see Origin's *Against Celsus*, 3, 36. Tatian is more sympathetic to Antinous himself, regarding him as a victim of Hadrian's tyranny and of slander (*Against the Greeks*, 10). Prudentius, writing about 385 CE in *Against Symmichus*, 1, 273–77, was the last to write against Antinous before the fall of the city.

103. Justin, *First Apology*, 27.

104. Tyson, *Study of Early Christianity*, 262–63.

105. Eusebius, *History of the Church*, 16, 16. We may contemplate the trial and execution of Justin as part of the long conflict between the mild and austere Cynics.

106. Tatian, *Against the Greeks*, 19. Crescens seems to have been involved in the prosecution of Justin and his martyrdom.

107. Eusebius, *History of the Church*, 22, 4.

108. Smith, *Clement of Alexandria*, 8.

109. Smith, *Clement*, 185.

110. Clement of Alexandria, *Stromeitais*, 3, 6–9, in Barnstone, *The Other Bible*, 648–50. The essential disagreement with Gnosticism among the Church Fathers was regarding their polytheism — these lesser angels function virtually as gods.

111. Clement in Barnstone, 649. The source that Carpocrates cites is Plato's *Cratylus*, 400C, but the idea had come to Plato from his Orphic-Pythagorean sources.

112. Carpocrates in Clement in Barnstone, 649–50.

113. Smith, *Clement*, 82.

114. The term is repeated in condemning homosexuality in *Theophilus to Autolycus*, 1, 2, 13 (written about 180 CE and using the Sibyllines) and Origin (died about 251 CE), *Commentary on Matthew*.

115. Everett Ferguson, "Didache," in Everett Ferguson, *Encyclopedia of Early Christianity*, 262.

116. "The Church Fathers also developed the habit of using 'natural law' simply as a term for whatever idea they wanted to recommend," says Gerald Watson ("The Natural Law and Stoicism," 235).

117. Quoted in Watson, 236.

118. D.F. Wright ("Homosexuality," in Ferguson, *Encyclopedia of Early Christianity*, 435–36) provides a good source for lists and a useful bibliography. However, Wright's statement that the Council of Elvira (Illiberis in Spain, meeting about 310 CE) condemned homosexuality (Canon 71) is based on a mistranslation the text of that council's decisions. Canon 71 only condemns bestiality. Fone (*Homosexuality*, 103) picks up and repeats this error.

119. The subject of the confluence of Greek thought and early Christian thought is one far too vast to be touched upon here. An old but very useful and readable study is Edwin Hatch, *The Influence of Greek Ideas and Usages upon the Christian Church*.

120. Dodds, *The Greeks and the Irrational*, 154–55. Dodds doubts this idea was originally in Empedocles, but it is certain that Hippolytus found it in a work he believed to be genuine.

121. James E. Goehring, "Asceticism," in Ferguson, *Encyclopedia of Early Christianity*, 104–107. Downing, *Cynics and Christian Origins*, states the matter succinctly: "Ascetic practice is an assertion of freedom over against social convention," and "Our freedom is diminished by our love of pleasure, desire for gain, dislike of loss; it is curtailed by public opinion and custom and the resultant social inequalities and above all in legal slavery" (285).

122. For example Shenute of Atripe (about 400 CE), the head of the great White Monastery near Panopolis in Egypt, warns against and curses both homosexual and lesbian activity, as well as any heterosexuality. See Brooten, *Love Between Women*, 348–51.

123. Saint Basil, *De renuntiatione saeculi*, 23–24.

124. "For Augustine it would be a mistake to doubt that marriage is not sinful" (Brooten, 354, commenting on Augustine's *de bono coniugali*, 11).

125. Lord Kinross, *Hagia Sophia*, 20–21. It is significant that this church was built on the foundation of what had been the Byzantine temple of Aphrodite. No trace of the structure is known to exist today.

126. Ramsey McMullen, *Constantine*, 197.

127. McMullen, 192.

128. Ferdinan Lot, *The End of the Ancient World and the Beginning of the Middle Ages*, 98–99.

129. Leviticus 21:9 says that the daughter of a priest who acts as a prostitute shall be burned with fire; this seems to be the only reference to this quaint custom, outside the Roman context, in the classical world.

130. *Encyclopædia Britannica*, 1945, s.v. "Constantine."

131. Michael P. McHugh, "Lactantius," in Ferguson, *Encyclopedia of Early Christianity*. In his *Workmanship of God* (written 303–304), Lactantius shows considerable acquaintance with the Sibylline Oracles. Perhaps Lactantius reached the high point of his rhetorical ability in his treatise *On the Wrath of God* (written 313–14).

132. McMullen, *Constantine*, 192.

133. Gibbon, *Decline and Fall*, 20, 5, and n115. Decisions of councils such as Elvira entered into the body of "penitential jurisprudence," taking homophobia with them. For penitential literature in the Church Fathers, see Boswell, *Christianity*, 180–83. Boswell notes that the penances were relatively light. For information on the large body of early medieval penitential literature, such as the Canons of the Synod of Llanddewi-Brefi and the Penitential of Thorlac Thorhalson, see Fone, *Homosexuality*, 124.

134. Downing, *Cynics and Christian Origins*, 256–57. He cites Athanasius as a prime example.

135. William C. Frend, *The Archeology of Early Christian History*, 231, 250.

136. Gibbon, 28. The source for this is *de Caesaribus*, by Sextus Aurelius Victor, Roman governor of Pannonia. He calls Constans "a minister of unspeakable depravity."

137. Cantrella, *Bisexuality*, 175. This is the interpretation of the difficultly worded laws by Gothfredius of Mantua in 1714.

138. Cantrella, 177 and 181.

139. Greenberg, *Construction of Homosexuality*, 232.

140. Boswell, *Christianity*, 174–76. Boswell predictably tries to minimize the impact of this law.

141. Boswell, 176 n25.

142. Fone, *Homosexuality*, 131.

143. Other paired saints include Perpetua and Felicita and Polyeuct and Nearkhos. See Boswell, *Same Sex Unions*, 139–56. It hardly need be said that no erotic relationship is attributed to such saints in any of the early texts, with the single exception cited by Boswell of Sergius and Bacchos.

144. E. Hoade, "Saint George," in *New Catholic Encyclopedia*. Saint George "replaced Adonis" in the East, where he was often called simply "El Khader," "the Living." Few facts survive of the historical Saint George, whose legend may have absorbed the myth of Perseus. See also Langdon, 336–41, which discusses the matter fully.

145. Ralph H. Brewster, *The 6,000 Beards of Athos*, 66–70, 106–07.

146. Boswell, *Same Sex Unions*, 180–98.

147. Germanic peoples at the time had a violent horror of effeminate men. For a full discussion of the development of homophobia in the ancient Germanic peoples, see Greenberg, *Construction of Homosexuality*, 242–49.

148. Gibbon, *Decline and Fall of the Roman Empire*, 32.

149. Holland L. Hendrix, "Thessalonika," in Ferguson, *Encyclopedia of Early Christianity*.

150. Boswell, *Christianity*, 347.

151. Brown, *The Body and Society*, 306.

152. Robert Wilken, "John Chrysostom," in Ferguson, *Encyclopedia of Early Christianity*.

153. Brown, 308–09.

154. Brown, 313.

155. John Chrysostom, "Sermon on Matthew," 47, 4; Brown, 311.

156. John Chrysostom, Homily IV on the Epistle to the Romans, in *The Nicene and Post Nicene Fathers*, vol. 2, 355–59. There is a translation of part of this sermon in Boswell, *Christianity*, 359–62.

157. John Chrysostom, 357. The editors note that the idea that the insane may harm themselves unknowingly and seem to enjoy it goes back to Plato's *Thaetetarus*.

158. John Chrysostom, 358.

159. John Chrysostom, 357. However, John Boswell notes (*Christianity*, 157 and n85) that Chrysostom says in his *Sermons on I Thessalonians*, 3, 8, that "there are ten thousand sins equal and worse than this one." Absolute consistency in preachers is not always found.

160. John Chrysostom, 356.

161. John Chrysostom, 356.

162. John Chrysostom, 357.

163. Chrysostom, "On Suspect Cohabitations," 9; Aline Rousselle, *Porneia: On Desire and the Body in Antiquity*, 135–36.

164. Wilken, "John Chrysostom," in Ferguson, *Encyclopedia of Early Christianity*. Wilken's book, *John Chrysostom and the Jews: Rhetoric and Reality in the Late Fourth Century*, is a sensitive and readable source on this difficult issue.

165. Brown, *The Body and Society*, 318.

Bibliography

Adams, J.N. *The Latin Sexual Vocabulary*. Baltimore: The Johns Hopkins University Press, 1982.

Adkins, Arthur W.H. *From the One to the Many: A Study of Personality and Views of Human Nature in the Context of Ancient Greek Social Values and Beliefs*. Ithaca, New York: Cornell University Press, 1970.

Adorno, Theodor, and Else Frenkel-Brunswick, Daniel Levinson and R. Nevitt Sanford. *The Authoritarian Personality*. New York: W.W. Norton, 1993, abridged edition.

Aeschines, "Timarchos."

Aelian, *Varia Historia*.

Albright, William Foxwell. *Archaeology and the Religion of Israel*. Baltimore: Johns Hopkins Press, 1968, 80–81.

Alciphron, Aelian and Philostratus. Trans. Allen Rogers Benner and Francis H. Forbes. Loeb Classics. Cambridge: Harvard University Press, 1949.

Alderlink, Larry J. *Orphism and Bacchic Mysteries: New Evidence and Old Problems of Interpretation*. Ed. W. Wuellner. Berkeley, Cal.: Graduate Theological Union, 1977.

Alter, David. *The David Story*. New York: W.W. Norton, 1999.

Alfoldi, Andreas. *Early Rome and the Latins (Jerome Lectures 7th Series)*. Ann Arbor: University of Michigan Press, ND.

Allport, Gordon W. *The Nature of Prejudice*. Garden City, N.Y.: Anchor Books, 1958.

Altheim, Franz. *A History of Roman Religion*. Trans. Harold Mattingly. London: Methuen, 1933.

Anderson, Daniel E. *The Masks of Dionysus: A Commentary on Plato's Symposium*. New York: State University of New York Press, 1993.

Andrews, E.A. *A Copious and Critical Latin-English Dictionary*. New York: Harper and Brothers, 1861.

Apollonius of Rhodes, *The Voyage of Argo*. Trans. E.V. Rieu. Baltimore: Penguin Books, 1959.

Aquinas, St. Thomas. *The Summa Theologica*. Trans. Fathers of the English Dominican Provence, revised by Daniel J. Sullivan. Vol. 2 of 2. Chicago: William Benton, 1952.

Aristotle, *Constitution of Athens*.

_____. *Metaphysics*.

_____. *Nicomachean Ethics*.

_____. *Physics*.

_____. *Politics*.

Arnold, Edward Vernon. *Roman Stoicism*. 1911. Reprint Freeport, N.Y.: Books for Libraries Press, 1971.

Arrian, *Anabasis of Alexander*.

Astin, A.E. *Scipio Aemelianus*. Oxford: Clarendon Press, 1967.

Astour, Michael C. *Hellenosemitica: An Ethnic and Cultural Study in West Semitic Impact of Mycenean Greece*. Leiden: E.J. Brill, 1967.

Athenaeus of Naucritus. *The Deipnosophists of Athenaeus of Naucritos*. Loeb ed. Trans. Charles Barton Gulick. Cambridge: Harvard University Press, 1937.

Babut, Daniel. "Les Stociens et l'Amour." *Homosexuality in the Ancient World*. Eds. Wayne R. Dynes and Stephen Donaldson. Vol. 1 of *Studies in Homosexuality*. New York: Garland, 1992.

Bacon, Benjamin Wisner. *The Gospel of the Hellenists*. New York: Henry Holt, 1933.

Bailey, Alan. *Sextus Empiricus and Pyrrhonean skepticism*. Oxford: Oxford University Press, 1959.

Baker, John W. *Justinian and the Later Roman Empire*. Madison: University of Wisconsin Press, 1966.

Barnstone, Willis, trans. *Greek Lyric Poetry*. Bloomington: University of Indiana Press, 1962.

Barnstone, Willis. *The Other Bible: Jewish Pseudopigrapha, Christian Apocrypha, Gnostic Scriptures, Kabbalah, Dead Sea Scrolls*. New York: HarperCollins, 1984.

Basil, Saint. *De renuntiatione saeculi*. Trans. M. Monica Wagner. Vol. 9 of *The Fathers of the Church*. Washington, D.C.: Catholic University of America.

Bauckham, Richard J. "The Apocalypse of Peter: An Account of Research." In *Aufstieg und Niedergang der romischen Welt*. Berlin: Walter de Gruyter, 1988.

Becker, Raymond de. *The Other Face of LOVE*. Trans. Margaret Crosland and Alan Daventry. New York: Bell, 1969.

Berkert, Walter. *Lore and Science in Ancient Pythagoreanism*. Trans. Edwin L. Minor, Jr. Cambridge: Harvard University Press, 1972.

———. *Structure and Story in Greek Mythology*.

Bieber, Margaret. *Alexander the Great in Greek and Roman Art*. Chicago: Argonaut, 1964.

Birley, Anthony R. *Hadrian: The Restless Emperor*. London: Routledge, 1997.

Bloch, Raymond. *The Etruscans*. London: Thames and Hudson, 1958.

Boardman, John. *Greek Sculpture: The Archaic Period*. New York: Oxford University Press, 1978.

Boswell, John. *Christianity, Social Tolerance and Homosexuality: Gay People in Western Europe from the Beginning of the Christian Era to the End of the Fourteenth Century*. Chicago: University of Chicago Press, 1980.

———. *Same Sex Unions in Pre-Modern Europe*. New York: Villard Books, 1994.

Bradford, Alfred S., compiler, translator, and editor. *Philip II of Macedon: A Life from the Ancient Sources*. Westport, Conn.: Praeger, 1992.

Brandt, Paul (as Hans Licht). *Sexual Life in Ancient Greece*. London: George Routledge, 1932.

Branham, R. Bracht, and Marie-Odile Goulet-Caze, eds. *The Cynics*. University of California Press, 2000.

Breasted, Henry. *Development of Religious Thought in Ancient Egypt*. Gloucester, Mass.: Peter Smith, 1970.

Breasted, James Henry. *A History of Egypt from the Earliest Times to the Persian Conquest*. New York: Scribner's, 1937.

Brehier, Emile. *History of Philosophy: The Hellenistic and Roman Age*. Trans. Wade Baskin. Chicago: University of Chicago Press, 1965.

Bremmer, John. "An Enigmatic Indo-European Rite: Pederasty." *Arithusa* 13, no. 2 (1980).

Brewster, Ralph H. *The 6,000 Beards of Athos*. London: Citadel Press, 1935.

Brooten, Bernadette J. *Love Between Women: Early Christian Responses to Female Homoeroticism*. Chicago: University of Chicago Press, 1997.

Brown, Arthur A. "Storytelling: the Meaning of Life and the Meaning of *The Epic of Gilgamesh*." Mar 14, 2002. http://ancienthistory.about.com/gi/dynamic/offsite.htm?site=http%3A%2F%2Feawc.evansville.edu%2Fessays%2Fbrown.htm.

Brown, Peter. *The Body and Society: Men, Women, and Sexual Renunciation in Early Christianity*. New York: Columbia University Press, 1988.

Bruce, F.F. *Jesus and Christian Origins Outside the New Testament*. Grand Rapids, Mich.: William B. Eerdmans, 1974.

Brumbaugh, Robert S. *Plato's Mathematical Imagination: The Mathematical Passages in the Dialogues and Their Interpretation*. Bloomington: Indiana University Press, 1977.

Brunnsaker, Sture. *The Tyrant Slayers of Kritios and Nesiotes*. Stockholm: Svenska Institute, 1971.

Bullough, Vern. *Sexual Variance in Society and History*. New York: Wiley, 1976.

Burnett, John. *Early Greek Philosophy*. 4th ed. London: Adam and Charles Black, 1930.

Burton, Carlin A. *The Sorrows of the Ancient Romans: The Gladiator and the Monster*. Princeton: Princeton University Press, 1993.

Burton, Robert. *The Anatomy of Melancholy*. New York: Empire State, 1924.

Bury J.B. *History of Greece*. 3rd ed. New York: Macmillan, 1970.

Bury, R.G. *Laws of Plato in Twelve Volumes*. Vol. I The Loeb Classical Library. Cambridge: Harvard University Press, 1968.

Calame, Claude. *Les choeurs de jeunes filles en Greece archaique I, Morphologies fuction religieuse et sociale*. Rome: Aten, 1977.

Callan, Terence. *Forgetting the Root: The Emergence of Christianity from Judaism*. New York: Paulist Press, 1986.

The Hellenistic Monarchies and the Rise of Rome. Vol. 7 of *The Cambridge Ancient History*. Ed. S.A. Cook, et al. Cambridge: Cambridge University Press, 1928.

The Cambridge History of Later Greek and Early Medieval Philosophy. Ed. Arthur Hilary Armstrong. Cambridge: Cambridge University Press, 1967.

Cameron, Averil. *Procopius and the Sixth Century*. Berkeley: University of California Press, 1985.

Cameron, Ron. "'What Have You Come Out to See?'" Characterization of John and Jesus in the Gospels." In *Semeia 49: The Apocryphal Jesus and Christian Origins*. Ed. Ron Cameron. Atlanta: Scholars Press, 1990.

Campbell, L., ed. *The Statesman*. Oxford: Oxford University Press, 1867.

Cantrella, Eva. *Bisexuality in the Ancient World*. Trans. Cormac O Cuilleanain. New Haven: Yale University Press, 1992.

Carcopino, Jerome. *La bisilque puthagoricienne de la Porte-Majeure*. Paris, 1926.

———. *De Pythagore aux Apostres*. Paris, 1956.

Carrier, Richard. "On Musonius Rufus: A Brief Essay." 1999. July 4, 2000. http://www.infidels.org/library/modern/richardcarrier/musonius.html.

Cartledge, P. "The Politics of Spartan Pederasty." *Proceedings of the Cambridge Philological Society*, 1981. 201.

Cato, Marcus Porcius. *Cato and Varro on Agriculture*. Trans. William Davis Hooper, revised by Harrison Boyd Ash. Cambridge: Harvard University Press, 1979.

Cicero, Marcus Tullius. *De Finibus*. Translated by lt. Rackham. Cambridge: Cambridge University Press, 2001.

_____. *De Officiis*. Trans. Walter Miller. Loeb Classical Library. Harvard: Heinemann, Harvard University Press.

_____. *The Nature of the Gods*. The Loeb Classical Library. Cambridge, Mass: Harvard University Press, 1979–1990.

_____. *Of Law*.

_____. *Philippic*, 2. Translated by Walter C.A. Ker. Cambridge: Cambridge University Press, 1928.

_____. *Tusculum Disputations*. Translated by S.E. King. Cambridge: Cambridge University Press, 1927.

Chadwick, Henry. *Early Christian Thought and the Classical Tradition: Studies in Justin, Clement, and Origin*. Oxford: The Clarendon Press, 1966.

Churchill, Wainwright. *Homosexual Behavior among Males: A Cross-Cultural and Cross-Species Investigation*. Englewood Cliffs, N.J.: Prentice-Hall, 1967.

Clarke, W.M. "Achilles and Patroculus in Love," 95–110. In *Homosexuality in the Ancient World*, edited by Wayne R. Dynes and Stephen Donaldson. New York: Garland, 1992.

Clement of Alexandria. *Paidagogos*. Translated as *Christ the Educator* by Simon P. Woods. Washington, D.C.: University of America Press, 1954.

_____. *Stromateis. Books 1–3*. Trans. John Ferguson. Washington: Catholic University, 1991.

Cobb, William S. "The Symposium and the Phaedrus." In *Plato's Erotic Dialogues*. Albany, NY: State University of New York Press, 1993.

Cohen, Martin Samuel. "The Biblical Prohibition of Homosexual Intercourse." *Journal of Homosexuality* 19, no. 4 (1990), 2–20.

Clay, Diskin. "Reading the *Republic*." In *Platonic Writings, Platonic Readings*. Charles L. Griswold, Jr., ed. New York: Routledge, 1988.

Collins, John J. *The Apocalyptic Imagination: An Introduction to the Jewish Matrix of Christianity*. New York: Crossroad, 1984.

_____. *Between Athens and Jerusalem: Jewish Identity in the Hellenistic Diaspora*. New York: Crossroad, 1983.

The Complete Gospels: Annotated Scholars Version. Ed. Robert Miller. Sonoma, Cal.: Polebridge Press, 1992.

Cook, S.A., F.E. Adcock, and M.P. Charlesworth, eds. *The Cambridge Ancient History*. Cambridge: Cambridge University Press, 1928.

Crisp, Quentin. *The Naked Civil Servant*. New York: Quality Paperback Book Club, 2000.

Crossan, John Dominic. "Divine Immediacy and Human Immediacy: Towards a First Principle in Historic Jesus Research." *Semi: An Experimental Journal for Biblical Criticism* 44 (1988).

_____. *The Essential Jesus: Original Sayings and Earliest Images*. New York: HarperCollins, 1994.

_____. *Four Other Gospels: Shadows on the Contours of Canon*. Minneapolis: Winston Press, 1985.

_____. *The Historical Jesus: The Life of a Mediterranean Jewish Peasant*. San Francisco: HarperCollins, 1992.

Cullmann, Oscar. *The Johanine Circle*. Trans. John Bowden. Philadelphia: Westminster Press, 1976.

Dank, Barry M. "The Homosexual." In *Sexual Deviance and Deviants*, ed. Erich Goode and Richard R. Troiden. New York: William Morrow, 1974.

Davis, David Brion. *The Problem of Slavery in Western Culture*. New York: Oxford University Press, 1988.

Demosthenes. *Demosthenes with an English Translation*, J.A. Vince, M.A. Cambridge, Mass.: Harvard, 1930.

Detienne, M. *Dionysus Slain*. Trans. Mirielle and Leonard Muellner. English ed. London and Baltimore: Johns Hopkins University Press, 1979.

Deissmann, Adolf. *Light from the Ancient East: The New Testament Illustrated by Recently Discovered Texts of the Graeco-Roman World*. Trans. Lionel R.M. Strachan. Rev. ed. Grand Rapids, Mich.: Baker Book House, 1978.

Dillon, John. *The Middle Platonists: 80 BC–220 AD*. Ithaca: Cornell University Press, 1977.

Dinarchos, *Orations*.

Diodorus Siculus, *History*.

Dio Chrysostom. *Discourses 12–30*. Trans. J.W. Cohoon. Vol. 2. Loeb Classical Library. Cambridge: Harvard University Press, 1961.

Diogenes Laertius. *Lives of Eminent Philosophers*. Trans. R.D. Hicles. Cambridge, Mass.: Harvard, 1964.

Dodds, Eric Robertson. *The Greeks and the Irrational*. Berkeley: University of California Press, 1951.

Douglas, Mary. *Purity and Danger*. London: Routledge and Kegan Paul, 1966.

_____. "Social Conditions of Enthusiasm and Heterodoxy." In *Forms of Symbolic Action: Proceeding of the 1969 Spring Meeting of the American Ethnological Society*. Seattle, 1969.

Dover, K.J. *Greek Homosexuality: Updated with a New Post Script*. Cambridge, Mass.: Harvard University Press, 1989.

Downing, Christine. "Athena." In *The Encyclopedia of Religion*, ed. Mircea Eliade. Vol. 1. New York: Macmillan, 1987.

Downing, F. Gerald. *Christ and the Cynics: Jesus and Other Radical Preachers in the First Century Tradition*. Sheffield, England: Sheffield Academic Press, 1988.

_____. *Cynics and Christian Origins*. Edinburgh: T. and T. Clark, 1992.

Driver, S.R. *An Introduction to the Literature of the Old Testament*. New York: Meridian Books, 1956.

Dudley, Donald. *A History of Cynicism from Diogenes*

to the Sixth Century AD. New York: Gordon Press, 1974.

Dumezil, George. *Archaic Roman Religion: With an Appendix on the Religion of the Etruscans*. Trans. Philip Krap. Two vols., consecutively numbered. Chicago: University of Chicago Press, 1970.

Earl, Donald. *The Moral and Political Tradition of Rome*. Ithaca: Cornell University Press, 1967.

Edman, Irwin. *Marcus Aurelius and His Times: The Transition from Paganism to Christianity*. Rosalyn, N.Y.: Water J. Black, 1945.

Eisenman, Robert. *James the Brother of Jesus*. New York: Viking Penguin, 1996.

Elia, John P. "History, Etymology, and Fallacy: Attitudes Toward Masturbation in the Ancient Western World." *Journal of Homosexuality* 14, no. 3/4 (1987).

Epicurus, "The Vatican Sayings." Trans. C. Bailey. In *The Stoic and Epicurean Philosophers*, ed. Whitley J. Oats. New York: The Modern Library, 1940.

Eunapius. *Lives of the Sophists*.

Eusebius. *History of the Church*.

_____. *Preparation of the Gospel*.

Evans, Arthur. *The God of Ecstasy: Sex Roles and the Madness of Dionysus*. New York: St. Martin's Press, 1988.

Feibleman, James K. *Religious Platonism: The Influence of Religion on Plato and the Influence of Plato on Religion*. Westport, Conn.: Greenwood Press, 1959.

Ferguson, Everett, ed. *Encyclopedia of Early Christianity*. New York: Garland, 1990.

Ferrari, Giovanni R.F. *Listening to the Cicadas: A Study of Plato's Phaedros*. Cambridge: Cambridge University Press, 1987.

Fitzgerald, Thomas R." The Murder of Hipparchus: A Reply." *Historia* 6 (1957), 275–86.

Fone, Byrne. *Homosexuality: A History*. New York: Metropolitan Books, 2000.

Forde, Nels W. *Cato the Censor*. Boston: Twayne, 1975.

Fornara, Charles W. "The 'Tradition' about the Murder of Hipparchus." *Historia* 17 (1968).

Foster, Benjamin R., Trans. and Ed. *The Epic of Gilgamesh*. New York: W.W. Norton, 2001.

Fowler, Miles. "Identification of the Bethany Youth in the Secret Gospel of Mark with Other Figures Found in Mark and John." *Journal of the History of Christianity* 5, no. 1 (spring 1998). <http://www.depts.drew.edu/jhc/fowler.html>. 30 May 2000.

Fox, Robin Lane. *Alexander the Great*. New York: Dial Press, 1973.

Frazer, James G. *Adonis Attis Osiris: Studies in the History of Oriental Religion*. Vol. 1 of 2. New York: Macmillan, 1951.

Freeman, Kathleen. *Ancilla to Pre-Socratic Philosophers: A Complete Translation of the Fragments in Diels, Fragmente de Vorsokratiker*. Cambridge, Mass.: Harvard, 1957.

Frend, William C. *The Archeology of Early Christian History*. Minneapolis: Fortress Press, 1996.

Friedlander, Paul. *The Dialogues*. Vol. 2 of *Plato*. Trans. Hans Meyerhoff. Bollengen Series LIX. Princeton: Princeton University Press, 1969.

Ferguson, William Scott. *Hellenistic Athens*. New York: Howard Fertig, 1969.

Fronto, Marcus Cornelius. *Correspondence*. Trans. C.R. Haines. Cambridge, Mass.: Harvard, 1982.

Gadget, Pierre. *Alexander the Great and the Hellenistic World: Macedonian Imperialism and the Hellenization of the East*. Trans. M.R. Dobie. 1928. Reprint Chicago: Ares, 1985.

Gaster, Theodore. *Thespis: Ritual Myth and Drama in the Ancient Near East*. New rev. ed. New York: Gordion Press, 1975.

Gellius, Aulius. *Attic Nights*. London: William Heinemann, 1968.

Gibbon, Edward. (Oliphant Seward, ed.) *A History of the Decline and Fall of the Roman Empire* in 3 vols. New York: Modern Library, n.d.

Gomperz, Theodore. *Greek Thinkers: A History of Ancient Philosophy*. Vol. 2. Trans. G.G. Berry. 1905. Reprint London: John Murray, 1964.

Goodenough, Edwin R. *Jewish Symbols in the Graeco-Roman Perius*. 8 vols. New York: Pantheon, 1953–1968.

Gould, Josiah B. *The Philosophy of Chrysippus*. Albany: State University of New York Press, 1970.

Gould, Thomas. *Platonic Love*. New York: Free Press, 1983.

Graff, Fritz. "Dionysian and Orphic Eschatology." In *Masks of Dionysus*, eds. Thomas H. Carpenter and Christopher A. Faraone. Ithaca: Cornell University Press, 1993.

Graham, Geoffrey. Correspondence with author. Dec. 2, 1996.

Grant, Michael. *The Ancient Historians*. London: Weidenfeld and Nicholson, 1970.

_____. *History of Rome*. New York: Scribner's, 1978.

Grant, Robert M. *A Historical Introduction to the New Testament*. London: Collins, 1963.

_____. *Miracle and Natural Law in Graeco-Roman and Early Christian Thought*. Amsterdam: North-Holland, 1952.

The Greek Anthology. English trans. by W.R. Paton. 5 vols., Loeb Classical Library. Cambridge: Harvard University Press, 1979.

Green, Peter. *Alexander of Macedon, 356–323 B.C.: A Historical Biography*. Berkeley: University of California Press, 1991.

_____. *Alexander to Actium: The Historic Evolution of the Hellenistic Age*. Berkeley: University of California Press, 1990.

Greenberg, David F. *The Construction of Homosexuality*. Chicago: University of Chicago Press, 1988.

Grenier, Albert. *The Roman Spirit in Religion, Thought and Art*. Trans. M.R. Dobie. New York: Cooper Square, 1970.

Gridlestone, Robert Baker. *Synonyms of the Old Testament: Their Bearing on Christian Doctrine.* Grand Rapids, Mich.: William B. Eerdmans, 1897.

Griffin, Miriam T. *Nero: The End of a Dynasty.* New Haven: Yale University Press, 1985.

Grimal, Pierre. *The Dictionary of Classical Mythology.* Trans A.R. Maxwell-Hyslop. Oxford: Blackwell Reference, 1956.

Gruen, Erick S. *Culture and National Identity in Republican Rome.* Ithaca: Cornell University Press, 1992.

Guthrie, Kenneth Sylvan. *The Pythagorean Source Book and Library.* Ed. David R. Fideler. Grand Rapids, Mich.: Phanes Press, 1978.

Guthrie, W.K.C. *Aristotle: An Encounter.* Vol. VI. *A History of Greek Philosophy.* Cambridge: Cambridge University Press, 1990.

_____. *The Early Pre-Socratics and the Pythagoreans.* Vol. 1 of *A History of Greek Philosophy.* Cambridge University Press, 1967.

_____. *The Greeks and Their Gods.* Boston: Beacon, 1955.

_____. *The Later Plato and the Academy.* Vol. 5 of *A History of Greek Philosophy.* Cambridge: Cambridge University Press, 1978.

_____. *Orpheus and Greek Religion: A Study in the Orphic Movement.* Princeton: Princeton University Press, 1993.

Hackforth, R. *Plato's Phaedrus.* Cambridge: Cambridge University Press, 1972.

Hadas, Moses. *Hellenistic Culture: Fusion and Diffusion.* New York: Columbia University Press, 1959.

_____, and Morton Smith. *Spiritual Biographies in Antiquity.* New York: Harper and Rowe, 1962.

Hallett, Judith P. "Female Homoeroticism and the Denial of Roman Reality in Latin Literature." *Yale Journal of Criticism* 13, no. 1 (1989), 209–27.

Hammond, N.G.L. *Philip of Macedon.* Baltimore: Johns Hopkins University Press.

Hardon, John A. *The Catholic Catechism.* Garden City, N.Y.: Doubleday, 1975.

Harris, R. Blaine. "Brief Description of Neoplatonism." In *The Significance of Neoplatonism*, ed. R. Blaine Harris. Norfolk, Virginia: The Internationals Society for Neoplatonic Studies, 1976, 1–20.

Hart, George. *A Dictionary of Egyptians Gods and Goddesses.* London: Routledge and Kegan Paul, 1986.

Hatch, Edwin. *The Influence of Greek Ideas and Usages upon the Christian Church.* Ed. A.M. Fairbairn. 1885. Reprint London: Henderson, 1995.

Heinemann, Uta Ranke. *Eunuchs for the Kingdom of God: Women, Sexuality and the Catholic Church.* Trans. Peter Heinegg. Hammondsworth, Middlesex, England: Penguin Books, 1990.

Hellenistic Philosophy: Introductory Readings. 2nd ed. Trans. with introduction and notes by L.P. Gerson. Indianapolis: Hackett, 1988.

Hengel, Martin. *Judaism and Hellenism: Studies in Their Encounter in Palestine During the Early Hellenistic Era.* Trans. John Bowden. Vol. 1. Philadelphia: Fortress Press, 1974.

Henneke, Edgar, and Wilhelm Schneemelcher, eds. and trans. *New Testament Apocrypha.* Vol. 2. Philadelphia: Westminster Press, 1963.

Herodotus. *Histories.*

Heurgon, Jacques. *The Rise of Rome to 264 BC.* Trans. James Willis. Berkeley: University of California Press, 1973.

Hoade, E. "Saint George." *New Catholic Encyclopedia.* New York: McGraw Hill, 1967.

Holsinger, Bruce W. "Sodomy and Resurrection: The Homoerotic Subject of the *Divine Comedy*." In *Premodern Sexualities*, ed. Louise Fraudenburg and Carla Freccero. New York: Routledge, 1996.

Hornung, Erik. *Conceptions of God in Ancient Egypt: The One and the Many.* Trans. John Baines. 1971. Reprint Ithaca: Cornell University Press, 1982.

Hrozny, Friedrich. "Hittites." In *Encyclopedia Britannica*, 1945.

Iamblichus. *On the Pythagorean Life.* Translated with notes by Gillian Clark. Liverpool: Liverpool University Press, 1989.

The Imperial Peace. Vol. II of *The Cambridge Ancient History.* Ed. S.A. Cook et. al. Cambridge: Cambridge University Press, 1936.

Inscriptiones Graeca. Berlin. Brandenburg Academy of Arts and Sciences, 1815–present.

Isay, Richard. *Being Homosexual: Homosexual Men and Their Development.* New York: Farrar, Straus and Giroux, 1989.

Iseos. *Orations.*

Jachmann, J. *Plautinshes und Attischos.* Berlin: n.p., 1913.

Jaeger, Werner. *Paideia: The Ideals of Greek Culture.* Trans. Gilbert Highet. Vol. I. 2nd ed. New York: Oxford University Press, 1945.

Jerome (Hieronymous). *Corpus Scriptorum Ecclesiasticorum Latinorum.* Editum consilio et impensis Academiae Litterarum Caesareae Vindohonensis. Vindohonae: C. Geroldi, 1866.

John Chrysostom, Homily IV on the Epistle to the Romans. *The Nicene and Post Nicene Fathers.* Vol. 2. 1st Series. *The Homilies of St. John Chrysostom.* Oxford: Oxford University Press, 1841.

Jowett, B. *The Dialogues of Plato. The Laws of The Dialogues of Plato translated into English with Analyses and Introductions*, in 5 vols., 3rd edition. Oxford: Oxford University Press, 1892.

Justinian. *Institutes*, trans. J.B. Moyle. Oxford: Oxford University Press, 1913.

Justinus, Marcus Junianus. *Epitome of Historiae Philippicae et totius mundi origines et terrae situs by Pompeius Trogus.*

Justin Martyr, *Dialogue with Trypho, a Jew.* In *Marcus Aurelius and His Times: The Transition from Paganism to Christianity.* Rosalyn, New York: Walter J. Black, 1945.

Juvenal. *Satires.*

Kerenyi, C. *Dionysus: Archetypal Image of Indestructible Life.* Trans. by Ralph Mankeim. Bollegen Series LXV-2. Princeton: Princeton University Press, 1976.

Kiefer, Otto. *Sexual Life in Ancient Rome.* Trans. Gilbert Highet and Helen Highet. New York: Barnes and Noble, 1952.

King, Katherine Callen. *Achilles: Paradigms of the War Hero from Homer to the Middle Ages.* Berkeley: University of California Press, 1987.

Kingsley, Peter. *Ancient Philosophy, Mystery and Magic: Empedocles and the Pythagorean Tradition.* Oxford: Clarendon Press, 1995.

Kinross, Lord, and the editors of the Newsweek Book Division. *Hagia Sophia.* New York: Newsweek, 1972.

Kirkpatrick, Walter. *The Family in Classical Greece.* Ithaca: Cornell University Press, 1968.

Klausner, Joseph. *From Jesus to Paul.* Trans. William F. Steinspring. Boston: Beacon Press, 1961.

Kleg, Joseph. *Hate, Prejudice and Racism.* Albany: State University of New York Press, 1993.

Klostermann, A. *Beiträse zur Entstenungsgeschichte des Pentateuch.* 1877.

Kostan, David. *Sexual Symmetry: Love in the Ancient Novel and Related Genres.* Princeton: Princeton University Press, 1994.

Krueger, Devek. "The Body and Society: The Shamelessness of Diogenes in Roman Imperial Culture." In *The Cynic Movement in Antiquity and Its Legacy,* ed. R. Bracht Branham and Marie Odile Gaulet-Caze. Berkeley: University of California Press, 1996.

Kus, Robert J. "Alcoholism and Non-Acceptance of the Gay Self: The Clinical Link." *Journal of Homosexuality* 15, nos. 1–2 (1988), 25–42.

Lambert, Royston. *Beloved and God: The Story of Hadrian and Antinous.* New York: Viking, 1984.

Lancell, Serge. *Carthage: A History.* Trans. Antonia Nevill. Oxford: Blackwell, 1992.

Lang, Mable. "The Murder of Hipparchus." *Historia* 3 (1954–55), 395–407.

Langdon, Stephen Herbert. *The Mythology of All Races.* Vol. V: *Semitic.* Boston: Archaeological Institute of America, Marshall Jones, 1931.

Leach, Marjorie. *Guide to the Gods.* Ed. Michael Owen Jones and Frances Chattermole-Tally. Santa Barbara: ABC CLIO, 1992.

Leapp, Gary P. *Male Colors: The Construction of Homosexuality in Tokugawa, Japan.* Berkeley: University of California Press, 1995.

Lehmann, Jean-Pierre. *Roots of Modern Japan.* New York: St. Martin's Press, 1962.

Leisegang, Hans. "The Mystery of the Serpent." In *The Mysteries: Papers from the Eranos Yearbooks.* Julius Baum et al. Bollengen Series XXX.2. Princeton: Princeton University Press, 1955.

Le Vay, Simon. *Queer Science: The Use and Abuse of Research into Homosexuality.* Cambridge: MIT Press, 1996.

Liddell, George Henry, and Robert Scott. *A Greek-English Lexicon Based on the German Work of Francis Passon.* New York: Harper, 1878.

Lilja, Saara. *Homosexuality in Republican and Imperial Rome.* Helsinki: The Finnish Society of Sciences and Letters, 1983.

Livy (Titus Livius). *(Ab Urbe Condita) History of Rome.* Trans. Evan. T. Sage and Alfred C. Schlesinger. Cambridge: Harvard University Press, 1979.

Lohmeyer, Ernst. *Das Evangelium des Markus.* Gottengen: Vanderhoeck und Ruprecht, 1930.

Lohse, Eduard. *The New Testament Environment.* Trans. John E. Steely. Nashville: Abington Press, 1976.

Long, A.A. *Hellenistic Philosophy: Stoics, Epicureans, Skeptics.* New York: Scribner's, 1974.

Lot, Ferdinan. *The End of the Ancient World and the Beginning of the Middle Ages.* Trans. Philip Leon and Marriette Leon. New York: Barnes and Noble, 1953.

Lucian. *Dialogues of the Courtesans.*

Lutz, Cora E. "The Roman Socrates." In *Yale Classical Studies,* ed. Alfred Bellenger. New Haven: Yale University Press, 1947, 3–150.

Macedon 401–301 BC. Vol. 6 of *The Cambridge Ancient History,* ed. J.B. Bury. Cambridge: Cambridge University Press, 1927.

Mack, Burton L. *The Lost Gospel: The Book of Q and Christian Origins.* San Francisco: HarperCollins, 1993.

Mair, Alexander W. *Encyclopedia Britannica,* 1945, s.v. "Polybius."

Maguire, Joseph P. "Plato's Theory of Natural Law." In *Yale Classical Studies,* ed. Alfred Bellenger. New Haven: Yale University Press, 1947.

Malherbe, Abraham J. *The Cynic Epistles: A Study Edition.* Missoula, Montana: The Scholars Press, 1977.

_____. *Paul and the Popular Philosophers.* Minneapolis: Fortress Press, 1987.

Markle, Minor M., III. "Support of Athenian Intellectuals for Philip: A Study of Isocrates' *Phillipus* and Speusippus' *Letter to Philip.*" *Journal of Hellenic Studies* 96.

Martial. *Apophoreta.*

Martin, Luther A. *Hellenistic Religions: An Introduction.* Oxford: Oxford University Press, 1987.

McDonald, J.I.H. *Biblical Interpretation and Christian Ethics.* Cambridge: Cambridge University Press, 1993.

McMullen, Ramsay. *Constantine.* New York: Dial Press, 1969.

_____. "Roman Attitudes to Greek Love." *Historia* 31 (1982).

Middleton, John. "Theories of Magic." In *Encyclopedia of Religion*, ed. Mircea Eliade. New York: Macmillan, 1987.

Mohr, Richard D. *Gay Ideas: Outing and Other Controversies*. Beacon Press, Boston, 1992.

Muller, C. and T. *Fragmenta historicorum graecorum, Vols. 1–4*. Paris Didot, 1885.

Murphy-O'Connor, John. "I Corinthians 11:2–26 Once Again." *Catholic Biblical Quarterly* 50 (1988), 265–74.

_____. *Paul: A Critical Life*. Oxford: Clarendon Press, 1996.

_____. "Sex and Logic in 1 Corinthians 11, 2–6." *Catholic Biblical Quarterly* 42 (1980).

Murray, Oswyn. "Life and Society in Classical Greece." In *The Oxford History of Classical Greece*, ed. John Boardman, Jasper Griffin and Oswyn Murray. Oxford: Oxford University Press, 1986.

Muscarella, Frank. "The Evolution of Homoerotic Behavior in Humans." *Journal of Homosexuality* 44, no. 1 (2000), 51–77.

Nepos, Cornelius. "Epaminondas." In De Virius Ilustribus.

New Oxford Annotated Bible with the Apocrypha. New York: Oxford University Press, 1977.

Newby, P.H. *Warrior Pharaoh: The Rise and Fall of the Egyptian Empire*. London: Faber and Faber, 1980.

Ng, Vivian. "Homosexuality in Late Imperial China." In *Homosexuality in the Ancient World*, ed. Wayne R. Dynes and Stephen Donaldson. New York: Garland, 1992, 76–78.

Niebuhr, Reinhold. "Love and Law in Protestantism and Catholicism." In *The Essential Reinhold Neibuhr*, ed. Robert McAfee Brown. New Haven: Yale University Press, 1986.

Nilsson, Martin P. *The Dionysitic Mysteries of the Hellenistic and Roman Age*. Lund, Sweden: CWK Gleerup, 1957.

Nock, Arthur Darby. *Early Gentile Christianity and Its Hellenistic Background*. New York: Harper Torchbooks, 1964.

Novem Testamentem Greaece. Ed. Alexander Souter. 1910. Reprint Oxford: Clarendon Press, 1953.

Nussbaum, Martha. *The Fragility of Goodness*. Cambridge: Cambridge University Press, 1986.

Oates, Whitney Jennings and Charles Theophilus Murphy, eds. *Greek Literature in Translation*. Trans. Gilbert Highet. New York: Longmans, Green, 1944.

O'Brian, John Maxwell. *Alexander the Great: the Invisible Enemy*. London: Routledge, 1992.

Olyan, Saul M. "'And with a Male You Shall Not Lie the Lying Down of a Woman': On the Meaning and Significant of Leviticus 18:22 and 20:13." *Journal of the History of Sexuality* 5, no. 2 (Oct. 1994), 179–206.

Ovid. *Metamorphosis*. R. Ehwald, ed. Leipzig: Teubner, 1982.

Pagels, Elaine. *The Origin of Satan*. New York: Random House, 1995.

Parker, Robert. *Miasma: Pollution and Purification in Early Greek Religion*. Oxford: Clarendon, 1983.

Parkinson, R.B. "Homosexual Desire in Middle Kingdom Literature." *Journal of Egyptian Archeology* 81 (1995).

Pausanius, *Tour in Greece*.

_____. *Tour of Greece*.

Pembroke, S.G. "Oikeiosis." In *Problems in Stoicism*, ed. A.A. Long. London: Atholone Press, 1971.

Percy, William Armstrong, III. *Pederasty and Pedagogy in Ancient Greece*. Urbana: University of Illinois Press, 1997.

Philip, James A. *Pythagoras and Early Pythagoreanism. Journal of the Classical Association of Canada, Supplementary*. Vol. VII. Toronto: University of Toronto Press, 1966.

Philo. English Translation by F.H. Colson MA. Cambridge, Mass.: Harvard University Press, 1966.

_____. *Philo of Alexandria: The Contemplative Life, the Giants, and Selections*. Trans. David Winston. Ramsey, N.J.: The Paulist Press, 1981.

_____. "Questions and Answers on Genesis." In Genesis 43, *Philo*, Supplement I. Loeb Classical Library. Translated by Ralph Marcus. Harvard: Harvard University Press, 1971.

Philostratus. *Life of Apollonius*. Trans. C.P. Jones, ed. G.W. Bowerstock. Harmonsworth, Middlesex, England: Penguin Books, 1970.

Pindar: Olympian Odes: Pythian Odes. Ed. and trans. by William H. Race. Loeb Classical Library. London: Harvard University Press, 1997.

Plato. *Laws*. Trans. R.G. Bury. Cambridge, Mass.: Harvard University Press, 1967–1968.

_____. *Republic*. Trans. and ed. Paul Shorey. Vol. I Loeb Classical Library. London: William Heinemann, 1969. 1967–1968.

_____. *The Statesman*. L. Campbell, ed. Oxford: Oxford University Press, 1867.

_____. *The Symposium*. Trans. Walter Hamilton. London: Penguin Books, 1951.

_____. *The Symposium*. Trans. W.R.M. Lamb. Cambridge: Harvard University Press, 1997.

Platthy, Jeno. *Plato: A Critical Biography*. Santa Claus, Ind.: Federation of International Poetry Associations of UNESCO, 1990.

Pliny the Elder. *Natural History*.

Pliny the Younger. *Letters*.

Plotinus. *Enneads*. Vol. 3 of *Plotinus*. Trans. A.H. Armstrong. Cambridge: Cambridge University Press, 1967.

Plutarch. "Against the Stoics on Common Conceptions." Trans. Edwin L. Minor, F.H. Sandbach and W.C. Helmbold. Cambridge: Harvard University Press, 1969.

_____. "Convivial Questions." Trans. Edwin L. Minor, F.H. Sandbach and W.C. Helmbold. Cambridge: Harvard University Press, 1969.

_____. "De esu charn." Trans. Edwin L. Minor, F.H. Sandbach and W.C. Helmbold. Cambridge: Harvard University Press, 1969.

_____. "De Stoic Repug." Trans. Edwin L. Minor, F.H. Sandbach and W.C. Helmbold. Cambridge: Harvard University Press, 1969.

_____. "The Dialogue on Love." Trans. Edwin L. Minor, F.H. Sandbach and W.C. Helmbold. Cambridge: Harvard University Press, 1969.

_____. "Life of Alexander." Trans. Edwin L. Minor, F.H. Sandbach and W.C. Helmbold. Cambridge: Harvard University Press, 1969.

_____. "Life of Amellius Paulus." Trans. Edwin L. Minor, F.H. Sandbach and W.C. Helmbold. Cambridge: Harvard University Press, 1969.

_____. "Life of Cato the Elder." Trans. Edwin L. Minor, F.H. Sandbach and W.C. Helmbold. Cambridge: Harvard University Press, 1969.

_____. "Life of Lycurgus." Trans. Edwin L. Minor, F.H. Sandbach and W.C. Helmbold. Cambridge: Harvard University Press, 1969.

_____. "Life of Marcellus." Trans. Edwin L. Minor, F.H. Sandbach and W.C. Helmbold. Cambridge: Harvard University Press, 1969.

_____. "Life of Numa." Trans. Edwin L. Minor, F.H. Sandbach and W.C. Helmbold. Cambridge: Harvard University Press, 1969.

_____. "Life of Pelopidas." Trans. Edwin L. Minor, F.H. Sandbach and W.C. Helmbold. Cambridge: Harvard University Press, 1969.

_____. "Life of Romullus." Trans. Edwin L. Minor, F.H. Sandbach and W.C. Helmbold. Cambridge: Harvard University Press, 1969.

_____. "Life of Solon." Trans. Edwin L. Minor, F.H. Sandbach and W.C. Helmbold. Cambridge: Harvard University Press, 1969.

_____. "Life of Theseus." Trans. Edwin L. Minor, F.H. Sandbach and W.C. Helmbold. Cambridge: Harvard University Press, 1969.

_____. "On the Fortune of Alexander." Trans. Edwin L. Minor, F.H. Sandbach and W.C. Helmbold. Cambridge: Harvard University Press, 1969.

_____. "Platonic Questions." Trans. Edwin L. Minor, F.H. Sandbach and W.C. Helmbold. Cambridge: Harvard University Press, 1969.

_____. *Plutarch's Moralia in Sixteen Volumes*. Trans. Edwin L Minor, F.H. Sandbach and W.C. Helmbold. Cambridge: Harvard University Press, 1969.

_____. "Roman Questions." Trans. Edwin L. Minor, F.H. Sandbach and W.C. Helmbold. Cambridge: Harvard University Press, 1969.

_____. "The Sayings of Kings." Trans. Edwin L. Minor, F.H. Sandbach and W.C. Helmbold. Cambridge: Harvard University Press, 1969.

_____. "Sayings of the Romans." Trans. Edwin L. Minor, F.H. Sandbach and W.C. Helmbold. Cambridge: Harvard University Press, 1969.

_____. "Table Talk." Trans. Edwin L. Minor, F.H. Sandbach and W.C. Helmbold. Cambridge: Harvard University Press, 1969.

Porphyry. *Life of Plotinus*. Sec. 15 of Plotinus, *The Enneads*, trans. Stephen Mac Kenna. 4th ed. New York: Pantheon Books, 1969.

Pseudepigrapha. Vol. 2 of *The Apocrypha and Pseudepigrapha of the Old Testament*. Ed. R.H. Charles. Oxford: Clarendon Press, 1913.

Pseudo-Diogenes. *Cynic Epistles*. Trans. Benjamin Fiore. Ed. Abraham Malherbe. Missoula: Scholars Press, 1977.

Pseudo-Phoclydes. Trans. Pieter Van der Horst. *Studia in Veteris Testamenta Pseudepigrapha* 4. Leiden: Brill, 1978.

Pseudo-Plato. *Erixias*.

Pseudo-Plutarch. *Moralia*. "Life of Lycurgos of Athens."

Preston, James J. "Purification." In *The Encyclopedia of Religion*, ed. Mircea Eliade. 16 Vols. Vol. 8. New York: Macmillan, 1978, 91–100.

Procopius. *On the Buildings*.

_____. *The Secret History*.

Quintus Curtius. *History of Alexander the Great*.

Randall, John Herman Jr. *Plato: Dramatist of the Life of Reason*. New York: Columbia University Press, 1970.

Ramsay, William M. *The Westminster Guide to the Books of the Bible*. Louisville, Kentucky: Westminster John Knox Press, 1994.

Reale, Giovanni. *From the Origins to Socrates*. Vol. I of *A History of Ancient Philosophy*. Ed. and trans. John Catan. N.p.: State University of New York Press, 1987.

_____. *The Schools of the Imperial Age*. Ed. and trans. John R. Cuthan. Albany: State University of New York Press, 1990.

_____. *The Systems of the Hellenistic Age*. Vol. III of *A History of Ancient Philosophy*. Ed. and trans. from the third Italian edition by John R. Catan. Albany: State University of New York Press, 1985.

Remains of Old Latin. Ed. E.H. Warmington. Vol. 4. Cambridge: Harvard University Press, 1979.

Renault, Mary. *The Nature of Alexander*. New York: Pantheon Books, 1975.

Richlin, Amy. *The Garden of Priapus: Sexuality and Aggression in Roman Humor*. New Haven: Yale University Press, 1983.

_____. "Not Before Homosexuality: The Materiality of the *Cinaedus* and the Roman Law Against Love Between Men." *Journal of the History of Sexuality* 3, no. 4 (1993).

Riefstahl, Elizabeth. *Thebes in the Time of Amunhotpe III*. Norman: University of Oklahoma Press, 1964.

Rigionos, Alice Swift. *Platonica: The Anecdotes Concerning the Life and Writings of Plato*. Leiden: E.J. Brill, 1976.

Rist, J.M. *Stoic Philosophy*. Cambridge: Cambridge University Press, 1969.

Rohde, Erwin. *Psyche: The Cult of Souls and Belief in Immorality among the Greeks*. Vol. 2. Trans. W.B. Hillis. New York: Harper Torchbooks, 1925.

Rome and the Mediterranean 218–133 BC. Vol. 8 of *The Cambridge Ancient History*. Cambridge: Cambridge University Press, 1930.

Romilly, Jacqueline de. *The Great Sophists in Periclean Athens*. Trans. Janet Lloyd. Oxford: Clarendon Press, 1992.

Rostovtzeff, Mikhail Ivonovich. *The Social and Economic History of the Roman Empire*. 2nd ed. Revised by P.M. Fraser. 2 vols., pages numbered consecutively. Oxford: Clarendon Press, 1957.

Rousselle, Aline. *Porneia: On Desire and the Body in Antiquity*. Trans. Felicia Pheasant. New York: Basil Blackwell, 1988.

Rowe, J.C. *Plato: Phaedrus, Translation with Commentary*. Warminster, England: Aris and Phillips, 1986, 204–05.

Russell, F.W. *The School of Plato: Its Origin, Development and Revival under the Roman Empire*. London: Methuen, 1896.

Rutherford, R.B. *The Meditations of Marcus Aurelius: A Study*. Oxford: Clarendon Press, 1989.

Samdmel, Samuel. *Philo of Alexandria: An Introduction*. New York: Oxford University Press, 1979.

Sandbach, F.H. *The Stoics*. New York: W.W. Norton, 1975.

Sandars, N.K. *The Epic of Gilgamesh: An English Version with an Introduction*. Hammondsworth, Middlesex, England: Penguin Books, revised ed. 1987.

Sarna, Nahum M. "Biblical Literature: Hebrew Scripture." In *The Encyclopedia of Religion*. Vol. 2. Ed. Mircea Eliade. New York: Macmillan, 1978, 158–59.

Satlow, Michael. "'They Abused Him Like a Woman': Homoeroticism, Gender Blurring and the Rabbis in Late Antiquity." *Journal of the History of Sexuality* 5, no. 1 (July 1994), 1–25.

Schibli, Herman S. *Pherekydes of Syros*. Clarendon: Oxford Press, 1990.

Sedley, David. "The Protagonists." In *Doubt and Dogmatism: Studies in Hellenistic Epistemology*. Oxford: Clarendon Press, 1980, 1–19.

Sellar, W.Y. *The Roman Poets of the Republic*. 1889. Reprint New York: Biblo and Tannen, 1965.

Seneca, Lucius Annaeus. *Epistles 93–124*. Trans. Richard M. Gummere. London: William Heinemann, 1925.

Seneca, Marcus [sic] Annaeus. *Controverses et Svasoires*. Paris: Garnier, 1932.

Septuagint. Ed. Lancelot C.L. Brenton. London: Samuel Bagster, 1884. Reprint Zondervan, n.d.

Sextus Empiricus. *Outlines of Skepticism*. Trans. Julia Annas and Jon Baress. Cambridge: Cambridge University Press, 1994.

Shelton, Jo-Ann. *As the Romans Did: A Sourcebook of Roman Social History*, 2nd ed. New York: Oxford, 1998.

Shorey, Paul. *What Plato Said*. Chicago: University of Chicago Press, 1933.

Silverstein, Thomas. "Did Someone Know the Vision of St. Paul?" *Harvard Studies and Notes on Philology and Literature*. 1937.

Smith, Morton. *Clement of Alexandria and a Secret Gospel of Mark*. Howard University Press, 1973.

_____. *The Secret Gospel: The Discovery and Interpretation of the Secret Gospel According to Mark*. New York: Harper and Row, 1973.

Spence, Jonathan D. *Emperor of China: Self-Portrait of Cawing Hi*. New York: Vintage Books, 1975.

Stager, Lawrence. "Why Were Hundreds of Dogs Buried at Ashkelon?" *Biblical Archaeology Review* 17 (Mar.–Apr. 1991), 24–43.

Statius. *Silvae*.

Stambaugh, John E., and David Balch. *The New Testament in Its Social Environment*. Philadelphia: Westminster Press, 1986.

Staub, Ervin. *The Roots of Evil: The Origins of Genocide and Other Group Violence*. Cambridge: Cambridge University Press.

Stephanos Bycantinos. *Ethnikon*.

Stevenson, Walter. "The Rise of Eunuchs in Greco-Roman Antiquity." *Journal of the History of Sexuality* 5, no. 4 (Apr. 1995).

Stewart, Andrew. *Faces of Power: Alexander's Image and Hellenistic Politics*. Berkeley: University of California Press, 1993.

Stobaeus. *Anthology*. In *Hellenistic Philosophy: Introductory Readings*. 2nd ed. Translated and with an introduction and notes by B. Inwood and L.P. Gerson. Indianapolis: Hackett, 1988.

Stobaeus, Johannes. *Eclogues and Anthology*.

Striker, Gisela. *Essays in Hellenistic Epistemology and Ethics*. Cambridge: Cambridge University Press, 1996.

Suetonius. In *The Lives of the Caesars*. Trans. J.C. Lolfe. London: William Heinemann, 1968.

Tacitus, *Annals*.

_____. *Histories*.

Taran, Leonard. *Parmenides: A Text with Translations and Critical Essays*. Princeton: Princeton University Press, 1965.

Taran, Sonya Lida. "EISI TRIXES: An Erotic Motif." *Journal of Hellenism Studies* 105 (1985).

Tarn, William Woodthorpe. *Alexander the Great*. Boston: Beacon Press, 1948.

Tarrant, Howard. *Thrasyllian Platonism*. Ithaca: Cornell University Press, 1993.

Taylor, Michael W. *The Tyrant Slayers: The Heroic Image in the Fifth Century BC Athenian Art and Politics*. New York: Arno Press, 1981.

Tejera, Victorino. *Plato's Dialogues One by One: A Structural Interpretation*. New York: Irvington, 1984.

Theissen, Gerd, and Annette Merz. *The Historical*

Jesus: A Comprehensive Guide. Trans. John Bowden. Minneapolis: Fortress Press, 1998.

Thesleff, Holgar. *The Pythagorean Texts of the Hellenistic Period*. Abo, Finland: Abo Akadem, 1961.

Thompson, George. *Studies in Ancient Greek Society*. Vol. 2. London: Lawrence and Wishart, 1955.

Thorbjornsrud, Berit. "What Can the Gilgamesh Myth Tell Us About Religion and the View of Humanity in Mesopotamia." *Temenos* 19 (1983).

Thucydides. *History of the Peloponnesian War*. Trans. Rex Warner. Hammondsworth, Middlesex: Penguin Books, 1954.

Tripp, Edward. *Crowell's Handbook of Classical Mythology*. New York: Y. Crowell, 1970.

Tuckett, C.M. "A Cynic Q?" *Biblica* 70 (1989).

Tyson, Joseph B. *A Study of Early Christianity*. New York: Macmillan, 1973.

Vacano, Otto Wilhelm von. *The Etruscans in the Ancient World*. Trans. Sheila Ann Ogilve. London: Edward Arnold, 1960.

Valerius Maximus. *Factorum et dictorum memoribilium, libri novem*.

Vlastos, Gregory. *Platonic Studies*. 2nd ed. Princeton: Princeton University Press, 1981.

Wallis, R.T. *Neoplatonism*. New York: Scribner's, 1972.

Walters, Jonathan. "Soldiers and Whores in a Pseudo-Quintilian Declamation." In *Gender and Ethnicity in Ancient Italy*, ed. Tim Cornell and Kathryn Lomas. Vol. 6. Accordia Specialist Studies in Italy. London: Accordia Research Institute, 1997. 109–114, 109.

Walters, Margaret. *The Nude Male: A New Perspective*. New York: Penguin Books, 1978.

Waterfield, Robin. *Xenophon: Conversations of Socrates*. Trans. and ed. with new material by Robin Waterfield and Hugh Tredennick. London: Penguin Books, 1990.

Watson, Gerald. "The Natural Law and Stoicism." In *Problems in Stoicism*, ed. A.A. Long. London: Atholone Press, 1971.

Weiser, Artur. *The Old Testament: Its Formation and Development*. Trans. Dorothea M. Barton. 1948. Reprint New York: Association Press, 1961.

Wilbank, F.W. Introduction to *Polybius: The Rise of the Roman Empire*. London: Penguin Books, 1979.

Wild, John. *Plato's Modern Enemies and the Theory of Natural Law*. Chicago: University of Chicago Press, 1953.

Winkler, John J. *Constraints of Desire: The Anthropology of Sex and Gender in Ancient Greece*. New York: Routledge, 1990.

Winston, David. Introduction to *Philo of Alexandria: The Contemplative Life, the Giants, and Selections*. Ramsey, N.J.: The Paulist Press, 1981.

Wolfson, Harry Austryne. *Philo: Foundations of Religious Philosophy in Judaism, Christianity and Islam*. Vol. 2. 4th ed. Cambridge: Harvard University Press, 1947.

Wunerlich, Hans Georg. *The Secrets of Crete*. Trans. Richard Winston. New York: Macmillan, 1974.

Xenophon. *Hellenica*. Trans. Carlton W. Brownson. Loeb Classical Library. Cambridge: Harvard University Press, William Heinemann, 1985.

Index

227